Married to Another Man

Married to Another Man

Israel's Dilemma in Palestine

GHADA KARMI

Pluto Press

LONDON • ANN ARBOR, MI

First published 2007 by Pluto Press
345 Archway Road, London N6 5AA
and 839 Greene Street, Ann Arbor, MI 48106

www.plutobooks.com

Copyright © Ghada Karmi 2007

The right of Ghada Karmi to be identified as the author of this work has been
asserted by her in accordance with the Copyright, Designs and Patents Act 1988.

British Library Cataloguing in Publication Data
A catalogue record for this book is available from the British Library

Hardback
ISBN-13   978 0 7453 2066 3
ISBN-10   0 7453 2066 X

Paperback
ISBN-13   978 0 7453 2065 6
ISBN-10   0 7453 2065 1

Library of Congress Cataloging in Publication Data applied for

This book is printed on paper suitable for recycling and made from fully managed
and sustained forest sources. Logging, pulping and manufacturing processes are
expected to conform to the environmental regulations of the country of origin.

10 9 8 7 6 5 4 3 2 1

Designed and produced for Pluto Press by
Chase Publishing Services Ltd, Fortescue, Sidmouth, EX10 9QG, England
Typeset from disk by Stanford DTP Services, Northampton, England
Printed and bound in the European Union by
CPI Antony Rowe Ltd, Chippenham and Eastbourne, England

Following the first Zionist Congress in Basel in 1897 at which the idea of establishing a Jewish state in Palestine was first mooted, the rabbis of Vienna dispatched two representatives to investigate the suitability of the country for such an enterprise. The men reported the result of their explorations in this cable to Vienna:

The bride is beautiful, but she is married to another man.

To their disappointment they had found that Palestine, though highly eligible to become the Jewish state the Zionists longed for, was not, as the writer, Israel Zangwill, later claimed, 'A land without a people for a people without a land'. It was already inhabited, spoken for by a native Palestinian Arab population whose homeland it already was.

Contents

Maps

Preface

My chief reason for writing this book was to lay out my vision for solving the Israeli–Palestinian conflict. This is both a personal and a political imperative. On the personal level, I had long felt I would never be at peace if I did not see this terrible conflict resolved in my lifetime, that a situation so dangerous and tragic could not be allowed to persist. I found the fatalistic opinion of many Arabs that 'in the fullness of time' all would be solved depressing, and the so-called 'realistic' political assessments that a durable settlement, given the balance of forces existing today, would take many decades if not a hundred years, disheartening. My quest for a solution was certainly tied up with my own origins as a Palestinian who had experienced at first hand Israel's creation in 1948 and was still living, along with millions of others, through its consequences. But on the political level, it seemed to me that the prevailing pessimism about finding a satisfactory solution was unwarranted if one thought through the logic of the situation. This book examines the various solutions to the conflict and concludes that, logically, only one is possible.

Married to Another Man is not about the one-state solution as such and yet it also is. Much of it is devoted to what I considered a necessary review and analysis of the previous history and events that led me to advocate the position I reached. Hence, the book discusses many areas relevant to this question (all of which, incidentally, could form the subject of separate books in their own right), and covers the origins of the conflict, its Arab, Jewish and Western dimensions, and the ways devised for its solution to date. This review, which was as exhaustive as the limits of a single book permit, led irresistibly in my mind to the only conclusion possible in the circumstances. As Sherlock Holmes put it to Dr Watson, 'Eliminate all other factors, and the one which remains must be the truth.'

I am conscious that, even though it forms only a small part of the book, the one-state solution is not easy topic to write about. It places one immediately amongst a marginal minority and attracts accusations of utopianism, antisemitism or even treachery. But such judgements are a lazy way out of having to think about ideas that conflict with what has become familiar, conventional and also serves vested interests. Yet it is a solution that must be faced squarely and subjected to honest debate because, as I will hope to show, it is the only way forward for both Palestinians and Israelis.

The difficulty of writing about a situation as dynamic and changeable as this means that some of the facts and allusions in the text will be quickly overtaken by events and may seem out of date. This is an uncomfortable situation for any writer but unavoidable in dealing with what is, in effect, history in the making. For the same reason I have used press sources for many of my references. I have relied in the main on the Arabic-language daily, *Al-Quds al-Arabi* (abbreviated to *Al-Quds*), for its exhaustive coverage of Palestinian affairs, and the Israeli daily, *Haaretz*, for its equally detailed reporting of Israeli affairs. Other press reports also feature throughout the book.

Acknowledgements

This book started out as a long essay but over time it stretched to become a far bigger enterprise. Consequently, the list of people who helped me with it grew longer and longer. I hope that those I omit from acknowledgement will forgive my forgetfulness and what may seem my ingratitude. I thank all of them in advance. First and foremost I should like to thank Roger van Zwanenberg, my publisher and exacting critic, for his support, friendship and fortitude, as well as the staff at Pluto Press for making the book a reality. Also and equally Adel Kamal for his painstaking editing, patience, advice and support over what must have seemed an interminable project. I am grateful to many kind friends who checked various parts of the manuscript: Raghid al-Solh, Tim Niblock, Richard Seaford, Norton Mezvinsky and Elfi Pallis. I must also thank Tim Llewellyn who supported me with textual advice and reference material; likewise Mortaza Sahibzada for his generous help, technical and otherwise, and many other friends and well-wishers. Thanks also to The Foundation for Middle East Peace and the Palestinian Academic Society for the Study of International Affairs, and also Ahmed Abu-Zayed, for the maps.

Finally, I must thank my daughter, Salma, for her enthusiasm and the advance publicity she gave the book among her young friends.

Introduction

When the Zionists resolved in 1897 to establish a Jewish state in Palestine, they were aware that it was already home to an indigenous non-Jewish population. How to create and maintain a state for another people in a land already inhabited? Squaring that circle has been the essence of Israel's dilemma ever since its establishment and the cause of the Palestinian tragedy that it led to. It could not have been otherwise, for what the Zionists envisaged was a project that was bizarre and, on the face of it, unworkable, namely to set up an ethnically defined, Jews-only collective existing on a land belonging to another people and to their exclusion. Moreover, this new creation was supposed, irrespective of native opposition, to prosper in perpetuity. It was inevitable that a project necessitating the appropriation of a land already inhabited by a people defined as ethnically unacceptable could only have been realised by a mixture of force and coercion. To have any hope of long-term success, the new state thus created would have to maintain itself through constant military superiority and powerful backing by its creator, the West. The corollary to this was that the Arabs would have to remain too weak and disunited to offer much resistance, with the calculation that Israel's powerful army would swiftly despatch any that arose.

This, in substance, is the Zionist project, whose main aims came to be realised in the creation of Israel in 1948, but which was never able to resolve the problem of 'the other man'. Its dilemma has nowhere been better expressed than by the Israeli historian, Benny Morris, in an interview with the Israeli daily, *Haaretz*, on 8 January 2004. In a lucid exposé of classical Zionist thinking, which merits quotation at length, he encapsulates all Zionism's major elements, its inherent implausibility as a practical project, its arrogance, racism and self-

1

righteousness, and the insurmountable obstacle to it of Palestine's original population, which refuses to go away. The conditions that must pertain for the Jewish state's creation and survival required the expulsion of the indigenous population and the need to maintain Israeli supremacy in the face of the inevitable Arab hostility. As he says,

> A Jewish state would not have come into being without the uprooting of 700,000 Palestinians. Therefore it was necessary to uproot them. There was no choice but to expel that population. If the desire to establish a Jewish state here is legitimate, there was no other choice ... The need to establish this state in this place overcame the injustice that was done to the Palestinians by uprooting them.

It follows that the future survival of Israel may necessitate further Palestinian population 'transfers'. Morris maintains the mistake the Zionists made was to have allowed any Palestinians to remain.

> If the end of the story turns out to be a gloomy one for the Jews, it will be because Ben-Gurion [Israel's first prime minister] did not complete the transfer in 1948. Because he left a large and volatile demographic reserve in the West Bank and Gaza and within Israel itself ... In other circumstances, apocalyptic ones, which are liable to be realized in five or ten years, I can see expulsions. If we find ourselves...in a situation of warfare...acts of expulsion will be entirely reasonable. They may even be essential ... If the threat to Israel is existential, expulsion will be justified.

Inevitably, Zionism resulted in the creation of hostility amongst its victims since the displaced Palestinians have never been reconciled to the Zionist project and 'can't tolerate the existence of a Jewish state'. Given this, Zionism could only have succeeded by the use of superior force. 'There is not going to be peace in the present generation. There will not be a solution. We are doomed to live by the sword.' He recognises that Zionism had unrealistic expectations: 'The whole Zionist project is apocalyptic. It exists within hostile surroundings and in a certain sense its existence is unreasonable. It wasn't reasonable for it to succeed in 1881 and it wasn't reasonable for it to succeed in 1948 and it's not reasonable that it will succeed now.' In the final analysis, Morris concludes, the Zionist project is faced with two options: perpetual cruelty and repression of others, or the end of the dream. For Zionists, the latter is tragically unthinkable.

Following this interview, liberal Israelis attacked Morris for what they viewed as his right-wing views. Yet, he should have been commended for his candour and honesty in articulating what most Zionists feel but do not say. In these extracts, he accurately reflects the anxieties and soul-searching that beset Zionism as the Jewish state approaches the sixtieth decade of its existence. The problem, already foreseen by the two Viennese rabbis, was also clear to Zionism's earliest leaders. One of the most important of these, Vladimir (later, Zeev) Jabotinsky, put it well in 1923 in an article entitled 'The Iron Wall'.

'Every indigenous people', he wrote about the Palestinian Arabs' expected reaction to the Zionist project, 'will resist alien settlers as long as they see any hope of ridding themselves of the danger of foreign settlement'. A voluntary agreement with the Palestinians was thus impossible. He ridiculed his fellow Zionists who thought such an agreement was a necessary condition of Zionism by saying that they might as well abandon the project. The alternative he advocated was for Zionist colonisation to develop 'under the protection of a force independent of the local population – an iron wall which the native population cannot break through.'[1] (The iron wall refers to a wall of bayonets.)

Moshe Dayan, a later leader and Israel's chief of staff many years on, reiterates these same ideas in a different way. Speaking in 1956 at the funeral of a young Israeli killed by an Arab 'infiltrator' near the Egyptian frontier, he said:

> Let us not today fling accusations at the murderers. Who are we that we should argue against their hatred? For eight years now, they sit in their refugee camps in Gaza and, before their very eyes we turn into our homestead the land and the villages in which they and their forefathers have lived. We are a generation of settlers, and without the steel helmet and the cannon we cannot plant a tree and build a home. Let us not shrink back when we see the hatred fermenting and filling the lives of hundreds of thousands of Arabs, who sit all around us. Let us not avert our gaze, so that our hand shall not slip. This is the fate of our generation, the choice of our life – to be prepared and armed, strong and tough – or otherwise, the sword will slip from our fist, and our life will be snuffed out.[2]

If Dayan had had foresight, he might have added that it was not just his generation but also all subsequent Israeli generations who would have to continue this tough stance or else have their lives 'snuffed out'. For the central issue confronting Israel has always been how to stem the tide of opposition to its existence. Inevitably, Arabs saw it as an alien body implanted in the heart of their region. They rejected it, just as the human body rejects a foreign organ graft. In such cases, doctors strive hard to suppress the body's rejection to save the patient's life, and this noble aim is generally taken to justify the medical effort and expense entailed in achieving it. Zionism sees its own struggle in similar terms: to fulfil an aim no less noble, that of maintaining a Jewish state as a solution to the long-standing persecution of Jews. In the furtherance of what is perceived as a self-evidently moral project, measures normally deemed to be unacceptable become tolerable as a means to an end no one could disagree with. And it is this which makes Zionism such a dangerous ideology. The conviction of moral rightness that lies at its heart has engaged most Jews and a substantial number of non-Jews in the liberal West. Shortly after issuing his famous Declaration, Arthur Balfour, the British foreign secretary, expressed it long ago in this way:

> Zionism, be it right or wrong, good or bad, is rooted in age-long traditions, in present deeds, in future hopes, of far profounder import than the desires and prejudices of the 700,000 Arabs who now inhabit that ancient land.[3]

That was in 1917. In the ensuing three decades, the Nazi Holocaust had completed the task of persuading Zionism's Western sponsors that a haven for persecuted Jews was an imperative. And few people in the West have ever seriously disagreed with this proposition since then. It is inextricably bound up with the general perception of Palestine as the rightful and necessary home of the Jews, a view that runs very deep within the hearts and minds of virtually all Jews, however liberal, and a majority of others in the West. To challenge this concept, to argue that the Jews (or any other foreign group) had no right to Palestine whatsoever as a *state* and, no matter what their sufferings, were not justified in dispossessing its people is tantamount to sacrilege. The campaign to equate anti-Israel criticism with antisemitism, shrewdly instigated by the Zionists and vigorously pursued today, has compounded this situation. Add to this the fact that a linkage between Jews and the Holy Land already existed in the minds of Western Christians, whether practising or not, and the case for Israel seems unassailable.

Truly, for the Palestinians, who were the chief victims of the enterprise, to take on this mixture of received wisdom, psychology, emotion and entrenched beliefs is a monumental task. Their case has been so effectively subsumed in the dominant Israeli narrative that they are not expected even to question or resist it. They and the rest of the Arab world are supposed to share everyone else's view of Israel as a moral project and not to object to its creation. Hence, Arab hostility to Israel appears mysterious or just spiteful and it has only been since the start of the second Palestinian intifada in 2000, with the brutality of Israel's occupation exposed, that Palestinians have been legitimately permitted to object. The parameters of these objections, however, are strictly limited by an implicit consensus on what Palestinians can legitimately hope for: that Israel may be expected to ease its occupation and that the end of the process can be a Palestinian state of sorts in the post-1967 territories. The latter is regarded as the pinnacle of Palestinian ambition, with any claim to the land lost before 1967 totally excluded from the equation, as if there had been no Palestinian history before 1967 and Israel had always been a natural part of the landscape.

Such a scenario may be superficially convincing, even comforting, for Israel and the West. It implies that Palestinians can delete the past and their own grievances, that they can be content with a small portion of their original homeland and that the refugees and other displaced people who are currently lodging in various countries will altruistically and unilaterally give up on their hopes of repatriation. It is only possible to think in this way if one entirely disregards the feelings and reactions of the people in whose midst the Jewish state was set up. This essentially colonialist and racist thinking imbued the Balfour Declaration that gave the impetus to the whole process. The idea that a foreign people could be invited into another land without the knowledge or permission of the native population would now be regarded as outrageous. But it still informs the Western approach to the Arabs in this conflict. And under the weight of this pervasive view, many Arabs have begun to doubt themselves, to feel that their rejection of Israel is somehow unfeeling and ungracious.

After nearly six decades of Israeli nationhood, maintained through superior power and ceaseless Western support, a change in the Arab position vis-à-vis Israel is clearly discernible. Matters have moved on significantly since the days of Nasser, Egypt's president until 1970, and the refusal of Arab states to recognise or deal with Israel. Today, there are peace plans that extend recognition and full acceptance to Israel as a normal part of the region, of which the 2002 Saudi peace plan is the latest. Normalisation of relations with Israel is proceeding apace at the formal and informal level. This is the more remarkable, when one considers what the Arabs were required to do: to host an alien people who carved out a state for themselves on Arab land, and did so, moreover, with a Western support that was callously indifferent to the effects of this enterprise on those at the receiving end. And they were expected to do so without questioning its basic tenet: that there had to be a Jewish state in Palestine *as of right*. That Jewish/Western imperative was supposed to justify *to Arabs* every excess and every abuse that Israel meted out to them in the last six decades. That, despite this monstrous imposition, the Arabs allowed the Zionist project to flourish might suggest to many that it has finally succeeded.

But has it? The Palestinians are still there – damaged, fragmented, occupied and oppressed, to be sure – but still there, both physically and politically, and in fact more than ever before. Six decades of Israeli effort to destroy them and resolve the original Zionist dilemma have not succeeded. They still constitute an obstacle to Zionism that refuses to go away. There is still no peace agreement to end the conflict and Israel's supremacy in arms and technology, its powerful friends and devoted supporters have not bought it a normal, peaceful existence. The Jewish state is not a haven for Jews seeking refuge. It is more dangerous and unstable than anywhere else where Jews now reside, constantly under threat and unsure of its long-term future. Putting up the barricades against 'terrorism' and the Arab 'demographic threat' cannot dam the tide forever, and the attempt has converted Israel into a quasi-fascist state, embarrassing to its supporters and unloved by nearly everyone else. As the people living in Israel elaborate a new 'Israeli' identity, they will become ever more disconnected from the Jews outside, to whom already many of them appear alien.[4] Jewish immigration into Israel is increasingly difficult, as the pool of 'suitable' Jews dries up. The desperation to ward off the inevitable is discernible in the hunt for 'Jews', many of them converts, in Africa, Peru, India and elsewhere,[5] and the numbers of non-Jewish immigrants admitted to Israel as Jews (for example, thousands of Soviet immigrants are reported to be Christians).[6]

The damage, dislocation and suffering the Palestinians and Arabs of the region have been forced to endure in order to make the Zionist experiment succeed – even in the cause of solving the problem of Jewish persecution in Europe – are far in excess of what could reasonably have been demanded from any group of people. It was particularly deleterious to the Arabs in the first half of the twentieth century when Zionism was taking root, emerging as they were from longtime Ottoman rule to be dominated again almost at once by the Western powers. As such, they were singularly ill-equipped to protect themselves effectively against the Zionist intrusion. In many ways, they remain so today owing in no small measure, as we will see later, to the existence of Israel in their midst. The conflict thus generated was inevitable and entirely predictable. To date, all attempts to end it have failed.

This book will argue that the central cause for this failure is the Zionist imperative to create and maintain a Jewish majority in a land inhabited by non-Jews. The obsessive adherence to this imperative has led to a variety of Israeli initiatives, all of which aimed to minimise the Palestinian presence in the country and ensure that it did not re-emerge. Hence, a series of plans, combining expulsion (as happened in 1948 and 1967 and continues at a slower pace today) and territorial partition heavily in favour of the Jewish state were devised. This is a difficult task in a land the size of Wales, whose natural resources are scattered throughout. Trying to apportion these on a basis of inequitable sharing in a partitioned land has proved complicated and unworkable except as outright theft. No formulation has appeared so far that can satisfy Israeli demands and ensure Palestinian acquiescence in such a deal.

Nor can there ever be, for the 'peace' proposals are all flawed by injustice and gross inequality. Such deals may be imposed by the stronger party on the weaker one and may succeed for a while, but they will not last. A durable solution must address the issue of justice and, for Palestinians, so traduced in this conflict, this will mean affording them – all those inside and outside Palestine – a future life in dignity and equality in their homeland. As one of the Palestinians 'outside', the issue of justice is paramount in my thinking. The fact that I do not live under Israeli occupation, nor in a refugee camp, nor as an unequal Arab citizen of Israel, makes no difference to this position. All of us who grew up in the West were exposed to Western assumptions about the 'rightness' of Israel's creation and the careless dismissal of what that enterprise had meant for the natives of the country.

The two-state solution was touted for years as the answer to the problem, including by many Palestinians for their own reasons. Yet, how fair was it to the indigenous people of Palestine, most of whom had been displaced outside it in camps or in foreign countries, that their land should be unequally sliced, with the lion's share going to the invader? Why should they have been expected to accept solutions that took no account of the reality of their situation? It is clear that, had the two-state solution as proposed come into being, the majority of Palestinians (who live in the diaspora) would have been excluded. What would happen to these people? To solve their problem, Israel and its Western allies have come up with a hotchpotch of proposals, patriation for some, emigration for others and compensation for yet others – untidy solutions that can only cause further dislocation and hardship and compound the initial injustice. No peace agreement can last under these conditions.

Justice also requires that the Israeli Jewish community now living in that new homeland and no matter how it got there, be similarly entitled to dignity and equality. In the chapters that ensue, I will argue that the only possible solution that can provide these twin imperatives will be that of a single state in an unpartitioned land where both peoples may live together. There is no other sensible way to accommodate their needs and, had it not been for Israel's destructive and foolish pursuit of an ethnic state for Jews alone, the one-state solution would have been implemented long ago.

Chapter 1 will review the damage that Israel's creation inflicted on the Arabs, how it has retarded their development and provoked a reactive and dangerous radicalisation. Chapter 2 discusses the question of Jewish support for Israel and how its complexities have baffled Palestinians and other Arabs. Chapter 3 will discuss the nature of Western support for Israel and how this has complicated the search for a solution. Chapters 4 and 5 will review and analyse the variety of peace proposals for solving the conflict from 1967 to the Oslo Accords of 1993 and thereafter, and the reasons for their failure. Chapter 6 will deal mainly with the two-state solution, its history, significances and feasibility. The last section, Chapter 7, is devoted to the subject of the one-state solution, binationalism, secular democracy and its advantages and drawbacks. The Epilogue offers some reflections on the future.

There is no ideal way forward for this terrible conflict, nor do I pretend to have a magic formula. A problem as complex as that of Israel, perpetuated by external interests and an uncompromising state ideology, has no solution as long as its basic parameters remain unchanged. Nonetheless a way must be found if the acute crisis in the Middle East is to end. In the pages that follow I have set out my arguments for what that way should be. I intend through these to invite the reader to accompany me on a journey that I hope will lead him or her to the same destination that I have reached.

1
The Cost of Israel to the Arabs

The profound damage done to the Arab world by Israel's creation is a big, untold story in the West. For the Arabs, Israel's presence in their midst has quite simply been an unmitigated disaster. This may come as a surprise to the average Western reader, encouraged over many decades to regard Israel as a natural part of the Middle Eastern landscape and to disregard in equal measure what Arabs feel about it. Likewise Western policy makers traditionally place Arab perceptions low down on their list of priorities. Yet, an understanding of Israel's impact on the Arab world is crucial to the search for a resolution to the conflict. The fact that this complex relationship has usually been dismissed in the most superficial terms – 'Arabs hate Jews', 'they're both as bad as each other', 'wars are not the answer' and the like – is a major factor in the failure to find a solution. To understand the true dimensions of the problem it is necessary at this point for the Western reader to set aside the Israeli narrative of events and its accompanying propaganda image of Arabs as fanatical, backward warmongers bent on destroying the modern, democratic and peaceable state of Israel for no conceivable reason. The following account aims to look at the issue from the Arab point of view.

The reality for Arabs is that Israel confers no conceivable benefit on their lives or wellbeing, but on the contrary, its existence has led to a series of depredations and crises with profound impact on the Arab region. This chapter will describe Israel's deleterious effects on the Arabs and thus set the scene for the basic argument in this book. The term 'Arab states' is ambiguous in this context, since they were not all similarly damaged by Israel's existence, and needs explanation. A disproportionate degree of damage was borne by the frontline states of Jordan, Syria, Lebanon and Egypt, and the following account applies mostly to them. However, Iraq, the Gulf States and North Africa have all been affected in various ways, as has Arab society in general.

On each visit there, the Arab world's immense resources, its varied geography, history and customs strike me. One has but to think of the stretch of the Arab region, from Yemen, through the Gulf, to the Levant, then sweeping by way of Egypt and Sudan to its westernmost point in Morocco to appreciate how stunning is its kaleidoscope of landscape and people. Such marvellous diversity that yet retains a collective identity could have made this area the wonder of the world, physically beautiful, self-sufficient and wealthy. I would sometimes think that, in such a region, no Arab need travel anywhere else, so satisfying and broad is its appeal. Instead of which it is a place of backwardness, poverty and divisiveness. This is by no means all Israel's fault, but its existence in their midst has contributed powerfully to the Arabs' decline. Israelis and their apologists dismiss such assessments as conspiratorial and seeking to avoid the Arabs' responsibility for their own backwardness. It has even become fashionable for the Arabs themselves to decry their failure as self-induced. And though, as will be argued later, there are faults endemic to the Arab world, ignoring Israel's signal role in the story is both wrong and misleading. We will discuss in what follows the major ways in which Israel has damaged the Arab region and continues to do so.

In 1948, the Arab world found itself confronted with a new creation which was alien to it in every sense. Its governing ethos was European and the bulk of its population was also European. (The 'Arab' Jews, who augmented the existing Palestinian Jewish community, came later, but were subsumed into the ruling Western structure.) As such, Arabs could neither understand it nor deal with it. That year, 1948, was immensely traumatic for the Arabs. Not only were they powerless to prevent Israel's creation, but they also failed to defeat it in the war that immediately ensued. Their ill-trained, ill-equipped token armies, prevented by the colonialist powers who still dominated them from anything more than a security role at home, stood little chance against the much larger, highly motivated, trained and better equipped Jewish forces. But it made no difference to their sense of failure.[1] They were impotent to protect the Palestinians from dispossession, something that at the time shocked and appalled every Arab who watched it happen, and just as impotent to halt Israel's expansion and growing power in the region. By early 1949, the Israelis had seized over 20 per cent of the land allocated to the Palestinians by the UN Partition Plan (see Map 1). 'The problem is not that Israel is so great,' an Israeli friend once told me, 'but rather that it's a mirror in which the Arabs see their own weakness.' The implied contempt for Arab sensibilities and welfare of those who helped set up Israel amongst them was an additional insult, which only rubbed salt into the wound. It was especially galling to see the West's most powerful states, having implanted Israel at the heart of the Arab world, devotedly nurturing and indulging it in ways that would have been unthinkable for these powers with any Arab state. Few people, blinded as most Westerners were by widespread projections of Israel's helplessness and vulnerability, realised how extensive and generous that support was, and how, without it, the Zionist experiment might have ended before it had begun.

Nurturing a Fledgling Israel

The first decade of Israel's existence was seemingly precarious, confronting Arab hostility and international demands to repatriate the Palestinian refugees. But, much as Israelis might not have perceived it like this, in fact there was little actual danger from these quarters, and it looked as if the Zionist project in Palestine, implausible and unreasonable though it was, might really proceed unhampered. Between 1948 and 1964, Arab and Palestinian reaction was confused and ineffective, and opposition beyond the rhetorical, was minimal. The neighbouring Arab states even put out several peaceful feelers towards the Jewish state, as we shall see. At the same time, Western powers, most notably the US, were strongly supportive of Israel. This is hardly surprising, since it was set up with their active participation (as in the case of Britain) and maintained with their military and financial support (Germany, France and later the US). The last is today Israel's staunchest ally and most generous benefactor.

American endorsement of the Zionist project was far from wholehearted at first. Although up until 1947, successive American presidents supported the idea of a Jewish homeland in Palestine, the state and defense departments, as well as the Central Intelligence

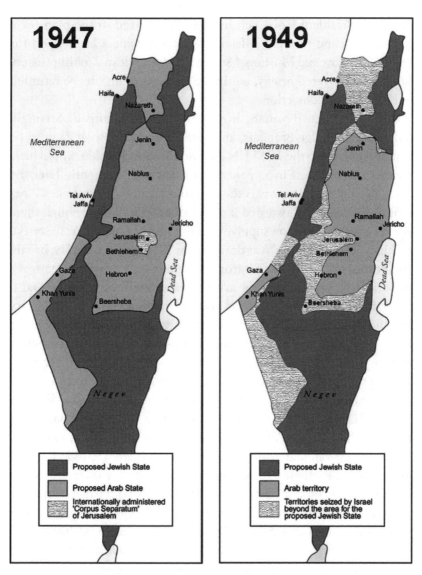

Map 1. UN Partition Plan of 1947 and Israel/Palestine in 1949 (Source: The Palestinian Academic Society for the Study of International Affairs)

Agency, were opposed to the creation of Israel on the grounds that it would be a source of instability and danger in the future.[2] Indeed the American-inspired King–Crane Commission of 1919 reported that the Zionist project would violate the principle of self-determination and Arab rights.[3] And so the US remained largely detached from the scene before 1947, albeit with periodic expressions of sympathy for

Zionism. President Roosevelt in fact disapproved of the plan for a
Jewish state and thought Palestine should become a Holy Land for
Jews, Christians and Muslims.[4] Subjected to American Zionist pressure
for this, he wavered briefly, but in the last year of his life, he returned
to his previous conviction.[5]

With President Truman, however, matters changed. Strongly
influenced by Judge Brandeis, an ardent American Jewish Zionist, he
lent his support to the 1947 UN Partition Resolution that would have
created a Jewish state in 55 per cent of Palestine.[6] Six months later, the
US under his presidency was the first to recognise this state in 77 per
cent of the land and awarded it a sum of $200 million. Though there
was an arms embargo on supplying arms to Israel (and the Arab states),
a 'Tripartite Declaration' was drawn up in 1950 between the US, Britain
and France to protect Israel's frontiers and provide it with armaments
up to the level permitted by the arms balance agreement with the Arabs.
When Israel started to develop its nuclear programme in 1956, contrary
to America's opposition to the proliferation of nuclear weapons, the
latter turned a blind eye. Recently declassified CIA documents show
that, by 1961, the US was certainly aware of Israel's nuclear weapons-
making capacity.[7] The American stance of pretending not to know what
Israel was up to in the nuclear field has been maintained ever since.

It was France in fact that started Israel on the nuclear path. The
French, who had been arming the Jewish state since 1953, gave it its
nuclear reactor in that year to be installed in the late 1950s at Dimona
in the Negev. Partly in revenge against the Arabs for their support of
the Algerian revolution, they co-operated closely with Israel on nuclear
arms research, elevating it to the ranks of the tiny number of nuclear
states at the time. Consequently, Israel today has a reported 200 nuclear
warheads or more. This help was more than matched by Germany's
support for Israel, in atonement for the sins committed against the
Jewish people in the Second World War. German reparations, which
started in 1953, provided the Jewish state with one-eighth of its
total revenue and accounted for a third of its investments. Within
14 years, West Germany had given Israel DM3.45 billion as 'global
compensation', 2.4 billion of it in the form of goods and services.[8] By
1978, the figure had risen to DM22 billion with an additional 10.47
billion projected for the year 2000.[9] And that was in addition to the
annual $130 million given to 500,000 Israeli Jewish individuals in

restitution, boosting Israel's economy further. By 1957, 20 per cent of German reparations were made payable in weapons and the building of weapons factories in Israel, and indeed West Germany became a secret conduit for US arms to Israel until the 1960s.[10] The Germans built Israel's commercial fleet and provided 50 per cent of investment in its railways; in 1966, German reparations alone accounted for 4 per cent of Israel's GNP. Within 19 years, German reparations provided a quarter of Israel's imports and 16 per cent of its capital investments.[11] Such payment to the state and to Jewish individuals living there has continued ever since.[12] Germany's unstinting support for Israel has most recently been expressed through the supply of sophisticated nuclear submarines in 2005 without a thought for the threat this poses to the Arab world.

It is noteworthy that this marked generosity to Israel was not matched by an equal obligation towards Poland and Russia, both of which lost many more of their citizens during the war and also lodged claims with Germany. Nor has anything like the same favour been bestowed on any Arab country to date. For Germany, Israel was a very special case and remains so, although, strictly speaking, the Jewish state (as against the Jews whom Nazism harmed) has no legal claim against Germany. It did not exist at the time when the offence was committed.[13] It is also worth remembering that the Zionists collaborated with Nazi Germany during the 1930s over the emigration of German Jews to Palestine through the so-called Haavara agreement whereby German Jews were encouraged to leave for Palestine with a proportion of their assets.[14] Zionism in fact pronounced itself in ideological sympathy with the aims of the Hitler regime at the time, drawing a parallel between the rebirth of national life in Germany and that of Jews in Palestine.[15] But in view of the mass murder of Jews, none of this has made any difference to the German determination to support Israel; indeed to even question it in today's political climate would be seen as tantamount to antisemitism. Yet in trying to atone for its sins against the Jews, Germany has in effect been helping to strengthen Israel against the Arabs. Thus, by improving conditions for Israelis, Germany has worsened them for Arabs.

Not all the major Western powers supported Israel so strongly. Relations with the now defunct USSR were not always smooth. But in the beginning, the USSR was amongst the Zionist project's supporters.

In 1947, it voted for the UN partition plan, which might not have been passed otherwise, and, in 1948, sent arms to the Zionists via Czechoslovakia, Hungary and Romania.[16] The Soviets sought to weaken the Anglo-American hold on the region by helping to create in Israel a state loyal to them. For the same reason they recognised Israel in 1948, immediately after the Americans. But relations soon soured over Israel's overt approaches to America and the Western capitalist camp, although they improved again in 1953, and a year later the Soviets signed a trade agreement with the new state. However, matters deteriorated once more during the 1956 Suez campaign, which the USSR formally opposed, and the agreement was suspended. In 1967, the Soviets severed all relations with Israel and adopted a hostile policy towards it, although the Soviet Union always maintained the right of Israel to exist.[17] With the appearance of Mikhail Gorbachev on the scene and the demise of the USSR in 1989, free exit for Soviet Jews to Israel was instituted and diplomatic ties with Russia were restored in 1991. Today, the two states enjoy good political and diplomatic relations, and Russia is a major sponsor of the 'peace process'. Many agreements on trade, tourism and cultural exchange have been drawn up between the two sides.

Overall, therefore, Israel enjoyed enormous support from the major Western powers, which crucially enabled the Zionist project to 'bed down' in a hostile and alien region. The fact that this Western stance was motivated more by self-interest than an endorsement of Zionism as such was irrelevant for Israel; the important point was that the West provided the means necessary to the project's survival. The same reasoning underlies the alliance between Zionism and the Christian right in the US today. While the latter sees the return of the Jews to the Holy Land and the annihilation of those who fail to convert to Christianity as a necessary prelude to the Messiah's second coming and hence support Israel, the Zionists are happy to go along with this in exchange for their vigorous defence of the Jewish state. This is not difficult to understand, since Zionism always had to be opportunistic in order to ensure Israel's survival.

Israel's Damage to the Palestinians

The deleterious effects of Israel's establishment on Palestinian soil are well documented. It is not the purpose of this book to detail once again that dismal story with its seemingly endless ramifications that have blighted the lives of generations of Palestinians and continues to this day. The cardinal factor, which started the Palestinians on a tragic and downward course, was their dispossession. Between 1947 and 1949 most of them lost their homes.[18] This terrible event ensued on a protracted indigenous struggle that started in the early 1920s against the Zionists and the British, who ruled the country under the Mandate, during which Palestinian hopes for independence were crushed and subordinated to the needs of the incoming Jews. Some early Zionists, perhaps foreseeing some of this, imagined a different scenario for Jews and Arabs in Palestine. They included such figures as Judah Magnes, the Hebrew University's first president, Martin Buber and Arthur Ruppin representing a small Zionist minority which saw Arab–Jewish co-existence as possible and desirable.[19] They established Brit Shalom in the 1930s, an organisation devoted to these ideas. (At one point, its members invited my father, an official in the Mandate's education department at the time, to join them in the struggle for Arab–Jewish co-operation.) They envisaged a shared state between Jews and Arabs, and were interested in unification between the Arab states, in which the Jews could become a component. As will be seen in Chapter 7, some of this group did not want a Jewish state at all, but rather the freedom to express their culture. David Ben-Gurion himself put forward a plan in 1934 for a union of Arab states to which the Palestinians could be linked, allowing for a Jewish majority to develop in Palestine without conflict (and become a state, though he did not communicate this to his Palestinian interlocutors).[20]

But the majority Zionist drive towards statehood (in which Ben-Gurion became a prominent leader) overtook these attempts at accommodation and co-existence. Long before the UN Partition Resolution was passed in 1947 (which the Zionists eagerly accepted),[21] Ben-Gurion was clear on his ultimate goal of a Jewish state to replace Palestine. In 1937 he wrote in a letter, 'Erect a Jewish state at once, even if it is not in the whole land. The rest will come in the course of time. It must come.'[22] It is tempting to speculate how differently things might have turned out had it been the Brit Shalom faction and not Ben-Gurion's that succeeded.

The 1948 *nakba*, or catastrophe, did more than dispossess the Palestinians. It destroyed their whole society and led to their fragmentation and dispersal. Today, they live as disparate communities, between three and four million in refugee camps; approximately one million as Israeli citizens in Israel; three and a half million in the West Bank and Gaza under Israeli occupation; and the remaining two to three million as exiles in a variety of countries around the world.[23] Altogether over ten million Palestinians were sacrificed in order to accommodate five million Jews, most of them until recently from distant countries. From 1964 until 1993, the Palestinians managed a sort of unity under the umbrella of the Palestine Liberation Organisation (PLO), which enabled them to feel a sense of cohesion. But after the signing of the Oslo Accords in 1993 and the return of Yasser Arafat and most of the Palestinian leadership to Palestinian territory in 1994, the PLO was effectively marginalised and, by 2005, existed in barely more than name.[24] This left millions of exiled Palestinians leaderless and fragmented once again. At the same time, those who lived under Israeli occupation experienced daily privation and hardship on a scale unimaginable to most people. So often repeated was this fact, it became almost banal, and people were virtually inured to the daily reports of Palestinian suffering, however horrifying. According to the World Bank, the Palestinian economy in 2004 was 'one of the worst in modern history'.[25]

Thus, the creation of Israel converted a settled, mostly agricultural society into a nation of refugees, exiles, second-class citizens and communities under military occupation. From 1948 onwards, every attempt was made to erase all traces of the Arab presence in the new Israel so as to destroy the Arab character and distinctive history of the old Palestine. Place names were changed from Arabic to Hebrew as a deliberate policy instituted in 1949 by Ben-Gurion, one which aimed to find ancient or biblical equivalents for the Palestinian towns and villages and produce a 'Hebrew map' of Palestine.[26] The same policy continued after 1967 with the renaming of Muslim and Christian sites in the Old City of Jerusalem.[27] Buildings and villages were demolished, and in their place new European-style structures and settlements sprang up. So effective was this erasure that the locations of many of the old villages are scarcely recognisable, and it has become the task of Palestinian historians like Walid Khalidi and the researcher, Salman Abu Sitta, to try and re-map them.[28] More recently, settlements built directly above Palestinian villages use the village names with the addition of the

Hebrew word for 'upper', and often the Arabic has been distorted to make it unrecognisable as such. In time, it may be difficult to remember which of the two had been the original, and the Palestinian village will have been in effect effaced.

Aspects of indigenous culture, most prominently in food, were adopted and labelled Israeli. I remember feeling a sense of outrage when I first came across 'Israeli' *falafel*, a staple snack in Egypt and the Levant, and 'Israeli' *hummos,* another Arab dish widely used in the area; even in Western countries, restaurants serving 'Israeli food' are found to be offering none other than the same Arab dishes, appropriated without attribution. I could not repress my annoyance every time I passed a Jewish snack bar in Golders Green, where I lived (an area of north London with a large number of Jewish residents), selling blatantly Lebanese/Palestinian dishes as 'oriental Jewish food'. 'Why don't you go there?' the Jewish drycleaner on Golders Green Road once asked me, 'You'd like it. The food's very similar to yours I expect.' Equally annoying to me was the shop next door, which displayed Palestinian pottery plates and jars, with their distinctive colourful patterns, as souvenirs 'from Israel'. The *hora,* an Israeli folk dance, first introduced by Jewish immigrants from Eastern Europe where it originated, and which acquired over the years many features of the traditional Arab *dabka,* is another example of this cultural 'borrowing'. Some might see in this a benign Israeli attempt to integrate into the regional culture, but for Palestinians it was yet another part of the process that sought to expunge their existence from memory.

The Israeli campaign against the Palestinians was a systematic assault on the collective memory, identity and cohesion of a whole society that aimed to extirpate the idea that anything coherent and non-Jewish had predated Israel. The damage this has done to the Palestinians in physical, social and psychological terms is incalculable and has yet to be assessed. In the early years of the state, for example, Israel instituted a policy deliberately aimed at destroying the cohesion of Palestinian society. Israeli agents secretly incited conflict amongst Palestinians, armed and otherwise favoured certain groups amongst them, and devised ways to prevent the emergence of a Palestinian educated class and the formation of a Palestinian leadership.[29] There were ongoing oral history projects aiming to document the 1948 experiences and their consequences, since few written records were made of this tragic story.[30] Though such projects were gaining momentum, the work was still at an early stage. That these efforts to salvage the facts before the generation that lived them disappeared took so long to take shape was itself an indication of the trauma that the nakba caused.

One small example should serve to illustrate the point. A little-publicised feature of the nakba was the forced labour camps that the new Israeli state set up during the 1948–9 war. According to the International Red Cross, there were five such camps for males aged between 10 and 60 which housed over 5,000 Palestinians captured during the war. The men were used to build Jewish settlements and transfer stones from destroyed Arab homes to build new Jewish ones. The prisoners remained in the camps for between two and five years, and most were released in 1955. Many of the camp guards were German Jews who had escaped from Nazi Germany, and possibly from German prisoner camps themselves. No Palestinian captive spoke of this experience later and the story only surfaced in later research.[31] It was as if no one could articulate for years the enormity of suffering that the experience of loss, insecurity and dislocation had caused. So, people got on with the business of survival and did not look back.

Israel's Damage to the Arab World

It was not only the 1948 Palestinians and their descendants who have paid a heavy price for Israel's creation. The Arab world was transformed by its imposition in their midst. While the so-called frontline states of Egypt, Jordan, Syria and Lebanon have been the most affected, the consequences of Israel's presence have reverberated throughout the region. No other conflict has lasted as long as that consequent on Israel's creation. There has not been a single decade since then when Israel has not been in combat with its neighbours. This has damaged the political process in the Arab world, which has come to look to and depend on its army generals for leadership and to admire military strength and violence. The establishment of the Jewish state in 1948 must rate as the single most cataclysmic event to hit the Middle East region since the First World War. As noted earlier, this traditional Arab view of Israel has recently been challenged by alternative critiques that see the Arabs themselves as responsible for much of their own misfortunes.

These assert that Arab regimes have found it convenient to blame Israel and the West for the sorry state of the Arab world, so as to disguise their own backwardness and incompetence. The Egyptian commentator, Amin al-Mahdy, wrote in *Al-Hayat* (9 September 2002) that the Palestinian conflict had always been 'the basic source of legitimacy for the Arab military republics' and the constant excuse for their lack of modernity.[32] In 2004 a group of influential Arab intellectuals, dubbed by many as 'the new liberals', came together in Alexandria to discuss the question of Arab social and economic backwardness, not as a consequence of foreign factors, but purely in terms of the local context.[33] The Arab Human Development Report prepared for the UN Development Programme (UNDP) in 2002, which revealed the extent of the Arab world's retardation in several key areas, was seized on by Western observers as evidence for this view. *The Economist* (4 July 2002) observed that the report had avoided blaming the Arab–Israeli conflict for the Arab region's failings. Yet, the authors of the report were also quite clear that the Israeli occupation cast a pall over the region's entire political and economic life, posed a threat to all Arab countries and that the Arab–Israeli conflict was 'a major impediment to human development in the region'.[34]

The Cost of Militarisation

The Arab states, struggling with post-independence at the time of Israel's establishment, should have been focused on their own political and social development. The frontline states were instead dragged into wars, which diverted their resources into armaments and surveillance. Since they did not win these wars (the 1973 war is seen by Arabs as a possible exception), they were set back each time with loss of territory or a failure to regain all of it, as in the 1973 war, and a need to rearm even more extravagantly than before. This arms build-up was aggravated by the willingness of the major weapons-exporting states – America, the former Soviet Union, France and Britain – to sell arms to the region. The Middle East is the biggest per capita spender on arms in the developing world. Arab military spending in the late 1990s accounted for 7.4 per cent of GNP, three times the world average of 2.4 per cent. Arms expenditure in Arab countries has grown by an annual 5 per cent since then.

This was hardly surprising. Modern warfare necessitated the purchase of ever more sophisticated weapons, with correspondingly high military expenditure. As Israel acquired such arms from the US to satisfy its 'security needs', something that the Western world seemed to have adopted as legitimate, the Arab states were pushed into trying to keep up at increasing expense. But the difference was that the arms the US (and Britain) sold to the Arabs were not ones they could use without US or British technical assistance. Such sales were thus more designed to benefit Western arms industries than enhance the ability of the Arab states to protect themselves against aggression. Arms for what one might call real use were rarely forthcoming from the West from the 1950s to the 1970s but rather from the Soviet Union. For example, when Egypt's Nasser requested such arms from America to help fend off Israeli attacks on Egypt in the 1950s, his request was rejected and he had to turn to Czechoslovakia, then under Soviet control. After the Camp David agreement, when Egypt ceased to be a threat to Israel, the US has supplied real-use arms to it.

It is not difficult to see why states of conflict, especially those involving war, disable a region's economies. In the Arab–Israeli case, the conflict led to five major wars and a continuous state of hostility with consequently heightened military expenditure on arms purchases and on maintaining armies in and out of combat, not to mention the indirect costs of diverting expert and other skilled labour to service these arms. Furthermore, situations of instability and conflict discourage foreign investment with predictable ill effects on the economy. Forced migration of skilled labour to other places, consequent on this situation, are further aggravating factors; while labour remittances from outside benefit overpopulated countries such as Egypt, they also suffer from the loss of their skilled workforce for domestic development. The effect of sequential wars with Israel has thus been to exhaust the frontline Arab states and weaken them. At the same time, the average Arab expenditure on health and education combined was running at only 3.7 per cent of GNP in 2002.[35] Lacking a Western sponsor, as in the case of Israel, which would fund these military extravagances, the frontline Arabs states have ended up with economies grossly distorted in favour of the needs of militarisation at the expense of social and economic development.[36]

Yet, the Arabs could not have resisted the need to militarise. They had no choice in the face of what they saw as a clearly expansionist Israel, bent on taking their land. Israel's first leaders made no secret of these designs. David Ben-Gurion declared, in 1948, that the Jewish state had been established on only a part of the 'Land of Israel'. 'To maintain the status quo will not do,' he said. 'We have to set up a dynamic state bent upon expansion.'[37] He regretted ending the 1948–9 war with the Arabs because it set a brake on the Jewish state's expansionist aims. Yigal Allon, a prominent military commander at this time, would have preferred the borders to run from the Litani river in Lebanon to the Sinai desert and blamed Ben-Gurion for halting the Jewish army's advance.[38] Israel did not set its borders with Egypt until 1979 and not at all with Syria or Lebanon to this day (the Shebaa farms, partly in Lebanon and partly in Syria, were still in dispute and under Israeli occupation in 2006), indicating, as the Arabs felt, that it had left the possibility for expansion open. The Zionist attitude to Arab land, moreover, seemed to be that it was there to be used for Israel's security, agriculture and water needs, for example, in the Golan Heights or Lebanon, disregarding the question of Arab rights to the land and its resources. From an Arab perspective, Israel's only moral position appeared to be, 'if you want it, take it'.

Israel's Stance on Peace

At the same time, the Arabs could also see that Israel wanted no peace with them. The reasons for this were obvious. Israel needed time to consolidate its diverse population into some sort of homogeneity. After all, and despite the claims of Zionism, there was no single Jewish nation ready to populate the new state; a myriad of individuals and groups who came from a variety of countries with different languages and customs hardly constituted a nation. If Israel had allowed itself to be accepted into the surrounding region by making peace with the Arabs before it had amalgamated its entire people into something cohesive, there would have been no Jewish state. Newly arrived immigrants might have returned, Jews from Arab lands might never have come, and the rest would have assimilated. If the Zionist project was to succeed, Israel could literally not afford to make peace with the Arab world. As will be discussed in the rest of this section, Israel thus rejected every peaceful Arab advance, starting as far back as September 1948, barely four months after it was established. Though Israel's outward posture in these contacts seemed flexible, in reality it was nothing of the kind and its policy remained driven by the need to keep the Arab world at bay until the time was right. Thus, it was no accident that it took 30 years for Israel to sign its first peace treaty with an Arab state, the 1979 Camp David Accords with Egypt, entered into because it was under US pressure to do so and saw the advantage of removing Egypt out of the fray, but also because by then it had become firmly established.

Despite their belligerent public stance, the Arab states made numerous overtures to Israel for negotiations and/or a peaceful resolution of the conflict, but to no avail (see below).[39] Even before the 1948–9 war they were ready to accommodate the Jewish state on certain conditions, and the Arab League decided on military intervention only at the end of April 1948, two weeks before the war began, although the possibility of such intervention had been discussed in 1946.[40] It should be borne in mind that in making peaceful approaches to the Jewish state, Arab rulers were taking enormous risks. Not only did their populations harbour a powerful anger and hatred towards Israel for its treatment of the Palestinians, but they were also betraying an agreed pan-Arab position on the principled basis of the rights of the Palestinian refugees. The Arab League's official view was that the rights of the Palestinians could not be harmed 'without prejudice to and stability in the Arab world' and, the Palestinians having no government to represent them, the League took up the case on their behalf.[41] None of this impressed Israel's leadership, however, intent as it was on maintaining the newly-forged integrity of the Jewish state. But this rejectionist position was not enough to implement Israel's expansionist strategy for land and resources. It was necessary to provoke the neighbouring Arabs in order to make use of the resulting conflict.

From 1951 onwards there was constant unrest on the armistice lines with Syria and Jordan, a string of incidents always instigated by the Israelis and followed by an Arab response ranging from placation to hostility.[42] The usual pretext for Israeli military action was that 'infiltrators' – unarmed, displaced Palestinians mostly, trying to get back to their land or belongings – were an existential threat to Israel, which retaliated with disproportionate military force against the host country. The Arab governments responded with strenuous – some would say, shameful – attempts at curbing the Palestinians, but Israel remained unimpressed, maintaining an attitude of injured innocence and victimisation.

These early skirmishes were sufficient for a while to assist Israel in its campaign of 'bedding down'. But more needed to be done, as the wars of 1956 and 1967 demonstrate. Both of these were the result of deliberate and/or opportunistic Israeli action, serving the same agenda: to destroy or neutralise Arab opposition to the Jewish state and force the Arabs to negotiate peace with Israel on its own terms or else pay a heavy price. In so far as the Israelis had identified Egypt's president, Gamal Abdul Nasser, with his vision of a pan-Arab unity, to be their greatest threat almost as soon as he was in office, they set about finding ways to defeat him. The story of the Suez war is well known, how it was instigated by deliberate Israeli aggression against Egypt, acting in collusion with France and Britain, and how it was only by concerted US–USSR action through the Security Council that Israel was made to withdraw from Egyptian territory.[43]

The Suez adventure backfired on Israel; far from destroying Nasser, it only raised his status and prestige amongst the Arabs. The job was unfinished. Whether the next war in 1967 was also a direct result of Israeli design or not has formed the subject of much argument. But it is clear that the Israeli strategy of relentless attacks on Syrian positions and the creation of illegal farming settlements in the Israeli–Syrian demilitarised zone, coupled with Israel's verbal threats against Syria, which had driven it to sign a defence treaty with Egypt in 1966, and its pointed taunts at Nasser, played a decisive role in the escalation to war. Given Israel's anti-Nasser agenda, coupled with reports of Israeli troop concentration along the Syrian border, it is difficult to accept that the 1967 war was an unintended consequence of Arab 'provocation', which was in fact reaction on Egypt's part.[44] Because of it, Israel achieved what it had not succeeded in before, Nasser's humiliation and with it the defeat of the region's hopes of Arab unity.

Israel had cause for enormous satisfaction at this outcome, which expanded its territory and swung the Western world to its cause more staunchly than ever before. Nasser's successor, the more pliant, pro-Western leader, Anwar Sadat, who went on to sign the first Arab–Israeli peace agreement in 1979, was an additional blessing for Israel. This removed the Arab world's most important state from the battle against

Israel and ensured that Egypt would never be a threat again. And indeed, since then, Arabs have never been able to regroup under a new leader and the classic anti-Israel front has been effectively and, it seems, terminally breached – a triumph for Israel and its crowning achievement.

But for the Arabs, it was a radically different story. Humiliated and stunned by the 1967 defeat, despised in the West and deprived of strong, nationalist leadership, they could only contemplate bitterly the damage that Israel had wrought in their midst. It was as if it had finally dawned on them that it would not just be the Palestinians who would be sacrificed for Israel but they themselves as well. The war and Israel's expansion into Arab territory vividly brought home the danger that it posed. With the demise of Nasser's pan-Arab vision, each state started to look to its own national interest. Disunity, unrest and fragmentation along increasingly ethnic and religious lines – always a danger in a region with numerous such minorities – have characterised the Arab region since then. This too fulfils a long-cherished Zionist aim, to see the region broken up into a collection of minorities among which the Jewish state would stand out as the most cohesive and powerful – a neo-Ottoman empire of ethnic-religious communities with Israel (instead of Turkey) at the centre.

This idea was already being implemented domestically with Israel's non-Jewish citizens categorised into Muslims, Christians and Druze, disrupting their collective identity as a national Arab group. It also made it easier to rule them by favouring some communities over others. The Druze, for example, received special treatment right from the beginning of Israel's existence. They had initially been willing to accept the Jewish state, and some of them had collaborated with the Israelis during the 1948–9 war and indeed were recruited to a special volunteer unit within the Israeli army. As an official in the Israeli foreign ministry, Yaacov Shimoni, commented at the time, the Druze would be used as 'the sharp blade of a knife to stab in the back of Arab unity'.[45] In 1963, Israel defined the Druze as an 'ethno-religious community', emphasising their difference from the other Arabs and Muslims and allowed them autonomy over matters of personal status and religious education and endowments (*waqf*). The Israelis tried to integrate them into Israeli society, conscripted them into the army and offered employment in the security services. By 1983 a survey showed that 33 per cent of Druze

men were in the army or other branches of the security services, and
by 1995, 42 per cent were employed by the security services.[46]

One of the ugliest results of this policy has been their recruitment
to the ranks of the notoriously brutal Israeli border guards. I was
detained by such a man at the Ram checkpoint between Ramallah
and Jerusalem in the summer of 2005. He was an Arab in all but his
Israeli military uniform and the large gun slung nonchalantly over his
shoulder. Had I resisted his detention of me in any way, I felt he would
have shot me without hesitation. It was on the tip of my tongue to ask
why he served such masters, especially since Israel had appropriated
acres of Druze land under various laws and regulations introduced
in the 1950s and 1960s. But for Druze peasant protests in the 1970s,
more would have been seized through bribery of their chiefs. Druze
villagers were forcibly resettled on rocky, infertile land. Petitioning the
Israeli government, they asked, 'Are we not citizen of the state? Are
our children not defending its borders like every Jew?'[47]

Factionalising the Arab World

The Zionist vision of factionalising the Arab world was articulated with
extraordinary bluntness in 1982 by a senior Israeli foreign ministry
official, Oded Yinon, writing in the World Zionist Organisation's
periodical, *Kivunim*.[48] In this he saw Israel as instrumental in bringing
about the dissolution of Jordan; the break-up of Egypt into separate
districts; the disintegration of Lebanon into five locally governed areas,
with a similar fate for Syria – Alawites against Sunnis – and Iraq along
ethnic and religious lines; the Druze would form a state in Hauran and
northern Jordan. Following that, the entire Arabian Peninsula would
be 'a natural candidate for dissolution'. Less flamboyantly, Ben-Gurion
during the 1950s had propounded a vision of a reorganised Middle East
wherein Jordan would be divided into an east bank going to Iraq (and
used to house the Palestinian refugees) and a west bank being joined to
Israel. Ariel Sharon, Israel's defence minister and architect of the 1982
invasion of Lebanon, embellished this vision with his earlier plan for
a forced exodus of the West Bank Palestinians into what remained of
Jordan. Lebanon would be split into a Muslim south and annexed to
Israel, while the rest would become a Maronite Christian entity, allied
to the Jewish state.[49] At about the same time, the Israeli Labour Party

European representative, Yoram Peri, wrote in the Israeli journal *Davar* (February 1982) that Israel was committed to destabilising the region, especially Lebanon, Syria, Jordan and Saudi Arabia, and imposing a 'new reality' through military dominance. At the time, there was no American receptiveness to such ideas, a situation that changed dramatically in line with Israel's wishes after the 2003 invasion of Iraq as will be seen below.

Even so, Israel's vision played an important part in the later invasions of Lebanon in 1978 and 1982. Bashir Gemayel, the Maronite leader, a strongly anti-Palestinian figure had been elected in 1982 to form the new Lebanese government, and had been identified by Israel as an ally. But, as he was assassinated shortly thereafter, the plan got no further. However, Israel's drive towards forging alliances with non-Muslim and preferably non-Arab minorities and states remained the same. The purpose of such action was to keep the Arab world divided in Israel's interest and was a central plank of pre- and post-state Israeli policymaking. This dictated Israel's interventionist behaviour on the Arab domestic front – by supporting minorities and penetrating ruling circles with bribes and inducements – and in the regional balance of forces, so as to establish its own hegemony. Lebanon provides a perfect example of both these types of intervention.[50] In its attempts to support Maronite dominance over the Lebanese state, Israel sought to plant a base from which it could offset Syrian influence and so further its hegemonic designs over the Levant. Lebanon, with its multi-confessional system and pro-Western stance, and the fact that its Maronite community had already forged friendly ties with pre- and post-state Israel was fertile ground for such policies. Even so, Israel's involvement in Lebanon is an instructive illustration of classic intra-state Zionist interventionism.

Israel's instrumental role in causing the enormous disruption that the Arab region is witnessing today is another facet of the damage the Jewish state has wrought on the Arabs. Nor should one be surprised that Israel chose such a strategy. It was the logical way to weaken its enemies and enhance its hegemonic status over them. The chaos created in Iraq after the US–British invasion in 2003 raised the real possibility of the country's fragmentation into Shia, Sunni and Kurdish areas as foretold in Zionist planning. Israel had long before been preparing the ground for Iraq's fragmentation by supporting Kurdish rebellions against the Iraq government throughout the 1960s and 1970s. After the American invasion, Israeli operatives became more active in the Kurdish areas (much to Turkey's alarm), funding and training Kurdish fighters to carry out intelligence gathering in Iran and Syria, which Israel identified as next on the list of hostile Middle Eastern sates to be destroyed or broken up. It was alleged that Israel used this intelligence to identify and kill off Shiite and Sunni insurgency leaders in Iraq. In 2004, Israel was also implicated in stirring up the violent Kurdish protests against the Syrian government, using these Iraqi Kurdish operatives.[51]

By 2005, Iraq's fragmentation was becoming a reality, which the new Iraqi constitution was bringing into being. Without mentioning partition by name, the constitution set in motion a process that could lead to it. A Kurdish president was elected, unprecedented for Iraq, but initially welcomed as evidence of ethnic integration and a symbol of the country's multi-ethnic character. However, there were fears at the same time that it was, in fact, a US policy-driven device, aiming to facilitate the process of Kurdish secession and the creation of a Kurdish state, with the rest of the country divided further into Shia and Sunni parts. From here, it was easy to see how these could become statelets in an Iraqi federation. The Iraqi president almost said as much by referring to the 'Union of Iraq' in a presidential address in April 2005, not once mentioning the phrase 'national unity'.

That Israel, which had already shown its inimical intent towards Iraq when it bombed the Iraqi nuclear reactor in 1981, was implicated in this scheme may be discerned in the activities of the neoconservative group advising President George W. Bush on his Iraq policy. The members of this group, all Jewish Zionists sympathetic to the right-wing Israeli Likud party, had been agitating for 'regime change' in Iraq since 1995, arguing that ousting Saddam Hussein was the key to transforming the balance of power in the Middle East in Israel's favour. David Wurmser, Middle East advisor to the US vice-president, Dick Cheney, and a principal member of the neocons, called for the region to be reorganised according to tribe and clan alliances. In such a region, Israel would be the leader and able to dictate terms to Syria and the Palestinians.[52] The neocons were principally concerned with destabilising Israel's enemies so as to secure its position, and saw that only US backing for such an enterprise could ensure the strategy's success. This was the thinking behind the 1996 paper produced by a US-based Israeli think tank, the

Institute for Advanced Strategic and Political Studies, and entitled, 'A clean break: a new strategy for securing the realm'. At its core was a plan to enable Israel (the 'realm'), to shape its regional environment to its own advantage. In this scheme, removing the Iraqi regime was the essential first step to this reconfiguring of the Middle East, with Syria (and Iran) to follow. The government of George Bush, departing from previous US policy to maintain Middle Eastern stability, embraced the strategy and by 2003 was executing it to devastating effect in Iraq. The fact that the neocon agenda coincided with Bush's own vision of a reshaped Middle East in which democracy and freedom prevailed and its enemies defeated was a fortuitous coincidence.[53]

The elections of 2005, which brought into power a government dominated by Shiites and Kurds were a further blow to Iraqi unity. By the middle of 2006, a sectarian civil war was developing to make this fragmentation even more of a reality.[54] The break-up of a major Arab country like Iraq would be a tragedy for the hard-won cohesion of this state and the failure of pluralism there would set an ominous precedent for other Arab states with sectarian minorities. It will also have dire consequences for regional stability, with the potential outcome of Iraqi Kurds inciting other Kurdish groups in Turkey, Syria and Iran to demand an alliance with them, and Iraqi Shiites linking up with militant Shiites in Iran, Lebanon, Bahrain and Saudi Arabia, so undermining the stability of these countries. Iranian support for the Arab Shiites could lead to its greater intervention in the affairs of the Arab world and add another dimension to the fragmentation process.[55]

The Destabilisation of Lebanon

Lebanon was severely destabilised by years of Israeli occupation and interference, its fragile confessional system of government repeatedly under stress. Lebanon's plight was Yinon's model for the entire Middle East. 'The dissolution of Syria and Iraq later into ethnically or religiously unique areas such as in Lebanon', he wrote, 'is Israel's primary target on the Eastern front in the long run.' Israel's protracted occupation of southern Lebanon (1982–2000) left indelible scars on the economic and social life of the local community. Amongst these may be mentioned the creation of thousands of Lebanese collaborators, many of whom have become outcasts both in Israel and in their home country.[56] Thousands of them emigrated to northern Israel where they caused friction with the local Palestinians. The southern Lebanese who had been recruited to trade with, and provide a range of services for, Israel needed to adjust to life following the Israeli withdrawal from Lebanon in 2000. A detailed study of the effects of Israel's occupation on Lebanese society in all its aspects is long overdue.

In 2005, the Syrian presence in Lebanon was ended by the intervention of the USA and other Western powers following the assassination of Rafiq al-Hariri, Lebanon's former prime minister, which was widely imputed to Syria. A situation of political instability ensued, damaging Lebanon's long-standing status as a liberal state and magnet for foreign investment. The evacuation of its army was a severe blow for the Syrians, who had sought to maintain a military presence in the Beqaa valley, as a safeguard against its use by Israel as an attack route. The long-term effects of these dramatic events have yet to be seen. But perhaps the 2006 Israeli attack on Lebanon was an early indication of future events. Syria's withdrawal had left a political vacuum and a weakened Lebanese state, with a strengthening of the anti-Syrian forces that already existed in Lebanon. Israel, which had always sought to weaken its neighbours or convert them into allies, saw the chance of fragmenting Lebanon further and possibly of reviving its old aim to foster the development of a Lebanese government friendly towards it. The Israelis attacked by air, sea and land following the capture, on 12 July, by the Lebanese Shia militia, Hizbullah, of two Israeli soldiers and the killing of eight others. Yet again, the mainly Shiite south of Lebanon bore the brunt of that war, with demolished villages and a massive number of cluster bombs, 100,000 at least, according to the UN (1.2 million according to an Israeli army commander), most of which were still unexploded after the ceasefire drawn up on 11 August 2006.[57]

After 34 days of war, Israel had killed 1,183 Lebanese, most of whom were civilians, and displaced 970,000 others (25 per cent of Lebanon's population). It destroyed thousands of homes and 80 bridges, bombed fuel depots and water storage, pumping and treatment sites, as well as Beirut airport and other civilian structures.[58] The bombing of large fuel depots in south Beirut caused a spillage into the sea of 15,000 tons of oil more than 2 cm thick. The polluted coastline would cost an estimated £34 million to clean up (none of it offered by Israel), and the damage done to marine life, let alone tourism, was likely to be considerable.[59] An air, land and sea blockade, imposed by Israel at the start of the war, was not fully lifted until the end of September 2006. This disproportionate assault on Lebanon (Israel also incurred losses, but to a far smaller extent),[60] was a typical illustration of Israel's use of overwhelming force against any Arab encroachment, and a vivid example of its deadly effect on its neighbours.

In this devastating attack on Lebanon, Israel was in fact aiming to demolish Hizbullah, a relatively recent player in the conflict and a more effective opponent than any other on the Arab scene, one which had had the temerity to fight Israel's occupation of southern Lebanon from 1985 to 2000 and win. Destroying Lebanon's infrastructure in 2006 was supposed to turn the Lebanese people against Hizbullah, to cut off its supply lines and to drive a greater wedge between Lebanon and Syria. And hence Israel's repeated protestations that it had no quarrel with the Lebanese people, but wanted to free them from the hold of the 'terrorists' of Hizbullah. It is ironic that it was Israel's own aggression and belligerence that had created the Islamist militia in the first place. Hizbullah, a Shiite Islamist party representing the large disadvantaged Shia minority, came into being in response to Israel's 1982 occupation of Lebanon, and especially its tenacious hold on the largely Shia south of the country.

By 1992, the party had entered into mainstream Lebanese politics through the election of its members to the Lebanese parliament, and in the 2005 election Hizbullah netted 14 seats out of 128 and one cabinet minister. At the same time, it functioned as an effective welfare organisation, dispensing essential services to the poor, especially in the south of Lebanon. Hizbullah's discipline, cohesion, fighting spirit and freedom from corruption had already won it the praise of many Lebanese and other Arabs throughout the region. But its military achievements against Israel, first in driving Israeli forces out of southern Lebanon in 2000, and then in putting up such resistance to Israel's assault in 2006 as to carry the war into Israeli territory – for the first time in the history of the Jewish state – and force Israel towards a diplomatic solution, engendered an adulation for Hizbullah amongst Arabs throughout the Arab world.[61]

For that very reason perhaps, and because Israel felt humiliated by the drubbing it had received at Hizbullah's hands, a psychological blow from which it might never recover without crushing the Lebanese militia, there were likely to be more Israeli attacks on Lebanon in future. If that happened, it would not only continue to destabilise and damage the country, which had lost the economic gains of the 20 previous years as a result of Israel's bombing, but it would also ensure that Hizbullah remained a fighting force. Demanding that Hizbullah fighters be disarmed, as the West did repeatedly through the UN, without taking into account Israel's role in provoking the need for defence on the part of this essentially Lebanese nationalist movement, was unreasonable and bound to fail.[62] The best way to achieve Hizbullah's disarmament would have been to stop Israel's attacks on Lebanon (UNIFIL, the UN force overseeing the ceasefire following the Lebanon war, for example, reported numerous violations of Lebanese airspace by Israeli fighter planes in October 2006) and enable the Shiite militia to integrate fully into the Lebanese political system.

Splitting Arab Ranks

Israel's policy of making separate deals with individual Arab states, so as to split Arab ranks, was another divisive strategy aiming to break up their resistance. A variety of diplomatic arrangements between Israel and the Arab states were actively pursued towards that end. Egypt, the PLO and Jordan concluded formal agreements with the Jewish state in 1979, 1993 and 1994 respectively (while Arab populations were becoming increasingly anti-Israel), and contacts at lower levels have been made in the last decade with all of Morocco, Tunisia, Mauritania, Qatar and Bahrain; latterly, secret contacts are also rumoured to have been commenced with Libya and Sudan. In an interview with *Haaretz* (22 May 2005), the Libyan ruler's son, Saif al-Islam Qadhafi, said that he saw no problem in co-operating with Israelis. In the period prior and subsequent to the evacuation of Israeli settlements from Gaza in August 2005, this process intensified and became more overt. In Dubai an Israeli representative office was due to be opened in the same year (it never was in the end); Kuwait gave clear signals of its intentions to make contacts with Israel, while Algerian and Saudi ministers were reported to be meeting with their Israeli counterparts.[63] Silvan Shalom, Israel's foreign minister, boasted openly that ten Arab states would be establishing relations with the Jewish state before long.[64]

In late 2006, it was alleged that a secret meeting was held in the Jordanian capital between the Israeli prime minister and top-level Saudi officials to discuss the Iranian threat to both countries as well as the Palestinian situation.[65] A visit to the region shortly after by the US secretary of state, Condoleeza Rice, followed up on this initiative by bringing together a coalition of Arab foreign ministers from 'moderate' Arab Sunni states in an attempt to counter the Arab Shiites whom, the US claimed, Iran was using to incite acts of terrorism and to wield its influence over the region. In this scheme, the US and Israel had identified Egypt, Saudi Arabia and Jordan as the 'moderate Arabs', Syria, Hizbullah and Hamas as the 'extremists' and the instruments of Iranian designs.[66] Whether this new alignment would succeed against Syria and Iran was not clear at the time of writing, but the attempt would certainly act as yet another device for fragmenting the Arab world in Israel's favour. Persistent rumours of Israel's clandestine involvement in the 2003 occupation of Iraq, in the torture regime of Iraqi prisoners and its intelligence operations with the Iraqi Kurds, where, according to many sources, Israeli agents have been especially active since the US–British invasion, add to the picture of Israeli interference in the affairs of the Arab world. It has to be anticipated that a pro-American government in Iraq would attempt to establish relations with Israel as a matter of policy.[67]

In 2004 Israeli exports to Arab countries stood at $85 million, representing an increase of 68 per cent over the previous year. Of this amount, $2.5 million of exports went to Iraq. Imports to Israel from the Arab world in the same year totalled $42 million, representing an increase of 27 per cent over 2003.[68] This suggests that the economic boycott of Israel, instituted by the Arab League in 1951, was being circumvented (by those states that had no peace treaty with Israel). In a situation of collective Arab military and political weakness against Israel, the boycott had been one of the few instruments open to the Arabs to use against it. But that too was now crumbling. And all this was happening against the background of an intensified Israeli occupation of Palestinian land and repression of its inhabitants, not to mention the continued occupation of Syrian territory.

Encircling the Arab World

At the state level, Israeli strategy from the 1950s onwards aimed at creating a network of non-Muslim, non-Arab countries linked to Israel and especially those states opposed to pan-Arabism and Islam as a unifying factor. In addition, it sought to neutralise or win over those non-Arab states which supported the Arab cause. Hence, it cultivated clandestine contacts with pre-Khomeini Iran and maintained these for several years even afterwards, supplying weapons to Iran during its war with Iraq. Likewise, Israel established ties with Turkey, Ethiopia and the Christian south of Sudan, aiming to surround the Arab world with a ring of antipathetic states. Israel's relationship with Sudan was in fact quite complex and punctuated by periods of co-operation between the two states, especially in the early 1950s.[69] Even so, Israel maintained its policy of isolating Arab states by supporting the anti-government rebel movement in the south of Sudan with arms and training after 1957. In the early 1990s it cultivated John Garang, the leader of the southern Sudan's People's Liberation Army, sending him arms shipments through Kenya and, in 1994, he was reported to have gone to Israel to meet with Israel's prime minister, Yitzhak Shamir.

The same policy of encirclement became more overt over time, and resulted in a close liaison with Turkey, despite tensions following the US–British invasion of Iraq.[70] The Israeli presence in Ethiopia expanded to include a series of educational and development projects and, in 2004, following the Ethiopian foreign minister's visit to Israel, both countries signed an agreement to enhance cultural, educational and scientific co-operation. Israel's mission in Addis Ababa is the largest after that of the US. The alliance between the two countries was not always so close, however; with the rise of the Dergue regime under Haile Mariam Mengistu in 1974, all contacts with Israel ceased. Even so, Israel established links with anti-government insurgents and was able to execute the so-called Operation Solomon in which Israel airlifted 14,400 Jewish Ethiopians to the Jewish state in 1991. The fall of the Dergue government in the same year enabled Israel to resume relations with Ethiopia as before.

Neighbouring Eritrea also became the recipient of intense Israeli attention. In line with Israel's policy of breaking up all Arab or pro-Arab networks and creating enmity towards them, Israel aimed from the 1960s onwards to 'de-Arabise ' the Horn of Africa by inserting its own influence there, an enterprise in which it seems to have signally succeeded.[71] After decades of assistance to Ethiopia in its war against Eritrea, Israel succeeded in reversing Eritrean hostility towards it. An Israeli embassy was opened in Asmara, in 1991, to which the Eritreans eventually responded by opening their own embassy in Israel, in 2003. This reversal in the Eritrean position, traditionally a sympathetic one to the Arabs (as was theirs towards Eritrea), and given Israel's longstanding support for the Ethiopians against Eritrea, must be counted among Israel's more remarkable diplomatic achievements. It is worth remembering that many Eritreans traced their ancestry to the Arabs of Yemen, many were Arabic-speaking and approximately 50 per cent were Muslim.[72]

Israeli military and agrarian experts became likewise involved in many parts of black Africa, providing them with military training and construction. Israeli technical assistance pointedly targeted those African states with significant Christian populations or which were pro-Western in approach, as, for example, Kenya, Ghana, Zaire, the Ivory Coast and Mauritius.[73] Between 1958 and 1971, there were 2,763 such experts based in African states. In the wake of the 1973 Arab–Israeli war, however, there was an interruption in this co-operative relationship when most African states, which supported the Arab side in the war, broke off relations with Israel. But they restored them later. By 1983, 4 per cent of Israel's exports were going to Africa, and Israel had established links with 30 African countries through which it enhanced its stature as an international player and gateway to US favour. Israeli military experts were reported to be active in Chad during its civil war in the 1980s, and talks were underway in 2005 to establish diplomatic ties between the two countries. The warming of relations between Israel and the African states owed something also to events in the Arab world after 1991, when the Madrid peace conference was held with the aim of achieving an Arab–Israeli peace agreement, and even more so after the signing of the Oslo Accords two years later. It was as if Israel, having gained greater Arab acceptance, released the African states from having to harbour any hostility towards it on that basis.

The same policy of encirclement and neutralisation of pro-Arab states underlay Israel's latterly cultivated relations with India, which, until 1992, had a staunchly pro-Palestinian position and no diplomatic ties with the Jewish state. Since the new detente under the Bharatiya Janata Party, which came into power in 1998, trade between the two increased and was reported to have reached an annual $2 billion by 2004, while India spent $1.8 billion on military purchases from Israel in 2004.[74] A close security relationship developed, with intelligence sharing and joint military exercises, threatening the neighbouring Muslim state, Pakistan. Consequently, the latter began to reconsider its traditionally hostile stance towards Israel. Although clandestine meetings between Israeli and Pakistani officials had been ongoing for years, in 2005, Pakistan's foreign minister had an unprecedented public meeting with his Israeli counterpart in Turkey and openly affirmed the change in relations between the two states.[75] The Pakistani president went on to address the American Jewish Congress in September 2005 and was preparing his people for a de facto recognition of Israel. In this Pakistan was aiming to counterbalance the close relationship between Israel and India on the one hand, and the one between India and the US on the other.[76]

Forcing Arabs to Normalise with Israel

The insistence on 'full normalisation of relations' between Israel and its Arab neighbours became a familiar phrase in the Israeli political lexicon and that of its Western backers. Egypt's peace treaty with Israel, for example, carried a provision for full normalisation of relations between the two countries; the same happened with the Israel–Jordan treaty, and negotiations over an agreement with Syria, though unsuccessful to date, always included such a condition. Normalisation of relations is indeed a desirable and accepted end point to peacemaking. But it usually comes about in the context of a settlement the parties view as fair. In Israel's case, however, the Arabs were required to normalise with it despite its occupation of Arab land and its treatment of the Palestinians, both now and formerly. Moreover, they had to accept and embrace it in their midst while it maintained a hegemonic status over them in arms and technology with the help of Western backers determined to give it an edge over its neighbours. In short, the Arabs were expected to make peace with Israel – and to love it as well.

Unsurprisingly, this did not happen. Israel's impressive penetration of Arab ranks acted as yet another factor in destabilising the region, for it was nowhere accompanied by an acceptance of Israel at popular level. As an Israeli writer complained in the mass circulation Israeli daily, *Yediott Ahronot* (10 October 2004), 'All over Egypt they hate us . . . The ground burns beneath the feet of the Israeli tourist in every Muslim state.' Indeed, no real normalisation of relations with Israel took place, not even in Egypt, after 27 years of formal agreement. On the contrary, relations between the two were more strained than even before.[77] Following the terrorist bombings of tourist resorts at Sharm al-Sheikh in October 2004, when Israel proposed Egyptian–Israeli security co-ordination, the Egyptian side was dismayed and refused the offer. As an editorial in *Al-Quds* pointed out on 11 October 2004, the majority of Egyptian military and security institutions still regarded Israel as an enemy and the largest threat to Egyptian security. At the start of the intifada, Egypt withdrew its ambassador to Israel, who was not returned until five years later. When Ariel Sharon was invited to Egypt in February 2005, large crowds of demonstrators in Cairo and Alexandria denounced the visit and burnt the Israeli flag (*Al-Quds*, 9 February 2005). Civil society, institutions and individuals, throughout the Arab world is generally hostile towards Israel, although there have been a number of specific initiatives between writers, academics and intellectuals.[78] When Ariel Sharon was due to visit Tunis for an international conference in November 2005, ten opposition parties and human rights groups described it, to government denials, as a move towards recognising Israel that would bring 'eternal shame' down on Tunisia (*Al-Quds*, 2 March 2005).

The Palestinian intifada in 2000 had already set back what movement there was towards normalisation with the Jewish state. As always in the past, Israel's maltreatment of the Palestinians coloured popular perceptions and augmented pre-existing Arab prejudice against it. Since the beginning of the intifada in 2000, popular feeling, expressed in the large and angry demonstrations that erupted in several Arab capitals, has been at odds with the friendly posture of Arab governments toward Israel. Morocco, which had an official policy of normalisation with Israel following the Oslo Accords, was forced by popular pressure to break off formal contacts with Israel after 2000. An international conference of rabbis and imams, due to be held in Morocco in 2004, had to be cancelled because of security fears of popular opposition.[79] Likewise, Jordan had to withdraw its ambassadors to Israel in 2000 (although he was subsequently returned five years later to popular dismay). In May 2005, a visit by Silvan Shalom, Israel's foreign minister, to Mauritania, which had long-standing diplomatic ties with Israel, was met by angry demonstrations demanding a severance of relations between the two countries (*Al-Quds*, 3 May 2005).

Calls were made to abrogate the peace treaties with Egypt and Jordan, and many cultural and diplomatic contacts with Israel had to be suspended. The Jordanian professional syndicates demanded that the government boycott the Sharon administration. An unprecedented display of placards at their headquarters in Amman calling for an end to normalisation with Israel were hastily removed by embarrassed Jordanian authorities (*Al-Quds*, 18 January 2005). In Bahrain, when in October 2005, the government announced it would close the Arab Boycott Office (a policy maintained since the 1960s as part of the Arab League ban on trading with Israel), there were massive protests against the decision. At about the same time, articles supporting closer ties with Israel appeared in the Kuwaiti press, to similar popular opposition.

Provoking the Rise of Islamic Fundamentalism

Despite these setbacks, Israel made considerable progress in disrupting the traditional Arab opposition to normalisation. So much so that by 2004, a former Israeli foreign ministry director-general, Yoav Biram, could claim that Israel had forged secret ties with Arab (and Islamic) governments, 'far more extensive than has been reported in public', but that such governments concealed the truth from their own populations.[80] The members of the provisional Iraqi government were said in 2005 to have signed a pledge to recognise Israel, but this was kept out of the public eye.[81] Dubai wanted its intention to open an Israeli liaison office kept secret, and there was a general ambiguity about the question of closer ties with the Jewish state at the official level.[82] This dissonance between governor and governed, so widespread in the Arab world, was not without consequences, and only exacerbated the long-standing tensions already existing in what were the essentially undemocratic societies of the Arab world. Israel's drive towards acceptance and popular Arab rejection of it were incompatible forces which, if ignored, must only lead to more extremism and instability.

As it was, the threat that Israel posed to the Arab world had already meant that generations of young Arabs were reared on an unhealthy diet of enmity and confrontationalism. Instead of looking to a normal, secure future in which to develop theirs and their countries' potential, they were instead focused on hostility, and this led to the growth of an array of radical non-state groups and movements opposing Israel and its backers. As the Israeli commentator, Guy Bahor, observed in *Yediott Ahronot*, 3 September 2006, a generation of young Arabs was growing up who saw Israel only as a hateful entity that was the cause of all their ills. In an illuminating account of his visit to Egypt at the time of the devastating Israeli incursions into Palestinian cities in 2002, the American journalist, Lawrence Wright, wondered what had turned the peaceable Egypt he knew towards violence. He recorded a woman at a Muslim Brotherhood meeting in Cairo asking how she could help the Palestinians. 'Teach your children to hate America,' was the answer.[83] In 2002, the director of the United Nations Population Fund, Thoraya Obaid, drew attention to the radicalisation of youth in the Arab world, growing up in a climate of war and military conflict. The long-running Israeli–Palestinian conflict and the sufferings of the Iraqi people under sanctions and occupation had affected these young people, and the double standards of imposing UN sanctions on Islamic countries such as Iraq, Syria and Iran, while failing to resolve the Israeli–Palestinian conflict, fired them with anger.[84] On his first visit to the Palestinian village of Faluja in 2002, the site where the young officer, Gamal Abdul Nasser, had been surrounded by Jewish forces in the 1948–9 war, the Egyptian writer, Ali Salem, recalls how this event affected the lives of millions of Arabs and set them on the road to a state of 'mental war' (against Israel), which has afflicted them ever since.[85]

The recruits for Osama bin Laden and al-Qaeda did not spring out of nowhere. Bin Laden had been an advocate of the Palestinian cause since the 1980s, when he organised a boycott of US goods in protest at US support for Israel. The Palestinian-born Islamist, Abdullah Azzam, with whom he worked closely on the anti-Soviet Afghani jihadist campaign in Peshawar in 1980, may also have influenced him in that direction.[86] But although bin Laden's focus shifted towards the ejection of the American military presence from his homeland, Saudi Arabia, after the Iraq war of 1991, he increasingly linked his cause with that of Palestine's liberation from Israeli occupation. In al-Qaeda's doctrine

Palestine was in any case a sacred land which held some of Islam's holiest shrines. It began to find a sympathetic following amongst some Palestinians in Gaza, which could only grow as the Israeli siege of Gaza worsens.[87] This trend, if continued, would change the Palestinian struggle from being nationalist into being Islamic and one, as Danny Rubinstein observed in *Haaretz* (28 August 2006), far more dangerous. In that sense, it would become a part of the shift towards political Islam that was sweeping the whole region, convulsed by increasing anger at America and its support for Israel.[88] The Lebanese Hizbullah, as we saw, came into being entirely in response to the Israeli invasion of their country in 1982.

But a more striking example of radicalisation was to be seen amongst Palestinians. From 1994 Islamist groups began to carry out acts of violence never seen before in Palestinian society, which had traditionally been secular and peaceable. Though Israel was not responsible for the initial establishment of a branch of the Muslim Brotherhood in Palestine in the 1940s, the later growth of Palestinian Islamic fundamentalism can be traced back to Israel's tacit encouragement after the 1967 occupation of the Palestinian territories. By turning a blind eye to the growth of these movements, which established a considerable network of welfare services in Gaza and the West Bank, it allowed them to become fully established and also armed. Israel's aim in supporting the Islamist groups was to use them as a counterforce to the overwhelmingly (secular) nationalist PLO.[89]

Israel was instrumental in creating Islamic fundamentalism in another way. As a Jewish state, it had established a concept of statehood based on religion, in contradistinction to the modern state whose citizens are not defined by their creed. It should be no surprise that this paradigm, promoted by Israel and its supporters so fervently, in time provoked a reaction in kind, with Islam as the counterpoint to Judaism. Hamas, formally created out of the Palestine Muslim Brotherhood in 1987, is a case in point. Initially encouraged and helped to develop with Israel's support in order to undermine the PLO, it turned to opposing Israel instead during the first intifada.[90] Its aim to establish an Islamic state in the whole of Palestine, which it regards as an Islamic *waqf* (land belonging to the Muslims in perpetuity), though not a concept invented by Hamas, may be seen as the mirror image to *Eretz Israel* (the land of Israel). This phrase refers to the Jewish idea that the land must be held as the patrimony of the Jewish people, and the whole of it must form the Jewish state. Nevertheless, most Palestinians were not fundamentalists and Palestinian society was generally lukewarm in its response to the Islamists. Support for these groups usually ran at some 10 to 20 per cent in the West Bank and 30 per cent at most in Gaza.

It was only since the start of the second intifada and the failure of the 1993 Oslo agreement and with it the collapse of secular resistance that Islamists have enjoyed increased support for their uncompromising opposition to Israel. This phenomenon accounts for the decisive election of Hamas in the Palestinian Legislative Council elections in early 2006. Aware of the secular nature of Palestinian society, the new leadership was at pains to maintain that it would not impose Islamic rule on the people.

Suicide Bombing

The phenomenon of suicide bombing, not confined to Islamic groups, was a late and particularly ugly manifestation of Palestinian reaction to Israel. Its routine condemnation by Israeli and Western observers was neither enlightening nor effective, and only served to obscure its true origins and *raison d'être*. Its Islamic colouration arose within a broader regional context in which Arab nationalism, weakened by decades of Western onslaught on behalf of Israel, gave way to religion as the primary intellectual motivation.[91] It is sobering to realise that by 2006 literally scores of young Palestinians, who should have wanted to embrace life, were, on the contrary, eager to kill themselves in order to damage Israeli society. That a traditionally peaceable, agrarian and family-centred people should have come to accept the sacrifice of their young men and women in the struggle against Israel was an eloquent and horrific testament to the way they were damaged by it. It is this that should have engaged the minds of Western politicians and prompted them to address the cause which did not stop at the Palestinians only.

For, through the narrow prism of their preoccupations, these desperate young people were expressing their rejection of something all other Arabs rejected too: the fact that they were made host to a state which ensured a continued hegemonic Western presence in their region – since Israel, as we saw, could never have been established nor survived except with Western support. It had stolen their land and resources and had schemed ceaselessly to control them, wooed their enemies, and worked against their interests in every field, from the use of water to their hopes of political unity. And it posed an ever-present military threat through its massive arsenal, including nuclear weapons.

The Western occupation of Iraq in 2003 was a project that Arabs saw as a fulfilment of Israel's wish to see every strong Arab state destroyed. The US-led campaign against Syria that intensified at the end of 2004 prompted speculation of the same kind. If not for Israel's benefit, why destabilise Syria, a weak state without military muscle, with threats of regime change, tough UN Security Council resolutions and US sanctions (imposed since 2003)?[92] Although the American reasons put forward for their attacks on Syria changed from initial accusations of possessing weapons of mass destruction to harbouring Baathist organisers of the Iraq insurgency and supporting terrorist groups killing Americans in Iraq, to masterminding the murder of the Lebanese prime minister, Rafiq Hariri, in 2005, none of it was convincing. It seemed far more likely that it was more to do with bringing Syria into line over holding renewed peace negotiations in a balance of power more favourable to Israel, and thus fulfilling the neocon agenda of creating a friendly regional environment for the Jewish state.[93] Seen in this light, the US insistence on Syrian troops evacuating Lebanon and its encouragement of the Lebanese anti-Syrian movement that started in the wake of Hariri's killing were in reality preambles to weakening Syria's hegemony over Lebanon. This had the additional advantage of potentially disrupting Syrian–Iranian relations, also to Israel's benefit, and of weakening Syrian support for Hizbullah, a thorn in the side of both Israel and, indirectly, the US.[94] The pressure exerted on Syria to end its interference in Lebanon, while Israel was permitted to remain in occupation of the Syrian Golan Heights, demonstrated a degree of Western bias against Arabs that was not lost on the Arab world.

What To Do About Israel?

The foregoing account, which has reviewed in summary Israel's malign influence on the Arab world, should not be understood to suggest that the problems the Arabs faced were all created by Israel, nor that the Arab world would have had an untroubled history but for Israel's existence. Indeed, in many cases Israel merely aggravated or exploited what was already there. The ground for the damaging divisions in the Arab world, for example, had already been laid by the major European powers at the end of the First World War. By creating borders and nation-states where none had previously existed, they sowed the seeds of future discord. We need look no further for proof of this assertion than the creation of Iraq in 1920, for example, whose borders were neither natural nor stable (as witness the 1990 Iraqi occupation of Kuwait on the basis that the latter was claimed to be part of southern Iraq).[95] Or to take another example, Lebanon, whose precarious confessional government was cobbled together by France in 1920 from the previous Ottoman administrative districts of Beirut, Tyre, Sidon and Tripoli, with the addition of the Druze stronghold of Mount Lebanon and the previously Syrian Beqaa valley. This arrangement was designed to maximise ethnic and religious divisions, and enable the Maronites, whom France cultivated as allies, to be the largest minority in the new state.[96]

The regional imposition of the Jewish state in this setting was but the most flagrant example of the same divisive and imperialist policy. The strategy of nurturing alliances with ethnic and religious minorities, which was a hallmark of Western imperialist control over the Arabs, was a further divisive factor. What Israel did in this context was to exacerbate these existing tendencies and to counter any Arab attempts, most notably, for example, Nasser's vision of pan-Arabism, that aimed to reverse them.

Nor did it help that some Arab regimes were dependent on Western support, without which they would have been considerably worse off. Western policy towards the Arab world was chiefly dictated by the need to protect its own strategic and economic interests and also to protect the Jewish state. In so doing, Britain, France and the US always strove to support or help install regimes in the Arab world which would be compliant with their interests, even at the expense of those of the Arab populations of these states. The pattern in each of these Arab states was familiar: once installed, pro-Western regimes maintained their dominance through a strong military class and state security apparatus to stifle popular dissent. The history of the region after the fall of the Ottoman Empire is replete with examples of this policy.[97] And on this reading (as opposed to the religious motivation of British Christian Zionists like the Victorian philanthropist Lord Salisbury), Western policy in Israel's case was strategic rather than ideological. The installation of the Jewish state as the local agent of Western regional self-interest was an effective way of dividing the Arabs, so as to ensure that they remained dependent and subjugated. This proved a successful policy to attain Western ends and was but another example of the same self-interested policy.

Egypt, the most important frontline state with Israel, and the one that in the past posed the greatest danger to it, had become a tame tiger. It benefited from annual US aid of $2.1 billion, paid since the signing of the 1979 Camp David peace treaty in line with the US strategy of helping those states that had peace treaties with Israel. In 2005 US aid amounted to $1,795 million, $1,300 million of it in the form of military aid.[98] However, the economic aid came with several strings attached. It was specifically to go towards developing democracy, human rights and good governance, as an implicit way of creating a more amenable climate for co-operation with Israel, and be implemented through organisations not subject to prior Egyptian governmental approval.[99] Needless to say, no such conditions applied to US aid for Israel. Compromised by the Camp David peace agreement that formally barred it from open hostility to Israel, Egypt played a role alternating between passivity towards oppressive Israeli policies and diplomatic manoeuvring to preserve its integrity as the foremost Arab state. This was responsible for the seeming contradictions in its behaviour, attempting to be an impartial mediator in the conflict between Israel and the Palestinians, as if it had not been an Arab state which had itself been damaged by Israel in the wars of 1956, 1967 and in the war of attrition (1968–1972). At the same time, and despite the raging intifada on its doorstep, Egypt continued co-operation with Israel, though, in view of popular protest, not as consistently as before.[100]

Jordan was more dependent on the US, receiving some $460 million annually and maintaining a strong pro-Western stance. Having been created by a Western power in the first place, in 1923, it owed its survival thereafter to the West. Thus, the Jordanian regime could never have taken an independent stand against Israel on this count, let alone its historical complicity with the Zionists. Like Egypt, its 1994 peace treaty with Israel precluded it from any hostile action against its neighbour, even had the political will been there. In the midst of the current intifada that threatens Jordan's internal stability more than any other Arab state, and in spite of the Palestinian preponderance in the Jordanian population (conservatively estimated at 60 per cent), Jordan embarked in 2004 on a major Israeli–Jordanian science and technology centre to provide education and training for Israeli and Jordanian students, and 'possibly' Palestinians as well.[101]

The Gulf States owed their existence either directly to Britain or to Western support in the technological, military and intelligence fields. Most of them were under British tutelage until independence in 1971, and thereafter began to draw closer to the US, whose interests they served faithfully in the two wars against Iraq. American bases, expanded after the closure of the ones in Saudi Arabia, were maintained in Bahrain, Qatar and Kuwait, without which the US could not have waged these wars. The fact that the West could have enticed Egypt and Syria to join in the force that attacked a fellow Arab country in the 1991 Iraq war attests to this Arab docility, which was also shown in other ways. For example, when the first conference of Arab and South American states was held in Brazil in 2005 to initiate a new alliance opposed to US hegemony in both regions, it was notable that only five Arab states attended, the rest reportedly intimated by American pressure from joining. As a result, a valuable opportunity for co-operation over energy and markets from which the Arabs would have gained considerably was lost.[102]

In February 2005 Jordan's ambassador to Israel was returned after five years of protest against Israel's maltreatment of Palestinians, although this had not abated, and more importantly for Jordan, nor had Israel freed the Jordanian prisoners incarcerated in its jails. The prisoners went on hunger strike, demanding that their government have them released, or at least that its ambassador to Israel have their harsh conditions ameliorated, but to no avail. On a visit to London in 2004, Yemen's president pledged in an address to the Three Faiths Forum, a Jewish, Christian and Muslim dialogue group, that his country would protect the rights of Yemen's small Jewish minority without once making reference to Israel's maltreatment of Muslims and Christians under its occupation.[103]

The Arabs' sorry state became the object of fierce home-grown condemnation and criticism. Such views became more boldly expressed, despite the fact that free debate in the Arab media (with the exception of the Al-Jazeera TV channel), was usually absent or subject to censorship. When I published an article in the Arabic daily, *Al-Hayat*, in 1998, on the historic connection between the Jordanian Hashemite monarchy and the Zionist leadership, I was advised against travelling to Jordan for a year afterwards in case I was apprehended at the airport. Conversation at most private Arab gatherings soon turns to this subject, and I have always found something pathetic about the mixture of anger, helplessness and resignation expressed on such occasions, as if to say, 'We hate our plight, but can do nothing except sound off against our leaders.'

As one bold Arab commentator noted bitterly in 2005, the Arab states' only preoccupation was how to please America, and that applied equally to the so-called 'radical' states, strong on anti-American rhetoric, but nothing else.[104] An *Al-Quds* editorial on 23 March of the same year declared that the Arab League was in final decline. Another writer wondered who was responsible for the abject submissiveness of the Arabs: the Arab regimes or the Arab people who had 'entered the intensive care unit', or both?[105] Yet another castigated the Arab rulers for being 'the agents of American and Israeli imperialism' and responsible for the 'slaughter' of Arabs from the (Atlantic) ocean to the (Arabian) gulf.[106] A strongly-phrased comment article, also in *Al-Quds*, decried the total surrender of the Arab order to Israeli and US wishes and described what it saw as a 'marathon race' amongst the Arabs in the rush to win American favour. 'Is this [state of affairs] reality?', it asks, 'or a terrible nightmare from which we will awake to a common Arab destiny and a shared solidarity?' Alas, it concludes gloomily, events have shown that it is all too true and that 'we are living through the worst age of Arab decline'.[107]

At the same time and ironically enough, a myriad cultural initiatives tie the Arab world to the US. Higher education in most Arab universities is modelled on the American system, and Arab elites look to the US for ideas and aspire to American models of progress. Young middle-class Arabs imitate American norms in dress, music and lifestyle. Many of them express affection for the American people whom they distinguish from the American administration, and enjoy visiting or studying in the US. At one time, the Arabs also felt an affinity for Americans on the basis that, however biased they were towards Israel, they were in the end 'People of the Book' (a Quranic term for Jews, Christians and Muslims) who were to be treated equally with each other. By contrast, they viewed with disapproval the godless Soviets who had indeed offered aid, especially in Nasser's time, to the Arab world, but were uncompromising atheists. Arab–US cultural co-operation continued, despite the strictures imposed on Arabs and Muslims visiting America after the events of 9/11. A project to establish a branch of America's Georgetown University in the Qatari capital, Doha, was established in 2005.

Viewed like this, the paradox of the situation becomes clear. In fighting Israel, Arab regimes might have alienated their foreign sponsors and, in effect, might have helped to weaken their position at home. It was improbable that any ruling regime, however anti-Israeli, would so willingly relinquish its own power. It was a paradox that defied solution and whose effect was necessarily to undermine every effort to alter the fundamentals of the situation. Furthermore, it was often argued, these regimes had in any case benefited from Israel's existence, since they could deflect public anger away from their own deficiencies onto Israel's persecution of the Palestinians. Sheltering behind anti-Israel rhetoric, Arab governments cynically exploited the Palestinian cause for their own ends, while doing little to resolve it. Though this was true to some extent, a more useful approach was to see these official Arab reactions as part of the general inability to deal with the problem of Israel and the effects of its presence on the region. Had it never existed, their mettle would never have been so tested.

Arab Reaction

Since Israel does exist, we will never know how the Arabs might have fared without it. But we can observe that, faced with this imposed state whose every act since its creation seemed to demonstrate ill will towards them and a desire to exploit their region – and had the military force and advanced technology to do it – they found themselves up against a huge problem. How to deal with such a state (their attack on the fledgling Israel in 1948 had been a dismal failure), one, moreover, with powerful Western sponsors so committed to its security, irrespective of the cost to the Arabs? What could they (or anyone else in the same situation) have done to solve such a problem? Much as Israeli propagandists tried to ascribe all hostile Arab reaction to innate anti-Jewishness (antisemitism hardly seems an appropriate term in this context, since the Arabs are semites), the reality was that even a far more politically sophisticated, socially advanced protagonist than the Arab world would have found Israel a formidable challenge.

As it was, the Arab response wavered between war and appeasement. From the start, there were only two theoretical options before them: either to dismantle Israel (*as a state*) or to accommodate it in some way. Going down the first route had clearly failed; in any case it could never have succeeded, given Arab military weakness and disunity of purpose, Arab dependence on Western powers and the latter's determination to prevent Israel's destruction. Apart from a brief demonstration of Arab military and economic power when, during the 1973 October war, an oil embargo had been imposed by the Gulf States, there had been no effective use of Arab power against Israel. On the contrary, Arab regimes fought each other (Egypt's futile war in Yemen, the Syrian conflict with Iraq, Iraq's invasion of Kuwait, for example) and weakened their position vis-à-vis Israel. That left the second option, which entailed a range of possibilities. At one end was full, unresisting acceptance of Israel and all it did. This could never have been acceptable to Arab populations, even if Arab leaders had felt differently. And at the other were compromise arrangements of various kinds: non-belligerency treaties, negotiations over borders and resources, and a resolution of the Palestinian problem, including that of the refugees, so leading to full diplomatic recognition and normalisation of relations. For this option to succeed, it required a readiness on the part of Israel, no less than that of the Arabs, to do the same. It would also have required that Israel view itself as a Middle Eastern state, not just *in* it, but *of* it.

In the event, we had the worst of all outcomes. The Arabs did not succeed in defeating Israel, nor did any of their efforts at peaceful accommodation work either. As mentioned above, despite their rhetoric to the contrary, the Arab states initiated a number of conciliatory moves towards Israel after their defeat in the 1948–9 Arab–Israeli war. Foremost among them was the Hashemite Kingdom of Jordan, which had in any case sought peaceful co-existence with the Jewish state long before its establishment and continued this tradition more or less thereafter. To appease Israel, the Jordanian authorities strove hard to prevent Palestinian infiltration over the border after 1949, as indeed did Syria, Lebanon and Egypt, at least at the beginning. For nearly two years after the termination of the 1948–9 war, Syria maintained a scrupulously peaceful border with Israel when it might have been expected for anti-Israeli hostility to be at its most acute. At the same time, Syria tried until 1953 to pursue peace negotiations with its new neighbour, despite Israeli settlement-building on the demilitarised zone between them and Israel's incursions into Syrian territory.[108] The talks broke down finally, principally because of Israeli insistence on retaining exclusive rights to the waters of the Sea of Galilee and the River Jordan.

Peaceful contacts with Egypt were initiated soon after the fall of the Egyptian monarchy in 1952. The young Colonel Nasser made secret overtures to the Israelis in 1953, hoping to secure a reciprocal deal and co-operation that could ultimately pave the way for a final settlement with Israel.[109] Israel responded with demands that would have exposed the Egyptian position prematurely and caused it to deviate from its pan-Arab stand on Israel, and the talks failed. Even then, and despite continuing punitive strikes by Israel along its borders with Jordan and Egypt in response to the infiltration of Palestinians from those areas, the Arab countries, as was noted above, made considerable efforts to control these infiltrators and keep the peace. After the 1967 war the Arabs made a series of formal efforts aimed at reaching a peace settlement. All of these relied on the framework set by UN Security Council Resolution 242, which established for the first time the basic parameters for an Arab–Israeli settlement. It was for that reason that in 1970 Nasser spoke for the first time of the possibility of a durable peace with Israel if it evacuated the Arab territories acquired in the 1967 war and settled the refugee problem. In 1971, Nasser's successor, Anwar Sadat, offered a full peace with recognition of Israel, based on its withdrawal from Arab territory as before.[110] In 1972, Jordan proposed a confederation with the West Bank and a comprehensive peace with Israel.

All these were attempts at accommodation with Israel and all failed. In the aftermath of the 1973 war, Syria and Egypt were willing to exchange land for peace, and Jordan again offered a full peace treaty. Three years later, a UN Security Council resolution backed by the three frontline Arab states (and the PLO) to recognise Israel (and a new Palestinian state) within the pre-June 1967 borders was tabled and then vetoed by the US. In 1977, Egypt, Syria and Jordan offered to sign peace treaties with Israel. It was only after American pressure on Israel that the Sadat initiative of 1977 led to the first Arab country to negotiate a peace agreement with Israel at Camp David two years later.[111] I well remember watching on TV Sadat's historic visit to Jerusalem in November 1977 that kicked off the whole process. Seeing his lonely figure standing at the rostrum in Israel's parliament, in the very heartland of his enemies, so to speak, was shocking but also strangely moving. He intoned verses from the Quran about the ancient Israelites at his audience, people collected from all parts of the globe, most of whom, I judged, had neither knowledge nor interest in his scriptures.

Further peace overtures were made in 1981 when the so-called (King) Fahd peace plan was put forward at Fez. For the first time, the Arab states implicitly recognised the Jewish state by calling for peaceful co-existence between Israel and a Palestinian state in the West Bank and Gaza. Israel rejected the plan. Earlier, the PLO had also offered its own recognition of Israel through the Palestine National Council meeting of 1977, which called for a Palestinian state, implicitly separate from Israel, but that was also rejected. The 1991 Madrid peace conference under US and Russian sponsorship, designed to reach a comprehensive peace between Israel and the Arab world, met with no success. In 1993, the PLO formally accepted Israel's existence in 78 per cent of Palestine and signed a separate peace deal with it, the Oslo Accords. In 1994, Jordan followed suit with the Israel–Jordan peace treaty. Even Syria, Israel's longtime bitter enemy, exchanged peaceful contacts with Israel through the US in 1994 and again in 1999, although they came to nothing.[112] And in 2002, the Arab states, meeting at the Arab League summit in Beirut, put forward the Saudi peace plan, the most comprehensive proposal of all Arab peace plans to date. This spelled out the terms of a final peace agreement with Israel, based on Israeli withdrawal to the 1967 borders, a division of Jerusalem into Arab and Jewish parts, the creation of a Palestinian state and a settlement of the refugee problem (without elaborating). In return, the Arabs pledged full diplomatic recognition of Israel and normalisation of relations with it.

Israel ignored the offer, but it should not have, nor should the West have dismissed this demonstration of Arab commitment to a peaceful settlement by endorsing the Israeli view that the demand for full withdrawal to the 1967 borders, including East Jerusalem, was extreme. They ignored the fact that it was more than balanced by something that the Arabs thought equally extreme: settling for only 22 per cent of the original Palestine and pledging full normalisation of relations with Israel. The Saudi plan was a landmark in the historical evolution of the Arab world from outrage and hostility at Israel's establishment in 1948 to its large-scale accommodation and acceptance 54 years later. The Arab states, albeit bludgeoned and coerced into submission by Israeli force and Western manipulation, had nevertheless come a long way from the postures of the past.

Israel's response was to persist in its oppression of the Palestinians and the appropriation of their land. At the same time, it maintained its occupation of the Syrian Golan Heights. Only in 2000 did it vacate the south of Lebanon, which it had occupied since 1982, because it had failed to vanquish Lebanese resistance. Meanwhile, it consolidated its hold on Jerusalem as its 'eternal capital' and repeatedly threatened its neighbours, such as bombing Iraq's nuclear reactor in 1981 and mounting an air raid on Syrian territory in 2003 under the pretext that it was attacking a terrorist training camp. Rumours of Israeli complicity in the war on Iraq and America's threatening stance towards Syria since 2003 completed the picture for the Arabs of a relentlessly hostile state that refused to be accommodated peacefully into the region.

Facing this reality, the Arab states remained as baffled and divided about the best way to deal with Israel as they always had been. Neither war nor peace had succeeded and they ended up with a variety of unsatisfactory and uneven arrangements vis-à-vis Israel, all of them characterised by a common resignation and impotence. Syria was officially at war with Israel while unable to eject it from the Golan Heights; Lebanon, part of whose land Israel had occupied for nearly 20 years and was still the object of Israeli attack, remained at war; Egypt, disabled by its peace treaty with Israel, was forced to accept its inferior status as the former regional power in the face of Israel's military and technological superiority; Jordan had long ago accepted the permanence of the Jewish state; the Gulf States had evidently come to the same conclusion and would have no difficulty in recognising Israel openly once a respectable formula was found; some of these countries, in any case, had until the outbreak of the second intifada hosted low-level Israeli official representation; Morocco had openly encouraged co-operation with the Israeli establishment and welcomed many Israeli officials as well as former Moroccan Jewish citizens, now domiciled in Israel, to the country; Libya was rumoured to be making secret overtures to Israel;[113] and numerous contacts were established between Israeli and Arab businessmen from several Arab countries during the 1990s and were still continuing. Co-operation between Arabs and Israelis in other spheres – amongst scholars, artists and writers, for example – was also ongoing.

Still No Solution for the Palestinians

The heart of the problem, meanwhile, remained what it always was: the conflict between Israel and the Palestinians, with the additional complication that the world assumed it was up to the Arabs to solve it. This unjust imposition, resented by Arabs, needs to be borne in mind when assessing their performance in this regard. The fact that Israel continued to abuse the Palestinians and deprive them of their basic rights set a limit on how far the Arab states could go down the route of accommodation. One Palestinian right in particular, the right of return for refugees, presented a special problem for the Arab states. For 59 years, Israel had been able to evade its responsibility for creating the refugee problem and for its resolution. It was the frontline Arab states, instead, that bore the brunt of Palestinian displacement, sometimes at great cost to their own economies and stability. I can recall as a child witnessing the chaotic scenes when the refugees from Safad in northern Palestine flooded into Damascus in May 1948, rapidly overwhelming the services that an ill-equipped, underdeveloped country like Syria could provide.[114]

Lebanon was a case in point, where the Palestinian refugee camps had engendered a guerrilla movement that gave rise to cross-border attacks on northern Israel, provoking massive military retaliation and an 18-year Israeli occupation of the south of the country. In doing this, Israel used the Palestinian raids also as a pretext to realise its old designs for 'regime change' towards a more Israel-friendly Lebanese government, as discussed above. The 1982 Israeli bombing and six-month siege of Beirut led to the loss of some 20,000 Lebanese and Palestinian lives. Israel's army destroyed ministries, institutions and homes, as if aiming to wipe out the Lebanese state itself. For years the Israeli self-styled 'security zone' in the south of Lebanon cut it off from the rest of the country, and turned it into a battlefield with ruined farmlands and a flood of refugees going northwards to Beirut. The cost of all this to Lebanon was unquantifiable, but must have run into billions of dollars, none of which was ever recovered in compensation from the Jewish state (or anyone else).

Jordan was home to the largest number of Palestinian refugees, estimated in 2001 at 1.6 million out of a total 3.5 million who were registered with UNRWA. A further 800,000 Palestinians, displaced as a result of the 1967 war, also took refuge in Jordan. The cost of maintaining the camps, where many refugees had lived since their original displacement in 1948, was borne by the host country and the international community through UNRWA (for refugees registered with it, which did not represent the total number). For example, it was estimated that in 1998 the Jordanian government was spending an annual $250 per refugee on education, health and employment to UNRWA's $56, and in 2001, Jordan's expenditure was five times that of UNRWA's.[115] Such costs, especially given the chronic deficit in UNRWA's budget (due to donor reluctance to fund it in recent years), were a considerable burden to the small economies of states like Jordan and Lebanon. Nor did the estimates take account of the additional social, political and security costs incurred by the presence of a displaced, politicised population with a commitment to fight for its rights. The Palestinian presence in the countries that were host to it was not one of immigrants seeking a better life. It was an uncomfortable, potentially destabilising intrusion into the body politic of these states which had to accommodate it in different ways, all of which entailed some degree of disturbance to them. At no time did Israel offer compensation to these countries, but on the contrary demanded restitution for its Jewish citizens allegedly made refugees by various Arab states.[116] From an Arab (as apart from a Palestinian) point of view, a resolution of the situation without further Arab cost was long overdue.

Even had Arab governments, tied as they were to Western powers, wished to ignore Israel's treatment of the Palestinians, their own public opinion was always a factor to be taken into account. The mass of Arab people, even those as far away as Morocco,[117] was deeply sympathetic to the Palestinian cause. The official Arab position on the Palestinians was one of declared support and solidarity precisely because of this factor. The 2003 war on Iraq, widely unpopular among Arabs, and the blatant partisanship that the Bush Administration displayed towards Israel only reinforced popular feeling. (One possible exception was Kuwait, whose people were outraged by Iraq's 1991 invasion and grateful for the US liberation of their land.) Arab governments, moreover, were not unaware of the danger to themselves from the rise of extremist Islamic movements that espoused the Palestinian cause. The growing instability inside Arab societies that reflected dissatisfaction with their governments' lack of public accountability, reliance on the enemies of the Arab people (the West and through it, Israel) and, by extension, colluded with the oppression of the Palestinians, was conflated under several banners, including the twin causes of Iraqi and Palestinian liberation. It followed that a resolution of the Palestinian problem would crucially remove one of the prime ingredients of this dangerous cocktail.

So the Arab regimes' conundrum was how to effect this, given the restrictions on their freedom of manoeuvre by, on the one hand, their dependence on Western aid, technology and trade, and especially on American favour, itself tied to their acquiescence in accommodating Israel – not as a normal state in the region, but as a regional superpower with a military and economic edge over them – and, on the other, there was Israel's uncompromising and threatening stance and its rejection of all efforts at Arab accommodation except on its own unacceptable terms.[118] It was an unenviable dilemma which their floundering, disunited policies and unco-ordinated reactions did little to resolve.

This irresolute and wavering stand had the result that by late 2006, Israel was poised to impose its unique version of 'peace' on the Arab world, with all the Arab states pacified or disabled, including the potential challenger, Syria, and the Palestinians almost bludgeoned into submission. It must have looked to the Western powers, which were instrumental in helping Israel to attain this achievement, as if they had finally succeeded in forcing Israel down the Arabs' throats, no matter what the Arabs themselves might have hoped or wished for.

2
Why Do Jews Support Israel?

The imperative to create a Jewish state in place of Palestine led, as we have seen, to enormous suffering and disruption for the native Palestinians and, to a lesser extent, the Arabs of the frontline states. Why did a project, which was, on the face of it, implausible in the first place and inevitably destructive of others, succeed so well? Just as importantly, why did it continue to receive support, despite a clear record of aggression and multiple breaches of international law against its neighbours that ensured its survival – not just as a state but *as a disruptive force*? This was a conundrum that bewildered the Palestinians who saw that they were exploited for the advantage of others, but who remained, despite much theorising and debate, largely ignorant of the full extent of the problem that had been foisted on them. To comprehend the complex phenomenon that is Israel and those who support it demanded a familiarity and empathy with European history and culture that was simply beyond the majority of Palestinians. Despite the Westernisation that some experienced living in exile, the mass of Palestinians were not in touch with the foreign influences that shaped Israel and continued to accord it such importance. I myself, reared in an area of London full of European Jews, among whom were indeed 'some of my best friends', have struggled to grasp the ramifications. How much more difficult must it have been for a typical Palestinian coming from an Arab culture and world-view to deal with the complexities of European Jewish history and psychology.

And indeed, it was difficult to find a phenomenon, historical or modern, comparable to the case of Israel. Here was a state, more in concept than actuality (that is, irrespective of the reality on the ground), with a unique appeal to religious, historical and psychological sentiment and an army of devoted followers, unprecedented in scale, working diligently on its behalf. The multifarious and many-faceted nature of this support was truly striking, as if a number of disparate issues and factors – the Holocaust and its associated trauma and guilts, the exigencies of Western regional policy, especially during the Cold War, religious mythology, etc. – had tacitly come together to promote the cause of Israel.

More powerful still was the emotional and psychological underpinning of this support, not least because it was more difficult to define and address. Analyses of the phenomenon of Israel have conventionally neglected this dimension, although it constituted arguably the greatest obstacle and the most resistant to a final resolution of the Middle East conflict. The extent to which ordinary Jews, citizens of European countries, usually without the least intention of emigrating to Israel, nonetheless identified with it as an ideal, was astonishing. In 2002, I had occasion to participate in a meeting organised by the British charity Oxfam, which aimed to bring together members of the 'three Abrahamic faiths' with the hope of initiating a campaign to alleviate the ill effects of the Israeli occupation on the Palestinians. None of the Jewish representatives was Israeli, and yet the passion with which they defended the Jewish state was striking. During discussion, a point was made about the lack of moral equivalence between Israeli and Palestinian behaviour: is the violence of the occupier equivalent to that of the occupied? Can one judge the oppressor and the oppressed, whatever their actions, by the same standards? 'In saying that there are two sides to every story, that Israelis and Palestinians each have their own justifications and arguments', a sympathiser with the Palestinians said, 'Would you judge that a murderer, for example, had as much of a case as his victim?'

The Jewish response was one of dismay and anger. A Jewish participant from London told me afterwards that he felt he had been personally assaulted by that remark, that having Israel attacked was like hearing his own mother described as a slut. Long before this incident, an Israeli friend and political activist, Akiva Orr, recounted the following story. It was at the time of the 1967 Arab–Israeli war and Akiva was in London. He recalls that his landlord, a German Jew who was a British national and had lived in England for thirty years, asked him in distress and alarm what would happen. 'Will they [the Arabs] destroy us?' he said, and clearly he meant 'us Israelis', as if he had been one of them there and not a Londoner here.[1] This identification first became overt, or for some Jews may have even started, in the wake of the Six-Day War. It was commonplace to see members of the Jewish community in America and in many European countries volunteering to provide all sorts of services for the embattled Israelis (as they saw them), despite the latter's lightning military success right from the start.

Nor did this personal fervour for Israel amongst such European Jews decline in more recent times. A well-known London journalist and avid supporter of Israel, Melanie Phillips, wrote an illuminating piece following a visit she had made to the occupied Palestinian territories in February 2004. In this, she absolves Israel of all blame in the fight against Palestinian 'terrorism', commenting that the Israeli occupying army 'picks its way from house to house to kill or arrest terrorists while trying to avoid innocent civilians, despite thereby incurring far greater casualties'. The 'terrorists', she asserted, had deliberately demoralised the Israelis so as to make them overreact and thereby cause the Palestinians to seem like the victims. That kind of wilful denial to the point of absurdity in the face of the evidence is not unusual amongst Zionist apologists. But it is yet another psychological facet of the almost desperate need some Jews have to support Israel, right or wrong.[2] For, to do otherwise, to draw the conclusions which the logic of the facts on the ground would dictate, could lead to a denunciation of Israel which would not be psychologically tolerable. This cognitive dissonance, as one might call it, when two narratives are incompatible and so a third has to be elaborated to explain the contradiction was a marked feature of the Zionist attitude towards Israel.

The American Jewish community in particular had shown itself to be ardently Zionist and was a major direct donor to Israel as well as its active proponent in US society and politics. Many American Jews came to the US from Eastern Europe and brought with them a distinctive religious/ethnic culture, which defined them in religious and national terms. At the same time, they were exposed to secularism; so Zionism, by combining this aspect with religious tradition must have been an immensely attractive ideology. Israel became the focus of identity for all American Jewish groups, gave them a sense of communal cohesion and created power networks amongst them. It also made them feel 'normal', almost like other immigrants in America who had a home country they could visit or 'return' to. Such psychological attachment is hard to forgo. It intensified after the 1967 and 1973 wars, reinforcing the perception that the Jews were about to be annihilated again for a people still profoundly affected by the Holocaust.[3] In the last 30 years it is estimated that US Jewish organisations bought Israeli bonds worth over $50 billion.[4] Washington's foremost pro-Israel lobby, the American Israel Public Affairs Committee (AIPAC) campaigned energetically on Israel's behalf in the American Congress and collaborated with the Confederation of Presidents of Jewish Organisations, a powerful US group which co-ordinated the efforts of Jewish organisations on Israel's behalf.[5] For these Jews, even at their most liberal, Israel had taken on a mythic quality, part-identity, part-religion, and its dissolution, *as a Jewish state*, became psychologically and emotionally unthinkable. The obverse of this coin was of course a paranoid suspicion and hatred of anyone who threatened Israel in the slightest way. The head of the Movement for Jewish Reform in Britain expressed this feeling well in 2005. 'When attacked,' he wrote, 'we [Zionists] respond by equating anti-Zionists with anti-Semites . . . [It] wells up out of anger and frustration at not being allowed to be ourselves.' If Israel no longer existed, he said, it would be the end of Judaism too.[6]

Though many Zionist supporters were later prepared, especially with the ascendance of the Likud government in Israel after 2001, to criticise Israeli policies and display considerable sympathy for Palestinian suffering, all this was still predicated on the crucial assumption of the rightness and necessity of Israel's existence. Such people would not have felt constrained to find fault with Israel under a more benign regime. These attitudes spawned a number of movements aiming to draw Jews and Palestinians together on a shared platform to find 'peace'. They also led to the appearance of Jewish individuals and groups, and most particularly, after the 1993 Oslo Accords, rushing to do good works with disadvantaged Palestinians. At its most generous, this Jewish constituency offered to work for a Palestinian state on the 1967 territories with a shared capital for the two states in Jerusalem.

However, none of them would have contemplated any proposal which entailed breaching the integrity of the Jewish state, as, for example, the unitary state idea (to be discussed later), or a return of the Palestinian refugees. Indeed, in my experience, even the mention of such a possibility provoked reactions bordering on hysteria. In a meeting in London in

2004 with Moshe Dayan's widow, Ruth Dayan, the subject of the right
of Palestinian refugees to return to Israel was brought up. This was a lady
with a long history of benevolent interaction with Palestinians which
she paraded with pride. At the time of our meeting she was being hosted
with great hospitality by a Palestinian family whose lands in Jerusalem
had been appropriated by the Jewish state after 1967. She evaded my
questions about the refugee issue, asking her why Palestinians could
not return to Israel, since Jews claimed this right for themselves. When
I persisted she resorted with alarm to the old Zionist narrative of an
empty Palestine, the Arab presence there due to wandering tribes that
came into the country later, and a war unjustly forced on Israel in 1948
by hostile Arabs. For such mainstream Zionists, even if a final settlement
were to entail a slightly smaller Israel, the loss of some land was still
preferable to compromising the 'Jewish character' of the state.

That was the thinking that led Israel's prime minister, Yitzhak Rabin,
to conclude the Oslo Accords with the PLO in 1993 and that underscored
an emerging broad Israeli consensus for the creation of a Palestinian
state, even if its exact size was still undetermined. (At the same time,
Rabin was careful to ensure that Israel would pay the minimum price
for this new departure from traditional Zionist policy. Under the Oslo
Accords Israel retained its sovereignty over the Palestinians' land, though
they were allowed autonomous rule.) The so-called Geneva Accords,
drawn up between Israelis and Palestinians at the end of 2003, were
in line with the same thinking. These were the result of unofficial talks
between the two sides, which were widely welcomed by European and
American politicians who promoted them enthusiastically. The Accords
provided for an Israeli withdrawal from most of the territories captured
in 1967, with Israel retaining the major settlement blocs in the West
Bank, a shared capital of Jerusalem, and an end to conflict. Inevitably
and conspicuously absent from all this and previous proposals was the
Palestinian right of return. And logically so, for allowing a return of the
displaced Palestinians to Israel would endanger the 'Jewish character'
of the state and spell the end of Zionism.

Israel's Significance for Israeli Jews

Jews inside Israel, with the possible exception of a tiny minority of anti-
Zionists – contemptuously labelled 'self-hating Jews' – naturally feared

the end of Zionism. For them, the dissolution of a state predicated on exclusive Jewish membership, not withstanding the 20 per cent Arab minority (and the non-Jewish Soviet immigrants), and preferential treatment of Jews, was not an option. The reasons are not mysterious. For the majority of them, Israeli citizenship conferred the economic benefits and advantages of a privileged group psychologically predisposed to see itself as superior to the non-Jewish 'natives' that is common to all coloniser communities. In Israel's case, these privileges were hugely augmented by US funding ($5,700 per person since 1973, more than £3 billion annually) and world Jewish support.[7] Not least amongst these were the non-ideological settlers in the 'commuter settlements' of the West Bank, where inducements of cheap housing, tax breaks and jobs in Israel drew large numbers of young people who could not otherwise have attained the same standard of living in Israel or outside.[8] In many of the settlements I have seen, the houses were well laid out with neat roads and trees and, built on hills as they were, the views were often very beautiful. Where could such people dream of being so comfortably and picturesquely housed? Likewise, the settlements built on Syria's Golan Heights had yielded prosperity for those Jews who had farmed them since 1967.[9] Even though the economic situation suffered some reversals due to the 2000 intifada, with poverty levels in Israel higher than at any time before, the average Israeli household still enjoyed a considerable edge over its Arab neighbours.[10] Such Israelis would have vigorously rejected any threat of change to this special situation.

In addition, the Palestinians, if allowed to return, would have formed a particularly unwelcome group, since most Israelis looked down on them. Racist attitudes amongst Jewish Israelis were well known; they were both institutional and social.[11] Anti-Arab racism affected many areas of life in Israel, from education to marriage legislation. The Israeli party, Yisrael Beitenu (Israel Our Home), which contested the 2006 Israeli elections, called openly for the expulsion of Israeli Arab citizens. On a visit to Haifa in the spring of 2004, I was struck by the discrimination, both subtle and overt, against Israeli Arabs. This could be seen in the poor housing, inferior jobs and greater poverty amongst the Arabs. The government's budgetary allocation for Israeli Arabs was less than that for Israeli Jews, for example, and in 2002 the Jewish settlements in the West Bank and Gaza received three times the funding of the state's Arab communities.[12] Their subservience towards the Jewish majority was a clear effect of this discrimination. Even an Ethiopian refuse collector I came across, who was part of the influx of Ethiopian Jews and themselves objects of Israeli discrimination, made no secret of his contempt for Arabs. It was well known that Sephardi Jews (from an oriental origin), Moroccans, Yemenis and Iraqis, treated native Palestinians far worse than their Ashkenazi counterparts, replicating the discrimination perhaps they themselves were subjected to in an Israeli society that prized European Jews above others. The elevation of Amir Peretz, a Moroccan by origin, to the ranks of the Israeli Labour Party's leadership in 2006, or indeed the prominence of some other Oriental Jews, in no way detracts from the truth of this statement. In an Israeli hierarchy where European Jews formed the elite and to whose culture, power and way of life the rest aspired, Sephardi Jews came next and black Jews were lower still, with Palestinians at the bottom of the heap.[13] Indeed, the definition of Zionism itself seemed to have changed over time from being an ideology that excluded non-Jews in general to being specifically anti-Arab. This could be seen in the discrimination against Palestinian labour in favour of specifically imported foreign workers, despite the social problems that it created for Israeli society. It was also seen in the campaign to convert non-Jews to Judaism so as to settle them in place of Palestinians.[14]

Within this general context specific sectors of the Israeli Jewish population had their own additional reasons for wanting to preserve the status quo. Religious Jews, and especially those amongst them who formed the bulk of religious settlers in the West Bank colonies, believed passionately in the concept of 'Eretz Israel', that every Jew had a God-given right to the whole land between the river and the sea, (variously meaning from the Euphrates river in Syria to the northern shore of Sinai in Egypt, or, less ambitiously, from the Jordan river to the Mediterranean). The Naturei Karta and several other small ultra-orthodox Jewish sects, which abominated the state of Israel as an act of sacrilege, were a notable exception, but formed a tiny minority amongst religious Jews.[15] To the latter, the Jewish state was a theological imperative and, as evidenced by their strident opposition to the government evacuation of Jewish settlements, however small, in the Sinai in 1979 and those in Gaza in 2005, they could barely conceive of giving up any part of the land they considered Jewish. (In fact they did accept the generous government offer of financial compensation after the Gaza evacuation in the end, but neither Sinai nor Gaza held the same religious significance for them as the West Bank.) Some of them threatened to assassinate Ariel Sharon, the then Israeli prime minister, for bringing about the Gaza evacuation, praying he would be struck down dead in Gaza,[16] and of course it was just such a religious zealot who assassinated a previous prime minister, Yitzhak Rabin, in 1995 for his alleged surrender of 'Jewish land' in the Oslo Accords with the PLO.

These settlers formed some of the most vociferous, intractable and hardline supporters of the Jewish state. Mostly fanatical ultra-orthodox Israelis or Jewish immigrants from the US, they were widely feared by Palestinians for their unprovoked aggression against them and vicious anti-social behaviour. Such people, whom I always suspected had probably failed to make adequate lives in their places of origin, or were socially maladjusted, acquired status and a mission in life when they emigrated to Israel. Tormenting the indigenous population became almost like a sport through which they could 'act out', to borrow a psychoanalytic phrase, their aggressions, feelings of inferiority and social exclusion. A perfect example of this was to be seen in the adulation accorded by such people to Baruch (formerly Barry) Goldstein, the ultra-religious fanatical Hebron settler of American extraction (and interestingly enough a man with a previously normal social history), who murdered 24 Arab Hebronites at prayer in the Ibrahimi mosque in February 1994. After his killing by angry Arab worshippers as a consequence, other settlers of Goldstein's ilk (and many secular Jews in addition) went on to idolise him and revere his tomb, which became a shrine for them.[17] The settlers' notoriously sadistic harassment of Palestinians in Hebron provided further evidence of this behaviour.

But quite apart from all this, Israel had acquired a population of Israelis, and especially the younger generation born there, so-called 'Sabras', who regarded Israel as their natural home, and, indeed now had nowhere else to go. Not long before, the number of those born in the state was lower than those born outside, but by the 1990s that was no longer the case.[18] Although in the years since the beginning of the second intifada, a considerable number of Israelis emigrated abroad, said to be higher than at any time since the founding of Israel, the bulk of the Israeli Jewish population stayed.[19] It may be speculated that, if matters got worse, more Jews with the means to would leave. But a large majority would still remain, for whom the survival of the state was an existential necessity, if nothing else.

The Zionist Narrative's Hold on Jews

While all the above factors were of relevance in maintaining domestic Jewish allegiance to Israel, the success of Zionism in creating this allegiance lay also at another deeper, more psychological level. This quotation from a right-wing writer in *Haaretz* illustrates the point:

> Our right to Eretz Israel and our right to establish a sovereign national entity on it does not depend on our numbers, and on whether we are a majority or minority. This land was our country when we were a small, isolated minority . . . Legislators should settle this point in clear, categorical terms without any qualms of conscience or moral compunction. *Absolute justice holds that the state of Israel is, and has always been, the only Jewish state, and this country has been solely that of the Jewish people.* (Emphasis added.)[20]

The sentiment in these lines is not merely based on biblical belief, but on a set of interconnected, implicit ideas that need to be deconstructed. The writer is saying that no matter who and how many live in Palestine at any one time makes no difference to the immutable fact that it has always been the land of the Jewish people – in the same sense as one might say that an object legally belonging to a person remains his even if stolen, pawned and not redeemed, or borrowed. This is self-evidently true, but how can the same thing possibly apply to the notion of a country, Palestine, which historically has been home to an admixture of populations, among them the ancient Israelites at one time, being the sole possession of 'the Jewish people'? Clearly it cannot, yet for Zionists it made a compelling case that brought together a variety of religious and historical arguments, as may be inferred from the quotation above. If we analyse these, we find, first, the biblical concept of the Promised Land, wherein God gave the land of Canaan to Abraham (who actually came from Ur in Mesopotamia) and his seed, that is the Jews (Muslims hold that Ishmael, or Ismail, Father of the Arabs, as they call him, and also Abraham's issue, makes them equally his heirs); second, the idea that the Jewish inhabitants of Palestine, duly living in the land long before given them by God, were dispersed from it by the Romans in AD 70 and went into exile, but, despite the passage of 2000 years, remained essentially the same people; and to this may be added a third

Zionist argument, that a Jewish minority continued to exist as part of the Palestinian population throughout the time since the original dispersion, and hence proof of original title to the land. Underlying all this was the essential concept of a 'Jewish people' in the sense of a separate, definable race, nation or homogeneous ethnic group.

On the face of it, and especially for the non-religious, these ideas as a legal title to ownership of Palestine are absurd. The biblical argument is a matter of religious belief and cannot be accepted as proof of anything else, and, in any case, are today's Jews the same as the ancient Israelites? The mass dispersion of the Jews from Palestine is historically questionable. In AD 70 the Jews of Judea (who formed only one of the groups inhabiting the country), rebelled against the Romans and were expelled partly into the Diaspora outside Palestine, but mostly to the Galilee in the north of the country.[21] A large Jewish Diaspora of ex-slaves and ex-mercenaries was already living in the Mediterranean lands of the Roman Empire since the Hellenistic period, estimated at the beginning of the Christian era to be four million people, or three times the number of Jews in Palestine.[22] In other words, the 'mass dispersion' was small and mainly internal and, although some Jews ended up joining the Diaspora communities, the majority remained inside Palestine. Some of the descendants of this community subsequently converted to Christianity and then to Islam, and the rest formed the Jewish minority that existed in Palestine until the twentieth century.

The idea that any human group can remain unchanged through the course of centuries is untenable; in the Jewish case, it becomes nonsensical. The increase in size of Jewish communities subsequent to the supposed dispersion and their physical resemblance to the societies they lived amongst is most plausibly explained by the processes of conversion and intermarriage. Nor has the existence of a large reservoir of Jews in Russia and Eastern Europe ever been satisfactorily explained, if their origins were indeed Mediterranean. By the nineteenth century more than half the world's Jews were to be found in Lithuania/Poland.[23] How did they get there in such large numbers? It is improbable that a Middle Eastern people would have gone out of choice to settle in the harsh, cold climate and environment of Eastern Europe so different from their own, although we do know that Jews, fleeing persecution under the Byzantine Empire, had gone to the Caucasus in early mediaeval

times. But their numbers were small, and some other explanation must
be found.

Where Did European Jews Come From?

There would appear to be two explanations for the Jewish presence
in Eastern Europe. The development of a Jewish merchant class in
the early Middle Ages led to the movement of Jewish traders into
the Mediterranean and Western Europe. Jewish mercantile groups
settled along the Rhineland and in western Germany, where during
the fourteenth century, they developed a strong sense of community
and a new language, Yiddish, a combination of mediaeval German and
Hebrew. It is believed that persecution in Germany subsequently drove
them eastwards towards Poland, where they settled in the sixteenth
century, although no one knows for sure if that was the real story.[24]
Acting as agents for Poland's landowning elite, Jewish communities
penetrated into the Ukraine in 1660.[25]

Arthur Koestler's thesis, drawing on Dunlop's earlier work and on
mediaeval Arabic sources, that the East European Jews were in fact
the product of Khazar conversions in the eighth century, is the other
main explanation for this phenomenon.[26] Koestler was not a historian
and the evidence that he marshalled to prove his case was considered
inadequate by many scholars. And so the idea that so enthused him was
never widely taken up.[27] Nevertheless it was thought-provoking and
not without historical validity. The Khazar kingdom of south Russia,
which flourished between the seventh and tenth centuries, stretched at
its zenith from the Caucasus to the Volga. Its peoples, Turkic/Finnish
shamanists, began to convert to Judaism around the middle of the
eighth century, having been exposed to contact with Jewish refugees
from Byzantine persecution, who had been in their kingdom for at least
a century before. Many of these were active proselytisers, something
that Jews had engaged in vigorously during the early centuries of the
Christian era. The Khazars were also familiar with Jews through the
Jewish trading communities, which had established prosperous trading
colonies along the Caspian Sea. By the tenth century, Judaism had
become the official Khazar state religion, and at least a part of the
population had converted. With the decline of the Khazar state in the
twelfth century, many of its people migrated into neighbouring Russia

and Poland. Hence, on this theory, it was these Jewish migrants and their descendants who were responsible for the large Jewish presence in Eastern Europe.

Palestinians and their sympathisers, seeking to vindicate their case that European Jews did not originate in Palestine and so could not 'return' there, seized avidly on Koestler's book during the 1970s. Though his thesis was not adopted by mainstream scholarship, it was not wholly refuted either, and in 1999, Kevin Brook published an authoritative and carefully researched reconfirmation of Koestler's thesis.[28] Marc Ferro's collection of essays, *Les Tabous de l'histoire*, published in 2002, also dismissed the idea that Jews were a race originating in the Middle East, pointing to the role of conversion in creating the Jewish communities of North Africa. It was the large-scale Berber conversions, where whole villages in the Atlas Mountains embraced Judaism and the Moroccan Jewish kingdom of Ouja was set up, that created the Jewish communities of Morocco and Algeria.[29]

Not surprisingly, Zionists and some others who dismissed them as unconvincing or fanciful largely ignored these writings. The Khazar Jewish converts, it was argued, were irrelevant because their numbers were largely confined to the ranks of the ruling classes and so never formed more than a small minority amongst the Khazars.[30] And it must be said that the relative contribution of each source to the origin of East European Jews remains unclear. Were they mainly, as Koestler posited, converted Khazar descendants and other Slavic converts, or were they mainly the consequence of Jews migrating from Western Europe? We do not know for sure, but most plausibly they must have been a mixture, with the majority of them converts, whether Khazars or other European peoples. What is not plausible, however, is that an unbroken chain existed between the Jews of Palestine and those of Europe, albeit with several stations in between, as if they had been sealed packages posted from one place to the other, their contents unchanged over the centuries. Put like this, the absurdity of the idea is obvious, but that in fact was the proposition Zionists wanted people to believe in order to justify the Jewish 'return' to the 'homeland'. Accepting anything else would have invalidated a central plank of the Zionist claim to Palestine, which had been instrumental in marshalling Western Christianity to its support.

Looking for a Connection with Palestine

Because the Zionist claim rested on such shaky grounds, Jewish researchers, who were aware of this problem, tried to use genetics as a way of demonstrating a link between European (Ashkenazi) Jews and their supposed Middle Eastern origins by way of finding a common ancestry with Middle Eastern Jews. They also sought to establish a genetic connection between Jewish groups of different countries to support the case for the existence of a single Jewish nation. One study in particular, purporting to demonstrate an unbroken genetic chain for the Cohanim, or Jewish priestly caste, from their Palestinian origin to modern times, excited great attention.[31] Its scientific grounds were open to question, but it provided much comfort in a field with a dearth of such evidence. Overall, however, and as one might expect, the weight of genetic evidence was in favour of a separate ancestry for Ashkenazi Jews (Turkic/Slav), and also of genetic similarities between Jewish groups and the societies they lived in.[32]

On these and other grounds, it could not be said that there was such a biological, racial or national entity as 'the Jewish people'. This was also the position of the American Council for Judaism; a small but influential group founded in 1942, which considered Jews to be a religious community, not a nation.[33] And how could they be when each Jewish community was self-evidently akin to the nation it lived amongst? If it had been otherwise, how to explain the black Ethiopian 'Jews', to name one glaringly divergent group? Or the 'Jewish' Bantu tribesmen of Uganda, an interesting case of a Jewish community in the making? The Bantu adopted Judaism in the early twentieth century and went on to establish four synagogues and a Jewish school. They prayed for the State of Israel and married amongst themselves, and, no doubt, in time, they would develop physical characteristics that distinguished them from the non-Jewish Ugandans, as had happened with other social sub-groups (see below). They became an object of study for genetic researchers seeking to find significant differences between them and the larger society, but they should instead be seen as an instructive illustration of how other, especially European, Jewish groups came into being.[34] What made a real mockery of the Jewish nation idea, however, was the reported mass conversion by Israeli rabbis of immigrants from India and Peru transferred as 'Jews' to populate West Bank settlements, not to mention the thousands of non-Jewish Russians from the former USSR.[35]As we saw earlier, this was primarily meant as a device to expand the State of Israel at the expense of the native Palestinians, even if it meant having to populate it with fake Jews.

The confusion over the question of whether Jews formed an ethnic group or not persisted because many Jewish communities, by reason of the historical social strictures placed on them in various societies, often lived together and intermarried, perpetuating certain religious and other customs, as well as physical characteristics. These did not amount to actual genetic changes by which they could be distinguished from others, but to the fact that the same physical characteristics can be passed on amongst families or other close groupings, rather as in the commonplace observation that family members resemble each other. I remember as a child in England noting that some of the Jewish girls at my school looked 'Jewish'. It was some indefinable mixture of facial characteristics that I learned to recognise. Indeed Jews themselves must have shared this view if the old joke they told about the Jewish old lady on the bus was anything to go by. She kept asking a young man sitting next to her whether he was Jewish, refusing to accept his repeated denials. In the end, exasperated and wanting to shut her up, the young man said he was. 'Funny,' she said, 'you don't look Jewish!'

With the possible exception of the East European Ashkenazim whose claim to ethnicity was the strongest, Jews might at best have been described as societal sub-groups or sects, like the Punjabi Sikhs, who have developed a strong ethno-national identity but yet are not a nation, or the American Amish. This is a Christian sect whose members live in communities spread across 22 American states. They keep themselves separate and interact minimally with the surrounding society. Conversion is rare and marriage outside the faith is forbidden. As a result, some of them, like Ashkenazi Jews, now suffer from various inherited disorders (see below). One can see how such a group can come to occupy a special category, neither a separate nation nor quite native.

So are Jews a Nation?

However that may be, it was undeniable that many Jews saw themselves as part of a nation, race or at least of one people in a way that Christians or Muslims did not. This is a complex subject that has exercised the minds of many writers, Jewish and otherwise, and only a summary of its main features can be given here. But it was at the same time of crucial importance for Arabs to understand, given the fact that they were the principal victims of this belief. There were several components to the view that Jews were a separate people. In part it had to do with the Orthodox Jewish position that Jews were only those born of a Jewish mother, which when adhered to, gave Jews a peculiar genetic/religious character. Such people were considered Jews even if they converted or renounced the faith, in which case they became 'apostates'. According to the Talmud, 'A Jew who has sinned still remains a Jew.'[36] Partly it was due to the Classical Reform view, largely faded in modern times, that Jews were those who practised Judaism, in other words, performed the *mitzvot*, a large number of daily religious duties the faithful must fulfil. And partly there was the view that antisemitism was the glue that defined Jews and made them stick together as one people.

Arabs, however, always saw them as a religious group, especially in Palestine where they were regarded as ethnically part of the community; they spoke Arabic and had an Arab culture. As the Palin Commission set up by Britain to investigate the 1920 Arab–Jewish riots in Jerusalem remarked, 'The Orthodox Jew of Palestine was a humble, inoffensive creature . . . hardly distinguishable from the rest of the peasant population.'[37] Anyone familiar with Israelis from Arab countries will observe how culturally 'Arab' they are, or at least the older generations. The European Jews, however, who began to infiltrate Palestine from 1880 onwards, struck Arabs (and also the indigenous Jewish minority in Palestine) as foreigners and quite unlike what they termed as 'our Jews'. They looked different, behaved differently and spoke other languages. Israel's sometime prime minister, Ariel Sharon, for example, could easily have been taken for an Aryan.

For Arabs, it was apparent that Eastern and Western Jews were so dissimilar as to throw doubt on the whole notion of their being one people. And yet, from my own observation growing up amongst European Jews in London, it was clear they genuinely believed themselves to be just that. And they were right in the sense that many of them could say they belonged to a loose affiliation of Ashkenazi East European Jews with similar histories, culture and a Yiddish language that the older generation all spoke. The people, who gave birth to political Zionism, first established it in Palestine and dominated the

Jewish state from its inception, were all members of this group.[38] They mostly came from the countries of Eastern Europe where most of them, especially those from Lithuania/Poland, Russia and Ukraine, had developed a strong sense of ethnic identity. This was based on 'Yiddishism', a socio-political movement to develop Yiddish culture in Eastern Europe that aimed for cultural autonomy within the states where the Ashkenazim lived. In time this community produced an impressive Yiddish literature and a thriving popular culture, as well as an important research institute at Vilna (Vilnius). There was moreover some genetic basis to their ethnic claim in the frequent association of certain inherited disorders, for example, Tay-Sachs disease, with Ashkenazi Jews. Even so, and although there was enough of a shared cultural and historical experience between them as to persuade many of them that they were a national group, it would be wrong to see them as a homogeneous or single community.

It was this Ashkenazi culture that was described to me as 'Jewish', when growing up in Britain in the 1950s. One could recognise it in its 'Jewish jokes', a black humour which recalled life in the *shtetl* (Yiddish for townlets in Eastern Europe to which Jews were confined), its strange linguistic constructions of English mixed with Yiddish, its cuisine (chopped liver, gefilte fish, bagels) and its tradition of orthodox Jewish attire for men; the sight of black-coated orthodox Jews in silk breeches and round fur hats, as if they had just stepped out of eighteenth-century Poland, walking to synagogue on Saturdays was typical and familiar to me living in Golders Green, at the time London's most Jewish suburb. Little did I understand when I met the Jewish girls at my school there with their German surnames and Yiddish vocabulary that their forebears or relatives bore a responsibility for my expulsion from Palestine. Unwittingly putting my finger on the essence of the problem, I saw not the faintest connection between them and my homeland and therefore no reason for any hostility between us. A popular film made in America in 1971, *Fiddler on the Roof*, after Shalom Aleichem's Yiddish novel, *Tevi and His Daughter*, portrayed Jewish life in a Russian shtetl and epitomised this culture for non-Jews. Ashkenazim became familiar in the West after the great waves of Jewish immigration from Russia and Eastern Europe at the turn of the twentieth century, and their culture dominates many aspects of life in the US today. Had it remained like that, they might have gone down in history as a remarkable and interesting community with a rich culture to add to the wealth of human experience, but no more.

As it was, political Zionism intervened with a definition of Jewish nationhood that was in reality nothing other than the ethnic Ashkenazi identity grafted onto the rest. In other words, the East European Ashkenazim reinterpreted themselves as the pan-Jewish nation, an imagined community with a fabricated unifying narrative. (Israel's national anthem, it may be noted, was nothing other than a medley of nostalgic Russian tunes.) It was for that reason that generations of non-Ashkenazi Jews who were brought to populate the new Jewish state after 1948 were subjected to what one might call 'Ashkenazification', an acculturation process to make them more like 'real' or European Jews. It was also the reason for the widespread racism still directed at them by Ashkenazi Israelis.[39] During a visit to Haifa in 1991 I was told that such Israelis would rather their children married an Arab than a Sephardi Jew (although these attitudes have mellowed over time and especially amongst the younger generation of Israelis). I also noted the pathetic attempts of many such Jews to emulate their Ashkenazi superiors, deliberately distorting their Hebrew pronunciation to ape that of the (less authentic) European version.[40] But the most egregious aspect of this false Ashkenazi representation of 'the Jewish people' was the claim it then made for a primordial connection with Palestine. That this became, as we shall see below, the received wisdom amongst Jews (and others) after Zionism had taken hold, makes it no less absurd and, for Palestinians, no less pernicious.

A Persuasive Zionist Myth

The arguments for the existence of a Jewish nation and the refutations of it are familiar to most readers. They were reviewed at some length here because of the persuasive power that the myth of Jewish nationhood had in promoting the takeover of Palestine. But the main point of course was none of this. Even had it been true that the origin of Jews in the world today, wherever they lived and no matter what they looked or sounded like, had been in Palestine 2000 years ago, it is inconceivable that such a fact could ever have conferred on them the right of claiming it for themselves after all this time and to the detriment of its indigenous inhabitants. The history of mankind is littered with the movement of peoples and tribes from place to place, with changing patterns of habitation and repeated migrations. No one, other than the Zionists and their supporters, suggests that reversing this history would be either workable or desirable.

Yet the idea of a homogeneous Jewish people whose physical origin lay in the Middle East took tenacious hold of Jews themselves, irrespective of their personal histories, mother tongues or secular cultures. A prominent Jewish psychiatrist whom I knew during the 1990s in London once told me that when he looked at himself in the mirror he could see an ancient Sumerian (that is Mesopotamian and not even semitic!), origin to his features and the shape of his head. This man's parents were Lithuanian, and thus Ashkenazi, immigrants to England in the early decades of the twentieth century and he himself had been reared in Glasgow. He was by no means a stupid man, but he spoke in perfect seriousness. When once I complimented a Jewish woman friend whose parents were Czech and Viennese respectively (although she herself was born in London) on her handsome suntan, she said, 'Oh it's my Mediterranean skin I expect.' In similar vein, while at a North London dinner party with a Jewish anti-Zionist friend born in England of mixed Polish/Russian descent, I found myself drawn into a discussion about the Jewish claim to Palestine. My friend's brother, an accountant who did not share his brother's political views, declared that he had no interest in Israel as such, 'despite our originating from there'. The man himself, with light brown hair and blue eyes, could not have looked more English. For Middle Eastern, so-called Oriental Jews, to think of themselves in this way would be understandable and also legitimate, but why the people in the examples above (of which there are many more) think the same is the question.

Part of the answer lies in the very definition of Jewishness. To be a member of the Jewish faith is not just to subscribe to a set of religious beliefs; it also means laying claim to a specific history – the history of the Israelites according to the Old Testament, from their Abrahamic origins in the region we call the Middle East today, through to their 'dispersal' from it. This is reflected in the major Jewish religious festival of Passover which commemorates supposed historical events, in this case the Israelites' exodus from Egypt; the festival of Tisha b'Av marks the destruction of the Jewish temples in Jerusalem, and several other less important Jewish festivals also relate to biblical/historical accounts.

To be a Jew is to be physically descended, however distantly, from this chain of *historical* events, that is, to be the bearer of a specific history, even if it is not accompanied by religious belief. When Khazar converts to Judaism visited the Prince of Kiev in 986, they told him that their native land was Jerusalem and that they were a part of the dispersion of the Judeans.[41] And hence arose the concept of a 'secular Jew', which would otherwise be meaningless if Jewishness could only be defined by religion, and hence also presumably the idea of a single, definable 'Jewish people'.

Grasping this fact is essential to understanding the nature of the situation, which is quite unlike that of the other major religions. To be a Christian or a Muslim is to subscribe to a set of precepts as laid out in these religions; it is not to say that Christians or Muslims are physical descendants of the Virgin Mary or the Prophet Muhammad or had any historical link with Palestine or the Arabian Peninsula respectively. Thus, conversion to these religions merely entails accepting relevant beliefs, but in the Jewish case orthodox and conservative doctrine has it that the convert must undertake to adopt the Jewish religious way of life and be accepted *as a member of the Jewish people*. He or she makes a commitment to integrate into the Jewish community by changing his/her religious *and ethnic* identity. This is problematic, since historical linkage cannot really be transferred. Yet to inherit this particular history was an essential component of being a Jew. This is encapsulated in the Jewish religious teaching mentioned above, which stipulates that a Jew remains so even if he converts to another faith or becomes an atheist.

Zionism and Jewish Assimilation

Such ideas no doubt helped promote the concept of a biologically linked, single people. But it was not just Jews themselves who nurtured these beliefs. They were immeasurably assisted, some would say created, by Christian attitudes towards them, especially in Europe. For centuries Jewish communities were regarded as foreign bodies in the societies in which they lived, were confined to specific localities and frequently described in racial terms. The 1922 White Paper, the so-called Churchill Paper, that defined Britain's responsibilities to a Jewish national home in Palestine as propounded by the Balfour

Declaration five years before, sought the establishment of 'a centre in which the Jewish people as a whole may take, on grounds of religion *and race* an interest and a pride' (emphasis added). Their position was anomalous and ambiguous, neither in nor out of the society. Because of this feeling of difference, they developed their own dialects, and hence the appearance of Judaeo-Spanish (Ladino), Judaeo-German (Yiddish) and several other such hybrids. They also intermarried as a rule and this may well have contributed, as pointed out above, to the emergence of a specific facies that became denoted as 'Jewish'.

It was not until the European Enlightenment that ushered in liberal and egalitarian social ideas that Jewish communities in the eighteenth and nineteenth centuries started to break free of the confinement of the ghetto and to integrate with the larger society. Jewish emancipation in Europe thus followed the spread of these liberal ideas and was most pronounced in Western Europe, where after the French Revolution Jews were granted equality before the law.[42] With the separation of church and state, official Jewish activity was confined to the religious sphere and the stereotyping of Jews as foreign elements began to break down. Increasing assimilationist tendencies amongst Jews, most marked in Germany, France and Britain, led to a greater identification between them and the national groups they lived amongst. For example, German replaced Yiddish in Germany and by the eighteenth century, Jewish children were beginning to receive a secular education.[43]

The assimilation process faced much greater barriers in Eastern Europe, where the hold of traditional Judaism was strong and the Jewish communities there had a quasi-ethnic identity of their own. The mass of East European Jews lived in ghettos, apart from their non-Jewish compatriots, and traditionally led separate lives. As the Russian socialist revolutionary movements developed during the nineteenth century, Jews became particularly active participants and were gradually secularised. Towards the end of the century, they had broken through into Russia's economy and culture, although not as deeply as Jews had done in Western Europe.

At the same time Jewish assimilationism in Europe provoked the worsening or creation of powerful anti-Jewish movements in Russia and elsewhere, to which the term 'antisemitism' was first applied in modern times. There was a complexity of reasons for this discrimination against the Jews, made official policy in nineteenth-century Russia and in the

Austrian Empire, where they had the status of citizens of the second or third category.[44] But the overall trend amongst Jews was emancipationist and a move away from the segregation and ghettoisation of the past. How this trend might have developed into our own time we cannot know, since it was dramatically interrupted by the appearance of Nazism in central Europe, culminating in the Holocaust that was to be a seminal event in halting, or even reversing, the process. Zionism, itself a response to the episodes of antisemitism that continued to plague Jewish communities in Europe, and though it attracted only a minority of Jews until the 1940s, was a phenomenon striving towards the same de-assimilationist end. Since its establishment, Israel has acted as a counterweight to Jewish assimilation, which is the greatest threat to Zionism.

As is well known, most Jews were not initially interested in Zionism, seen as a fringe movement, or in emigrating to Palestine. Its earliest opponents were no less than the Jewish Bund, the nineteenth-century Russian socialist party, which believed the Jewish homeland, if there were to be any, should be set up, not in Palestine, but in the Pale of Settlement (stretching from Lithuania to Poland and Ukraine).[45] Only a tiny percentage of the millions of East European Jews who fled the Russian pogroms before the First World War went to Palestine. The majority of those that remained preferred universalist solutions to the narrow ideals of Zionism.[46] The German Orthodox and Reform Jewish communities also opposed it, as did the majority of European Jews, who saw no reason to leave their comfortable homes for a malaria-ridden backwater like Palestine. Nazism in Germany and the Holocaust had an enormous impact in reversing this reluctance, and Jewish immigration into Palestine and support for Zionism increased dramatically during the 1930s and in the wake of the Second World War. Jews began increasingly to identify with Israel's cause from its establishment in 1948, thanks to an active campaign funded by US Jews to promote this result. But it was not until 1967 that the process and the de-assimilation it led to became so marked. The Six-Day War, and perhaps more significantly, the war of 1973 in which the Arabs fought better, engendered in Jews an acute concern for Israel's survival. As the American Jewish writer, Michel Novick, noted, 'The hallmark of the good [American] Jew became the depth of his or her commitment to Israel.'[47]

The Jewish state came to assume a special status for the majority of Jews as the place of origin, the reference point and the untouchable ideal whose maintenance and survival were a sacred duty. Elie Wiesel, the ardent defender of Jewish Holocaust victims, who lived in America, summed up this extraordinary commitment, 'I feel as a Jew who resides outside Israel I must identify with whatever Israel does – even with her errors. That is the least Jews in the Diaspora can do for Israel: either speak up in praise, or keep silent.'[48] Did this come about because of a multi-million dollar Zionist propaganda effort, or for some other reason? There is no doubt that a massive campaign of publicity, persuasion and arm-twisting was fought ceaselessly on Israel's behalf. Every sector of the Jewish community and the wider society (whose collective guilt over the Holocaust was expiated in this way), was drawn into this propaganda effort – delegations to visit Israel, youth groups, academic exchanges, networking with centres of influence and power, media presentations, pro-Israel events and the like. 'Birthright Israel', for example, was an organisation that aimed to lure young Jews to holiday in Israel free of charge. This was considered an effective way to bind the Jewish Diaspora to the 'homeland'. Without these unrelenting efforts, some have argued, support for Israel might have waned, and Jews living outside might have continued their lives much as before.

Jewish Identification with Israel

Such tactics doubtless form an important part of the story, but they also build on a psychology that was already there amongst Jews, both religious and secular. The Israeli Marxist writer, Akiva Orr, has argued that the aim of political Zionism, a secular movement that arose in Eastern Europe, was to solve the identity problem of non-religious Jews. (For the religious, he wrote, it was not an issue: their reference point was Judaism and its rituals.) It was the secular Jews who had the problem, the product of a history of exclusion and alienation in European society. They saw themselves as different, even when there was no persecution, but could not define their identity with reference to religion, especially after the emancipation which weakened the hold of Judaism as an identity; hence their need to establish a nation state which would provide an alternative secular identity for Jews like them.[49] Zionism therefore strove to provide a non-religious definition of Jewishness, and hence the emphasis from the beginning on Israel being a state like any other, 'as Jewish as England is English' (to quote Israel's first president, Chaim Weitzman), with a national, secular identity. Orr concludes that this still does not solve the problem of 'who is a Jew?' nor of those Jews living outside the State of Israel whose identity remains ambiguous. As Eitan ben Elyahu wrote in *Yediott Ahronot* (17 May 2006), only in Israel could a Jew acquire a 'Jewish national' identity. Yet, beyond, a Jew could also retain his Jewish identity wherever he was; so which of them was the more 'Jewish'?

However that may be, there was a need amongst European Jews for recognition of their separateness, not by way of the ghetto, but as a distinct group with a long tradition and a history of intellectual achievement. And behind that was the background of an accepted narrative about the continuity of the 'Jewish people', their ancient origins in biblical Palestine and worldwide dispersal from it, that greatly assisted the ideology Zionism had created to take hold. As Ben-Gurion said apropos of the newly drawn-up Israeli Law of Return in 1951, 'This right originates in the unbroken historical connection between the people and the homeland.' Though this appealed more to religious Jews, the concepts were familiar and to a certain extent influential with the non-religious as well. The Israeli writer, Irit Linur, refers to this phenomenon in acknowledging that Zionism started as secular, but 'the religious connection to "the land of Zion and Jerusalem" served as a powerful subterranean fuel . . . If it had not existed, to this day we would still be looking for land in Uganda.'[50]

As has been explained to me in interviews, such people, rejecting any theological affiliation with Judaism, nevertheless, would identify themselves as 'cultural Jews'; that is, belonging to a community with a shared history and 'ethnicity' and one with an outstanding contribution to Western society. This conviction, which is chiefly found amongst Ashkenazi Jews, apparently defies questions of differences in geography, mother tongue, customs, physical appearance or local conditions. A non-religious Jewish writer of Polish parentage living in London illustrated this when she asserted to me that whenever she came across a Jew anywhere in the world, 'whether black-skinned or slant-eyed', she felt an instant affinity. This feeling, which was clearly genuine amongst the communities in parts of Europe, did not explain where they thought Oriental Jews, so un-European, fitted into this 'culture'.

After 1967, a majority of Jews came to accept Zionist dogma at face value and also to see Israel as a safe haven from persecution, real or imagined, despite it being the unsafest place on earth for them. It had already fought four wars or been in a state of war with all of its neighbours for most of its existence. Jews who had had no opinion on Zionism, or even opposed it previously, also held this view. A striking example of this was a well-known British biologist of Jewish extraction I knew in London, who was brought up by a socialist father with no time for nationalism of any kind, including Zionism. He was astounded to find this same father changed into an avid supporter of Israel in his declining years. He travelled to Israel for the first time in the late 1980s. 'You must cherish Israel with all your heart. It's our home and our refuge,' he told his son.

In fact, these feelings were already in evidence long before 1967. I saw a typical example of this in the case of a Brighton man whose father had been an Austrian Jew living in Britain since the 1930s and whose mother was a Christian and an Englishwoman. The father was totally non-religious and uninterested in even socialising with other Jews and the son had been brought up as a Christian in complete ignorance of his father's Jewish origins. In 1955, when he was 15 and the State of Israel was just seven, he accompanied his father on a holiday to Switzerland, where, to his astonishment, his father suddenly confided to him that he was in fact Jewish (despite the fact that as his mother was non-Jewish and, according to Jewish religious law, he could not be a Jew). But his father told him not to worry about it, now that there was a Jewish state; he must never fear for the future, secure in the knowledge that all Jews had a refuge there if they needed it. The man was entirely serious, leaving my friend shocked and confused. The need for security and refuge from persecution amongst Jewish communities in Europe after the experiences of the Holocaust, whether justified or not in all cases, was a powerful factor in maintaining their tenacious support for a Jewish state.

The Jewish identification with Israel, however, came at some cost to the process of Jewish assimilation. The son of the Jewish psychiatrist who believed in his Sumerian origins, as in the story above, was born of an Irish Catholic mother but reared as Jewish. I recall how he took passionate issue with me over my writings in 2003 about Zionism. The bitterness of his assault and his fanatical defence of Israel were astonishing, but he had evidently been sold the same myths that animated his father. Such a young man, though born of Europeans – and not even Jewish according to religious (Halachic) laws – and English by language and education, yet felt himself a misfit in his surroundings, and presumably unhappy because of it. In this sense, the establishment of Israel, in trying to solve one problem may well have created another. Growing up in Britain after 1949, I could see the transformation from 1967 onwards in the Jewish community which had until then merged into the fabric of British society with considerable success. It had been a difficult process and anti-Jewish sentiment still survived in certain institutions and amongst individuals until the 1960s, but the general climate of opinion was favourable and had become increasingly liberal towards Jews over the last three decades. However, many Jews started to identify with the cause of Israel as 'the motherland' and to make no secret of their affiliation to it to the point that they took on its moral values as well. Such Jews regularly defended Israeli human rights violations and were able to find a justification even for its savage assault on Lebanon's civil infrastructure in the Lebanon war of 2006.

The consequences of this tendency may be seen in the attitude of the young man in the example above and those like him, who could have felt a sense of natural belonging to Britain but have come to see themselves as located elsewhere. It is difficult to see how such a psychological suspension between two societies could be of ultimate benefit to non-Israeli Jewish communities. Nor could this phenomenon be divorced from a rising rate of attacks on Jews and Jewish institutions in countries both East and West. Some of these at least were anti-Israeli in motivation, consequent on Israel's record of human rights abuse against the Palestinians, since Jews outside Israel were commonly and wrongly identified as universal supporters of the Jewish state as well as potential Israeli citizens. The 'ingathering of the exiles' was, after all, the central theme of Zionism. It should be no surprise that some non-Jews drew the obvious inference and targeted those they saw as surrogates for Israel. While the need for Jewish global solidarity amongst a people which had suffered from persecution was understandable, it was a phenomenon of the past, not the present, no matter what sporadic antisemitic incidents there had been in recent times. By supporting Israel so blindly on that basis, many Jews became, in effect, collaborators with it.

Dual Loyalty

The Zionist imperative to categorise all Jews as members of a separate and distinct race or nation, irrespective of where they lived, inevitably led to a blurring of the distinction between Israeli and non-Israeli Jews – and hence to view them as responsible for or complicit in Israel's policies. The tendency amongst many non-Israeli Jews to assume different identities as it suited them – now potential citizens of Israel, now English (or Italian or French or whatever) – only made this worse. When I worked as a general medical practitioner in an inner London practice, I had a Jewish senior partner. This man, who had a son studying at Oxford – 'our elite universities are wonderful, you know' – proudly put himself about as an Englishman. But each time there was a Middle East crisis he would declare his readiness to go to Israel's aid, saying that 'we' were being threatened. Such a seamless swapping of identities was commonplace in Jewish circles, and I had no doubt that my colleague genuinely saw himself as belonging to Britain and at the same time as a member of another group of people represented by Israel. This dual identity is not unusual in today's pluralist Western societies, but in the Jewish case where 'Jew' and 'Israeli' or 'Zionist' are the categories of the second identity, it was not surprising that 'Jews', as a collective, should increasingly have become targets of hostile attacks against Israeli policy. This phenomenon led rapidly to Jewish accusations that anti-Zionism was being used as a surrogate for antisemitism.[51] But the reality was that so long as the drive towards Jewish de-assimilation and closer ties with Israel continued, Jews would continue to be surrogates for Israel and hostile attitudes towards them for that reason would harden and increase.

The spate of well-publicised cases of Jewish espionage in America since the 1980s became a further spur to the popular identification of Jews with Israel, inviting charges of dual loyalty and potentially provoking 'antisemitic' hostility. In fact, there had been a long history of Israeli espionage against the US from the 1950s and well known to FBI officials and others.[52] The issue came to public prominence in 1985 with the Pollard case. Jonathan Pollard, a Jewish American working for US naval intelligence, was indicted on charges of passing information to Israel on matters regarding chemical, biological and nuclear weapons in Syria, Iran and Libya. Despite strenuous Israeli efforts to have him released, he was still in prison 20 years later and was unlikely to be released for years more. In the summer of 2004, the FBI launched an investigation into Larry Franklin, an official at the Pentagon, on suspicion of spying for AIPAC. Franklin worked for Douglas Feith, a prominent pro-Israel Jewish neoconservative and a top Pentagon official until 2005. He was charged with passing classified information on Iran to AIPAC, which in turn passed it to the Israeli embassy in Washington.[53] AIPAC itself had been under investigation for several years before that, two of its most senior officials accused of dealing with a 'foreign country'.[54]

Whether true or not, it reinforced the perception that AIPAC was indeed acting as an agent for a foreign power, while claiming to be an American organisation, a view that helped to reignite the debate about dual loyalty.[55] The suspicion that pro-Israel officials at the top of the administration had pushed the US into war against Iraq in order to protect Israel (as will be discussed further below) was another serious provocation to anti-Jewish resentment. To many Americans it appeared that American Jews were using their privileged position of access to distort US foreign policy in the interests of Israel – and this, despite a unique American largesse towards Israel. Though such sentiments were commonplace at the anecdotal level, they were rarely aired in public. Nevertheless, some US commentators were provoked into voicing their resentment, as in this example published on the Internet in late 2004. The writer questions the fuss over the AIPAC spying affair because, 'among informed people, it is taken as a given that virtually everyone in relevant top positions, within the executive branch of the US Government, as well as virtually all members of Congress, are Israeli agents – at least in a moral and functional sense'.[56]

All this was undoubtedly unfair to those Jews who did not support Israel and who deplored its abuse of the Palestinians, and they may well have felt themselves to be the victims of antisemitic racism yet again. But the predicament today needs to be seen more in the context and as a consequence of Zionism than as an abiding hatred of Jews. Many Jews, however, and especially those in Israel, drew precisely the latter conclusion from these events. The rise of anti-Jewish attacks in several European countries was seen as the resurgence of an old gentile affliction. In fact, such attacks in Europe increased sharply with the second intifada, suggesting a linkage with Israeli policy, and in Britain the Community Security Trust, a Jewish organisation that monitors levels of antisemitism, found that a quarter of 532 such attacks in 2004 had an 'anti-Israeli' motivation.[57] In the first four months of that year, eleven separate attacks on cemeteries were recorded in France. According to the *Guardian* (11 August 2004), the desecrated tombs were Jewish, but also Muslim and Christian. Many such incidents were usually imputed to National Front sympathisers, neo-Nazis and similar fascist groups, following a familiar European pattern, and even of exhibitionists, or, bizarrely, Jews themselves.[58]

In July 2004, Israel's prime minister, in a bid to play up these incidents as old-style antisemitism, urged French Jews to emigrate, and indeed, 200 people did so in one week alone. In this anxiety over old-style antisemitism, an important feature of this resurgence was ignored. Increasingly it seemed to originate with Muslims, as the European Union's Monitoring Centre on Racism found in its report of 2003.[59] The cause for this pattern was not the antisemitism familiar to the history of Europe, but rather it stemmed from anger amongst Muslim communities about perceived anti-Islamic aggression. The spectacle of fellow Muslims subjected to Israeli aggression in Palestine was a powerful incentive to feelings of hostility towards Israel and, by extension, towards all those who supported it, including non-Israeli Jews. The same mechanism may be assumed to have operated amongst Muslim immigrants everywhere, though in varying degrees, and needed to be understood in this context. American blanket support for Israel only added fuel to the Islamic fire.

3
Why Does the West Support Israel?

The previous chapter dealt with Jewish support for Israel. It is my purpose now to turn to the question of the non-Jewish dimension of this support which has played such a crucial part in maintaining the Jewish state – the bedrock on which Israel's wellbeing rests. Indeed, it may be argued that without it, all the Zionist machinating and Jewish sentiment in the world would not have saved the Israeli project. And this is the nub of the problem. Why did the world's most powerful state back Israel so blindly? Why did the West in general follow suit? These questions exercised all those Palestinians, Arabs and others, who had tried to make Israel accountable for its actions and brought down to its natural regional size, only to be vitiated by the fact of this support. Edward Said's *The Question of Palestine* wrestled with this problem in 1979 and many others have since tried to do the same. No matter what explanations were put forward, it remained perplexing. This chapter will review the various explanatory arguments that have been offered to explain this phenomenon, but none of them was able to settle the question decisively. For Palestinians, however, trying to understand it was no intellectual game but a matter of life and death.

But, irrespective of the causes of this phenomenon, the inference was clear: it was Israel's backers who needed tackling if the Arab–Israeli problem was to be solved. This realisation hit me hard while visiting the US in the spring of 2004. In Gaza the Israelis had just killed Abdul Aziz al-Rantisi, the second-in-command of Hamas; a few weeks earlier, they had killed its leader, Sheikh Ahmad Yassin, against the backdrop of a massive military onslaught on the Palestinian population under Israeli occupation. As if this were all happening on another planet, I saw huge billboards in San Francisco showing pictures of pleasant, ordinary-looking folk of all skin colours and ages, with the reassuring slogan, 'Israelis are people like us'. I was struck by this blatant advertising for Israel, as if it were not a foreign country but an American domestic concern. And that of course is what it had become, as even the most cursory examination of the situation in the US amply demonstrated. Such far-reaching penetration into the world's most powerful state at every level filled me with a sense of impotence, and I could see no hope for any activism which did not tackle this problem first.

The US and Israel

What was the nature of American support and why was it so necessary to maintain the Jewish state, *in its supremacist form*, no matter what the cost to the indigenous inhabitants, the region, or Western interests there? Various theories were elaborated in numerous studies and observations on this phenomenon. While Britain was the first to help establish the Zionist project and enable it to take hold in Palestine, it was later America that was Israel's foremost and most committed backer. US support, financial, military and political, was vital to Israel's existence, so vital that, like a patient on a heart-lung machine, any interruption in the power supply would have been fatal. Israel itself seemed to be aware of this and had tried to reduce its economic dependence on the US. In 1998, in an effort towards independence, Israel volunteered to phase out its annual subsidy from America over the next ten years. However, little happened and there appeared to be no imminent danger of a change in US support for Israel. This statement by the Democratic presidential candidate, John Kerry, in the 2004 US elections, said it all. 'We are not secure while Israel, the one true democracy in the [Middle Eastern] region, remains the victim of an unrelenting campaign of terror . . . American leadership is needed to bolster Israel's security at home as well as in the region.'[1] Having already pledged support for every plan the Sharon government had put forward in 2004 – the separation wall, the recognition of the West Bank settlements and the denial of the Palestinian right of return – he went on to detail even more supportive measures. These included a remarkable promise to set up a state department special office to combat and monitor antisemitism worldwide.[2] The entire tone of the statement comes across as grovelling and subservient, but it was also an illuminating illustration of the profoundly pro-Israeli posture that animated the top levels of US leadership.

Such blind allegiance had been gathering pace since the time of President Kennedy and was spread across the whole of the US political spectrum, both conservative right and liberal left. (That incidentally was why the Palestinian case had been so difficult to promote amongst US politicians, where it was blocked by both sides.) It became axiomatic that no politician, actual or aspiring, in the American system could afford to alienate Israel's supporters. The latter managed to impose such total censorship on both houses of Congress, that no senator or congressman dared make a critical speech about Israel. Those that did so faced the threat of losing re-election, with money going to support their opponents. Paul Findley's experience as a US congressman in the 1980s is instructive in this regard. An Israel supporter for 22 years while in Congress, he deviated from that course towards the end of the 1970s as he began to understand something of the Palestinian question. But criticising Israel, though in relatively mild terms, brought down on his head the wrath of Israel's supporters. He lost the battle for re-election to Congress in 1982, thanks to a massive campaign mounted by the pro-Israel lobby to unseat him.[3]

The Israel Lobby

There was no mystery about this at least. Pro-Israel groups, of which there were some two score active in the US, maintained a close watch on government, lobbying decision makers and funding politicians who might have been induced to push Israel's case in the US Administration. The contributions from such sources ran to hundreds of thousands of dollars to candidates in direct proportion to their commitment to the cause of Israel. Some of the recipients were Jewish themselves, as in the case of Joseph Lieberman or Frank Lautenberg, but by no means all.[4] The power of the Zionist lobby in America was legendary.[5] In March 2006, a detailed study of its workings was published by two American professors of impeccable academic credentials. The study, which was not well received by pro-Israel sympathisers with accusations of anti-semitic bias, makes fascinating reading and throws light on a topic that was normally glossed over precisely for that reason.[6] A later and even more detailed exploration of the same subject leaves the reader in little doubt about the immense power of the Israel lobby over American politics.[7] The best known and most effective of the Israel lobbyists was undoubtedly AIPAC, whose position was quite simply one of uncritical support for whichever Israeli government was in power. AIPAC worked most successfully through the US Congress, ensuring that Israel's case was promoted through direct and indirect means, funding congressmen and senators and working through sympathetic congressional aides.

Later on, AIPAC started to adopt an increasingly right-wing posture, both in its support for the Likud party in Israel and the political right in the US, including the Christian Zionists. The fanatical support of these groups for Israel was of crucial help in making AIPAC even more effective. This effusion by the influential evangelist, Pat Robertson (and supporter of AIPAC) during a visit to Jerusalem in 2004, illustrates the point well. If Bush were to 'touch' Jerusalem, Robertson told his Israeli audience, evangelists would abandon the Republicans and form a 'third party'. He had been on a tour of the Holy Land to support and pray for the people of Israel. Having called for the abolition of UNRWA (the UN agency concerned with Palestinian refugees), which he accused of perpetuating the Palestinian refugee problem, he warned of the threat a Palestinian state would pose to Israel. 'A Palestinian state with full sovereignty would be a launching pad for various types of weapons, including weapons of mass destruction,' he declared.[8] Not only did this powerful Zionist–Christian alliance lead the US Congress to adopt whatever pro-Israel position AIPAC dictated, but it also worked to prevent any semblance of equivalence in US dealings with the Arab world. Weapons sales to Arab states were repeatedly held up or cancelled as a result of AIPAC lobbying. The Stinger missile case is a famous example. When the US decided to sell defensive Stinger missiles to Jordan and Saudi Arabia in 1984, there was such opposition from the Jewish lobby that President Reagan allegedly had to beg the United Jewish Appeal for support. He never got it and the sale never went through.[9]

In the 1980s, AIPAC set up the Washington Institute for Near East Policy (WINEP). The fact that its director in 2006 was Dennis Ross (the erstwhile envoy of President Clinton to oversee the Israeli–Palestinian peace process), was in itself a reflection of the strongly partisan character of American dealings with the Palestinians in the peace negotiations.

WINEP was a pro-Likud organisation which hosted associates on the far right of Israeli politics, the likes of Martin Kramer and Daniel Pipes; the latter was notorious in the American academic world for his immoderate pro-Israeli stance. He and other AIPAC operatives were responsible for a major project to silence academics on US campuses critical of Israel. AIPAC generously funded programmes to monitor university activities related to Israel, and in 2002, Kramer and Pipes established 'Campus Watch'. This organisation drew up dossiers on academics suspected of being hostile to Israel and encouraged students to spy on such people and report back.[10] The same project tried to induce Congress to pass legislation that would impose censorship of material in American university teaching programmes deemed to be hostile to Jews or to Israel, but had not succeeded as yet.[11]

An example of these bullying tactics was the targeting of New York's Columbia University. In 2004, pro-Israel students complained that professors at the university were preventing them from defending Israel; their cause was taken up by the local press with accusations that Columbia was 'awash with anti-Semitism'.[12] The pressure was such that the university's president was forced to hold an inquiry into the complaints. It found no evidence of antisemitism, but the complaints re-surfaced when the Palestinian historian, Rashid Khalidi, was appointed at Columbia in 2005. The same Zionist campaign had been ceaselessly waged against his predecessor, the foremost Palestinian-American academic, Edward Said, in the decade before his death in 2004, aiming to oust him from his post, discredit his standing and even to threaten his life.

The anecdotal evidence for instances of bullying and threats against academics who did not toe the pro-Israel line, their dismissal and the ruination of their careers is legion. When I visited Stanford University in California, a well-known centre of pro-Zionist activity, in 2003, I noticed the advertisements for Campus Watch that the student newsletter carried. Demonstrations and protests were regularly organised to oppose or discredit pro-Palestinian speakers and activities. Any action critical of Israel was dubbed 'antisemitic', without fear of contradiction. Worse still, I noted a widespread and fearful reluctance to complain about any of this in public. 'This situation is clearly intolerable,' I exclaimed. 'Why do you put up with it?' 'Because it's not worth the penalty if we speak out,' people responded.

AIPAC, through its arm, WINEP, was enormously influential in Washington. Personnel from the state department and the military were sent there for 'education' about the Middle East. Conversely, WINEP supplied advisors to Republican administrations where they promoted pro-Likud policies. It was such people who were said to have steered US policy towards invading Iraq and who later had Syria and Iran in their sights as the next targets. Much was written about the neoconservative cabal of Jewish Zionists, the likes of Richard Perle (previously chairman of the Pentagon's Defense Policy Board), Paul Wolwofitz (former deputy-secretary of defense) and Douglas Feith (former under-secretary of defense for policy), who previously operated in senior policy positions within the Bush Administration. All three were either known – or had been investigated for – transmission of classified intelligence material to Israel.[13] The fact that the neocons were highly influential in determining US foreign policy with regard to Iraq and the Middle East, until the summer of 2005 at least, seemed hardly in doubt. That such policy was significantly geared to protecting and promoting Israel's interest was not in doubt either.

The Role of the Neoconservatives

In 1996, the neocons had been involved in drawing up a now famous policy paper on the 'Project for the New American Century' at the Jewish Institute for National Security Affairs (JINSA). This advocated the doctrine of pre-emption in US foreign policy and a strategy for removing Saddam Hussein from power as part of Israel's regional defence. The suspicions of a number of intellectuals and analysts that the last was the real motivation for the invasion of Iraq have gained support from a number of official sources. According to Ariel Sharon, speaking on Israel Radio in March of 2002, US Vice-President Dick Cheney assured him that the US would invade Iraq to protect Israel. In a speech to the National Press Club in Washington in April 2004, General Tommy Franks, who had led the war on Iraq, said that the threat of a missile attack on Israel was one reason justifying a pre-emptive strike against Iraq. 'We did not want to subject ourselves and Israel to the potential consequences of a long-range missile from being fired into Tel Aviv or Jerusalem,' he said.[14] Further confirmation came from Philip Zelikow, a senior White House official with close ties

to the Bush Administration and a member of the President's Foreign
Intelligence Advisory Board from 2001 to 2003. On the eve of Iraq's
invasion, Zelikow publicly acknowledged that the real Iraqi threat was
the one against Israel – 'the threat that dares not speak its name', as
he put it – and that the war's chief aim was the desire to protect the
Jewish state.[15]

By the time the Iraq war started, it was becoming strongly rumoured
that the whole enterprise had been the creation of some 30 neoconservative intellectuals, most of them Jewish, with a far-reaching agenda
for the Middle East and a profound penetration into the Bush Administration. Many of these people were also friends who shared and
collaborated over political ideas. As it emerged that none of the formal
reasons for going to war was valid – no weapons of mass destruction,
no links to al-Qaeda, no terrorism – the role of Israel working through
these supporters gained credence. In other words, it must have been
Israel's security that was the motive for attacking Iraq, in the absence
of any other. In an unusually outspoken comment on the Iraq war,
Senator Ernest Hollings dismissed the Iraqi WMD pretext for war on
the grounds that, had it been true, then Israel would have been the
first to know since its very survival would have been at stake. So, with
Iraq no threat, why go to war? The answer for him was clear: in order
to secure Israel in fulfilment of the neoconservative hardliners' grand
strategy for the region.[16]

The plan for the new Middle East espoused by the neocons aimed to
promote democratic change there in America's image, the removal of
'despotic regimes' among which Syria, Iran and Saudi Arabia ranked
highest, and an aggressive policy of pre-emption. But it also aimed
to create thereby a safe environment for Israel, with its traditional
enemies neutralised or replaced by friendly governments, something
the Jewish state had never fully enjoyed before. Attempts to rebuild the
Iraq–Israel oil pipeline (closed since the 1950s) so as to supply Israel
with cheap oil, and the determination to install an Iraqi government
that would normalise relations with Israel, support this interpretation. It was no secret that numerous Israeli businessmen, intelligence
agents and 'advisors' were operating in Iraq, with the aim of furthering
Israel's influence over the country. To implement this plan, the American
occupation of Iraq was the essential first stage. As if to affirm the
Iraq–Israel link, the *New York Times* columnist, Thomas Friedman,

drew a parallel between the Iraq war and the Israeli attack on Jenin in April 2002. The cause of the violence that the population used against the invaders in both cases was in his view the mistake that Israel and America had made in sparing the non-combatant inhabitants. So it was justifiable according to that logic to use force against the population in both cases.[17] There were those, however, who did not believe that protecting Israel had been the motive for the US attack on Iraq.[18] They argued that deposing Saddam Hussein and replacing him with a militant Shiite government, which was bound to be allied with Iran and certain to be anti-Zionist, would, in fact, place Israel in far greater danger than before.

Who Controls America?

On this evidence, it is abundantly clear that the pro-Israel lobby was formidably powerful and influential in US politics towards the Middle East. But was it possible to go further and say that this influence had over-ridden the American national interest? Was US policy so controlled by Israel and its supporters that it was they who primarily dictated it, or was Israel but the imperialist arm of America (and the West) in the Middle East, as some have suggested? On the surface, it certainly looked as if the former were closer to the truth, as the Mearsheimer and Walt study had tried to demonstrate. The institutionalisation of pro-Israel influence throughout a myriad of American think tanks, lobbying organisations and government departments at the highest level it describes could not have been without significant effect on US foreign policy. As the authors say, '[The Israel lobby's] activities have shaped America's action in this [the Middle Eastern] crucial region.'[19]

We have already alluded to the power of pro-Israel lobbyists over Congress and the Senate, where no one could criticise Israel and keep the job. When Hilary Clinton was competing with her Republican opponent in the race for the US Senate in 2003, she was noted to have totally reversed her position on the Palestinians. When she visited Gaza with President Clinton, just one year before, she had embraced Yasser Arafat's wife and backed the establishment of a Palestinian state. On entering the senatorial race, however, she started to exhibit strong fervour for Israel, advocated moving the US embassy from Tel Aviv to Jerusalem (an illegal act that no US Administration had been prepared to implement) and demanded leniency towards the convicted spy, Jonathan Pollard, in compliance with Israel's long-standing wishes. It was significant that the main weapon her opponents deployed against her was to depict her as an 'Arab-lover', waving photographs of her embracing Mrs Arafat.

Some distinguished Americans publicly voiced their alarm at what they saw as this pro-Israel manipulation of the US political process. Kennett Love, distinguished former *New York Times* foreign correspondent and author of a definitive work on the Suez war, summed up these fears in a recent comment. He castigated the US for having lost control of its politics to a 'Jewish lobby that puts Israel's interests above our American interests', and the American Congress for a 'cowardly caucus touting their glossy partisan support for Israel against nearly the entire Muslim world and in defiance of public opinion in Europe and the rest of the Americas'. It was Israel that ran the special alliance and not America, and it was Israel that 'corrupted an American citizen named Pollard to steal our secrets for years'.[20] Even more forthrightly, Ralph Nader, the independent presidential candidate in the 2004 elections, declared the White House to be a puppet in Israel's hands. 'The Israeli puppeteer travels to Washington,' he said of a visiting Israeli head of state to the US. 'The Israeli puppeteer meets with the puppet in the White House, and then moves down Pennsylvania Avenue and meets with the puppets in Congress. And then takes back billions of taxpayer dollars.'[21] The same sentiments were echoed in a series of thoughtful reflections on American Zionists written by Edward Said for *Al-Ahram Weekly* in 2000. He concluded that most Arabs did not understand how completely a small minority of American pro-Likudniks with more extreme positions than those of the Israeli Likud itself controlled US policy.[22]

Pro-Zionist Influence and the Media

Alongside this political coercion, the striking prevalence of pro-Israel sympathisers in the American mass media and organs of public information had to be considered. American Jews were prominent in publishing, in the ownership of major newspapers like the *New York Times*, the *Washington Post*, the *Boston Globe* and *Newsweek*, and also of TV news channels, CNN/Time Warner, CBS and ABC.

Rupert Murdoch's Fox channel, which was not Jewish-owned but had a Jewish president and a Jewish second-in-command at Murdoch News, was notorious for its biased and sensational reporting of many issues, most prominently Israel/Palestine. It tried, for example, to rename suicide bombers, 'homicide bombers', in case the word 'suicide' elicited viewers' sympathy for young Palestinians driven to take their own lives. Much of its reporting was also factually incorrect and, unsurprisingly, as a recent survey found, Fox News watchers ended up both biased and ill-informed.[23]

A number of widely syndicated journalists writing in major newspapers, such as the *New York Times*' William Safire and the *Washington Post*'s Charles Krauthammer, were fervently pro-Zionist Jews. Many of Hollywood's most prominent figures were Jewish, a fact that had frequently led to the supposition that most of them would be pro-Israeli as well. Regardless of whether all this amounted to a real or imagined pro-Israel control of the US media, it was certainly the case that American commentators willing to oppose the pro-Israeli line were few and far-between. Those that did, became the objects of abuse, and the organs that published them suffered letter-writing campaigns and boycotts orchestrated by the Israel lobby such as to discourage them from doing so again.[24] All media outlets – film, TV, newspapers, journals – propounded Israel's case, which had become America's case, and censored out anything that countered it, including any reasonable coverage of or opinion on the Arab situation.

The effect of this was unavoidably to distort American public perceptions and help entrench unassailable 'truths' favourable to Israel, as, for example, its much-vaunted democracy, 'civilised values' and so-called liberal culture. Remarkably, the Israeli press was often far more openly critical of its government and policies than its American counterpart. The American journalist, Alison Weir, has tried to document this censorship in America in a painstaking recent study.[25] She found that news reporting about Israel regularly omitted coverage of its abuses of Palestinians and tended instead to emphasise Israeli suffering at the hands of Palestinian militants. During the second intifada, for example, National Public Radio (NPR), often absurdly accused of being 'pro-Palestinian', chose to report on the deaths of 89 per cent of Israeli children killed in the conflict but only on 20 per cent of Palestinian ones, even though the death toll amongst the latter was three times higher. In the first three months of the intifada, during which the Israelis killed 84 Palestinian children and not a single Israeli died, only one Palestinian death received coverage. A public survey taken at the end of 2000 that Weir cites, showed that 93 per cent of respondents either did not know which children had been killed in the recent intifada or believed them to be Israeli. Several other issues were similarly distorted or covered up: the staggering amount of taxpayer's money that went to Israel – over $10million a day – Israel's fearsome nuclear arsenal, the powerful lobbies working in Washington on its behalf and, most seriously of all, Israel's responsibility for the longest military occupation in modern times and the existence of six million people it had dispossessed.

What Did it All Mean?

The foregoing evidence strongly suggests that it was pro-Israeli Jewish domination that explained America's apparent subservience to and limitless support for Israel. This was a conspiracy view beloved of many Arabs and linked to their broader belief in the Jewish plan to take over the world. The most extreme form of this paranoia that I saw was in Jordan, where I was on a visit in 2003. A doctor I met there, who had lived in Germany for many years, told me that the Jews had worked to corrupt postwar German society through, of all things, shortening the hemline. By dominating the fashion industry, he said, they had introduced short skirts to seduce German men and hasten the decline of German society! The widely discredited *Protocols of the Elders of Zion*, for example, became extremely popular with Arabs, who took the book at face value.[26] This was not plain idiocy on their part but represented a need to explain to themselves their helplessness and impotence in the face of a triumphant Israel.

Yet, as many observers pointed out, the American Zionists were only one, albeit highly organised and effective, amongst a number of powerful lobbies that operated in the US political system. The Cuba lobby that wielded such influence over the Administration was but one such example. Israel's Jewish supporters constituted no more than 5 to 8 per cent at most of the American population, but they were well mobilised and highly motivated. They also faced little opposition, since most American citizens were not interested in the Middle East as such and were in any case poorly informed. There was a vacuum in the US political discourse on this and many other issues. The pattern of American politics was to mobilise various interest groups around a particular candidate or party, and the ethnic communities that made up American society were often actively wooed for their support. The Republican pursuit of the Hispanic community, which formed a sizeable bloc of potential voters, was a case in point. There was no reason why, on this logic, the Jewish community should have been any less appealing to politicians. Nor was there any reason why committed Zionists should not have taken advantage of this situation. Since Israel's wellbeing depended so acutely on US support, it would have been strange, perverse even, for its supporters not to have done so. Add to this the ineffectiveness and disorganisation of the American Arab community, the failure of Arabs to comprehend and exploit the American system, and the Zionists had a clear field in which to operate.

Even so, was this passive picture of the American political establishment prey to whichever lobby wanted to feed off it really true in the case of Israel? Was there a reciprocal, even if not equal, benefit to America from the existence of Israel? Certainly Noam Chomsky, America's leading intellectual and critic of US imperialism, always argued for such a view, seeing Israel as an indispensable part of US geopolitical strategy in the Middle East and elsewhere.[27] And there had been a general perception from early on that Israel could be helpful in promoting key US regional interests: securing the supply of oil from the Middle East and, in the era of the Cold War, containing Soviet influence in a strategically vital region. In this endeavour, Israel was to act as a barrier against Arab states friendly to the USSR and help to support pro-Western Arab regimes such as those in Jordan and Saudi Arabia. This would in turn serve to offset the danger of Soviet designs on oil in the Gulf, which the US believed should always remain under its own control. Israel's alliance with the Shah of Iran during the 1970s was another means by which US oil interests in the Gulf region were protected.

Israel's other major usefulness, according to Chomsky, was in the fight against radical Arab nationalism, which if not defeated could have threatened American interests and drawn in Soviet support. Israel's early alliances with pre-Khomeini Iran, Turkey and Ethiopia, ringing the Arab world with unfriendly states, were a part of this endeavour. Israel served US interests also in playing a facilitating role for American influence in the penetration of Black Africa (described in Chapter 1). From the 1960s to the 1980s Israel became active in Central America, providing arms and technology to US client states there. Acting at the time as a proxy for America, which wanted to avoid congressional bans on selling arms to states that violated human rights, Israel became the chief arms supplier to Zaire, Liberia, Burma, Argentina, Brazil, Chile, Honduras and Guatemala, all ruled by notorious despots.[28] The picture that emerges from Chomsky's 1983 account of these contacts was of an Israel acting as an American agent on a global scale – and incidentally terrifying to Arabs. It showed them just how deeply entrenched at the highest geopolitical level Israel was and what an integral part of the world's only superpower's global strategy it had become. Grappling with Israel as a regional actor was difficult enough for the Arabs, but trying to deal with it at that global level was going to be impossible.

The thesis that Israel was a US 'strategic asset' which commenced in the 1950s became accepted dogma when Henry Kissinger, President Nixon's secretary of state, did much to advance it during the 1970s. He regarded Israel as an extension of American power and supplied it with a massive infusion of economic and military aid, as well as absolute political and diplomatic support. The two states went on to form a formal strategic alliance in 1985 through which they shared intelligence on terrorism, weapons proliferation and other matters of mutual interest.[29] Other bilateral agreements followed on military planning, weapons development, combined military exercises and counter-terrorism strategies. Decades of US technology transfer to Israel and unstinting financial support enabled the Jewish state to become one of the world's largest arms suppliers and producers, even supplying the US military itself. Following the 2003 US invasion of Iraq, Israel provided counter-insurgency training for American troops in the Negev desert in the south of the country and became indispensable in the war on terror. By the turn of the millennium it was locked into a partnership of unrivalled closeness with the USA.

But it is important to remember that it was not always so. For a brief period, under the Eisenhower Administration, America had a less partisan approach towards Israel and was willing to control its wayward behaviour during the Suez crisis. The Administration was well aware of Israel's usefulness in countering the growth of Arab nationalism and Soviet influence in the Middle East.[30] But John Dulles, secretary of state at the time, was equally aware of Arab resentment over Israel's creation and sought to alleviate it through cultivating better US–Arab relations and increased economic and technical assistance. Israel, he believed, should see itself as part of the region and also accept a limited return of Palestinian refugees to its territory. In 1953, he held up a loan request from Israel because he did not approve of its de facto annexation of West Jerusalem. There were many other examples of this attitude towards Israel throughout the period of the Eisenhower Administration, all of which would be inconceivable now.[31] It is a measure of how partisan towards Israel America has become today that we can look back on the Eisenhower era and marvel at its fearlessness and resolve in the face of Israel and its supporters.

Even so, many observers were still prepared to make the case that America's special relationship with Israel could be explained mostly or solely on the basis of imperialism and power politics. In this scenario, as the American academic, Stephen Zunes, argued, Israel was but an agent of Western imperialism and should not be accused of manipulating America.[32] Chomsky, who as we have seen, was the arch proponent of this view, did not set much store by the Israel lobby argument. Though he recognised the lobby's power over the US political process, he doubted that it would have succeeded so well had it not been for Israel's perceived usefulness to the ruling elites in the US system. Furthermore, he and others of this school of thought argued that blaming the Israel lobby for American policy in the Middle East exonerated the US from responsibility for the ills inflicted on Palestine, Iraq and elsewhere in the Middle East. Far from being an innocent pawn in a game played by others, in reality, they argued, the US sought to protect its interests all over the globe and had done so by the most unsavoury means (most prominently in Africa and Latin America), using local agents to do its work. So why was Israel not just another of these agents, particularly useful and effective perhaps, but nothing more?[33] It is interesting that this school of thought did not acknowledge that the ills in the Arab region that Israel was supposed to cure on America's behalf – Soviet influence, radical nationalism, Islamic fundamentalism, the threat to the oil supply – were mostly provoked by Israel's existence in the first place. In other words, Israel had created the very conditions that made its services apparently indispensable. Nor was the opposite scenario considered, where it was the arrival of Israel and the powerful lobbies working on its behalf that forced successive US Administrations to find a use for it in their foreign policies.

In the Arab world the trend became increasingly weighted in favour of seeing Israel as part of a Zionist conspiracy against Islam. But during the 1950s and 1960s the predominant view of its role was different, that is was a proxy of Europe and the West, created to exploit and dominate the Arabs on their behalf. The latter opinion was still strongly held in some quarters. I remember a research fellow at the reputable Egyptian Al-Ahram think tank telling me in 1997, 'Israel will come to heel when America says so. Without America, Israel is nothing. Its power is America's power, nothing else.' This traditional attitude was in part responsible for the paucity of Arab expertise in Israeli affairs and the dearth of reputable centres in the Arab world, whether academic or governmental, studying Israel and Israelis – after all, what would be the point of studying a state that was merely an extension of Western power outside of that context? Understanding Israel better would not denude it of its favoured position or alter the balance of power in the Arabs' favour.

Israel and the Great Powers

It was of course true that the Zionist project was allied from the beginning to the great imperialist powers. Theodor Herzl, the founder of Zionism, approached numerous world leaders, including the Pope, the German Kaiser and the British colonial secretary, in his quest to implement Zionism. The early Zionists well understood that their project could only succeed and survive with the support of the great powers, and that they would have to offer services in return for their patronage. The patrons in their turn saw Zionism as useful to their plans in the Middle East region. This understanding has continued since with the US adopting the patron's role following Britain, and was well enunciated in the 1970s Nixon Doctrine. This aimed to avoid direct American involvement in the Third World, substituting it for regional proxies who would protect US interests. In the Middle East, especially after the fall of the Shah of Iran, Israel was the obvious choice, entrusted with the task of maintaining a regional 'balance' favourable to America.[34]

If Israel was indeed an American client state, should not its patron have been able to exert some control over its behaviour, much as a dog owner might bring his hound to heel if it misbehaved? With Israel so dependent on the US for its welfare, one would think this a reasonable supposition. It was certainly the reasoning behind the Arab states' ardent wooing of America's top officials, attempting to convince them that they, the Arabs, could have been just as, or more, useful to their interests than Israel. As Egypt's President Anwar Sadat put it in 1974, the US held '99 per cent of the cards'. Unfortunately, this ploy never worked with America, and Israel was not displaced in Western affections. The US perception, shared more or less with the Western European states, was that Israel remained their most dependable ally in a volatile region and best placed to defend their interests. Intransigent and self-serving as Israel was, it was still preferable to any of the Arab states, which were seen as backward, alien and unstable. Moreover, the ready compliance of their leaders with Western wishes ensured that Western support for Israel was cost-free, without at the same time endearing any of them to the West in return.

After the September 11, 2001 terrorist strikes on the US, a new dimension to the US relationship with Israel was added, namely, the identification with America that Israel cleverly claimed in their 'common struggle' against 'terrorism'. Always ahead of the game, Israel's leaders were quick to exploit any situation that bound America ever closer to their interests. This was compounded during George Bush's presidency by the influence of the Jewish neocons over the Administration that strove to embed Israel firmly into a new America-dominated Middle East. Israel's regional priorities seemed to have become America's, not least in the drive to attack and weaken both Syria and Iran. It was no secret that Israel considered its greatest danger would come from an Iranian nuclear attack and was anxious to engage the US in pre-empting such a possibility. During the second Bush presidency, there were signs that the US was seriously contemplating such a move, in the hope, it was claimed, that it would help Bush's chances in the November 2006 congressional elections. In this scenario, the rumours went, Israel would bomb Iran's nuclear facilities, much as it did Iraq's in 1981 when it attacked the Osirak nuclear reactor, a suspicion further fuelled by the Israeli acquisition of American bunker-busting bombs and long-range fighter aircraft.[35]

Likewise, Syria, another of Israel's regional bugbears, came under increasing pressure from the US. Pro-Israel pressure in the US Congress succeeded in effecting a sanctions policy against Syria at the end of 2003. At the same time, Israel bombed an alleged terrorist training camp outside Damascus, presumably with American acquiescence. US officials assured Israel that after Iraq America would 'deal with' the threat from Syria and Iran. In May 2004, President Bush labelled Syria 'an unusual and extraordinary threat' and promised to tighten sanctions even more. In September 2004, the UN Security Council pushed through a US-sponsored resolution demanding Syria's withdrawal from Lebanon. The ostensible reasons for this punitive Israel/US stance towards Iran and Syria was that both countries allegedly harboured or were planning to develop weapons of mass destruction; that they both supported 'terrorist' organisations, such as Hizbullah and Islamic Jihad; and that, at least in Syria's case, terrorist groups had been permitted to cross the border into Iraq and fight US forces there.[36]

These contrived justifications could not disguise the fact that it was Israel that had the most to gain from the subjugation of these states. For, what threat did Syria, a militarily weak state with a precarious economy, really pose to the US? And how would an attack on Iran, a much larger and stronger state, advance American interests in the region? On the contrary, both these steps would be conducive to greater regional instability, radicalisation and increasing anti-American violence, not to speak of the huge military and resource costs of such an effort. Destroying Iran's dispersed and well-guarded underground nuclear facilities would be no easy matter and risked vigorous Iranian retaliation, of which Iranian leaders had made no secret.[37] The range of options for Iranian action included interference in Iraq, helping install an Iranian-backed Shia government there, strengthening Hizbullah in Lebanon and launching a series of terrorist operations against US targets. In addition, an interruption in the Iranian oil supply would have a serious impact on the price of oil and Western economies. A US/Israel attack would also entrench the position of the conservatives in Iran whose people would see them as a regime defending a country under attack. None of this was to America's advantage. Just as in the case of Iraq, where the US invasion was neither wise nor justified on any of the grounds officially presented for it, it was Israel's imperatives that were the defining factor. That the neoconservative agenda converged with these same imperatives makes no difference to that fundamental fact. In any case, enough evidence has been adduced in previous sections about the overweening influence of its pro-Israel elements to make the neoconservative agenda no more than an adjunct to Israel's. Put another way, how likely was it that America would have attacked Iraq and then threatened the same towards its neighbours if Israel had not existed?

Israel in Control

It does not seem to me reasonable to conclude from the evidence that America uses, controls or benefits from the existence of Israel to an extent commensurate with its inordinate support for the Jewish state. The most dramatic illustration of this fact must surely be the case of the USS *Liberty*.[38] In June 1967, while the war between Israel and its Arab neighbours was in full swing, the *Liberty*, an unarmed US Navy reconnaissance ship, was sailing in international waters off the coast of Gaza when it came under intense Israeli air and sea bombardment. Israel asserted afterwards that it had been a case of mistaken identity, despite the fact that the US flag and the Navy's insignia were clearly visible, and all the survivors testified that the attack had been deliberate and intended to destroy the ship and all its personnel. Even as Israel did this, the US was rushing military equipment to help it in its war with the Arab states. The speculation was that Israel had wanted to draw the US into the war on its side by staging the assault to look like an Egyptian attack and leaving no survivors to tell the tale. Lyndon Johnson, US president at the time, immediately and inexplicably acted to protect Israel from censure by allowing only a limited inquiry into the incident and ordering its chairman to absolve Israel of guilt. Johnson also prevented testimony damaging to Israel from being published, and most documents relating to the assault remained classified. But over the years many people became aware that there had been a cover-up at the highest levels of US government in Israel's interest, and the *Liberty* attack survivors never ceased their fight for justice.

During the first gulf war, Israel was in fact an embarrassment and had to be bought off (with costly American patriot missiles and other military hardware) from joining the fight. Even if the argument that Israel was a pawn in a scenario of American hegemony had merit, this did not necessarily contradict the idea that the relationship between the two was not cost-effective for America. The supposed benefits of Israel's existence were massively obviated by its economic and political costs.[39] In the period before 1967 it was supposed, as we saw, to work as a junior partner to the US in blocking Soviet influence in the Middle East. But its success in this enterprise is open to question. Its aggressive regional behaviour drove the Arabs into the arms of the Soviet Union. Nasser's Egypt, for example, turned to the USSR after Israel's attack on Egyptian-controlled Gaza in 1955; Syria sought and received Soviet arms and advisors after Israel had attacked its forces in Lebanon in 1982. But even if Israel's role in the Cold War had been significant, the break-up of the Soviet Union in 1989 should have led to a diminution of Israel's importance to the US. In reality, the opposite was true.

And yet the Arab world was not inherently anti-American and, had wiser counsels prevailed, it would have been clear that the US strategic interest was far better served by closer ties with the Arabs than by a blind allegiance to the Jewish state. The consequence of this was to increase instability in the Middle East, where pro-American Arab regimes were more under threat from resentful and angry populations than ever before. Radical anti-American movements came into being under various guises, of which al-Qaeda was the latest, with mounting terrorist attacks on US lives and property in countries that backed America. This brand of terrorism was presented as 'international', but in reality its target was quite clearly the US and its allies. Hatred of America, because of its bias towards Israel, spread from the Arab East to the rest of the Islamic world. Radical pseudo-religious ideologies had immense appeal for the young, unemployed and impoverished populations of these lands – 60 per cent were under the age of 20 – and anti-Americanism found fertile soil amongst such youngsters.

On a trip to Pakistan in February 2003, I witnessed scenes of passionate popular support for the cause of Palestine, accompanied by intense anger against Israel and its American backer. There was nothing out of the ordinary in this; it drew on a long tradition of Pakistani fellow feeling for the Muslims of Palestine, as well as a resentment of Western interference in the affairs of their country since its establishment, and more especially, after the events of 11 September. The same may be said of other Muslim states. Even Turkey, the most officially secular and Westernised of them all, was witnessing a wave of anti-Americanism at the popular level: an opinion poll conducted in April 2004 found that over 80 per cent of those polled rejected US regional policies in Iraq and in Israel/Palestine.[40] Stating matters at their blandest, it could not have been helpful to long-term US interests to have such passions aroused.

Nor could a foreign state's penetration into the US system such as Israel's have been helpful at the domestic level. No matter how loyal an ally – and Israel had shown itself on many occasions to be the opposite (for example, its unauthorised sale of US military technology to China in 2005)[41] – its own interests would always predominate. This could only lead to a clash of interests, as shown by the cases of espionage in which Israel had been implicated. As we saw, criticism of Israel was still muted in the US because of fear of victimisation and damage to individual careers, but that could not be a healthy situation for any democracy and might be untenable in the long run, at least in theory. But such an outcome as far as Israel was concerned could not be taken as inevitable. Despite the discontents of a few Americans, muttered in closed circles or even boldly voiced in public, Israel's influence was still strong and, combined with neocon power over the US Administration, seemed unstoppable. Had the situation been one of rational, pragmatic common sense, where the facts could be examined and the logical conclusions drawn, then the American national interest would ultimately have prevailed over the forces working on Israel's behalf.

But that was not the situation. It was not just pro-Israeli manipulation and penetration into the organs of state that created the extraordinary bond between Israel and the US. Under the second Bush presidency, there was a confluence of shared strategic interests between the Israel lobby and the neocon decision makers. But there was something more to it. For Israel supremely benefited from the fact that there was a pre-existing empathy with the Zionist project as a rightful and necessary cause. This was based on a mixture of religion and culture in the Western Protestant states, especially in America. It was this immaterial, intangible dimension to Western support for Israel that made the problem so intractable and, from an Arab point of view, so daunting.

Christian Zionism

Much has been written about this phenomenon, not least because of its role in supporting the State of Israel. Whereas today's Christian

Zionism is usually associated with America, in fact it had its roots in the
Protestant Reformation of the sixteenth century. This created a new tide
of interest in the Old Testament and its fundamental connection with the
Jewish people, dramatically reversing the traditional Catholic emphasis
on the New Testament. England's Puritan movement was an early
manifestation of this phenomenon, which the Pilgrim Fathers brought
with them to America in the seventeenth century. The 'Restoration
Movement', which Protestant theologians began to preach at this time,
advocated the return of the Jews to Palestine. By the nineteenth century,
the followers of this creed (known also as millenarians because of their
belief in the coming kingdom of Jesus to last for a thousand years) had
become diversified into a number of new groups – christadelphians,
evangelicals, dispensationalists, Adventists and Plymouth Brethren.
Promoted in England during the nineteenth century by the charismatic
preacher, John Darby, Christian Zionism spread to America, where it
became hugely influential.[42] More groups emerged in the following
century: Jehovah's Witnesses, pentecontalists and fundamentalists. The
last category became loosely affiliated to a number of other American
denominations, Baptists, Lutherans, Presbyterians, Methodists and
conservatives, who subscribed to many of the same ideas.

In its basic form Christian Zionism referred to a specific set of beliefs
that derived from a literal reading of the Old Testament. Fundamental
to these was the return of the Jews to the land of Israel, which was
given them by God through his covenant with Abraham. Abraham's
legacy as bequeathed to the Jews denoted all the land between the Nile
and the Euphrates. The Jewish return to Palestine (Israel) was essential
as a prelude to Christ's Second Coming; in that sense, Jews were the
instruments by which divine prophecy would be fulfilled. However, they
were obliged to convert to Christianity and rebuild the Jewish Temple
in Jerusalem. Seven years of tribulation would follow, culminating
in a holocaust or Armageddon, during which the unconverted Jews
and other godless people would be destroyed. Only then would the
Messiah return to redeem mankind and establish the Kingdom of God
on earth where he would reign for a thousand years. The converted
Jews, restored as God's Chosen People, would enjoy a privileged status
in the world. At the end of all this, they and all the righteous would
ascend to heaven in the final 'Rapture'. The role of the Jews in this
equation was pivotal: put simply, it meant: Jews restored to Israel

and converted, leading to the Second Advent, leading to mankind's redemption.

This brief outline of Christian Zionism's core doctrine leaves out the many additional details and variations which have appeared with each offshoot of the original sect. And had it remained just that, a set of bizarre and colourful ideas with a cult following of weird people, it would have barely attracted attention. It was the way in which Christian Zionism was adopted by influential politicians, first in Britain and then in the US, and the political role it then played there that made it a force to be reckoned with in any analysis of the Israeli–Palestinian conflict. It was also the way in which Christian Zionist ideas and allusions came to permeate the consciousness of ordinary men and women in the Protestant world at a profound and unconscious level that added to their potency. Protestant religious teaching in schools and churches was saturated with the texts, stories and themes of the Old Testament in which the allusions were to Zion, to Israel, to places in the biblical Palestine and to the Jewish people. Sunday School, a system of religious education of children widespread in Britain from the nineteenth century onwards, indoctrinated them in these same teachings. The effect of this was to create a familiarity and acceptance of concepts essential to later political Zionism: the return of Jews to their ancestral home in Palestine, the words 'Israel', 'Israelite', 'Zion' and 'Zionism' and its notion of the 're-establishment' of the Jewish state in its ancient land.

As a young activist for the Palestine cause, I remember trying to lobby the famous left-wing British politician, Tony Benn, at the House of Commons, when he was an influential Labour minister in the 1970s. In what I realise now was a significant statement, he reacted to my plea to him for a better understanding of the Palestinian point of view by saying, 'Show me how your cause can overcome my childhood conditioning about Israel and the ancient Jews at Sunday School and I will help you. Until then, you haven't got a hope!' By the nineteenth century in England, which was a particularly religious and Bible-conscious period, second only to the Puritan age, such ideas had become normal currency. English art, poetry and literature are replete with Old Testament allusions, something that dates from 1611 when the authorised English translation of the Bible appeared. George Elliot's *Daniel Deronda* and Benjamin Disraeli's novels, especially

Alroy, are cases in point.[43] Even today, most Christmas carols refer to 'Zion', 'Royal David's city' and other Jewish associations with the Holy Land.

Lord Shaftesbury (1801–85), philanthropist and one of the most influential men of the Victorian age, did much to advance the cause of Christian Zionism in England from 1840 onwards. Out of a fervent and literal religious belief in the Bible, he was convinced that the restoration of the Jews to Palestine was an essential condition for the Second Coming and redemption, and worked with zeal towards setting up an 'Anglican Israel'.[44] He and other evangelicals worked enthusiastically for the conversion of the Jews, and a number of gospel societies were established for that purpose throughout the nineteenth century. Of course, this concern with the Jewish return to Palestine had little to do with the welfare of Jews as people; they were the chosen instruments of prophecy and that was all. Hence it was possible for antisemitism in English society to co-exist with Christian Zionism. Arthur Balfour, the author of the Declaration that created the problem of Palestine, was himself an ardent believer in the importance of Jewish restoration. Yet, as prime minister, he had pushed through parliament the Aliens Act of 1905, which barred the entry of Jewish immigrants from Eastern Europe. Jews in the flesh, so to speak, were undesirable. This same dichotomy also existed in the US.

In 1838, Shaftesbury managed to get a British consulate established in Jerusalem as the first step to 'restoring' the Jews to what he referred to as 'their ancient city'; the British consul then immediately placed the Jews of Palestine under British protection. The Jewish philanthropist and contemporary of Shaftesbury, Moses Montefiore, took up this theme and declared, 'Palestine must belong to the Jews and Jerusalem is destined to be the seat of the Jewish Empire.'[45] Britain's prime minister, Lord Palmerston, had meanwhile begun the official British intervention on behalf of the 'the Jewish nation' and its resettlement in Palestine. The details of these fascinating moves towards the creation of what became the State of Israel are beyond the brief of this book. Suffice it to say that, by the time of the Balfour Declaration of 1917, the cultural/ideological ground for Zionism had been well laid in Britain amongst leaders and populace alike. Arthur Balfour himself was immensely influenced by the Old Testament long before political Zionism appeared on the scene, and had an intellectual admiration for the Jews. He felt that Christian civilisation owed them a great debt and that they deserved to return to their ancient homeland. What his Declaration, calling for a 'Jewish homeland' in Palestine, set in train was taken up by a British administration deeply attached to the idea of Zionism. It was the combination of this factor with Britain's political interests that crucially made possible the organised Jewish settlement of Palestine from 1920 onwards and the eventual realisation of Jewish statehood in 1948.

For Britain's leaders saw Zionism also, or even primarily, as a useful tool for the promotion of British imperial interests. Indeed, they believed that a 'Jewish Palestine' would safeguard the Suez Canal and act as a pro-Western regional buffer state, and that Zionist Jews in Russia and Germany could play an important role in assisting the Allied effort in the First World War. Balfour's contemporaries, Mark Sykes and Lloyd George, who were key players in the steps towards the settlement of a Zionist colony in Palestine, certainly held this view, and the fact that Lloyd George was also a Welsh Methodist and devout believer in the Jewish restoration would only have helped. The notion of a felicitous marriage between these material strategic plans and the fulfilment of a Christian spiritual legacy must have been irresistible. As Rose puts it, 'here was a really exciting, romantic experiment for the British Empire to revive continuity in Western civilisation, which was after all rooted in the Judaeo-Christian tradition, and at the same time strengthen its presence in the Arab world'.[46] It is a sobering thought that, in Britain's support for this project, far more than strategic British interests was at stake. The very soul of Britain's elite was engaged in it, and Christian Zionists were subsequently to say of the Balfour Declaration that it was 'guided by the hand of God'.

Christian/Protestant Zionism, having spread to the US, came to constitute a source of support for Israel of awesome power and influence. The hold of these ideas was no less entrenched amongst American converts than they once were with their British counterparts. The tradition that started with the arrival of the Puritans from England in 1620 was enormously boosted by the later teachings of John Darby. But it was with William Blackstone, leader of the passionately Christian Zionist dispensationalist movement in America – when Blackstone travelled to Palestine in 1888, he marvelled at this anomaly of a 'land without a people' he believed he had seen – that Christian Zionism first entered American politics. In 1891, Blackstone and 413 prominent Americans petitioned President Harrison to help Russian Jews emigrate to Palestine and thus 'restore their land to them'. In 1916, he submitted another petition, signed by a large number of Protestant groups, to President Wilson promoting the case for restoring the Jews to Palestine.

These campaigns were highly effective in influencing attitudes, and allegedly led Woodrow Wilson to support the Balfour Declaration a year later.[47] In 1942, the conference of the American Board of Missions to the Jews affirmed the Jewish right to Palestine, even without the Jews' converting, as a 'partial fulfilment of prophesy', and agreed that the Jews had a God-given right to the whole country. However, not all these groups were uncritical of Israeli actions or, after 1948, politically active on behalf of Israel. Even so, the important point was that they were building, as in the case of Britain, on a broad Protestant consensus that had been implanted long before: a familiarity with and belief in the essential tenets of the Old Testament. To hold that Zionism was a fulfilment of prophesy and that Israel was the modern expression of the Jewish return so essential to it, was but a short step from there.

The modern Christian Zionist position in America may best be described as a doctrine with a number of components, all of which presented a terrifying prospect for the chances of peace either in Israel/Palestine or in the wider world. They may be summarised in this way: the Bible was to be interpreted literally; the Jews were God's chosen people and had a God-given right to the land between the Nile and the Euphrates; they must control this land and be its sole inhabitants before the Second Coming of Christ; Jerusalem was their exclusive capital where the Jewish Temple must be rebuilt; the Arabs living in the land of the Jews were the enemies of God's people and must either leave or be destroyed; and lastly, the world would soon end in the Battle of Armageddon, but those Christians who supported Israel's divine mission would be spared. All this had to happen before mankind's redemption and the final Rapture could take place.

It was estimated in 2004 that there were between 25 and 30 million Christian Zionists in America who believed in this doctrine either in whole or in part, although Pat Robertson, the ardent American fundamentalist supporter of Israel and president of the Christian Coalition, claimed a far higher number. They were led by some 80,000 fundamentalist pastors, with a thousand Christian radio and TV stations putting out their message.[48] Another estimate put the total number of Christian Zionists in America at between 40 and 70 million, of whom about 20 million were politically active; one third of congressmen were also Christian Zionists.[49] An opinion poll conducted in 2005 on behalf of the American Council for the National Interest Foundation found that 31 per cent of people believed partially or wholly in the ideas behind Christian Zionism: that Jews must have all of the Promised Land, including Jerusalem, to facilitate Christ's Second Coming. A Pew poll found that 53 per cent of Americans believed that God gave Israel to the Jews, and, according to a CNN/Time poll, 59 per cent believed that the prophesies in the Book of Revelations would all come true.[50]

The exact number of Christian Zionists, however, depends on how they were defined. Not all fundamentalists and evangelical Christians were Christian Zionist, although they were often included in this category, and for our purposes here, not all of them were influential over US policy in the Middle East. In addition, a proportion of them, as will be seen below, focused their activities on promoting Zionism in Israel and the occupied territories. In 2003, 16,000 churches in America participated in a one-day 'Stand for Israel' prayer service co-ordinated by Ralph Reed, the Southern regional chairman of President Bush's re-election campaign.[51]

It was the Reagan presidency that first gave an important boost to the Christian Right in the US and, with it, to the Christian Zionist cause. Reagan's Administration was, until then, the most pro-Israel ever and gave Christian Zionists important government posts. Leading proponents of the cause like Jerry Falwell, a Baptist minister and head of the Baptist Liberty University, Mike Evans, member of the Christian Israel Public Action Campaign, and Hal Lindsey, the most influential of all Christian Zionist leaders and best-selling author of books on this subject, came into close contact with national and congressional leaders and, at the same time, the International Christian Embassy was founded in Jerusalem in order to co-ordinate American lobbying activities with the Israeli government. One of their aims was to move the US embassy from Tel Aviv to Jerusalem. Thereafter, a union of 200 US Christian and Jewish organisations became active in encouraging Jews to emigrate to Israel, especially from Soviet territory, funding their travel and exit visas and helping them with documentation to prove their Jewish origins. The Chicago-based International Fellowship of Christians and Jews was the largest private funding organisation in America raising funds for Israel. In 2003, its 250,000 supporters gave $20 million to various Israeli philanthropic causes.

Christian Zionists were also active in promoting the Israeli expansion into the post-1967 Palestinian territories with economic and political support for Jewish settlements. They passionately advocated the judaisation of Jerusalem as the exclusive, 'undivided' capital of the Jewish people, and supported the destruction of the Aqsa Mosque and the Dome of the Rock and the re-building of the Jewish Temple in their place.[52] Aware of these activities, Israel's tourism ministry began targeting evangelical Christians to make up for the shortfall in the tourist trade, which had been economically damaging for Israel since the intifada began in 2000. The Israeli ministry bought time on Christian radio stations in America and sent representatives to US evangelical churches to spread the message that holiday tours of Israel were a way of supporting it in its time of tribulation. This campaign of 'ideological tourism' proved resoundingly successful.[53]

From the late 1970s onwards, right-wing Christian fundamentalists started to forge a close alliance with Israel's Likud party. Menachem Begin, Israel's first Likud prime minister recognised, in 1977 the potential power of the American Christian Zionists and began to develop an alliance with them. When criticised by liberal American Jews for courting these groups, he was reported to have said, 'I tell you, if the Christian fundamentalists support us in Congress today, I will support them when the Messiah comes tomorrow.' This cynical sentiment was echoed shortly afterwards by Lenny Davis, the sometime chief of research at AIPAC, who put it like this, 'Until I see Jesus coming over the hill, I am in favour of all the friends Israel can get.'[54] Israel's later Likud prime minister, Ariel Sharon, made sure he attended many fundamentalist conventions and told them they were Israel's 'best friends in all the world'. At a rally in Jerusalem in October 2003, he told a gathering of 3,000 visiting evangelical Christians: 'We love you!'

The ascendancy of the Republican Party in the US advanced this alliance considerably. Their dominance in the 1994 House of Representatives brought to power a number of right-wing Christian conservatives and helped turn Congress into the strong supporter of Israel it became thereafter. Uncritical of Israel, Christian Zionists saw the hand of God in everything it did. The Republican presidency in the White House after 2000 provided an environment of maximal friendliness to these supporters of Israel, not least because President Bush himself was a 'born-again' Christian who believed that promoting Israel was a fulfilment of God's will. He came to power mostly because of a devout white Protestant and Christian evangelical coalition, which made up three-quarters of his voters in the 2000 election. Jerry Falwell said that God had smiled upon America because of its support for Israel. After the events of 9/11, he and others like him saw Israel as one with America, 'joined at the heart', in the fight against terrorism.

These extravagant notions, when translated into direct political action, made American support for Israel, which was already strong, almost unassailable. As Stephen Sizer put it, the Christian Zionist belief in the Jews as God's chosen people for the fulfilment of prophesy led to a blanket endorsement of Israel's policies: the occupation and possession of Palestine; the status of Jerusalem as the exclusive Jewish capital in which the re-building of the Temple was a vital component; and, most seriously of all from an Arab point of view, the active hostility toward Palestinians and Muslims who would seek to obstruct the divine plan for the total Jewish restoration and the Second Coming incumbent upon it. Thus, many Christian Zionists denied the existence of a Palestinian people and justified their ethnic cleansing since 1948 on a number of spurious grounds, already well known from Zionist apologists. Arabs were described as barbarous and to be denounced as Jew-haters on a par with Hitler. After 2001, Muslims were increasingly demonised as terrorists, and their religion as sanctioning terrorism. Pat Robertson described Islam as a violent religion bent on world domination, and Muhammad as the first terrorist. In line with this logic, Christian Zionists publicly opposed any peace plan that endorsed Palestinian statehood or allowed a return of 'Jewish' land to the Palestinians. Supporters of such plans were seen as fighting against God, to be severely punished for their rejection of Scripture.[55]

It is worth noting here that the majority of American Jews were uncomfortable with the alliance of Israel and the Christian Zionists, who were also conservatives on domestic issues. Only 19 per cent of the Jewish vote went to Bush in 2000, while 79 per cent went to his Democratic opponent. Most American Jews described themselves as liberal in outlook and traditionally supported the Democratic Party.

When the right-wing Knesset member, Benny Elon, gave a speech in Washington, in 2002, advocating a Palestinian transfer out of Israeli-occupied territory, they could not endorse such a policy. Many were more embarrassed than encouraged by Christian Zionist zeal and were proud of the American tradition of religious freedom, which these extremists threatened to change.[56]

Europe and Israel

Protestant Europe was affected by the same sentiments, even if they later became more muted and less overtly intrusive in official policy. The British prime minister, Tony Blair, for example, was a devout Protestant with evangelical views who could not have been unaffected by Christian Zionist sentiments; the same was true of others at the top of Britain's government. Even when such people were not practising Christians, they were still influenced by the same broad Protestant concepts that gave them an empathy with Zionism, even if they did not agree with all that it has entailed. The same was true of the population at large. When this factor was added to the widespread ignorance about the origins of the conflict in Israel/Palestine and the counter-narrative put out so actively and ably by the Zionists, the picture that emerges was broadly supportive of the Israeli case. A 2003 survey of knowledge and attitudes amongst a sample of the British public about the Israeli–Palestinian conflict showed broad misconceptions and considerable ignorance about the basic facts; for example, many people thought that Palestinians occupied Israel, rather than the reverse. This was in large measure a consequence of BBC reporting of events in Israel/Palestine, which the study showed to be subtly biased in favour of Israel.[57]

The most relevant factor in regard to European attitudes towards Israel, however, was the Holocaust and the feelings of guilt it engendered. There is no question that, in this context, this was of monumental importance in shaping the Western European states' approach to the Jews and subsequently of Israel. The fact that a stream of films, plays, books and TV documentaries about Nazism and the Jews continued to appear with undiminished, if not increasing, momentum long after the end of the Second World War, played no small part in the perpetuation of a sense of obligation towards the Jews. Germany's massive and continuing reparations to Israel and to individual Jews has already been referred to; the spectre of antisemitism haunted Germans, who could not voice even the slightest criticism of Israel. Essential to this taboo was the rejection of demonstrations of any sympathy towards the Palestinians. When in 2003 an article of mine on antisemitism and the Arab world was published in the foremost German newspaper, *Die Suddeutsche Zeitung*, my reference to the Israeli occupation of Palestinian land was edited out.

A type of philosemitism, often as extreme as the antisemitism that preceded it, took over in a number of European countries. Israelis were treated with special care, and there was a widespread sensitivity to any expression of views that could remotely be interpreted as antisemitic. In London, a part of the Imperial War Museum was designated as a Holocaust memorial in 2001 with an official Holocaust Remembrance Day in January, inaugurated by Britain's top dignitaries. Steven Spielberg's film about the Holocaust, *Schindler's List*, became obligatory showing in many British schools, where teaching about the Holocaust was also obligatory.

A corresponding aversion to the presentation of the Palestinian case was the obverse of this coin. Showing films, publishing books and articles, or indeed any other activity sympathetic to the Palestinians was notoriously difficult in many European countries. A major film about the Palestinian story had yet to be made, not because there was no one to make it, but because of the insuperable obstacles of funding and distribution.[58] There was no *Garden of the Fitzi-Continis* or *Life is Beautiful* or any of the scores of other sophisticated, imaginative and affecting films made about the Jews to convey the tragedy and pathos of Palestinians life.[59] How differently the Palestinian case would have fared, had it been afforded a fraction of the sympathetic media treatment enjoyed by Israel and the Jewish case. As a result of the second intifada this bleak situation improved somewhat and a greater Western tolerance of Palestinian self-expression developed in a number of different arenas. But all this was still ultimately subject to the limits imposed by the obligatory adherence to post-Holocaust European attitudes towards the Jews. Perhaps, in terms of their suffering at European hands, most Jews saw this belated support for them as the very least that Europe could do to make amends for the most horrific crime ever perpetrated against them (or anyone else), and who could blame them?

Yet, at the same time, Europeans were not wholly uncritical of Israel. A survey of the 15 EU member states, undertaken in October 2003, found that nearly 60 per cent of European citizens believed Israel to be the biggest threat to world peace of any country. In the case of Holland and Austria, the figures were 74 and 69 per cent respectively.[60] These findings were greeted with the usual accusations of antisemitism by Israeli ministers, and the US-based Simon Wiesenthal Center demanded that the EU be excluded from the Israeli–Palestinian peace process. A similar British poll, carried out in January 2005, showed a majority selecting Israel as a danger to the world. European disapproval of Israel's policies against the Palestinians was also being expressed in other ways. The press was outspoken about the brutality of Israeli occupation in a way that would have been unthinkable in the US. Israeli products made in the illegal Jewish settlements were not permitted to enjoy the same suspension of import tariffs as other Israeli exports to Europe. EU ministers made their displeasure known to Israel at its frequent violations of this agreement. Europe consistently favoured the creation of an independent Palestinian state on the post-1967 territories and, unlike America, would have liked to see Israel reduce its military assault on the Palestinians and engage in peace negotiations with them ahead of a cessation of violence. The EU shouldered the greatest part of the financial burden for the Palestinian Authority's running costs and funded most construction projects in the occupied territories (which Israel's war on the Palestinians later destroyed). European leaders never accepted the marginalisation of the late Yasser Arafat imposed by Israel and supported by the US, and continued to deal with him as the Palestinians' legitimate leader.

A divestment and boycott campaign of Israeli goods and institutions started in some parts of Europe (and also in the US) with the beginning of the second intifada and gained strength following the 2006 Lebanon war. In Britain, an active campaign to boycott Israeli academic institutions that failed to oppose the Israeli occupation, was established in 2005 and led to the Association of University Teachers in Britain passing an unprecedented motion that year to boycott two Israeli universities (*Education Guardian*, 9 October 2006). It was later overturned by a narrow margin and under intense pro-Israeli lobbying, but the point had been made. A group of Irish academics, likewise, called for an academic boycott of Israeli universities in a letter to the *Irish Times* on

17 September 2006. Israeli companies complained that several of their European counterparts were refusing to co-operate with them (Ehud Kenan, *Ynetnews*, 27 September 2006). In February 2006, a group of prominent British architects were considering a boycott of Israeli architects and construction companies involved in building Israel's barrier wall (*Independent*, 10 February 2006). Most significantly, the Church of England, not noted for taking a stance against Israel, took a striking decision, in January 2006, to divest from companies assisting the Israeli occupation. A month later, the World Council of Churches meeting in Brazil considered a similar divestment programme.[61] In the US and Canada, a number of such initiatives were also under way, although to a lesser extent.[62] While none was yet decisive in its impact, it heralded a marked change in support for Israel at least in some sectors of Western society.

A Persistent European Affinity with Israel

It would have been wrong, however, to read too much into this apparent European benevolence towards the Palestinians. The vast majority of Europeans supported the existence of the Jewish state and their governments had strong ties with it. Political, commercial and cultural relations were solid; indeed Europe was Israel's largest trading partner, and there was a vigorous exchange and sharing on the academic, technological and intelligence levels. Israeli research institutes benefited from preferential European funding and assistance. The 'Sixth Programme' was a key part of the EU's strategy to create a true European Research Area, an Internal Market for science and knowledge in which Israel would play a full role. The 'Framework Programmes' permitted Israeli universities, research institutes and companies to participate in hundreds of research projects with their European counterparts.[63] EU member states continued to sell arms to Israel, despite its barely concealed use of such weapons against the Palestinians. Britain, which was supposed to have an arms embargo on such sales, got around it in various ways, and Germany, which was subject to a post-Second World War ban on exporting arms to crisis regions like Israel/Palestine, also sold arms to Israel. Its export sales for 1998–2001 to the Jewish state amounted to $900 million, and, according to the *Observer* (7 November 2004), in 2000 it supplied

Israel for free three submarines capable of carrying nuclear warheads and was planning to build another two. In supporting Israel in this way the EU broke its own codes of practice on refusing assistance to states that violated human rights. As signatories to the Fourth Geneva Conventions that govern the behaviour of occupying powers, they failed in their obligation to enforce the Conventions on Israel. And had Europe not supported Israel so staunchly, was it possible that it could have gone along with the callous US/Israeli policy of starving the Palestinian people after their election of the Hamas government in 2006? (See Chapter 5.)

The question of an even closer connection with Europe arose in the wake of Turkey's application to join the EU. If an Islamic state could join, the Israeli daily *Maariv* (20 September 2004) asked, why not Israel, which had a greater cultural affinity with Europe? The proposal on offer from the EU was for Israel, with six other nations, including the Palestinian Authority, to become part of its new 'European Neighbourhood Policy'. This would mean an exchange of free access to goods, services and people into the EU for reciprocal economic and political reform in the Neighbourhood countries. Israel stood to benefit through access to membership of institutions previously closed to non-EU members. Even so, it would not allow the EU to intrude into its weapons of mass destruction programmes or the peace process unless it had greater access to European scientific and technological programmes than that permitted to the other prospective members.[64]

Europe's continuing accommodation of Israel, no matter what it did, was based, not just on religious conditioning and Holocaust guilt, but on other factors just as potent. The widespread identification between Western Europeans and Israelis as 'people like us' was one of these. Indeed many Israelis had European origins and spoke European languages, and Israel had been adept at providing a range of representatives to put its case in Western countries drawn from such ranks. They came across as familiar and reassuring types who could be found in any Western institution, and the easy inference was that they were genuinely the people they seemed. What a contrast with Arab officials, who, with their alien looks and poor command of Western languages, were distinctly not 'people like us'. Israel was seen as a liberal democracy on the Western model with the same aims and values. The liberal left in Europe (and in the US) particularly identified with this view of Israel. The reality of its motley, ill-assorted and very un-European population and its many alien incongruities seemed to have escaped these dreamers. Attractive also to the European left was the long-standing association between socialism and Zionism, based partly on history but mostly on misconception. The latter is not difficult to understand. The participation of Jews in the major socialist movements in Russia and Eastern Europe was well known. The early Zionists established a 'Zionist-Marxist' party, Poale Zion, and the 1905 Russian revolution, which influenced them deeply, led them to believe that Jewish nationalism could be formulated along socialist lines which could be implemented in Palestine. The notion of Jewish labour and the egalitarian principles that created the Jewish trade union, the Histadrut, and shaped the kibbutz movement all originated in this conception.

Western socialists, who adopted Zionism as consonant with their socialism, ignored or did not understand that, for Zionists, Jewish nationalism was always more important than socialism. This meant that Jewish nationalist imperatives always superseded those of the Arabs of Palestine who were displaced, dispossessed and discriminated against, *as an essential prerequisite to the realisation of Zionism*. And while this misconception thrived, Israel was able to trade on its 'socialist' credentials as a natural ally to socialist individuals, political parties and institutions and in all other forums where it was useful. Though Israel's socialist cover was eventually blown, and indeed was no longer of much value to its wellbeing, the Israeli Labour Party was still described as 'left-wing' and a standing member of the Socialist International; even the self-serving opportunist politician, Shimon Peres, was still admired as a great socialist liberal on the left of Israeli politics.

What Did it all Mean for Arabs?

To summarise what has gone before, there was a Jewish and non-Jewish dimension to the support for Israel, both as effective and entrenched as each other.

1. Jewish insecurity and sense of persecution, an unresolved crisis of identity and the illusion of a Jewish nation originating in Palestine, were all profoundly important in perpetuating the need amongst Jewish

communities for a reference point and a 'refuge' in Israel. Added to
this was the existence of an Israeli Jewish population that had acquired
a feeling of belonging to the country and enjoyed all the privileges
of colonial power, even if this entailed some sacrifice for its defence.
The generation born there certainly regarded Israel as its exclusive
homeland, though a minority accorded Palestinians a share of the land.
In addition, religious fervour amongst some Jewish groups engendered
a fanatical obsession with 'Eretz Israel' and its exclusive possession
by Jews. Even when none of these factors operated to any significant
extent, Jewish people everywhere were, or became, psychologically
involved with the Jewish state, both as an idea and as a place of unique
importance that they cherished. Some of my most secular and politically
sophisticated Jewish friends saw themselves as part of a 'Jewish people'
with a distinctive character. Most confessed to feeling some kind of
tug at the mere mention of Israel, when they visited the country and
on seeing Jewish communities elsewhere.

2. Non-Jewish Western involvement in the establishment of the Jewish
state and in its maintenance had many facets: the Protestant backdrop
and its consequences from Balfour to the Christian-Zionist alliance;
the guilt over the European phenomenon of Jewish persecution and the
Holocaust and hence the need to make amends; the perception of Israel
as a strategic asset; pro-Israel control over the US decision-making
process and the US media; and the global phenomenon of Third World
Countries seeking to curry favour with Washington through making
alliances with and dispensing favours to Israel – in other words, to
paraphrase the famous women's magazines' advice to women, 'The
way to America's heart is through Israel'. India's friendship and arms
deals with Israel was one such example, and the Kuwaiti and Qatari
wooing of the Jewish state with business deals and close, if unofficial,
contacts was another. In a unipolar world dominated by a hugely
powerful USA, poor or weak states came to understand they had no
other choice.

Where did Arabs, and specifically Palestinians, fit into all this? None
of the factors – Jewish or non-Jewish – listed above had anything to
do with them. It was as if Israel and those who set it up and continued
to sustain it were a cast of actors in a play written and produced by

someone else but staged in an Arab theatre: the theatre was merely the physical venue for someone else's production. Jews and the West were engaged in a dramatic dialectic all of their own. The age-old Jewish question Europe never solved, its periodic bouts of savagery against the Jewish communities that lived within it, its dichotomous Judaeo-Christian religious identity and, finally, the appalling Nazi Holocaust, belonged firmly to Europe. And the Jews' persecution, the calamities inflicted on them, their dilemma of identity, and their determination to find compensation or exact revenge for all they had undergone, also belonged to Europe. When all these variables came together in the Zionist ambition to create a Jewish state, how eagerly the West seized that chance to absolve itself of guilt and simultaneously offload an unloved people, no matter how deserving, onto another, helpless to resist and in a land mercifully far away. This attitude had been abundantly clear at the 1938 Evian Conference, convened to discuss the problem of Jewish refugees fleeing Nazi Germany. Most Western countries were reluctant to accept them, and the conference even failed to pass a resolution condemning German treatment of the Jews. If sending them to Palestine solved this problem and also fulfilled biblical prophesy for devout Christians, then so much the better. The way that Zionism connected the Old Testament stories of an ancient Israelite tribe that once lived in Palestine with a modern community of Jews in Europe – such that the latter's 'return' to 'their ancient homeland' seemed natural and just – was nothing short of genius. It satisfied at once the needs of persecuted Jews and those of a guilt-ridden and anti-semitic Europe – and all at the expense of a third party.

Imposing the Zionist project on others in this way was a cruel and despicable act – the more so for Arabs since it was they who had been chosen for the sacrifice. To claim, as Zionists and their supporters did, that it was justified in a good cause, to rescue the Jews from persecution, did not alter its basic immorality and the cynicism of implementing this 'moral act' at the expense of a people that could not resist. Palestine was a backward place with a largely illiterate peasant population, quite incapable of resisting, let alone fully comprehending, the enormity of the danger from Zionism. The Arab world of the time was not much better-equipped, and had not progressed much further by 1948 when Israel was established. More than half a century later, the problem of Israel was, if anything, more complex and more difficult for the Arabs to deal with.

It was not just a question of brute force, though Israel's mighty army and fearsome nuclear arsenal were not to be discounted. It was more that the factors I have discussed above were beyond the knowledge and experience of the majority of Arabs. Palestinians who dealt with Israel at close quarters and those who lived in Western countries had more insight into its inner workings and contradictions. But even that was often not enough, and the rest of the Arab world was not adequately qualified to understand the situation. Most Arabs did not meet Israelis anywhere (or non-Israeli Jews for that matter). They did not read Hebrew and, as mentioned before, they had no sophisticated institutes or centres of study of Israeli affairs. Likewise, there were no such centres for the study of Israel's principal backer, America.

How could they have been expected to understand all the issues, complexities and nuances that made up Zionism and motivated its supporters? They were not Europeans, either by history or culture; they had no psychological or historical sense of the intricacies of the Jewish–gentile relationship in Europe, and no comparable tradition of cruelty against Jews to help them understand its effects on such people. In just a few decades, they found themselves hosting a tormented, suspicious, complicated and neurotically self-absorbed community, toughened by centuries of the need to survive. Not only were Arabs required to accommodate this community, which was alien to them in every way, but to love it as well. It would be hard to find any nation that would have accepted such a monstrous imposition, but the Arabs for reasons that have already been cited, were more unfitted to the task than most. Their very ignorance and naivety in the face of the challenge of Zionism was probably the most important factor that enabled the Israeli project to survive and even thrive in the region.

Israel's creation in the Arab world was a double-edged weapon, two faces of a coin. On the one side, Israel was a state with a complexity and a network of support like no other, one that would have been a huge problem for whoever had to host it; and on the other, it nested in an Arab world that had totally failed to deal with it. Could the Arabs, though handicapped by differences of culture, history and sophistica-tion, have performed any better? Of course we cannot know, but we can wonder if it was conceivable that the same project, inflicted on another people – say, the English or the Italians – would have succeeded as well.

4
The 'Peace Process'

In the previous two chapters I have tried to review the various factors that ensured the establishment of Israel and continued to nurture and support it, no matter what outrage or inhumanity it committed. It should be clear from the line-up of complex issues I have described – the Jewish imperative for Israel to survive, its many-faceted, powerful web of Western support, the inability of the Arabs to deal with it and their paralysing dependence on Israel's staunchest ally, the US – solving the problem that this totality of circumstances created would be a monumental task. And yet finding a solution for a conflict that had blighted the lives and future, not just of Palestinians, but of the Arab world (and of Israel too) was more urgent than ever. The Palestinians, whose situation worsened by the day, could not afford more time while yet more futile attempts were made to find a solution. Their depredations under occupation,[1] the unacceptable prolongation of refugee life for millions of them, the widening gulf between the various Palestinian communities, and the ongoing destruction of the Palestinian national cause were imperatives that demanded urgent action.

On a visit to Ramallah in the spring of 2004, I was subjected to what was a relatively minor inconvenience as a European passport-holder. There was no shooting, bombing, arrest, imprisonment or torture in my story. Before entering Ramallah I had to pass on foot through two checkpoints, while heavily armed soldiers examined my papers. The dinner I was invited to had to end before nine because the checkpoint out of Ramallah closed at that time. My hosts dropped me off some distance from it and hurried back for fear of being caught by the soldiers. By the time I crossed the two checkpoints, I found myself alone in the dark in an eerie no-man's-land with no taxi in sight to take me back and a menacing army presence all around. I began, unreasonably, to feel myself a fugitive from justice. Eventually and at some expense, I made it back to Jerusalem in a passing taxi, which I shared with an equally anxious, stranded passenger. But my friends could not return the visit because, like all West Bank and Gaza Palestinians, they were barred from entering Jerusalem. Occasional exceptions were made for those whose application for a permit, submitted well in advance, was successful. But even then, the reason for the visit had to be compellingly important, as say, for medical treatment, and might be withdrawn at the last minute. No reason needed to be given and there was no provision for appeal. For me, it had been a passing and relatively minor inconvenience, but for them this was a living, daily reality. Consequently, they went nowhere most of the time, since all exits from Ramallah were similarly restricted. So, they spent their days stiflingly confined in their small town.

Two years later, the situation was infinitely worse. The inconvenience of that experience seemed laughable by comparison with the iron restrictions at that same Ramallah checkpoint, transformed in 2006 into a quasi-international border that shut the Palestinians in even more firmly behind it. It struck me then how precious is one's freedom of movement, how unthinkable it would be to lose it, how we all take this everyday matter for granted, and how outrageous it was that it should be taken away from millions of Palestinians, as if it were a trifle. And yet, Israel imposed this monstrous regime (and worse) on a whole people with total impunity. At the same time, its power and dominance in the region and in the affairs of the world's only superpower grew, as did the threat it posed to regional stability and beyond. The exceptional indulgence lavished on the Jewish state by the West had nurtured in Israelis, not surprisingly, powerful feelings of invincibility, self-importance and inflated ideas about Israel's place in the world. They had come to believe that the norms of international behaviour did not apply to Israel, which must be immune from censure and sanction, no matter what it did.

A state armed with such beliefs and a powerful arsenal of conventional and nuclear weapons to boot, was a very dangerous thing and a neighbour much to be feared. Furthermore, Israelis, especially after the victory of 1967, had been reared in the conviction that the whole of historical Palestine belonged to them, the Palestinians had no right to it but were there on sufferance, and that Israel's needs, whether for land, resources or security, were paramount. Israeli popular support for some sort of Palestinian entity in the West Bank and Gaza was nothing more than a recent and pragmatic response forced on them by their fear of Palestinian 'terrorism'. It was not a belated recognition of Palestinian rights.[2] As such, every offering, however small, that Israel contemplated giving to the Palestinians was seen as a concession and a 'painful sacrifice' for peace. To use the popular jargon, there were two national narratives at work here, Israeli and Palestinian, in direct contradiction with each other. The power imbalance between the two parties ensured that the Israeli one supervened.

The Size of the Problem

How was the problem to be solved? In answer, one is tempted to echo the man in the old Irish joke, when a visitor looking for Dublin asks him for directions, and he responds, 'Well, I wouldn't have started from here.' But from here, one had to start. The situation in 2006 gave little rise for optimism. The principal protagonists were hopelessly unequal, with the balance of forces heavily weighted in Israel's favour. The Palestinians on the other hand were not only weak and vulnerable in themselves, but their only backing derived, as we saw, from an Arab world ruled by governments themselves prey to Western influence and incapable of confronting Israel. Indeed the very anomalousness of this position led Arab governments on occasion to attack or restrain the Palestinians, Israel's victims, when these were deemed to have caused internal disruption within Arab states.[3] It is a familiar human reaction, rather like kicking the cat, when one feels provoked and impotent at the same time. And it was difficult to avoid the conclusion that, given the line-up of forces and power and the Western imperative to defend its oil and strategic interests, in which Israel was looked for as a major player, the outcome was foreordained. Nothing could be done unless the whole imperialist structure was dismantled and the Arab clients despatched. Only then could the problem of Israel be resolved. This theory had its attractions and indeed, one of the PLO groups, George Habash's Popular Front for the Liberation of Palestine (PFLP), espoused this philosophy in the early 1970s. The PLFP held that struggling against Israel was futile while the Arab regimes remained in place.

From today's cynical perspective, such analyses owe more to history than modern reality. They were much in vogue, especially during the 1960s, amongst the Left in the Arab world (and elsewhere). Cogent as their logic was (and still is), they changed nothing, but on the contrary, they might even have induced a sense of apathy that absolved the Arab intellectual from responsibility for dealing with the real situation. This steadily deteriorated with time. The conflict with Israel was more intractable than at any time previously; numerous peace plans were put forward and came to nothing; Israel consolidated its hold daily on the remaining Palestinian territories outside the 'Green Line'.[4] The appropriation of land and resources was relentless; a separation wall was being built which aimed to make this seizure permanent, squeezing the Palestinians into ever-smaller areas or into emigrating; the ensuing Palestinian resistance, often violent, had met with brutal Israeli reprisals and widespread abuses of human rights. Such conduct exacerbated the tensions already existing in the region over Israel. After the start of the intifada in 2000, in particular, they spread farther afield, into the wider Islamic world. Popular feeling in this wider arena, already inflamed over Palestine, viewed the US–British invasion of Iraq in 2003 as part of the same high-handed, arrogant and exploitative Western policy towards fellow Muslims, whether in Palestine or Iraq. The large Muslim populations of Europe (especially in France and Germany) were similarly affected, and fear of alienating these communities could have contributed to European politicians' inclination to distance themselves from US policy at times.[5] The invasion of Afghanistan had already inflamed these passions, and if Iran and Syria became the next targets, it would confirm the thesis of an anti-Islamic Western crusade.[6]

Unabashed American support for Israel in such a volatile climate was almost incomprehensible in its folly and insouciance. The installation in 2005 of a new, 'democratically elected' government in an Iraq under US occupation, widely derided by Arabs as a charade, only built on the resentment. The rise of global anti-American terrorism could not be divorced from these factors; though not caused by the conflict over Palestine, it drew on the iconic status of this cause amongst the world's disadvantaged to rally its followers. When in 2003 rumours of a possible move to establish diplomatic relations between Pakistan and the Jewish state started to circulate, Pakistanis openly threatened to 'kill any Jew who dared show his face in Pakistan'.[7] Massive anti-Israel demonstrations took place across Indonesia in April 2005. Speakers attacked Israel's treatment of the Palestinians and demanded that the US stop funding and supporting the Jewish state.[8]

The US may have wished to believe and persuade others that 'terrorism' was a global phenomenon, like an epidemic disease whose causes were divorced from its own conduct or that of some of its allies. Yet, the signs were that the phenomenon was only too closely tied to its behaviour towards other nations, as even some of its own policy makers recognised.[9] As was discussed in Chapter 1, Osama bin Laden's chief grievance was what he and his followers saw as the American control of his country, Saudi Arabia, but he had been a supporter of the Palestinian cause from the 1980s onwards. He denounced the US–Israel alliance in scattered remarks from 1996 onwards, and spoke of 'America and Israel killing the weaker men, women and children in the Muslim world'.[10] In 1998, he declared that the 'crusader–Zionist alliance' attacking Iraq aimed at serving 'the Jews' petty state and [to] divert attention from its occupation of Jerusalem and murder of Muslims there'.[11] The linkage with Palestine increased further, however, after September 11, as his statement on 7 October 2001 to Al-Jazeera television indicated: 'Neither America nor the people who live in it will dream of security before we live it in Palestine.'

This is not the place to rehearse the deleterious effects of US intervention in Central and Latin America or in Vietnam and Cambodia under the Pol Pot regime or in many other parts of the world. The crisis in the Middle East, fuelled by the persistence of the unresolved conflict in Israel/Palestine and the associated regional instability and rise in extremism, was cause enough to merit urgent international attention. Finding a resolution to this conflict would have set in motion a series of changes that, on the foregoing logic, could only be positive – not just for Palestinians and Israelis, but for the whole region and beyond. In dim recognition of this fact, George Bush, re-elected in 2004, made clear his determination to solve the Israeli–Palestinian conflict, belatedly following the European lead established long before in the Venice Declaration of 1980.[12] This had declared that a just solution must finally be found to the Palestinian problem, which was not simply one of refugees. The Palestinian people were entitled to exercise fully their right to self-determination.

The Arab–Israeli Peace Process

There is no term in the political lexicon more bandied about and with less meaning than, 'the Arab–Israeli peace process'. Like the poor, it was always with us, without any end in sight. It used to refer mainly to a settlement between Israel and the Arab states, but after the Oslo Accords of 1993, it increasingly came to denote specifically the process between Israel and the Palestinians, with the rest of the issues left on hold. Yet, despite the passage of over half a century since the armistice of 1949 that ended the first Arab–Israeli war, no settlement, which ended all states of hostility and ensured a durable peace in the region, was achieved. Numerous peace proposals came and went, but none succeeded in ending for good the multi-layered enmity that existed between Israel and the Arabs. By 2006, there were only two formal and operational peace treaties, those between Israel and Egypt and Israel and Jordan. Diplomatic ties of various sorts were set up with several other Arab states and possibly more would ensue. But a state of war still existed with Syria and Lebanon, and the Palestinians were locked into an interminable 'peace process' with Israel, despite the formal peace agreement of 1993 that was supposed to provide a solution. After the Arab League Summit of 2005, reiterating the Saudi peace plan of three years before, the situation looked as if the Arab states were displaying an increasing willingness to normalise relations with their old enemy (so far without result).[13]

Why had no solution worked? Why did all the international and regional efforts, which often appeared so promising, fail to resolve the conflict? A review of the main peace proposals that have been put forward so far with varying degrees of success should help to answer these questions. Up until 1993, when the Oslo Accords were signed between Israel and the PLO, peace negotiations were not principally about the Palestinian issue, although it usually featured somewhere. Of course, there was always an awareness, especially on the Arab side, that this issue would have to be addressed, but it was not reflected in a primacy of commitment to it in any peace proposal, with the possible exception of the Fahd peace plan of 1981 which referred to the need for a Palestinian state. Somehow the Palestinians had become like poor relations you know you have to help, and, feeling embarrassed, you give them a little something to make them go away. If it is not enough, they will just have to wait for another time when you might give them a little more, as if their poverty and deprivation were valid alternative options. The prevailing attitude towards the Palestinian refugees was a good illustration of this: everyone knew in theory that they needed a just solution, but in practice, they were ignored, patronised or looked down on as lesser mortals. This principle constantly animated the approach to the process of Arab–Israeli peacemaking.

Resolution 242

The first example was the famous, but unimplemented, UN Security Council Resolution 242, passed after the 1967 war. The first serious international attempt at peacemaking between Israel and the Arabs, this resolution set the basis for all subsequent peacemaking efforts and reflected no mean achievement for the Jewish state. While whittling down the Palestinian issue to one of refugees in an obliquely worded phrase, 'a just settlement of the refugee problem', it offered Israel an end to the state of belligerency with the Arabs, a recognition of its sovereignty and territorial integrity and, by implication, opened the way to its eventual acceptance into the region.[14] In less than 20 years from its establishment, and in the face of tremendous Arab resistance and hostility, Israel was being awarded an almost instant conversion from regional pariah to regional legitimacy and acceptance, with the Palestinians safely out of the way as a humanitarian problem awaiting a just solution, whatever that might mean. Unsurprisingly, the PLO rejected the resolution on these grounds and the fact that it made no mention of Palestinian sovereignty over Gaza and the West Bank after their vacation by Israel.

By diminishing and marginalising the Palestinian problem in this way, Resolution 242 set the scene for subsequent Arab–Israeli peacemaking efforts. Israel's obdurate manoeuvrings in the aftermath of this resolution would also be the pattern for the future. Not satisfied with what was already offered, and oblivious of the Arabs' overwhelming sense of humiliation and defeat, it insisted on direct negotiations with the Arab states, one by one, without preconditions, such negotiations to lead to full peace agreements. The calculation was always the same and served Israel's strategy well: that the Arabs would not agree to such bilateral deals because they implied recognition of the Jewish state for no guaranteed reciprocal benefit, nor would they accept the exclusion from the talks of third parties to help secure any agreement reached. In the ensuing hiatus, Israel could continue to hold on to and settle Arab land, with resolution of the Palestinian issue deferred. The international community did little to counter these Israeli ploys effectively – rather it had been persuaded to collude with Israel's position – and their consequences have been with us ever since. No international mechanism was ever established to compel Israel to withdraw from Arab land and none to enjoin it to countenance Palestinian political and human rights.

Between 1967 and the Camp David Accords of 1979

Earnest attempts were made to circumvent these handicaps but they never came to anything. Much diplomatic activity followed the passing of Resolution 242. The UN appointed a special negotiator, Gunnar Jarring, to help implement peace moves. Despite offers of a demilitarised Sinai and guarantees of freedom for Israeli shipping through the Suez Canal and a full peace with Egypt, he was unable to resolve the disagreement over the extent of Israel's withdrawal from Sinai. Israel insisted that any efforts should be made to bring about direct peace negotiations with each of the Arab states separately; and that no territorial concessions could be contemplated without the prospect of a lasting peace. The Arab states and the Soviet Union maintained that there would be no direct talks with Israel and that withdrawals were a pre-condition for any further talks. Jarring could not resolve this impasse, and his mission ended in failure.

The US put forward the Rogers Plan in 1969, trying to satisfy Israel's wishes for bilateral talks with Egypt by asking for a withdrawal from Egyptian territory in return for a full peace, but Israel refused this too. By 1970, the US had come round to Israel's view, that only limited peace agreements with individual Arab states were possible. Golda Meir, Israel's prime minister at the time, declared that, even if she were willing to return land in Sharm al-Sheikh, Gaza or the Syrian Golan Heights, Israel would hold on to Jerusalem and the West Bank,[15] and indeed by 1972, Israel had built 44 settlements in the West Bank. Meanwhile, in this flurry of activity, the Palestinian issue had been put on the back burner. The PLO retaliated to this marginalisation of the Palestinian cause by initiating its campaign of armed resistance against Israeli targets, first from Jordan and then, when its forces were driven out of Jordan, the campaign would be launched from southern Lebanon. The damaging effect of this move on the stability of Lebanon, its economy and its people over the following decades is well known.

Had the international will prevailed in 1967 – to face up to Israel and ensure its compliance over the issue of occupied Arab land and the crucial matter of Palestinian rights – perhaps the Middle East might have been spared much subsequent turmoil, bloodshed, destabilisation and war. As it was, any progress in resolving the conflict between Israel and the Arabs only came about through a mixture of cajoling, bribery and coercion, always flawed by the insufficient attention paid to the Palestinian dimension. Every peace agreement was constructed at the expense of the Palestinians, although various parties tried to do something for them. Egypt's President Anwar Sadat in his (failed) 1972 offer of a peace agreement with Israel included a condition relating to a resolution of the Palestinian refugee problem, but it was turned down by Israel. Likewise, in an unusual and incisive 1975 document, William Saunders, US deputy-assistant secretary of state to Henry Kissinger, stressed the centrality of the Palestinian issue to the conflict and stated that the 'legitimate interests' of the Palestinians must feature in any Arab–Israeli peace negotiations. Israel rejected this too and the proposal was abandoned.[16]

In the same spirit, US President Jimmy Carter displayed an initial willingness to resolve the Palestinian issue. In 1977 he proposed an international peace conference in conjunction with the USSR on the basis of Resolution 242, which was to include a resolution of the Palestinian problem and recognition of 'the legitimate rights of the Palestinian people'. Israel would withdraw from the 1967 territories (though not all) and all states of belligerency would end, leading to a full peace and recognition between Israel and the Arabs states. Carter had even gone so far as to speak in the same year of the need for a 'Palestinian homeland'. Although this referred only to the refugees and was intended as a humanitarian, not a political gesture, Carter came under strong pressure from the state department, Israel and the US Zionist lobby and was forced later to withdraw the remark as well his recognition of the PLO, with which he had been dealing. For the same reasons, he also had to abandon the international peace conference idea, since he was not prepared, as had become usual by now in US dealings with Israel, to exert any pressure on it to accept. The story of Carter's climb-down in the face of Israeli pressure is depressing: to have displayed such high ideals over this conflict and abandon them so cravenly in the face of that pressure.[17]

The Camp David Accords

In the end, Egypt and Israel proceeded to conclude a separate peace deal in 1979. Even so, the Palestinian dimension played a part in the peace talks. An autonomy plan for the occupied territories was discussed during exhausting negotiations which dragged on until 1980. The plan stipulated that, after a period of five years, in which the Palestinians in the West Bank and Gaza (East Jerusalem was off limits) prepared for 'full autonomy', a self-governing authority would be set up by free elections. When this happened and the powers of the Authority were defined, Israel would 're-deploy' (relocate and not withdraw) its forces in the Palestinian territories. After three years from this point, final status talks would begin on such maters as security, borders and other issues. Meanwhile, the Authority would be allowed a lightly armed police force, which would co-ordinate its activities with Israel, Egypt and Jordan, and its tasks would include, *inter alia,* securing Israel from Palestinian attack. There was no mention of Israeli withdrawal from the West Bank or Gaza; Jerusalem's status was left uncertain; and no reference was made to Israel's illegal settlements, nor to Palestinian national rights.

This plan, with all its limitations, was the most that Israel's prime minister, Menachem Begin, would contemplate, and neither President Carter nor Anwar Sadat could prevail on him to improve his offer. The effort was finally abandoned, leaving it at a stipulation in the first part of the Camp David agreement, to establish a framework for negotiations to set up an autonomous self-governing authority in the West Bank and the Gaza Strip. It was less clear than the agreements concerning Sinai, and was later interpreted differently by Israel, Egypt and the US. Even Carter's request to the Israelis for a freeze on settlement-building on Palestinian land while the negotiations over Palestinian autonomy were taking place was turned down. Begin accepted only a three-month moratorium, following which settlement-building was vigorously resumed. In the five years between 1977 and 1982, the number of illegal settlements increased from 47 to 149, not including another six around Jerusalem. This sequence of events – American requests, or even entreaties, over the settlement programme, met by Israeli obduracy, leading to no shift of position – was to repeat itself many times thereafter. The one time an American president deviated from this pattern was in 1991 when George Bush senior held up a $10 billion loan guarantee to Israel to prevent the building of more settlements; the result was that Israel stepped up the building programme and Bush was not re-elected for a second presidential term.

The basic parameters of Israel's best position vis-à-vis the Palestinians were thus laid out at Camp David, as were the inability or unwillingness of other parties to make Israel change them. The main features of the Camp David proposal for the Palestinian territories would re-surface 14 years later, in the Oslo Accords of 1993 and its subsequent versions, with the same Israeli determination to cede little more, and the same impotence on the part of the 'international community' to compel it to do so. The Camp David agreement also meant that Israel had succeeded in deflecting all attempts at convening an international or regional peace conference, and set in train the practice of making separate peace deals with individual Arab states in line with its original wishes. But the most serious effect of the Camp David Accords from the Palestinian point of view was the way it granted Israel's hold on the Palestinian territories a spurious post hoc legitimacy. It was as if Egypt, in accepting a deal with Israel that concerned only Egyptian territory, had assented to all its actions in the other territories. This could not have happened had Egypt linked its signature on the treaty to an Israeli acceptance of its conditions over the Palestinian issue.

After Camp David

With the arrival in 1980 of Ronald Reagan, America's most pro-Israeli president up to that point, Israel grew stronger. Reagan's secretary of state, George Schultz, built a strategic alliance with the Jewish state so powerful that, as he said afterwards, the institutional arrangements binding the US to Israel that he created would make it impossible for a future incumbent less positive towards Israel than himself to undo them.[18] When in 1982 Saudi Arabia put forward an 'Arab' peace proposal in the shape of the Fahd plan, Israel ignored it. Yet, this was an important first step towards Arab acceptance of Israel, and one moreover which the Arabs themselves had put forward. The plan proposed that, in line with Resolution 242, Israel withdraw from the 1967 territories and the Palestinians be granted a state on the West Bank and Gaza with East Jerusalem as its capital, all states in the region 'to live in peace'. In other words, the Arabs were offering an implied recognition of Israel in its pre-1967 borders and acknowledging West Jerusalem as a Jewish city (in contradiction to the UN General Assembly Partition Resolution 181 of 1947 which assigned the city as neither Jewish nor Arab and administered by the UN).

As has previously been pointed out, it was not easy for Arab leaders to move to this position, which would mean ignoring their populations' deep resentment at what Israel had done to the region and to the Palestinians, a point usually lost on Western policy makers. Reagan followed the Fahd plan with his own proposal in 1982, which was much kinder to Israel. The latter would freeze all settlement-building and could not be granted sovereignty over the West Bank or Gaza. But in return, there was to be no Palestinian state or self-determination and no PLO participation, only an autonomy arrangement in confederation with Jordan. The Arabs responded by declaring the PLO the Palestinian people's 'sole legitimate representative'. Since the Arabs were in no position to enforce this or any other of their declarations, it made little impact. And the Palestinian issue remained marginal to the process of peacemaking.

Finally the Palestinians themselves declared their willingness to formally recognise Israel, although this had been implicit in their policymaking from 1974 onwards. Following King Hussein of Jordan's surrender of the West Bank to the PLO in 1987, the Palestine National Council (PNC) meeting held in Algiers a year later offered Israel mutual recognition and accepted what the PLO had previously always rejected, namely Resolutions 242 and 338. For the Palestinians, it was a major step and a world away from their previous ambition to liberate the whole of the land taken from them by the Zionists in 1948. I remember attending a 1979 PNC meeting, held in Damascus, when the talk was of the 'Zionist enemy' and the impossibility of reconciling the realisation of Palestinian rights with the existence of Zionism. The mood in Damascus was defiant and self-confident, perhaps too much so. From there to the PNC meeting in Algiers in less than ten years was a huge step and a reflection of the reality on the ground that the PLO could not ignore: a powerful Israel with powerful backers and a weak and disunited Arab front unable to fight Israel or support the Palestinians. The eruption of the first Palestinian intifada in 1987 had also forced on the PLO leader, Yasser Arafat, the realisation that the centre of the struggle had shifted from the diaspora to the Palestinians inside, and that would have to be the basis of the Palestinian state. Israel showed no interest in the PLO offer. It had been in occupation of the Palestinian territories for 20 years by then, had built settlements more like townships, was in possession of the water and other natural resources in the territories and had no intention of changing any of that – certainly not for a tinpot guerrilla movement that had caused it no more than minor inconvenience, whatever its protestations to the contrary.

The Madrid Peace Conference, 1991

Israel's strategy to strip the Palestinian cause of any meaning or significance, followed faithfully by the US against ineffective Arab opposition, seemed to be succeeding. Attempts to convene an international peace conference had come to nothing so far and Israel had been left unmolested to consolidate its hold on the Arab territories it occupied. But in the aftermath of the first Gulf war in 1991, the US, under the less partisan George Bush senior, was determined to resolve the Arab–Israeli conflict, as part of 'the new world order' he espoused. He was anxious to satisfy the Arabs states, which, having helped the Western coalition attack Iraq, expected no less. It was also a favourable moment for Israel to impose a solution on the PLO, weakened by the opprobrium it had earned from its Arab backers because of its stand with Iraq during the Gulf war. A major international peace conference was convened in Madrid, in October 1991. James Baker, the US secretary of state, strove determinedly to include the Palestinians in this effort, and Israel, under a surly and foot-dragging Yitzhak Shamir, was persuaded to attend with all manner of blandishments. To this end, the USSR offered to re-open diplomatic relations with Israel, suspended since 1967, and Shamir's team was permitted to deal with each Arab state separately on a face-to-face basis within the conference. The PLO, despite being the Palestinians' only legitimate national representative, was excluded from the proceedings in line with Israel's wishes. An absurd arrangement whereby West Bank and Gaza negotiators, who were overtly conferring behind the scenes with the PLO, took the place of the PLO officials who should rightly have attended. (It was this conference, incidentally, which launched the political career of the articulate and charismatic Hanan Ashrawi as one of the 'acceptable' Palestinian negotiators.) No Palestinian from East Jerusalem was allowed to attend either, because of Israeli sensitivities about Jerusalem's (illegal) status as 'Israel's eternal capital'. The fact that the Arabs had their own sensitivities and their own constituencies to address was deemed by the organisers to be of little importance.

The Madrid conference set up a series of multilateral talks, which sought to find solutions for major regional issues like water, arms control, trade and refugees, and these dragged on until 1993. As in the Camp David negotiations, the Palestinians were offered an interim agreement, which this time and because of their weakened position, they accepted on condition that it would lead to an independent state. But as before Israel refused, agreeing only to an autonomy arrangement while security and foreign affairs would come under its own control. Shamir, as he admitted later, was prepared to drag the negotiations on for another ten years while Israel continued to settle the occupied territories.[19] In the end, all these elaborate arrangements and diplomatic manoeuvrings came to nothing on the Palestinian and Syrian fronts (Israeli–Jordanian relations had experienced some positive progress), and the Madrid conference closed without a resolution of the conflict. Once again, Israeli imperatives had won the day and the Arabs would have to await another opportunity. Once again, the Palestinian issue was relegated to a secondary role, shabbily sidelined as of little account.

The Oslo Accords, 1993

In 1993, the Palestinians themselves took over the function of peacemaking. This marked an important turning-point in the history of this process. Although the PLO had been making proposals for co-existence with Israel since 1974 (all ignored), this time they were negotiating with it directly and not through the customary intermediaries. Even so, as will be seen, the process they were able to effect with Israel was marked by the same failure to address the basis of the conflict and they ended up as short-changed as previously. Reams have been written about the Oslo Accords, which attracted supporters and detractors in almost equal measure.[20] I have no wish to swell the extant literature, but it was certainly a landmark in the history of the conflict between Israel and the Palestinians with far-reaching consequences. The byzantine bartering, dishonesty, evasion, cheating and relentless degradation of the Palestinian position that Israel indulged in throughout the negotiation process and after bears close study as an arch demonstration of its demeaning and dismissive attitude towards the Palestinians. For Israelis, they were still 'non-people' and little had changed in that respect since the beginning of the Zionist project.

Overall, was this a good or a bad agreement? Whatever the true answer, it was probably inevitable, given the circumstances. By 1993, the PLO had become irrelevant and virtually bankrupt. Successive traumas – the expulsion from Lebanon in 1982, the banishment of its leadership and fighters to the periphery of the Arab world in Yemen and Tunis and the condemnation of its friendly stance towards Saddam Hussein in the Gulf war – meant that it had little reputation and little money left. The Palestinians of the occupied territories, who had risen against the Israeli occupation in the first intifada in 1987 independently of the PLO, were further unimpressed by its performance at the Madrid conference, the way it had meekly accepted its background role and the absurd offer of an interim agreement, which they could see gave Israel room to tighten its hold on their land. The fragmentation of the Palestinian front, which the intifada had sharpened, into those under occupation and those outside under an impotent and demoralised leadership, was proceeding apace. This was exactly in line with Israel's aspirations and many of its machinations over the years.

So when secret talks began between the PLO and Israel in 1992 in the run-up to the Oslo Accords, the standard interpretation had it that Arafat was looking for a role and wanted to make the PLO relevant again, while Yitzhak Rabin, Israel's Labour leader elected in 1972, was looking to offload Gaza, the rebellious, overcrowded and impoverished colony which was more trouble than it was worth. Arafat provoked the ire of many Palestinians who felt he had sold out to the Israelis for personal gain. One of his most unrelenting critics was the prominent Palestinian intellectual, Edward Said, who spoke for many when he wrote this soon after the agreement came into effect, 'Yasir Arafat and a few of his closest advisers had already decided on their own to accept anything that the US and Israel might throw their way, just in order to survive as part of the "peace process".' The major benefit of the deal was that 'it restored Yasir Arafat and a small band of cronies to relative power and authority'.[21] But behind that obvious logic, each leader had a bigger agenda.

Through the intifada, Rabin had comprehended that the Palestinians were not going to disappear or leave Israel undisturbed for good. The militant Islamist groups, Hamas and Islamic Jihad, had now become prominent as a force, and in late 1992 Rabin deported 416 of their members to South Lebanon. Something had to be done to deal with the uprising and forestall a repetition of resurgence. In addition, Rabin thought that the risk that the Palestinians would eventually threaten the Zionist nature of the Jewish state – by demographic increase, growing interchange between the two sides, perhaps even by the occupied Palestinians one day demanding equal civil and political rights with Israelis – was too great to ignore. He thus sought to preserve Zionism in a smaller geographical space if necessary as long as it left intact a 'pure' Jewish Israel. This he did by implementing the doctrine of separation (Hebrew, *hafradah*), that is, ensuring a clear, physical division between the two sides. Confined to their own space, the Palestinians were free to construct an entity of some sort which could take on all the appurtenances of a state and call itself what it liked. They could also, most conveniently for Israel, police their own people to ensure Israeli security. In granting this, the important task for Israel was to elicit Palestinian acceptance of these terms in the smallest and least desirable land area possible, leaving room for existing Jewish settlements and others yet to be constructed; and to negotiate a division of resources as weighted in Israel's favour as the Palestinians could be made to swallow. And that, of course, is what happened.

The Oslo Accords, signed in Washington in 1993 with the pomp and ceremony more fitting to a final and comprehensive resolution of the Arab–Israeli conflict than the limited deal it was, were concluded between a state, on the one hand, and an organisation, on the other. The proceedings were presided over by Bill Clinton, America's passionately pro-Israeli president, elected in 1992, whose Middle East advisors were anything but impartial. Prominent among these was Martin Indyk, an Australian Jewish Zionist and head of WINEP, whom Clinton appointed to the National Security Council as his Middle East analyst. (In order to make this happen, Clinton reportedly had had to rush through Indyk's application for US citizenship, without which he could not have served in that post.) The Oslo agreement meant that Arafat, supposedly representing the whole Palestinian nation, signed up before the world to recognise Israel's right to exist in peace and security (which he had already done, though in the far smaller PNC forum in1988), to renounce and control 'terrorism', and to delete the parts of the PLO Charter deemed hostile to Israel. Essentially, the PLO recognised Israel as a state, but received no reciprocal Israeli recognition of the Palestinian right to statehood.

And thereby, Israel had been awarded the greatest prize it could ever have hoped for, something that had eluded it since its establishment. At one stroke, in signing the agreement, Arafat had legitimised Zionism, the very ideology that had created and still perpetuates the Palestinian tragedy. Of course, Israel had managed quite well without the need for such Palestinian acceptance. Nevertheless, to have the blessing of the victim, especially without having earned it, is like the icing on the cake, an unlooked-for boon to the perpetrator. For those Israelis, Jews, and others who felt some guilt towards the Palestinians, however inchoate and unacknowledged, it was a great liberation. The victims themselves had let them off the hook and ended up, not just having lost their land, their history and their society, but even their grievances and the dignity of anger at their fate had been wrested from them. After Oslo, the Palestinians could truly be discounted.

I well recall the euphoria with which the Accords was greeted in the West, and most especially amongst Zionists. A new warmth emanating from such people was palpable towards those of us who had known nothing but distrust and dislike or worse from them. All kinds of approaches were made to Palestinians, both in the occupied territories and outside aiming to engage them in what was termed 'dialogue' with Israelis, to set up joint projects supposedly beneficial to them, and to advise and direct them. Youth contact groups abounded, parties of Palestinian and Israeli schoolchildren were invited abroad to summer camps and other joint activities, with the idea of influencing their young minds towards the 'culture of peace'. I have no doubt that there were well-meaning people somewhere in all this who genuinely imagined the end of the conflict had arrived. It must also be said that a large number of Palestinians viewed what had happened with equal hope and excitement. In the wake of the agreement's signing, they welcomed the same Israeli soldiers, who had oppressed and humiliated them on a daily basis, with flowers and joyful greetings in the belief that a new era had started.

Conversely, for a minority of 'liberal' Zionists who had been working with Palestinians before Oslo to acknowledge their equal right to statehood in the post-1967 territories, the Accords were the answer to a prayer. I remember awkward moments when I used to ask such Zionists in London if they would accept sharing the country, not just on a post-1967, but on a 50-50 basis. 'Why give us just 20 per cent of the land [as the area of Gaza and the West Bank would be], if you really believe we have equal rights with you?' A prominent member of this group was a London-based Jewish activist in the peace movement, who had set up a campaign in the 1970s to promote Jewish emigration from the USSR to Israel under the emotive slogan, 'Let My People Go'. Eager to make friends, she had suggested a meeting over lunch. In the course of this, she told me proudly of her successful work on the Soviet Jewry campaign, which had borne fruit in the immigration of a million Russian Jews to Israel.

'Do you expect me to congratulate you?' I asked. She looked genuinely puzzled and hurt. 'Don't you realise that those people are taking the place that Palestinian refugees should rightfully have?' 'That's different,' she replied briskly, and I saw that she genuinely thought so.

The powerful optimism that the Oslo Accords generated was accompanied by an equally powerful hostility towards its detractors who were condemned as 'enemies of peace'. I had this dramatically demonstrated to me in May 1995 at a Wilton Park conference on the peace process.[22] This was after the signing of Oslo 2, which was concerned with the setting up of a Palestinian legislative council and was the agreement that divided the Palestinian territories into areas 'A' (under Palestinian jurisdiction), 'B' (joint Palestinian/Israeli security control) and 'C' (sole Israeli control). I had been invited to give a Palestinian perspective on the Oslo process, and my Israeli interlocutors included the then Israeli consul to the US, Colette Avital, and Ron Pondak, the Danish Israeli negotiator involved in the talks with the PLO in Oslo. The Israeli delegation had a self-congratulatory air,

evinced in hearty handshaking and embracing of the Palestinian representatives, as if they had been the best of friends. They looked to me
like people who had struck a business deal so favourable they couldn't
believe their luck. The other conference participants, representing the
EU, Germany, the UN, in addition to journalists and experts, smiled
benignly on the proceedings.

At risk of spoiling this glowing atmosphere, I gave my analysis of
the Oslo Accords. I spoke with candour about its shortcomings: it
had no endpoint, recognised no Palestinian rights to statehood or
self-determination, did not limit Jewish settlement-building, deferred
all crucial issues – Jerusalem, the settlements, borders, security and
refugees – which gave Israel time to create more irreversible 'facts
on the ground'. I referred to the vast disparity of power between the
negotiating sides and how it doomed the process from the outset. I urged
the Israelis to show more generosity if they wanted the deal to succeed,
and finally, I stressed, not to exploit the pathetic acquiescence and hope
of a weak and vulnerable people, downtrodden and militarily occupied
Palestinians, as a form of psychotherapy to expiate their own guilt over
the crimes they had committed against them. Shocked silence greeted
my exposition, as if I had drawn a gun or threatened to throw a bomb
at the gathering. The Israeli consul and her associates then launched
a fierce personal attack on me, accusing me of antisemitism, unpro-
fessional conduct and calling into question my academic credentials.
They wondered why 'dinosaurs' and has-been 'warmongers' such as
myself had been invited to participate in a conference about peace
and the future. One of the Palestinians spoke up in my defence. No
one else supported me. When we broke up for dinner, I walked away
alone and found myself sitting down to eat alone. I had become a
peace pariah.

What was in it for the Palestinians?

The Oslo agreement – formally entitled 'Declaration of Principles
on Interim Self-Government Arrangements' – had started out as a
bold Palestinian attempt to take matters into their own hands and
confront Israel head on. But this was more difficult than they could
have imagined. Not only were they too weak to do so, but they were
also handicapped by their failure to comprehend Israel's complex

character and the multi-faceted nature of its support, as discussed in earlier chapters. Inevitably, their initial hopes were dashed by a series of disappointments almost as soon as the agreement came into effect. Israel repeatedly reneged on its deadlines and it became clear that the areas which were eventually handed over to Palestinian 'rule', enjoyed no Palestinian sovereignty at all. Even Arafat was required to have Israel's permission every time he flew his helicopter from one place to another, since the air space over the occupied territories was under Israeli control. All entry and exit to the territories was likewise controlled by Israel, despite a risible arrangement (which was formally deemed to make Palestinians feel better), where Palestinian officials would carry out the security checks on travellers while Israeli guards sat invisible behind dark screens to monitor them and could overrule their decisions at will.

Evacuation of Israeli forces from towns was constantly delayed by disagreements over the size of areas to be handed over and the line to which the army would withdraw; for example, the redeployment from Jericho, the most distant and docile of West Bank cities and the first to be handed over, was four months late because of such haggling. Even then, Israel erected checkpoints outside the areas it evacuated, dug a deep trench around the city to hamper movement even more, and reserved the right to invade at any time in pursuit of 'terrorists'. The interim Palestinian Authority, due to be set up in 1994, was not elected until 1996, and final status talks, scheduled to begin then and end in 1999, never took place, the process having finally broken down in the summer of 2000. As if to isolate the Palestinians further, Jordan and Israel signed a separate peace treaty in 1994. This required them to co-operate in 'combating terrorism' and to prevent 'cross-boundary infiltrations', all thinly disguised allusions to the movement of Palestinian fighters and members of resistance groups, including all incitement to violence from such sources.[23] Jordan's historic and often secret contacts with the Jewish state were now formalised, and this added another ill-fitting piece to the jigsaw of Arab–Israeli relations.

Meanwhile, Israel's agreements with the Palestinians left it in control of the borders, the air space and the settlements; its army could move freely along all roads and had security jurisdiction over every aspect of Palestinian life. Not surprisingly, the tortuous process of negotiation, with its stops and starts and offers made and then withdrawn, was punctuated by Palestinian violence against Israeli targets, each time provoking the traditional excessive Israeli mass reprisals. And each time, Israel would demand that Arafat 'control the violence' and 'fight terrorism', a refrain made familiar by its overuse from that time onwards. At the same time, there was no similar Israeli undertaking with regard to settler violence or indeed the violence of Israel's own troops. (Gaza, for example, was under curfew from June 1993 until January 1994.) This not withstanding, the main cities of Jenin, Tulkarm, Qalqilya, Ramallah and Nablus were eventually transferred to Area A and granted autonomy status over civil affairs. But Hebron, whose partial evacuation had to wait until 1997, was made to retain the provocative enclave of hardline Jewish settlers in the centre of the city, guarded by thousands of Israeli soldiers.

The plight of Hebron was truly tragic. It was one of the greatest casualties of the Oslo agreement. For the sake of the 500 Jewish settlers, everyday life for the 35,000 Palestinians, who resided in the same area, became a living nightmare. They were cordoned off from the other 115,000 Palestinians in the rest of Hebron in 'Area H-2', so-called because of yet another elaborate sub-division of the land agreed in the 1997 Hebron Accord. This area contained the old city and Hebron's commercial centre and was part of Area C, that is, under Israeli control; this meant that the Palestinians who lived there were at the total mercy of the settlers, the army and the notoriously brutal Israeli border police. It is extraordinary that Arafat agreed to this condition, since the settlers of Hebron were probably the most obnoxious and anti-Arab of all the rest. Many of them were followers of the racist rabbi, Meir Kahane, who was notorious for his open advocacy of Arab expulsion from 'the land of Israel'.[24] We have already alluded to one of his followers, Baruch Goldstein, the perpetrator of the Ibrahimi mosque massacre in Hebron in 1994 that killed 24 Palestinian worshippers in cold blood. Goldstein was inspired by a vision of cleansing the land of Arabs and believed he was on a righteous mission.[25]

On a visit to Hebron in July 1995, I had occasion to see some of the Jewish settlers in action behind their barbed wire and military guard in the heart of what had been the charming, historic souk in the centre of this old Palestinian city (and later destined to be Area H-2). I was part of a delegation of American and British Christians 'bearing witness', under whose cover I was able to conceal my Palestinian, Muslim identity so as to move about unhampered by interrogation. One of our numbers was the Reverend Michael Prior, a Catholic priest, scholar and well-known critic of Zionism.[26] We had been shaken by witnessing a group of settlers running amok in the souk, kicking over Palestinian vegetable stalls and grinding tomatoes and aubergines beneath their boots. The storekeepers immediately shut and bolted the doors of their shops, and those out in the street started to pull their produce hurriedly out of the way. One man showed us the fresh gash in his leg inflicted earlier by a settler's dog, apparently a usual form of assault on Palestinians. The Israeli soldiers, who took their time about appearing on the scene, eventually restored order. We walked over to the Jewish settlement, which blocked the end of the main souk street, transforming it from the vibrant main thoroughfare of Hebron that it had been, into a dangerous and barricaded dead end. The soldiers allowed us to go behind the barbed wire of the settlement and we found ourselves confronted by a thickset, bearded settler with an American accent, wearing a *kippah* (skull cap), a large rifle slung over his shoulder.

'Why are you here?' asked a red-faced, angry Reverend Prior, fresh from the disturbing spectacle of bullying and anarchy we had just witnessed. 'You don't belong here. See those people?' – pointing to the Palestinians in the souk behind – 'This is their place, not yours,' he said. I thought the man was going to shoot him right there and then. 'You got it the other way around, Father,' he replied sarcastically, sneerily emphasising the word. 'This is the land God gave us. It's them who got no business being here and we're going to get them out.' Others of us stepped in at this point, thinking to argue with him. But three other settlers, also armed, drew up threateningly. 'And you know what,' continued the first settler prodding Prior in the chest so hard he almost fell over, 'there ain't nothing you can do about it!' And the whole group of settlers laughed raucously.

As the situation in Hebron continued to worsen, Arabs were indeed leaving. The pernicious and unrelenting attacks on them and the laxity of security control by army and police, who also participated in the attacks, had taken their toll. By 2003, 43 per cent of Arab Hebronites had left, 2,000 businesses and shops had closed, and three schools, which had catered for thousands of pupils, were taken over by the Israeli army.[27] Hebron's unemployment and poverty rates were among the highest of all the occupied towns. Donald Macintyre's report for the

Independent (21 April 2005) brings these statistics to life in his horrific picture of Palestinian suffering at the hands of the settlers. Though it had started two decades before, much of the later deterioration of Arab Hebronite life could have been anticipated following the Hebron Protocol. Signed between the PLO and the Netanyahu government in 1997, this returned 80 per cent of the city to the Palestinians but allowed the Jewish settlements inside the city to stay. Plans made public in 2005 to partition the city between the settlers and the Arabs, allotting the old city and the Ibrahimi mosque to the settlers and cutting them off from Palestinian life, was another logical outcome of the agreement.[28] Arafat's acquiescence in this was as apparently mysterious as his acceptance of the network of Israelis-only bypass roads all over the West Bank that Israel was allowed to build after the Interim Agreement on the West Bank and Gaza (Oslo 2), signed in 1995.[29]

Hearing about it in 1997, I could not believe that Arafat had abandoned the Hebronites to the mercies of those brutal settlers and their protectors. He also left the exact size of Area C to be determined by Israel: how much of it Israel would ultimately give back and when. Talks on water sharing ended with an unequal arrangement, whereby Israel would take the lion's share and leave the Palestinians an amount too small for their needs. The outcome was that the Palestinian Authority would control 90 per cent of the people but only 30 per cent of the land, and much of that was under joint Israeli control. The settlement-building programme, which had never stopped, picked up with renewed vigour after Oslo 2, especially with regard to the area around Jerusalem, which was expanded further to the north towards Ramallah and to the south towards Bethlehem. This artificially enlarged area was designated by Israel as part of 'Greater Jerusalem' and non-negotiable.

Arafat's Agenda

Why did Arafat and his colleagues accept all this or indeed agree to the Oslo arrangements in the first place? Various reasons were put forward: Israel had recognised the PLO and thereby acknowledged the existence of a Palestinian people who needed a solution; Resolution 242 had been agreed as the basis of the peace process, emphasising the formula of land-for-peace which should apply to the Palestinian territories as well; and issues that Israel had managed to make taboo subjects –

Jerusalem, settlements and refugees – were firmly on the negotiations agenda.[30] Indeed, following the Accords, Arab educational and cultural institutions in East Jerusalem like the nineteenth-century Husseini residence (Orient House) were turned over to the Palestinians. These implications of the Oslo Accords were quite true, strictly speaking, but any optimism they might have generated was in the event short-lived. Palestinians could see for themselves in the expansion of settlements, the checkpoints and bypass roads that the reality was different. It was not that Arafat ignored these facts or, in his apparent acquiescence with Israel's creeping colonisation, was in the process of betraying the Palestinian cause, as some accused him. His real agenda transcended these considerations. He truly believed in the foot-in-the-door approach, that if Israel could be prevailed on to allow a Palestinian rehabilitation, in the shape of the modest steps towards the independence the Palestinians sought and thereby accord them recognition as a nation with rights, then this would form the first stage in a continuous process. And that would lead inexorably on to statehood.

So wedded was he to this concept that he subordinated every objection he might reasonably have made to Israel's hegemonic demands to the greater aim of maintaining the momentum towards inevitable statehood, as he saw it. He displayed an unseemly eagerness to accept every crumb that fell from Israel's high table and a reluctance to use any kind of leverage against it to attain a better deal.[31] Arafat's basic premise was that Israel was too powerful to be directly challenged. The only way to achieve Palestinian aims was to hoodwink it into entering a process, which, despite itself, would ultimately end in a Palestinian state. It was for this reason that the Palestinian Authority assumed the trappings of statehood, appointing ministers and establishing institutions, flying the national flag and creating a Palestinian currency and passport. At first sight ridiculous in a situation of colonial occupation, it is less so when understood as the Palestinian version of 'creating facts', projecting an image to the world of a state-in-waiting which, however unpropitious the conditions seemed, would be difficult to set aside thereafter. It was an understandable strategy but naive in the circumstances. It under-estimated the tenacity with which the Israeli side clung to its acquision of Palestinian land and its determination to defeat every attempt at Palestinian independence. In the end, Arafat paid the ultimate price for his naivety, imprisoned and degraded by Israel and finally meeting a suspicious death in 2004 widely imputed to Israeli machinations (see below).

Rescuing the Oslo Process

The pursuit of this policy drew the Palestinian leadership into a downward spiral of ever greater retreats, giving up more and more of their previous conditions for the sake of some settlement with Israel, and developing an abject dependence on the good offices of its powerful patron, America. Like Anwar Sadat before him (as well as all other Arab leaders), Arafat believed that America had all the cards and sought its appeasement at almost any price. (Arafat's refusal to acquiesce in the US/Israeli terms at the Camp David talks in 2000 was the first such exception.) But as always before, Israel, which was aware of this position, took increasing advantage of Arafat's weakness and Palestinian vulnerability to push its demands further for more concessions. Consequently, while the peace process ran into increasing delays and difficulties, a number of attempts were made to resuscitate it. None of these met with any success as they were all similarly flawed: they dealt with the two parties as if they were equal, arguing the position, not from a previous reference point based on principle, but from the point it had reached at that moment. Israel, which was adept at moving the goalposts each time, was the obvious beneficiary, and the Palestinians found themselves having to accept the new terms each time. And as before, Israel had the power to suspend or amend any part of the process as it deemed fit. The old pattern of attempting to impose a settlement at the Palestinians' expense was now evident once again.

By 1998, a Likud government was in power in Israel with an uncompromising Binyamin Netanyahu at its head. None of the Israeli redeployments promised in Oslo 2 or the Hebron agreement had taken place and the peace process was stalled. To re-start it, the US convened a meeting between the two parties at the Wye River plantation, which produced a Memorandum of that name.[32] This stipulated that the Palestinians had to first fight terrorism and 'incitement to violence'; for this the CIA was deputed to provide training for the Palestinian police force, and remove clauses offensive to Israel from the Palestine National Charter. In return, Israel was to redeploy its forces as per the previous agreements, allow the Gaza airport to open, desist from security searches of Arafat's private plane and commence final status talks as soon as possible. The Palestinians tried to fulfil their side of the agreement, hurriedly convening the PNC in Gaza in order to ratify the Charter's amendment (in President Clinton's presence), and accepting CIA 'trainers' for their police force. The regime that was instituted for checking their security procedures, in which Israel played the third partner (thereafter called 'security co-operation'), was extraordinarily intrusive and blatantly designed to suppress Palestinian resistance to Israel's occupation. It is astonishing that Arafat should have co-operated with it, going so far as to arrest a number of suspects in moves that angered many of his own people.

Israel, on the other hand, dragged its heels over its commitments, quibbling over percentages of land from which it would redeploy, whittling the 13 per cent agreed in the Hebron agreement down to 9 per cent, and even that proceeded incrementally in stages of 1 or 2 per cent at a time, and tagging its redeployment rate to how well it thought the Palestinians were controlling 'terrorism'. Any action by Hamas fighters was pounced on as an excuse for holding up progress, even though it was obvious that Palestinian violence (resistance) was a consequence precisely of that lack of progress. Israel demanded oversight of all flight lists and schedules in and out of Gaza airport and asked the US to release the convicted spy, Jonathan Pollard, a condition which Netanyahu knew Clinton could not agree to. No one mentioned the matter of occupation, a persistent omission in all the Israeli–Palestinian agreements, as if it had been an irrelevance. On the contrary, Clinton had to offer Israel inducements to get it to agree to even the modest moves it had signed up to. He increased the USA's already generous military and financial assistance to cover the costs of Israel's redeployment and bypass roads. The details of Netanyahu's prevarications and duplicitous posturing, American persuasion and Palestinian subjugation make painful reading.[33] The result of all this was that the Wye Memorandum achieved negligible gains for the Palestinians: Israel withdrew from just 2 per cent of the land and allowed the Gaza airport to open. Final status talks were promised, but before much more could happen, the Netanyahu government collapsed in early 1999, to be replaced by the Labour Party under Ehud Barak.

The Camp David Talks

The peace process having stalled once again, a meeting at Egypt's Sharm al-Sheikh was convened between Israel and the Palestinians in September 1999, which produced what became known as the Sharm al-Sheikh or Wye II Memorandum.[34] The US secretary of state was in attendance, as well the Egyptian leader, the Jordanian king and representatives from Russia, the EU, Norway and Japan. President Mubarak's involvement in this meeting was to herald a new pattern in Israeli–Palestinian peacemaking in which Egypt was increasingly to act as a mediator between the two sides. The underlying assumption of this arrangement was curious: that an Arab state should be called on to act as a supposedly impartial broker between another Arab side and that side's non-Arab protagonist who was occupying Arab land and abusing fellow Arabs. A mediator who belonged to neither camp and could be neutral would surely have been the proper choice. It would seem obvious that Egypt was deliberately recruited for the job to put pressure on the Palestinians, who would respond more positively to Arab mediation than otherwise. That the Arab world's most important state should have accepted such an ignoble role, or at least its semblance, which it continued to play with vigour, was further evidence of the deplorable dependence of Arab regimes on the US and the need to curry favour with it through serving Israel.[35]

Like the Wye River Memorandum, the Sharm al-Sheikh meeting aimed to restart the peace process by implementing outstanding agreements and initiating final status negotiations. A schedule for further Israeli redeployments, consisting of the customary small percentages vacated at intervals, was set and a framework for Palestinian prisoner release established. Israel agreed to the construction of a Gaza seaport and discussed complicated arrangements for safe passage between Gaza and the West Bank via bridges (in order that Palestinians be kept out of Israeli-held territory). Final status talks were to be completed in one year from then. This was all accompanied by assurances to the Palestinians from the US and the EU that they would guarantee the process, and Barak, who was busy presiding over the expansion of Jewish settlements, spoke about his hopes of concluding 'a peace of the brave'. (Arafat reiterated this phrase many times, presumably to encourage the Israelis, but he would always render it as 'the peace of the braves'. He had no idea how funny this sounded, and I remember telling one of his aides to point the error out to him.) Barak meanwhile embarked on reactivating the stalled Israeli–Syrian peace talks, which resumed in late 1999, but failed a few months later. Throughout, Israel tried to use the same tactics of prevarication, ambiguity and obstructiveness as with the Palestinians – but with the difference here that the Syrian leader, Hafez al-Assad, was not prepared to acquiesce. He would not fall into the same 'peace' trap as Arafat, he said, who had signed a peace settlement with Israel and then failed to get either the West Bank or 'a capital in Jerusalem'. Seeing the Israelis' conduct, he walked out of the talks, which were not renewed during his lifetime.[36]

By the end of the first year of Barak's premiership, little had progressed on the Palestinian front. Final status talks had not begun and the settlement–building programme was proceeding as briskly as ever.[37] The Camp David negotiations of July 2000, instigated at American behest to try and achieve a final settlement, took place against this stalemate. Like the Oslo Accords, this summit has attracted a large volume of writings and reports, not least because of the conflicting accounts that were given about it at the time.[38] Barak and Arafat faced each other across the negotiating table at Camp David with President Clinton trying to be simultaneously referee, patron and host. The Palestinians went there unwillingly, as Arafat had made clear in June of that year to Douglas Ross, the US peace envoy to the Middle East, and again to the US secretary of state, Madeleine Albright. Since preparatory talks on the final status issues had not progressed at all, he argued, a trilateral summit to deal with them in a definitive way was premature. These misgivings were ignored and the Palestinians were made, as always, to bow to other people's deadlines and priorities. Israel judged them to be at their weakest and likely to be coerced into an agreement at any price, while Clinton was anxious to arrive at a successful Middle East settlement before his term of office expired.

The meeting, which involved an exhausting 14 days of the most intensive negotiation, arm-twisting, intimidation and coercion ever aimed at the Palestinians, ended in total failure. Akram Hanieh's detailed account of the wrangling and manoeuvrings at the summit, published in Arabic in the Palestinian daily, *Al-Ayyam* (of which he was the editor), makes fascinating reading.[39] Following the summit's termination, the Israeli side quickly put out their version in hints and innuendos and leaks to the press about what had happened – to the effect that it had all been Arafat's fault. He had rejected Barak's 'generous offer' to return most of the occupied territories as well as a deal on Jerusalem, and later wilfully incited his people to violence against Israel. Foolishly, the Palestinians did not publish their own account first, nor even after the Israeli allegations appeared, dutifully honouring a promise to Clinton that he extracted from both sides to keep the Camp David proceedings secret. Amazingly, no formal record of proceedings was published, no maps or proposals presented in writing. The much-vaunted Israeli concessions have never been defined in any document, and whatever ideas Israel did put forward were communicated to the Palestinians through the US. And yet, they were expected to accept the terms, vague and undocumented as they were, to be a general basis for negotiations. That issues of such importance to the Palestinians' future should have been dealt with in so cavalier a manner is a graphic illustration of their continuing denigration in a long history of so-called peacemaking.

What did happen at the Camp David talks? If we piece together the various accounts as they emerged later, it is possible, even with these caveats, to draw a reasonably accurate picture of the proceedings. It is well to remember at the outset that the land that was the subject of negotiation (and of Barak's 'generous offer') was already by then extensively colonised by Israeli settlements, bypass roads and 'security areas'. More than 400,000 Jewish settlers lived in the West Bank and around East Jerusalem, and 80 per cent of the land was dotted about with checkpoints. The Palestinian Authority had control, in whole or in part, over only 42 per cent of it. Israel proposed to annex 10–13 per cent of the West Bank, containing 90 per cent of the settlements. These were constituted as three massive blocs in the north, centre and south of the area, and were to be expanded and connected to each other and to Israel via bypass roads that took yet more Palestinian land. Not by accident, the Israeli-held areas were precisely those where the main West Bank water sources were located, so as to keep them firmly under Israeli control. In addition, parts of the Jordan Valley would be retained as Israeli military areas, amounting to another 14 per cent of West Bank territory, for 12 to 20 years. The Palestinian areas would be connected by a series of tunnels and bridges, and Hebron would remain divided. The result would be a non-contiguous

Palestinian territory, with enclaves separated by strips of Israeli-held land. The arguments that subsequently arose over exactly what land percentages Barak had offered seem to me irrelevant in the light of this fragmented arrangement.

The convoluted proposals for East Jerusalem were no better. They aimed to project an accommodation of the Palestinian aspiration to make it their capital, but were transparently designed to consolidate Israel's hold on the city. A bewildering series of ideas were put forward: Israel would have control over the Haram al-Sharif, but the PA would have 'custodial sovereignty' with a 'sovereign compound' for Arafat and his administration near the Haram; the PA could have 'vertical sovereignty' over the surface of the platform where the Haram stood and Israel over what was underneath it; inside the Old City, Palestinians would be sovereign over the Muslim and Christian Quarters, and Israel over the Jewish Quarter and the Western Wall. The districts outside the walls would be given a variable status, depending on their distance from the Old City: the nearest, like Sheikh Jarrah, Salah al-Din Street and the Damascus Gate, would have Palestinian 'functional' self-rule, and the neighbourhoods beyond (which had never formed part of Jerusalem before 1967 anyway), like the villages of Abu Dis, Isawiyya and Beit Hanina, would become subject to Palestinian partial or complete sovereignty. The American officials adopted unquestioningly Barak's passionate insistence on Israeli control of the Haram (Temple Mount) because of its Jewish *religious* significance.

The last and thorniest issue in the talks was that of the Palestinian refugees. In brief, Israel rejected any suggestion of responsibility for them, either historically or morally. If there was to be a right of return, then it might be to a future Palestinian entity, although even that would have been in doubt, since Israel controlled all borders and airspace and would take measures in case of such infiltration. Any refugee return to Israel was to be at its own discretion entirely, and Barak spoke of a programme of gradual family reunion for a maximum of 10,000 refugees. Compensating the rest was acceptable, provided it came from an international fund at no cost to Israel (and from which, he proposed, Jews expelled from Arab countries after 1948 should also benefit). Not even a verbal apology or acknowledgment for the refugee tragedy was forthcoming from Barak. And after all that, the Palestinians were asked to sign a document declaring the conflict at an end and cancelling forever all outstanding claims they had against Israel. One must agree with Reinhart, that Barak and his team had come to Camp David intending neither reconciliation nor even a closing of the gaps between them and the Palestinians.[40] How Arafat, or any Palestinian leader, could have been expected to accept such humiliating terms, whether over the division of land, the status of Jerusalem or the right of return that was at the heart of the conflict, is a mystery only to those who support Israel blindly.

Even had no details about the talks been available and on a prima facie basis alone, a glance at the political context in which they took place is enough to show why a successful outcome would have been impossible. The protagonists' position on all the permanent status issues were diametrically opposed, and the only arbiter who could minimise the differences was a party already deeply committed to Israel's imperatives and welfare. As became clear, Israel was not prepared to withdraw to the pre-1967 borders, would not remove the settlements, would not relinquish East Jerusalem and rejected the Palestinian right of return. The Palestinians, who felt they had compromised enough already by giving up 78 per cent of their homeland to Israel, wanted a full withdrawal to the 1967 lines, a removal of the settlements which had gobbled up more than half their remaining land, a capital in East Jerusalem and Israeli recognition of the right of return with compensation.

To bridge such divergent positions fairly was clearly going to be a Herculean task. In the event, nothing like this was even attempted at the Camp David summit, which seemed designed to draw the Palestinians into a dialogue based on an unequal relationship with Israel, weighted even more by the addition of the US as arbiter, and so, in effect, pitting one against two. This could mean only one thing: that the Palestinian side would be pressured into more concessions. The truth of this is borne out in Hanieh's description of the bullying tactics Clinton used to harry Arafat during the talks and to persuade Arab leaders, whom he telephoned repeatedly, to do the same. The net result was a breakdown of the process, with Arafat unable to sign up to what was demanded of him.

The Camp David proposals were an insult to the Palestinian cause. They were offered in the same mean spirit that had characterised the Oslo Accords seven years before. As ever, the parameters were those of pauper and prince: the Palestinians must be grateful for whatever they could get, not as of right, but as largesse from Israel. If they asked for more, they might find themselves, like Oliver Twist, castigated for greed. That was the basic reality beneath the statesman-like rhetoric at Camp David and the pretence of a proper contractual process between equal parties it projected. That this just and legal cause should have been so traduced by the insatiability and arrogance of an over-confident Israel, backed by a pliant US, was a shaming indictment of all those who allowed it to happen. A review of what was negotiated at Camp David shows how paltry were the offers made to the Palestinians. Only those who saw them as paupers without rights, lucky to get anything at all, could possibly have thought otherwise.

Salvaging Camp David

The failure of the Camp David talks was an outcome of the utmost gravity for both Palestinians and Israelis. It led to the outbreak of the second intifada in 2000, which this time was armed and more violent than the last. In the ensuing six years, several attempts were made to halt the violence and return the parties to the negotiating table. Reviewing these peace proposals, necessary here in order to complete the story so far, fills one with weariness and a sense of futility. It seemed not to strike Israel or its supporters that making peace on the basis of unequal power with a biased sponsor and minimal offerings was not a winning formula. Even more pointless, the sine qua non of all the plans put forward was the cessation of Palestinian violence. The PA had first to control the militants, its success judged by Israel (and third parties), before reciprocal peace moves could be made. Israel and the CIA were to assist in this effort through 'security co-operation', with Egyptian and Jordanian help as appropriate. The fact that Palestinians had no reason to trust either the Israeli security services or the CIA and were afraid to lay down their arms in the face of military occupation did not deter anyone from making such proposals. The aim of this doublespeak was of course to put an end to Palestinian resistance and ensure a compliant and submissive partner in the Israeli plan for resolving the conflict in line with its own wishes.

The real irony was that Israel itself, which ceaselessly affirmed its desire for peace, never initiated any of the peace proposals with the Palestinians. Left to itself, it was content to continue appropriating land

and resources and building settlements with a minimum of interference. It was the Palestinians under occupation who were desperate for a solution. All the follow-up to Camp David was US-inspired and Israel acquiesced either reluctantly or opportunistically. In January 2001, a meeting took place between Israeli and Palestinian representatives at Taba in Egypt to try and continue the unfinished business of the Camp David summit.[41] This was more productive, and measurable progress was made on substantive issues with the aid of a map, which both sides accepted. Israel would give up 95 per cent of the West Bank and reduce the size of the settlement blocs it wanted to retain. The Palestinians would be assured of a contiguous territory with full sovereignty – a breakthrough in the Israeli position – and most of East Jerusalem would become their capital. This looked like a genuine advance on the Camp David talks and, according to some interpretations, might have reflected Israel's recognition of its need to do more to reach a reasonable settlement with the Palestinians. But no American, Israeli or Palestinian leader was present, no documents of the meeting were ever produced, and it was far more likely that with the Barak administration on its way out by then, it was under no pressure to put any of the points agreed into effect, even had it wanted to.[42]

With the election of a new Israeli government under the hardline Ariel Sharon, all negotiations ceased and the intifada raged on. A US-initiated fact-finding committee under the chairmanship of former Senator George Mitchell was sent to investigate the causes of the violence. Their report, published in May 2001, is strongly reminiscent of the numerous commissions that the British government used to set up to investigate Arab–Jewish unrest in Mandate Palestine. Like theirs, it purported to start its inquiry *de novo*, as if nothing of the situation had been previously known or could be inferred from the obvious dynamics of occupier and occupied.

The recommendations of the Mitchell Report continued the now familiar tradition of Israeli–Palestinian peacemaking which, firstly, assumed the existence of two equal parties and, secondly, accepted the Israeli occupation as a given and sought only to deal with its consequences as if the two were unconnected. Hence, the PA was to make an 'all-out effort' to control Palestinian violence and 'be seen by the government of Israel as doing so'; to this end, security co-operation with Israel was to be resumed. In return, Israel was to freeze settlement-building and 'consider' withdrawing its forces to their positions as on 28 September 2000, the eve of the start of the second intifada. Israel was also to carry out confidence-building measures as, for example, lifting closures, desisting from destruction of trees, orchards and houses, and returning tax revenues collected from Palestinian workers in Israel and long owing to the PA. The parties were to return to the negotiating table, 'in a spirit of compromise and reconciliation'.[43] There is no doubt that Mitchell and his colleagues worked hard and meant well in this report, but apparently they could see no asymmetry in the demand that the occupied Palestinians lay down their arms in the face of occupation and the parallel request that Israel observe a modicum of decency in desisting from destroying their homes and livelihood, and returning revenues legally owing to the PA that it should never have retained in the first place.

The Mitchell recommendations were non-binding but were immediately accepted by the Palestinians who hoped for some improvement of their situation, however modest, now that a harsh Sharon government was in power. Israel did not comply with any of them and the CIA director, George Tenet, was called in next to deal with the situation. The Tenet Plan, which he produced in June 2001, was another attempt to stop the violence.[44] It called for an immediate ceasefire, security co-operation between the PA, Israel and the US with weekly co-ordinating meetings and commitments from the protagonists similar to those in the Mitchell Report, only more stringent and with greater monitoring of both parties' performance. The PA was to carry out pre-emptive operations against 'terrorists' among its own people and pass on the names of fugitives and suspects to the tripartite security committee; it was to confiscate their weapons, with Israel's help, and prevent arms manufacture and smuggling. Israel, meanwhile, was to refrain from 'pro-active' attacks on Palestinian civilian targets and attacks on Arafat's compound, Palestinian police buildings and prisons. As before, it was asked to withdraw its troops to the lines of 28 September 2000 and minimise the number of security checkpoints. A confident Sharon ignored all this, resisting any restriction on his army's actions against the uprising and the US as usual did nothing to force him.

A year later, in June 2002, President Bush stepped in with a declaration that if the Palestinians would undertake to reform their system of governance (including their leadership), then he would help enable a 'viable, credible Palestine state' to emerge. He emphasised the need for terrorism to be defeated, following which Israeli forces would withdraw to the 28 September 2000 positions. When Palestinians created a democratic political structure and a constitution, Israeli settlement activity would stop. For all its lack of balance, one must concede that this declaration was a landmark in US policy. It was the first time that an American president had explicitly and publicly spoken of a Palestinian state.[45] The fact that it was weighted in favour of Israel, which was required to do very little until the other side came up to scratch, shedding its historic leader, Yasser Arafat, in the process, did not detract from its political significance. Many Arabs did not see it in that light, however, but thought it a ploy to distract them from the impending US attack on Iraq in 2003. The fact that Bush's vision came to nothing, with no Palestinian state in sight, would tend to support this opinion.

The Road Map

The Road Map was the name given to the next formula for Israeli–Palestinian peacemaking, widely accepted in the international arena. Emanating from Bush's call of 2002, it was elaborated into a phased plan leading to the creation of a Palestinian state. Its implementation was to be supervised and monitored by the 'Quartet' – the US, Russia, the EU and the UN – within a short time frame, starting in 2003 and ending with the creation of a Palestinian state in 2005.[46] It was a detailed and precise plan with defined stages, each of which was to be judged in terms of how the parties performed. Its three phases set out within specified time intervals a series of actions which both sides must undertake and, upon the satisfactory performance of each of these, the next phase would begin.

Phase One (30 April 2003–31 May 2003) was concerned with ending Palestinian violence and 'terror', normalising Palestinian life and building institutions in preparation for statehood. Israel was to help in these efforts by improving the humanitarian situation and slowly withdrawing its forces to their positions before 28 September 2000. It was also to freeze all settlement activity as called for in the Mitchell Report. Phase Two (June–December 2003) was a transition phase aiming to create a Palestinian state with 'provisional borders and attributes of sovereignty', as a sort of dress rehearsal for actual statehood. This goal was subject to a satisfactory Palestinian security and reform performance under a leadership, 'acting decisively against terror'. During this phase, the Arab states would be asked to restore the links with Israel they had severed since the intifada. Phase Three would deal with final status issues: the establishment of permanent borders for an 'independent, democratic and viable' Palestinian state and the end of conflict. The Arab states would then fully normalise relations with Israel.

The Road Map's reference to the 'right' Palestinian leadership was of course a thinly disguised demand for an end to Arafat's presidency which, it was hoped by then, Mahmoud Abbas, the new prime minister (whose appointment had been more or less imposed on the PA), would replace. Despite this, Arafat and the Palestinian leadership, feeling they had no choice, accepted the Road Map. Israel, however, immediately listed 14 objections to it, which the Bush Administration was forced to accommodate in order to get progress. At the same time, the Sharon government encouraged the pro-Israel US lobby to mount a vigorous opposition to the Road Map, and the right-wing extremist Israeli party, Moledet, reacted by calling for a transfer of Palestinians out of the West Bank.[47] Though later Sharon made a public statement to the effect that he accepted the idea of a Palestinian state, and that the occupation must end, it made no substantive difference to the outcome. The Road Map has not been implemented to date, though it is still formally invoked by the Quartet and the Palestinian leadership as the basic framework for a settlement of the conflict. Yet, it was as flawed as all the other peace plans that had gone before it.

Like the Oslo Accords, it employed a gradualist approach, already shown to be futile, which concentrated on process more than substance. It came with no enforcement mechanism to ensure the compliance of the parties that was essential to its progress, and, despite the grandly named Quartet of four major players as supervisors and arbiters, most of whom might have genuinely meant well, the real decision lay, as ever, with one of them, the US. It made the same mistake of demanding that the Palestinians act to end their violence while Israel was allowed to continue its house demolitions, targeted assassinations and settlement-building undisturbed. Contrary to the requirement of the Road Map,

Sharon refused to remove even the small, so-called 'illegal' settler outposts, often no more than a caravan or two, established on the West Bank since March 2001. Bush accepted this. By March 2003, the US was engaged in the Iraq war anyway, and distracted from the Israeli–Palestinian conflict, all of which aided the Sharon government to maintain its programme of settlement and occupation secure from interference. To this was added a new infraction: the barrier wall, constructed mostly on West Bank land, ostensibly to protect Israel from terrorist infiltration.

The Wall

No Israeli violation of Palestinian life or international law was as visible or as shocking as the barrier wall. It raised the question of what sort of society it was that could contemplate its future only by walling off those it loathed or feared, as if to pretend that what was out of sight was out of mind. The wall took different forms depending on locality. In some areas, notably around Arab Jerusalem and the West Bank town of Qalqilya, it was an eight-metre high solid concrete structure with surveillance towers at 300-metre intervals, and in other places it was an electrified fence with sensors, razor wire and trenches up to four metres deep.[48] When I visited Qalqilya in the summer of 2005, I saw a town totally enclosed, rather like the quaint walled cities of the Middle Ages. But unlike them, the wall that surrounded Qalqilya had no charm or function other than to imprison and isolate. Its huge shadow loomed at every point and every street I walked stopped abruptly before its dead, slate-coloured concrete slabs. The one exit from the town was under Israeli military control, its times of opening and closing entirely arbitrary. Even on that short visit I could feel myself suffocate and could only guess at what the people of Qalqilya endured every day of their lives.

Israel planned for the wall to be 680 km in length, of which a third had been built by 2005. The greatest part of the wall, 80 per cent, was to be inside Palestinian territory, taking up 9.5 per cent of it, and trapping an estimated 242,000 Palestinians between it and the 1967 border. The sections already built showed that the intention was to enclose the Palestinians in reservation-like cantons, swallowing up acres of their agricultural land and destroying any chance of an

Israeli withdrawal to the pre-war borders of 1967. In July 2004, the International Court of Justice at The Hague condemned the wall as illegal because it confiscated Palestinian land, prevented free movement of people and goods, and violated the right of Palestinians to seek work, health and education. A year later, the UN General Assembly passed a resolution acknowledging the International Court's opinion and demanding that Israel comply with it. The resolution was passed by 150 states, including the 25 EU member states.[49] Israel ignored the ruling and pressed on with the wall's construction. By 2006, it planned to erect eleven gates in the separation wall. These would control Palestinian access to Israel from the West Bank and that of Palestinians living in Jerusalem travelling the other way. Part of the funding for this project was to be provided by the USA.[50]

Conclusion

No Israeli–Palestinian peace deal had worked to date. Nor was any likely to so long as the parameters of peacemaking that became conventional in this conflict remained unchanged. Essentially, these were that it was not possible to make a settlement which downgraded the Palestinian issue and delimited Palestinian rights while at the same time prohibiting the use of meaningful pressure on Israel to concede anything that went against its own wishes. Consequently, all the proposals put forward sought to satisfy Israel by sidestepping the Palestinian issue, ignoring its fundamental importance in the conflict, and proposing peace terms that were always at the expense of Palestinian rights. Even when finally the Palestinians themselves entered the process of peacemaking, their leadership was coerced into adopting the same parameters, so compromising their fundamental rights – the right of return was a case in point – in order to gain concessions from Israel. This process, which started with the gradual erosion of the aim to liberate the whole of Palestine into accepting a part of it, culminated in Arafat's capitulation to the terms of the Oslo Accords for the reasons discussed above. Having taken this route, the decline into further Palestinian concessions and diminishing expectations was inevitable. This long history of Palestinian marginalisation, part imposed but later also self-generated, created in the minds of policy makers and in popular perception the idea that a solution which in fact fell far short of meeting the basic requirements of justice for the Palestinians would be sufficient.

If we put these two concepts together – the validity of undermining the Palestinian case in a peace agreement and the inadmissibility of pressure on Israel to concede – and bearing in mind the gross asymmetry of power between the two sides, the only settlement possible under such conditions would be one that was imposed by the stronger party. And that in effect was what the 'peace process' between Israel and the Palestinians was trying to do. Aware of this, the Palestinians reduced their demands considerably in line with what they saw as politically possible in the present situation. But Israel's offers always fell short of even these reduced expectations and were therefore unacceptable to the Palestinian leadership, no matter how accommodating. The intifada should have been understood as a popular Palestinian rejection of this Israeli parsimony and the injustice of the whole system. People came to understand that the peace negotiations were no more than a cosmetic cover for Israel's real demands: an outright Palestinian surrender of their rights, including the right to resist – hence Israel's repeated insistence on the destruction of the 'terrorist infrastructure' as a prerequisite to any deal. Of course, Israel could not articulate all this so bluntly. It had to operate within certain constraints that forced it to engage in the 'peace process'. But this was more a matter of going through the motions for the sake of maintaining a peaceable façade for public consumption, especially in the West, and to placate the US, than a substantive position.[51]

But even if an Israeli–Palestinian peace deal, constructed in these circumstances, had been successful, by its very nature, it could only have produced a short-term political fix, not a durable peace agreement. And without that, regional instability and hostility towards Israel were likely to remain. Yet, this reality continued to be ignored by policy makers who, as we have seen, repeatedly tried to fob the Palestinians off with the minimum possible. This practice led to the impasse of today: (a) a Palestinian community fragmented into various parts – under Israeli occupation, in Israel as second-class citizens, refugees in camps and those dispersed in various countries – all of whom want a resolution of their problem; (b) a rapidly diminishing territory on which to build the Palestinian state that was supposed to meet at least some of these needs; and (c) an all powerful Israel used to getting its own way.

5
Destroying the Palestinians

Reviewing the long and tortuous history of peacemaking efforts to resolve the Israeli–Palestinian conflict, as we have done, leads logically to the question: is a solution to the conflict in fact possible? Many people certainly thought so at the beginning of 2005. The long quest for peace, which started in 1967, had led by then to what seemed to be a turning point. On the surface, things were looking up for the Palestinian cause. For the first time, America and Europe were united in open support of an independent *and viable* Palestinian state; Western public opinion had become familiar with that concept and accepted it as a valid aspiration; popular sympathy for Palestinian tribulation under occupation was high – there was much anecdotal evidence for this and many of us could discern the change amongst people at all levels of British and European society; the word 'Palestine', which had vanished from the political vocabulary throughout my early life in Britain in the 1950s, was now bandied about by politicians at the highest level; and anti-Israel sentiments were stronger and more widespread than they had ever been. According to Tel Aviv University's study of antisemitic violence, the incidence of attacks worldwide on Jewish targets in 2004 had increased more than six-fold since 1989 and 'virulent anti-Israel propaganda and anti-Americanism . . . continued to be the main factor inciting anti-Jewish violence'.[1]

A new Palestinian administration was installed in January 2005 under the 'moderate' leadership of Mahmoud Abbas, whom Israel and the US favoured over the much-reviled Arafat, and was showing itself seriously prepared to combat corruption and violence in line with Western requirements. Following Arafat's death in mysterious circumstances in November 2004, Israel and the US made clear their insistence on the instatement of Abbas as his successor, to carry forward a programme of 'reform' of Palestinian governance and control of 'terrorism'. From the Palestinian point of view, Abbas was no successor to Arafat. He lacked his charisma, popular base and nationalist credibility. Arafat's diplomatic manoeuvrings and consensus building amongst a notoriously fragmented and difficult constituency of highly politicised, hypercritical and fractious Palestinians were skills that neither Abbas nor any other Palestinian leader could match. I remember seeing them in action at a meeting of Palestinian businessmen in Tunis in the spring of 1990. They came from every corner of the globe, many alienated by a long exile, and some spoke only halting Arabic from disuse. Though Arafat and his colleagues faced us from a high platform, he managed to imbue the hall with a feeling of inclusive intimacy and a warm camaraderie that were truly remarkable. I can think of no other Arab leader who would have behaved with such informality and egalitarianism. It was hard not to respond to him, and he managed to achieve the meeting's agreement on the main points.

It was these same abilities that made it possible for Arafat to enlist the support of a widely dispersed Palestinian constituency for what were often highly unpopular policies. Few can doubt that the Oslo Accords and their subsequent accretions would have won the acquiescence, if not the enthusiasm, of the Palestinian people, both inside and outside the territories, without his adroit manoeuvrings and persuasive authority. The same tasks now faced Mahmoud Abbas, with much less likelihood of success. Though he was a contemporary and fellow revolutionary of Arafat, he simply lacked the same command over the community. If Israel's aim had been indeed to resolve the conflict, surely it would have been more in its interest to have negotiated seriously with a Palestinian leader who could deliver as Arafat had done. In fact, Israel's behaviour suggested that the opposite was the case. Plans to ensure that he could never again negotiate with Israel were laid several years before his death. The story of his deliberate and cynical destruction and that of the Authority he had built up after 1993 at the hands of Israel and the West's slavish acquiescence in it, is one of the most despicable in a history of such acts against the Palestinians. It was also the clearest demonstration of Israel's reluctance to reach a peace settlement with the Palestinians.

Arafat's Destruction

Israel's campaign against Arafat started in earnest after the failed Camp David talks in July 2000 and the resulting outbreak of the second intifada. The idea that both these events were caused by Arafat was strongly promoted by Israel and its supporters. By October 2000, plans had been drawn up to topple him and his Authority.[2] The Barak government published a detailed record of his alleged non-compliance with the peace agreements and his pivotal role in the violence against Israel. According to this, he had never abandoned terrorism and had 'given the green light' to Hamas's suicide operations. While it was true that Arafat turned a blind eye to military operations against Israel with the appearance of Ariel Sharon's harsh regime, it was not the case that he had any hand in instigating them. As Ami Ayalon, the head of Israel's Shin Beth (security service) under Ehud Barak, stated repeatedly the Shin Beth had no evidence of Arafat's involvement in planning the violence. Ayalon described the second intifada as a spontaneous eruption of Palestinian anger, which the Shin Beth had predicted long before.[3] On the contrary, all the evidence, according to Barak's chief of army intelligence, Amos Malka, was that Arafat wanted a permanent two-state settlement and would have signed up to one if his demands at Camp David had been met. There was no foundation to the accusations that he planned to eradicate Israel.[4]

Yet, the Barak allegations against him took such firm hold that, by the time of his death, Arafat had been made to take the total responsibility for all acts of terrorism by Islamist groups and others alike. The suffering of ordinary Palestinians was likewise laid at his door. He was said to have cynically exploited the deaths of Palestinian children, 'caught in the crossfire' on the frontline, to discredit Israel. This was at a time when the world was shocked by the haunting picture of Muhammad al-Durra, the Gazan child cowering in terror behind his father as Israeli soldiers shot at both of them, resulting in the father being wounded and the boy being killed before the camera. The success of this blatant inversion of the facts was remarkable. In Britain, people began to wonder why the Palestinians 'sent their children out' in front of Israeli tanks, as if this, even had it been true, exonerated the Israeli army from shooting them. The very term 'crossfire', implying a battle between two armies, was itself a deliberate misnomer.

With the election of Ariel Sharon as prime minister in February 2001, the campaign against Arafat gained real momentum. Discrediting his leadership and edging him towards political oblivion were aims openly discussed in Israeli government circles, and by the summer of 2001, the Israeli army had drawn up a plan for an all-out assault to smash the Palestinian Authority and force Arafat out.[5] In separate incidents in July, August and November of that year the army assassinated several Islamist and one PFLP leader, provoking violent Palestinian retaliation. Arafat attempted to calm the situation in his December appeal for a truce, declaring he condemned suicide missions, and had his security forces arrest several members of Hamas. The militants obeyed the call and held the truce for a period of six weeks, in which time Arafat was said to be close to a decision to abandon military for other forms of resistance. As if none of this were happening, Israel went on to assassinate another militant leader in January 2002, and the cycle of violence resumed.[6]

Meanwhile, and ignoring Arafat's efforts to control the Palestinian violence, the Israeli army imprisoned him in his Ramallah compound, and Sharon announced that he was 'no longer relevant'. In March, following the Palestinian suicide bombing which shook the Israeli public, the Israeli army moved into the West Bank cities and refugee camps in a large-scale assault. Within weeks, the army had destroyed all the Palestinian Authority institutions, killed many of its police and security men and laid waste to the major Palestinian cities.[7] Arafat's compound was bombed, all his means of communication with the outside world were severed, and even water and electricity were cut off for a while. The two rooms left standing in the compound, which was never rebuilt, remained Arafat's prison for the rest of his life. People said afterwards that these conditions must have contributed to his death. Going to visit him in April 2004, I was shocked by the sight of the wreck of the building which housed the Palestinians' national leader, with the rubble around it and its sparsely guarded entrance, as if the army of followers that used to surround him had also deserted him.

By that time, the chorus of denunciations against Arafat that Israel had carefully orchestrated, was being faithfully relayed in the US and Europe. Undeterred by the fact of his physical isolation, the destruction of his PA infrastructure and police force, both of which rendered him impotent, they kept calling on him 'to act to stop terror' in tandem with Israel. Living in the West, I could detect the gradual change in tone and attitude towards Arafat as it approximated to the one Israel had instigated. Even the Palestinians were affected. All those with a grievance against him, personal or political, legitimate or not, picked up the prevailing hostile mood. Genuine dissatisfaction with his style of leadership found a focus in this hostility. The Arab states, several of which had cause to dislike or distrust Arafat for past misdemeanours, also joined the campaign to marginalise him. The *New York Times* reported on 9 May 2004 the king of Jordan's call to the Palestinian leader to consider 'if his presence helped the cause of his people', and Egypt's president wrote to Arafat in June of that year, threatening that if he did not delegate security responsibilities to his prime minister (Mahmoud Abbas), Egypt would be unable to protect him (against Israel).[8] To its discredit, the Arab League, meeting at the Beirut summit in March 2002, did not protest against the Israeli refusal to allow Arafat to attend. He was forced to participate through a live video link from his prison.

In the months just prior to his death his isolation was complete. To the accusations of terrorism, new charges were added and endlessly harped on: his undemocratic administration and the corruption of his officials. European politicians, however, still insisted on dealing only with him, despite Israeli displeasure, but not all. Even to his supporters he was a spent force, if only because, however unfairly, Israel and the US refused to deal with him, and the peace process was therefore paralysed. It was a situation that defies sanity: here was a legally elected Palestinian leader of unique stature amongst his own people,[9] with a proven track record of peacemaking unprecedented in Israeli–Palestinian relations, being made deliberately impotent so as to disable him from pursuing that process – by the very Israelis who never tired of proclaiming their longing for peace. The worst aspect of this was the way in which everyone else seemed to have forgotten how the situation arose in the first place, and behaved as if it were received wisdom. The *only* reason for Arafat's unlawful incarceration, denigration and 'irrelevance' was the calculated Israeli campaign to put him in that position. As we saw, this had proved so effective that, by the autumn of 2004, Israeli officials were openly talking of 'eliminating' Arafat or expelling him from the Palestinian territories. And indeed, in October of that year, he fell ill with a mysterious ailment that remains undiagnosed to this day, dying in a Paris hospital in November 2004, far from his homeland and under the shadow of a vilification which, whatever his faults (and they were not inconsiderable), was undeserved.[10] The humiliation of his final years, accepted with little demur from the international community, embodies to my mind the demeaning attitude to the whole Palestinian question, which has never quite gone from Western psychology or discourse.

What Did Israel Want?

The important issue in all this was not how defective or otherwise Yasser Arafat's leadership was, but what it was that Israel wanted from the Palestinians. The exaggerated emphasis placed on the competence and performance of their leadership, which started with Arafat and continued with his successor, was a deliberate diversion from the real issue: what was Israel's agenda? If it were to seek a genuine peace with the Palestinians, then Israel should have grasped with both hands the golden opportunity provided by the Oslo agreement. This should have been an offer Israel could not refuse. For this agreement, with all its imbalance and inequality for the Palestinians, could have led to Israel's acceptance and integration into the region, with all the dividends that would bring the Jewish state in social, economic and military terms. Here were the defeated Palestinians, accepting on trust, meagre terms they had always rejected before; not insisting on proper safeguards or taking expert advice (which meant they could be bamboozled into signing unfavourable agreements); not asking for a neutral guarantor who could have ensured Israel's compliance; and offering Israel, *as of right*, the title to the majority of their homeland – and all this in return for a small remnant of that land, and an implicit promise (since it was never written into the agreement), to be allowed in time to make it into an independent state. It was virtually certain that, on the back of this, Arab recognition would have soon followed, probably with a formula worked out for future peace agreements with Syria and Lebanon.

For the Jewish state, still in a formal state of war with the Arab states, excepting the two that had peace treaties with it, and facing a growing popular radicalisation in the Arab world, this breakthrough should have been viewed as a lifeline to ensure Israel's wellbeing in the region. (Writing twelve years later about the Saudi peace plan, the

Knesset member, Roman Bronfman, understood that Israel's future lay in regional integration and normalisation of relations with the Arabs, and could only come about with an end to the 1967 occupation.)[11] Israel's actual response to the Oslo breakthrough was dealt with in the previous chapter. A new, 'approved' Palestinian leadership in 2005 and a fresh international determination to help resolve the conflict should have induced a change of response. However, the evidence, up to the time of writing, showed that the old pattern was set to continue.

The Sharm al-Sheikh Agreement

This was the result of a meeting between Mahmoud Abbas and Ariel Sharon at Sharm al-Sheikh on 8 February 2005 in the presence of the Egyptian president and the Jordanian monarch. It aimed to re-activate the stalled Road Map, and was convened in an atmosphere of cautious optimism. It had been nearly one year since Israel announced its intention to withdraw from Gaza and remove the 21 settlements it had established there. This 'unilateral' step was warmly welcomed by the international community, which saw in it a courageous reversal of traditional Israeli policy and the beginning of the end of the conflict. A *New York Times* editorial of 24 February 2005 described it as a 'giant step' towards peace in the Middle East and 'Israel's bold initiative to bring security and peace to its people'. By proposing it, Ariel Sharon, hardline man of war, was transformed virtually overnight into a man of peace. His willingness to meet his Palestinian counterpart in an apparent spirit of compromise was interpreted as a reflection of this transformation. Both sides agreed to halt all acts of violence against the other forthwith. Abbas undertook to bring in strict controls of illegal arms ownership and the activities of militant groups, and Sharon offered the release of 900 political prisoners out of a total of 8,000 (later reduced to 400, who, as it happened, were due to be released shortly anyway). Israel was to redeploy from five of the eight West Bank cities and allow the return of 69 Palestinians whom it had expelled to Gaza and Europe in the wake of an attack on Bethlehem in 2002.

These were significant offers, but even so, the gulf between Sharon and Abbas remained wide. Sharon still put the onus on the Palestinians to control the violence first; Israel would not negotiate, he said, until Abbas had disarmed the militant groups and destroyed their infrastructure. In other words, little had changed from Arafat's time, but Egypt and Jordan immediately behaved as if it had. They agreed to despatch their ambassadors (who had been withdrawn at the start of the intifada in 2000) again to Tel Aviv, apparently under American pressure to do so as a gesture of goodwill.[12] Abbas took determined steps to show his commitment to fulfilling what was required of him. Early in his administration, he sought to distance from it many of the previous Arafat loyalists and those implicated in corruption scandals. At the same time, he endeavoured to bring in younger technocrats to push through an agenda of economic transparency and democratic reform. He wanted to adopt an approach which substituted political patronage in the appointment of ministers (as had happened under Arafat's rule) with expertise and efficiency.[13] He accorded priority to the control of violence and the imposition of the rule of law. Meeting with the militant groups in Cairo in March 2005, he was able to enlist their agreement to a ceasefire.[14] To ensure their adherence to it, Abbas ordered the use of force against anyone violating it, especially during the period of anticipated Israeli withdrawal from Gaza.[15] Significantly, the largest of the factions, Hamas, agreed to participate in local and legislative council elections and become integrated into the mainstream political system. Hundreds of fugitive fighters were co-opted into the security services or other institutions, as Abbas endeavoured to reform the chaotic security situation.[16]

He tried to streamline the 12 disparate security services he had inherited into three – no easy matter, since it meant trying to bring 58,000 men with separate allegiances to their own commanders under one authority. At the same time, he mounted a drive to end corruption in the security services. Unflinchingly (given the effect of such a thing on Palestinian society), the PA demolished a number of houses built illegally on public land on the Gaza beach front by security officials, and pensioned off more than 2,000 civil servants who had been too long in office. He ordered a massive crackdown on lawlessness in Gaza, banned the carrying of weapons in public, and called in all 'unlicensed' weapons, that is, those not accredited to the security services.[17] But he rejected Israel's demand to disarm the militants who were not licensed to carry weapons either.[18] Throughout this time, Abbas repeatedly called for a cessation to all forms of attack on Israeli targets, and was largely obeyed. His success has to be measured in terms of the difficulties of the task of dealing with an occupied people, fragmented into non-contiguous parts and without freedom of movement. The Palestinian infrastructure, including security institutions, that was necessary to implement the reforms effectively, had been largely demolished by Israel. And, most important of all, the line between armed resistance and terrorism was not clear-cut. Where did legitimate operations against an enemy that did not itself distinguish between the fighters and civilians amongst its victims end and terrorism begin? Were suicide bombings justified in the war between Israel and the Palestinians (which is what it was), or only some of them or none? This ambiguity led to much soul-searching amongst Palestinians and blanket condemnation by everyone else.

In trying to fulfil his part of the agreement with Israel, Abbas, although he cracked down on corruption and tried to control the security situation, did no more in essence than Arafat had done in the seven years before Israel discarded him. There is something brave and pathetic about these heroic Palestinian attempts to jump through the hoops set for them by Israel and its allies and yet achieve something meaningful for their people. How many tests would the Palestinians have to pass in order to qualify for a reasonable peace settlement? As the anecdote attributed to George Habash, the head of the PFLP, goes when he warned at the time of the 1993 Oslo Accords: 'They'll start off by wanting you to take off your jacket, but they'll have you taking off your trousers by the end.' Within a context of such powerlessness, the Palestinian contortions and concessions to achieve a settlement since then, seem either desperate or hopelessly naive.

Israel's Response

How did Israel fulfil its side of the Sharm al-Sheikh agreement? In brief, it did not, but on the contrary, it carried out a series of provocative acts, which seemed designed to frustrate the ceasefire and the other terms of the agreement. The prisoner release, hugely important for the Palestinians, remained at 400 and did not take place until June, when 398 men were let out. Sharon's invitation to an early follow-up meeting with Abbas, after the Sharm al-Sheikh agreement, was re-scheduled for June. Though Abbas's efforts at dealing with violence were acknowledged in Israeli circles, they were still not considered sufficient. A suicide bombing in Tel Aviv at the end of February reinforced this belief. Abbas had not disarmed the militants (who had fired home-made rockets at Israel from Gaza during early May), and so Israel refused to redeploy from five of the eight Palestinian cities, as it had promised.[19] The *Jerusalem Post* (13 April 2005) reported Sharon's statement during his meeting with President Bush in April 2005 that Abbas's failure to 'dismantle the terror organisations' was holding up progress on the Road Map – a real piece of irony since he had himself ignored it from the start. The Israeli policy of arbitrary arrests and assassination of militants continued. During April, 328 Palestinians were arrested in Israeli attacks and searches, adding to the total of 8,000 detainees already in jail. To cope with this high number, detention camps had to be converted into prisons. At the same time, and despite the period of supposed calm, Israeli forces carried out daily assaults on the Palestinians of the West Bank, Gaza and Jerusalem, as if there had been no agreement.[20]

By May 2005, 312 Israeli violations of the ceasefire had taken place.[21] Seven Palestinians were killed in this period, including two teenagers from the West Bank village of Beit Laqiya, shot on 4 May by the army as they demonstrated against the separation barrier. The village had seen much of its land destroyed by the building of the wall and held daily demonstrations and protests. Contrary to Israeli undertakings at the Sharm al-Sheikh summit, there was no easing of Palestinian hardship. The 680 barriers (checkpoints, roadblocks, metal gates, earth mounds and trenches) transecting the West Bank and Gaza and strangling Palestinian life, remained in place. (In fact, Israel removed 75 in deference to the agreement, but soon replaced them with new ones.)[22] Meanwhile, construction of the barrier wall went on unabated. By July 2005, the wall would surround Jerusalem and cut it off from the West Bank. It had already enclosed Tulkarm and Qalqilya in the north. In February 2005, shortly after the Sharm al-Sheikh meeting, the Israeli government approved the southward extension of its route. Some 237,000 Palestinians would be trapped between the wall and the Green Line and a further 160,000 on the other side would lose their land. Small adjustments of the wall's route, proferred by Israel in response to Palestinian concerns, would reduce this number by 340 persons only, but were cleverly presented to the West as convincing evidence of Israel's compliance with the law.[23]

Settlement expansion continued. At the end of 2004, the settler population was already 250,179 (excluding 180,000 in East Jerusalem) living in 160 settlements. Sharon announced that he had received American endorsement for his plan to retain most of them in three main blocs under Israeli sovereignty, and, he claimed, for their continued expansion.[24] Indeed, President Bush had agreed in April 2004 that it was not 'realistic' to ask for an Israeli withdrawal to the 1949 armistice lines, taking into account that the settlements had become in effect heavily populated towns.[25] As if encouraged, the Israeli government decided in March 2005 to expand the largest of these, Maale Adumim on the Jersualem-Jericho road, by an additional 3,500 housing units. This would have the effect of linking it directly to Jerusalem, cutting off the West Bank and destroying geographic continuity between its northern and southern halves. Most importantly, it would effectively terminate crucial Palestinian commercial, professional and social ties with Jerusalem and prevent its eastern part from forming the capital of the Palestinian state.[26] By the time the barrier around Jerusalem was built in July 2005, and a new government ruling requiring them to hold permits before they could enter or leave the Palestinian territories came into effect, the isolation of the 240,000 Arab Jerusalemites inside would be complete. Unchecked, these changes would lead to the destruction of Jerusalem Arab society.

In disregard of the Road Map requirement that the status of Jerusalem be left to the final status talks, the judaisation of the city intensified. The Israeli government was helping ultra-religious Jewish settler groups move into the Arab houses of the Old City and the Arab neighbourhoods, either purchasing them (usually through fraudulent means by using middlemen claiming the purchasers were Arabs) or forcibly occupying them, in greater numbers. They moved into the narrow lanes around the Jewish Quarter and in the vicinity of the Church of the Holy Sepulchre and by Herod's Gate, where a new Jewish development of 30 housing units and several synagogues was planned.[27] They were to be found in the heart of Sheikh Jarrah and Musrara, staunchly Arab areas that had hitherto withstood the settler onslaught. Building on a new Jewish 'neighbourhood' in Jabal al-Mukabbir (the site of the British high commissioner's residence under the Mandate), started in 2004 and also in the suburbs of al-Walajah and Ras al-Amud, all densely populated by Palestinians. Threats to destroy the Aqsa and

Dome of the Rock mosques on the Haram al-Sharif were ever more insistent. A motley group of ultra-religious groups, like the Temple Mount Faithful and the followers of Meir Kahane, had worked for years to 're-build' the Jewish Temple on the Haram. Ran Peretz, writing in *Maariv* (29 July 2004) asked why Muslims should be allowed to hold the Haram sacred while Jews were denied the right to build their Third Temple there. These were unquestionably serious threats and the Israeli authorities had mounted a guard over the site to prevent such an attack. That the Israeli police were hardly the best protectors of the Islamic places only added to Palestinian anxieties.[28]

The nearby village of Silwan, where the settlers had been seizing Arab houses for years, using some of the most obnoxious and aggressive tactics of any visited on the Arabs, was threatened with a demolition order of a further 88 houses, according to *Haaretz* (31 May 2005). Resulting in 1,000 residents becoming homeless, this was to be the largest demolition since 1967, whose purpose, the Jerusalem municipality alleged, was to 'restore it to its landscape of yore', when it was 'David's city' 5,000 years ago. In fact, the decision harked back to a 1977 municipal plan to clear the whole area around the Old City and replace it with parks 'without Palestinian residents'. One of the fanatical religious groups, Ateret Cohanim's aims was to create a 'Jerusalem shield' of Jewish neighbourhoods between the Old City and the Arab population.[29] With the proposed expansion of Maale Adumim and the completion of the barrier wall, Jerusalem would be totally encircled, its contours changed irrevocably, and Israel would have won the battle for the city that started with its conquest in 1967.[30]

Every visit to Jerusalem left me more depressed. Its Arab half was a forlorn place without vitality or centre. The few remaining Arab streets were dead by evening, like England on Sundays in the 1950s. The narrow lanes of the Old City, formerly clean and well cared for, were now dirty and littered. Many shops, whose business had been destroyed by high Israeli taxes and by Israeli guides diverting tourists to the Jewish areas with tales of Arab swindlers and cheating merchants, were closed or open for short periods only. Orthodox Jews in black coats and hats swaggered along the alleyways, as if they owned them, jostling Palestinian shoppers out of their way, protected by watchful Israeli soldiers. To my eyes they looked grossly incongruous in that Arab place, and the tension was palpable. I often wondered how the city's people could stand this intrusion, why they were so docile, how they could suppress the urge to lash out at these invaders. Perhaps it was this unexpressed anger that fuelled the increasing drug abuse amongst the Arabs of the Old City, so shocking and so alien to Palestinian experience. I used always to love Jerusalem, the place where I was born, but found I scarcely recognised it in the ugly, soulless and plundered place it had become.

Israel's policy of creating facts on the ground so as to establish its control over the geography of the West Bank, was in evidence elsewhere. Hebron, already damaged by the settler enclaves at its heart and the partition of the Ibrahimi Mosque into Muslim and Jewish halves, a desecration of what had been a single, harmonious sacred space, was to be further assaulted by the building of a barrier wall, which would cut off the Old City from the rest permanently. The army defended this defacement of the historic city by claiming it as the most effective way of preventing the intractable violence between the two sides. Had that been true, removing the settler enclaves would have been the best way to solve the problem. In reality, of course, partition would entrench the Jewish presence in the best part of Hebron, making it as Jewish as Jerusalem was made to be Jewish.[31] The widespread appropriation of sites sacred to Muslims elsewhere and reconsecrating them as 'Jewish' in an ostensible religious fervour – as for example, 'Rachel's tomb' outside Bethlehem with its hideous Israeli-built concrete enclosure, and 'Joseph's tomb' near Nablus – were acts of the same kind.[32]

US Collusion

By May 2005, the evidence that Israel was complying neither with the Sharm al-Sheikh agreement nor the Road Map was overwhelming. Egypt conveyed its concerns over this non-compliance to the members of the Quartet, urging them to support Mahmoud Abbas, who needed tangible results to show his people, or be brought down.[33] But as before in the history of the 'peace process', there was no one to enforce this compliance. Rather, the US and its allies acted as if they were in collusion. The primacy placed on a satisfactory Palestinian security performance and a demonstrable financial probity in any progress towards a peace agreement formed the basis of that collusion. The imposition of American CIA operatives, working with Israeli officers, to 'train' and monitor the Palestinian security services during the years following the Oslo Accords – in other words, controlling Palestinian resistance to occupation – had institutionalised this arrangement and made it legitimate. No public pronouncement by Western leaders omitted a knee-jerk reference to Palestinian 'terrorism', and the Quartet's closing statement at the London conference, convened in March 2005 to promote Palestinian 'reforms', urged the Palestinians to work for the prevention of terrorism.[34] US Secretary of State Condoleeza Rice, speaking at the same conference, called on the Arab states to help disband the 'terrorist infrastructure' and stop all funding to terrorists. It was no wonder that in this climate of opinion Israel could hold up progress to any agreement on the basis of alleged PA security breaches and non-compliance – and frequently did, citing US support for its position. These claims were never contradicted.[35]

The PA repeatedly warned that it would need tangible results to maintain its domestic credibility. The $200 million pledged by Bush in March 2005 to 'support Palestinian political, economic and security reforms', which could have helped, never materialised. As the *Washington Post* reported (5 May 2005), the US Congress voted to prevent any of it from directly reaching the PA; $50 million was allotted to Israel to build services at its checkpoints in the Palestinian territories, $2 million, set aside for health care, was to go to a US Zionist women's organisation; $5 million was to be used to scrutinise the PA's accounting procedures, and the rest would be funnelled through a variety of NGOs. A vice-president of the pro-Zionist American Enterprise Institute testified that the Palestinians 'were not ready to absorb a huge infusion of aid' and Congress must not 'throw money down a toilet'. Congress diverted an earlier US pledge of $20 million to the PA after Arafat's death in November 2004 towards paying off debts to Israel's electricity company. The American position was later amended at the Abbas–Bush meeting in Washington, on 27 May 2005, with an offer of a paltry $50,000 as a direct payment to the PA.

Undoubtedly, though, the US agreement in April 2004 to keep the West Bank settlements under Israeli sovereignty was the most serious example of its collusion with Israel. By effectively legitimising Israel's colonisation of Palestinian land, this reversed the decades-old US position on their illegality and contravened the international legal position. It also gave the green light to Israel's plan for the West Bank which was, as Sharon's close advisor, Dov Weisglass, disclosed in a *Haaretz* interview, on 8 October 2004, to freeze the peace process for decades following the Gaza withdrawal (see below), and give the West Bank over to Israel to settle permanently. To Palestinian consternation, Bush also agreed to an Israeli proposal of recognising a Palestinian state with temporary borders and creating 'a provisional authority' in Gaza.[36] The danger that Palestinians saw in this was that it might lead to Gaza becoming the future Palestinian state, a not unreasonable inference – shared also by many Israelis – that surely could not have eluded the US Administration.[37]

The mixed messages from Washington were confusing. On the one hand, this subservience to Israel's agenda and on the other, Bush's avowed support for a Palestinian state as a way of demonstrating that the US military adventures in the Middle East would have a positive outcome. The diplomatic respect he accorded to Mahmoud Abbas, so unlike his attitude to Arafat, however, was not matched by a single concrete action to reverse the reality on the ground. Meanwhile, the other members of the Quartet, also aware of these US–Israeli moves, colluded in their own way. Though the EU view remained that the settlements and other Israeli actions in the occupied territories were illegal, and was willing to provide large-scale funding for the PA, there was no action to oppose Israel's plans or US support for them. On the contrary, in April 2005 Sweden funded an extensive training programme for the members of Fateh, the main Palestinian organisation, in civic responsibilities and the 'culture of peace'. Perhaps this was an inevitable consequence of the dichotomy in the character of Fateh that the Oslo Accords had introduced: was it a revolutionary organisation or a political party? Nevertheless, Palestinians interpreted the Swedish project to be a move towards converting Fateh from a resistance organisation into a civil society institution and neuter its ability to oppose the occupation, with nothing in return from Israel.[38]

Israel's Agenda

As we saw, Ariel Sharon won international plaudits for announcing, in February 2004, that Israel would 'unilaterally' withdraw from Gaza and remove its 21 settlements there. Holding his ground in the face of stiff domestic opposition, including death threats from religious

Jewish extremists, only added to the approbation. The members of the Quartet, and to a lesser extent, the PA, welcomed the Israeli move. Western politicians took it at face value as a simple withdrawal from Palestinian territory, hopefully with more to come. On the back of this approval Sharon won a respite from international criticism over the building of the wall and his army's brutal tactics in the occupied territories, as well as US support for the retention and expansion of the West Bank settlements. Just as importantly, Israel, which had been ostracised by the Arab states for its treatment of the Palestinians since 2000, found itself on the way to being accepted by them. As previously noted in Chapter 1, there were many moves to bring Israel and the Arab states together. *Haaretz* (22 February 2005) reported that, according to the Israeli foreign ministry, ten Arab states were willing to establish full relations with Israel following its withdrawal from Gaza. The Spanish foreign minister, Miguel Moratinos, announced in March 2005 that Saudi Arabia was ready to establish diplomatic relations with the Jewish state.[39] Jordan's king meanwhile worked for a 'softening' of the 2002 Saudi peace plan to take into account Israel's 'fears' about the Arab states' hostile position towards it, as he said. *Al-Quds* (12 March 2005) reported Shimon Peres meeting in Madrid with Morocco's king (incidentally, the head of the Arab League's Jerusalem Committee, which is opposed to Israeli actions in the city), an unnamed senior Sudanese minister, and the Algerian president, whom Peres allegedly embraced warmly. Not coincidentally, Tunisia's invitation to Ariel Sharon to attend an international conference was issued in the same month, November 2005.

These were no mean achievements for something that had never happened before and might never do so. (Several commentators expressed doubts about Sharon's true intentions regarding withdrawal from Gaza because no arrangements were seen to be made by the Israelis to rehouse the Gaza settlers, but their suspicions proved wrong as the evacuations did take place in August 2005.)[40] Whatever everyone else saw in the disengagement plan, for Sharon the aim was clear: to sacrifice 7,500 settlers and an area 1.3 per cent of the size of pre-1948 Palestine, full of noxious, poverty-stricken Palestinians who were costly to control, for the sake of keeping the West Bank permanently. As his defence minister, Shaul Mofaz, put it on 12 May 2005 (BBC website), the pullout would enable Israel to maintain Jerusalem as its 'united capital', and the West Bank settlers would say in future that they had 'helped establish the eastern frontiers of the state of Israel'. To those who wanted to believe it, the 'unilateral' withdrawal seemed generous, but Israel, having trashed Gaza, with systematic destruction of its institutions, homes and physical environment (even Gaza's small zoo was bulldozed in May 2004), planned to leave a place that was incapable of independent life, its borders, airspace and sea outlets all under Israeli control.

The period between the announcement of the disengagement plan in February 2004 and the beginning of 2005 was the most destructive that Gaza had seen since the beginning of the intifada. (There was to be another ferocious assault on Gaza in the summer of 2006, with another wave of death and destruction.) The army killed 614 people, assassinated between 26 and 45 suspected militants (depending on the statistical source), and demolished 3,084 houses, leaving thousands homeless by the end of 2004; the total made homeless in Gaza since 2000 was 28,483 people.[41] A giant prison already inside a wall originally built in 1994 and fitted with cameras and electronic devices, Gaza would be encircled by a second electrified wall to be built before the Israeli evacuation. The Israeli army prepared a multi-pronged plan of surveillance and attack for the post-evacuation phase, and a water-filled trench was to be constructed along the length of the Gaza–Egyptian border – purportedly to prevent arms smuggling, but in reality making the Gazans' only route to the outside world impossible so as to keep its people penned in and subjugated.[42] As B'tselem noted in a report, published in March 2005, the Gazans' forced isolation separated families and even spouses from each other. The humanitarian situation would not improve after the disengagement, since Israel intended to relinquish its responsibility for Gaza under the Geneva Conventions (which was little noted in the rush of congratulations to Sharon over his initiative). The word 'withdrawal' was thus meaningless, since the Israeli army would be encamped just outside Gaza's borders, as before, ready to invade at any time.

Those who imagined that the Gaza withdrawal heralded the start of the end of Israeli settlement did not understand the history of Israel's colonisation of Palestine before and after 1967, how relentless and unstoppable it was, and how faithfully Ariel Sharon adhered to it. His disengagement plan, though possibly conceived in response to the ferocity of Palestinian resistance in Gaza as the Israeli analyst, Uzi Benziman, suggested in *Haaretz* (8 May 2005) and as the Palestinians strongly believed, fitted into his geo-strategic vision for the rest of the territories.[43] He spelled this out in interviews with the Israeli journalist, Aluf Benn (*Haaretz*, 26 April 2005). Facts on the ground were being created to delineate the final border on the West Bank: the Israeli-controlled settlement blocs would be territorially connected to each other and to the Jordan Valley. The Palestinian centres would be linked by a series of tunnels and bridges so as to make them appear contiguous. The disengagement in Gaza was meant to save the West Bank for Israel. To that end, he would put off talks with the Palestinians *sine die*, continue settlement-building and avoid dismantling any of them there. What this meant for the West Bank, as the Palestinian cartographer, Khalil Tufakji explained, was a 'Greater Jerusalem' on 10 per cent of the West Bank. This did not include the additional land taken up by the bypass roads and 'security areas'. A passageway connecting Tel Aviv with the Jordan Valley, taking up yet more land, would be set up thus cutting off the northern from the southern West Bank.[44]

Sharon's Vision

Sharon, like the early Zionist leader Vladimir Jabotinsky before him, believed that the solution to the Arab–Israeli conflict would only be possible when the Arabs accepted Zionism and recognised the 'Jewish right to a homeland', established as a Jewish state in the Land of Israel (including the West Bank, 'the cradle of the Jewish people'). Only brute force and maintaining superior military strength would bring this about.[45] To counter the Arab 'demographic threat', it was necessary to build the separation wall, which would shut out Arab population centres, and settle more Jews on the land. Sharon intended to settle a million immigrants from the former Soviet Union, France and 'poor' American Jews in the Arab-populated Galilee, Negev and Jerusalem. A Jewish majority was essential to the existence of the Jewish state, and it had to be preserved at all costs. The worst nightmare for Israelis would be to wake up one morning and find that 3.5 million Palestinians (from Gaza and the West Bank, excluding East Jerusalem) had been added to the Jewish state if 'Eretz Israel' were to be realised. Indeed, Sharon's majority support amongst the Israeli public was in part motivated by demographic anxiety. Israelis were becoming aware that keeping hold of the whole of 'Eretz Israel' was incompatible with preserving a Jewish majority.[46] The fear of losing this was always very real and certainly not fanciful, if population projections were true. In 2005, these predicted that by 2020, Jews would form a minority of 6.5 million people out of a total of 15.1 million in Israel/Palestine. The same fear had motivated Yitzhak Rabin who thought to contain the demographic threat by giving up territory to the Palestinians and keeping them separate. Sharon improved on this with his own formula for solving the problem. The Palestinians had to be removed, ideally by physical means, but since that had become impractical in the current political climate, it would be done by making them 'vanish' politically.[47] As the prominent Israeli sociologist, Baruch Kimmerling, describes it, this 'politicide' was a process of gradual military, political and psychological attrition whose aim was to destroy the Palestinians as an independent people with a coherent political and social existence.[48] They would be made to vanish by their fragmentation and irrelevance.

As we saw in the last chapter, the process was already under way with the Palestinians' marginalisation in all the peace negotiations and agreements of the last four decades. When, like the 'other man', they refused to go away, but rather reasserted their existence with the Oslo Accords, the Israeli effort focused on their dissolution by different means. For Sharon, Palestinians had always been of little account, except as a hindrance to the Zionist project. Since they were powerless, they could be manipulated and kicked around. His whole history attests to this attitude, from the raid he conducted on the village of Qibya in 1953, through the attacks his units carried out on the refugees of Gaza in the 1970s, the Sabra and Shatila massacre of more refugees in 1982 for which he was ultimately responsible, to the brutal repression of the Palestinians under occupation today.

The techniques used to drive Palestinians out or make them otherwise absent, were multifarious, even sadistically creative. One of the most important effects, if not the main purpose, of the closures, checkpoints and the entrapment behind and within the barrier wall was to cause such hardship as to propel people into leaving. Saree Makdisi describes the misery that the wall engendered in a vivid and moving account for the *London Review of Books* (3 March 2005). He cites the tragic case of Qalqilya, whose people, predominantly farmers who worked the fertile fields and orchards, but could no longer reach them, as I also noted on my later visit there, because of the wall enclosing their city like a vice, its gates too narrow to let farm vehicles through. Israel appropriated most of their land, and what was left lay untended and unwatered because they could not reach it. Using a Machiavellian device previously exploited by the British against the Palestinians during the Mandate, the Israeli authorities reactivated the old Ottoman laws regarding land ownership; land left uncultivated for a period of time (which Israel could specify) reverts to 'public ownership' (now translated as Israeli ownership). The fact that the land was uncultivated because farmers had been prevented from working on it by the restrictions imposed on their access to it was disregarded, and Israel appropriated it just the same. Here was a seemingly respectable legalistic nicety to deprive the Palestinians of their territory, one which would yield dividends as the closures tightened and the wall was completed.

Not only land but also farm animals suffered under this strangulation. In nearby Jayyous, farmers watched helplessly during the Christmas of 2004 as their sheep died, starved of food and water because the farmers were prevented from reaching them. Appeals to the Christian world to save the animals, reminding them of the season's peace-loving message, went unheeded. In the villages outside Hebron, Jewish settlers were reported to have poisoned Palestinian farming lands with chemical toxins in the spring of 2005, killing 20 sheep and damaging the farmers' livelihood in an attempt to drive them out. Amnesty International's call to the Israeli government to investigate the reports was ignored, despite the fact that nearly a year before the Israeli police had accused the settlers of poisoning water wells in the same area.[49] Other villagers were even worse off. Those who lived on land between the wall and the Green Line, which Israel declared a closed area, were required after 2003 to apply for 'residency permits' from the authorities to be allowed to stay there, as if they had been visitors or tourists. As with the Palestinians of Jerusalem, who became 'residents' after the Israeli occupation of 1967, this was another example of turning facts on their heads: the foreign settler becomes the native and the native the intruder.

The policy of causing grinding hardship began to succeed, and people were leaving. In such situations it is the more affluent and educated classes who tend to go first, and the Palestinian case was no different, only more serious because the loss of such people deprived Palestinian society of its potential leadership. Sharon hoped that those left behind would be a lumpen-protelariat rump, incapable of resisting. At the outbreak of the intifada, in October 2000, hundreds of Palestinians emigrated, aided by the Israeli foreign ministry and foreign embassies.[50] In June 2001, 150,000 more people left for Jordan and more would have followed but for the Jordanian authorities' closure of the border. Anecdotal evidence spoke of far greater numbers emigrating since then. It is certain that the burden of daily survival – coping with food shortages and blocked access to medical help and education, protecting one's family against shootings and arrests or getting shot – is incompatible with the growth of a strong, united and healthy society, able to fight against its oppression. The cruelty of this regime is not difficult to imagine, even without the host of vivid accounts that appeared from numerous official and personal sources, including Israeli ones.[51] The Israeli journalist, Amira Hass, wrote in *Haaretz* (9 March 2005):

> Just as Israel robbed the Israeli Arabs of their lands to give to Jews, and did the same in the West Bank with the common land, which became a synonym for Jewish settlement land, here it is seizing the land around the wall. The operation of [settlement] building, tree uprooting and destruction of water wells combines arrogance with contempt for non-Jews and the international position – in the context of a major policy, declared and undeclared, to seize the land.

Palestinian politicide intensified after the start of the intifada, though the ground had been well laid long before. The massive incursions and destruction that Israel unleashed on the territories from September 2000 onwards, and especially in March 2002 (Operation Defensive Shield), was a major part of this campaign. By April 2002, there was little left of the infrastructure the PA had built towards creating the putative state. The policy of targeted killings effectively destroyed the Palestinians' military and political leadership without which no organised resistance was possible. The Palestinian people were deliberately rendered alone and vulnerable, since no Arab state or international body intervened on their behalf. Even the UN mission to investigate the 2002 Jenin refugee camp massacre was aborted under US/Israeli pressure. And, as we saw, the other prong of Sharon's policy was also working well: to so lower Palestinian expectations as to bring them into line with his meagre vision for them.

Consequences for the Palestinians

The Palestinian position in 2005 was a world away from the aim of total liberation through revolution that Fateh proclaimed in 1965. A friend still has on his wall a plaque bearing the Fateh slogan in beautiful Arabic calligraphy: 'Palestine is ours to liberate! Revolution until Victory!' When I see it now it looks like a sad relic of a bygone age. Forty years of Israeli politicide had done its work on the Palestine question as a national cause. The Palestinians, already in an unenviable position of physical fragmentation after 1948, became politically fragmented with the Israeli occupation. Understandably, the priority for those under occupation was its termination, and as the noose of hardship that Israel had imposed tightened, even its relative amelioration by such measures as removing checkpoints, easing access from place to place, lessening the daily humiliations meted out by Israeli soldiers, was an urgent aim to be pursued no less eagerly. Israel, aware of this, would lift some of the restrictions from time to time as a 'concession' or a reward, and indeed, after some particular ordeal, it felt like that. By contrast, those in the camps and the diaspora still clung to the letter of UN resolutions and international law that underpinned the Palestinian case, increasingly out of step with this thinking. The overall effect was to divide the community, inevitably pitting one set of priories against the other, and to break up the national consensus.

By 2005, the PLO, which had previously linked those inside and outside Palestine in one national cause, was defunct. While it still maintained its offices in Tunis under the leadership of Arafat's longtime associate, Farouk Qaddumi (the head of Fateh and the PLO's political committee), it had become increasingly irrelevant after Arafat's departure for Palestine. Palestinians spoke of the PLO in the past tense and scarcely noticed that its remnants still existed. Splits appeared between Qaddumi and Mahmoud Abbas soon after the latter's election. These surfaced in March 2005 over the appointment of Palestinian diplomats, a task properly part of Qaddumi's brief as PLO foreign minister. Bypassing him, Abbas's newly appointed foreign minister, Nasser Qidwa, took over this function. A bitter public quarrel ensued, leaving Qaddumi (and the PLO with him) firmly marginalised.[52] Of course the Abbas–Qaddumi quarrel was about more than appointing diplomats. It was rather an indication of Abbas's desire to transform the Palestinian Legislative Council (PLC) into the PA with himself at its head, so as to position the Palestinian struggle under one authority. And that had to be inside Palestine and not anywhere else.

He saw the creation of an independent state as the overriding aim of the Palestinian movement. Like Arafat, he suborned all other considerations to it, and his efforts to 'reform' Palestinian governance, deal with corruption and enlist the co-operation of the militants so as to prevent them giving Israel a pretext to backtrack on the Road Map (in his view, the only route to the Palestinian state), were all designed towards that end. Until that happened, the PA would play the game by the rules set by the Western powers in return for their help in establishing the Palestinian state. In this Abbas was doing no more than following Arafat's policy. Like Arafat, he was creating facts on the ground – his insistence on the PA and not the PLO appointing Palestine's ambassadors, like any sovereign state, was a case in point. The series of top-level foreign visits he made as 'president of the Palestine state' in April and May 2005 was another. The existence of a parallel Palestinian organisation, the PLO, could only dilute this message and divert energy away from its fulfilment. The imperative to suspend violent resistance against Israel, because this would alienate Western support for the creation of the state and help Israel to delay its withdrawal indefinitely, was part of the same policy.

At first glance, this seemed a reasonable strategy. What it obscured was the price it had cost the Palestinian national cause already, and how much more would follow in future. Who would have guessed in 1948 when UNGA Resolution 194, affirming the right of the displaced Palestinians to return to their homes, was passed, that 58 years later this right would have become a potential bargaining chip to be sacrificed for a promise of an 'independent' entity on less than a fifth of the homeland? I remember the 1948 exodus, as we fled to Damascus, the disbelief of my family and the other displaced Palestinians when it looked as if we could not return home. People said: 'It can't happen! The UN, Britain, the world will not allow it! We will, we must be back soon.' And indeed, it seems inconceivable that something so natural and human as a people's wish to return to their country after a time of conflict would come to be seen as a threat to the Israelis and a luxury to the Palestinians that should be set aside in the interests of 'practicality' and 'realism'. Or who, in the anguish of losing Arab Jerusalem to the

Israelis in 1967, could imagine that Palestinians in 1995 would accept giving up most of it, to retain a foothold in a part of the Old City and a few outlying villages, given the name of 'Al-Quds' (Arabic for Jerusalem) as a fig leaf?[53]

These depredations in the Palestinian position did not happen spontaneously. Ever since 1948, when the international community recognised that Palestinian dispossession had to be addressed, Israel worked, with Western complicity, to frustrate this aim and to downgrade Palestinian national demands. It worked tirelessly to prevent any Palestinians returning and to render their right to do so a meaningless slogan. Regular reiteration of Resolution 194 at the UN (it was passed no less than 110 times in 50 years) became an empty formula which no one was prepared to implement or challenge Israel over. From its inception the PLO fought hard against this Israeli campaign, keeping hope alive in the refugee camps by recruiting refugees to the national struggle and giving them a sense of importance. The 1948 UN demand to return the refugees to their homes, and the PLO's aim of liberating the homeland to become a 'democratic state for Muslims, Christians and Jews' set a benchmark for the Palestinian position at the end of the 1960s. But within a few years the organisation recognised that, given the powerful forces ranged against the Palestinians, downward shifts in this position, though it was just and legal, were inevitable. By the nature of the power imbalance, these Palestinian shifts became new starting points for the next set of negotiations. The political realities of a powerful Israel and a weak Arab world led the PLO to announce, in 1974, that its aim was to liberate a part of the homeland. This was translated into what later became the struggle for a state on the post-1967 territories, with the rest of the land implicitly left to Israel. Throughout all this, however, the right of return remained sacrosanct.

But with the Oslo Accords of 1993, the Palestinian official discourse began to change. Arafat was convinced that it would take significant Palestinian concessions to produce any result from an all-powerful Israel. Accordingly, he agreed to put the refugee issue (along with Jerusalem) on the back burner until the 'final status' talks, and the unthinkable – that the right of return might become a bargaining chip in the negotiations with Israel – crept onto the political agenda. This chimed in well with Israel's own wishes but also with those of Europe and the US, who sought to find alternative solutions for solving the refugee issue, so long as none of them disturbed Israel.[54] The Palestinian leadership came to accept the idea that refugees could 'return' to the Palestinian state-to-be. However, they insisted that Israel take in a token number of returnees and acknowledge its responsibility for creating the problem. Even with this debasement of the previous PLO position, Arafat was not willing to concede further on the right of return, as Israel wished him to at the 2000 Camp David summit. By January 2001, however, his emissary accepted a small advance in the Israeli position on the issue at the Taba talks, that 25,000 refugees could return annually for three years as part of a family reunion scheme.[55] And the Abbas leadership looked as if it would continue along the same path, raising acute anxieties in the refugee camps and in the diaspora at large. An angry Israeli Arab journalist spoke for many Palestinians when, following rumours that Abbas was considering amending the right of return, he wrote:

> Abbas in this represents only himself. He may renounce his own right to return to his city, Safad. But he is not entitled to abolish anyone else's right. Unfortunately, in taking this position, Abbas has adopted the conventional American and Israeli position [aiming to] eradicate the great problem that the right of return poses for them.[56]

The Election of Hamas

At the beginning of 2006, Palestinian politics took a radical departure from the traditional Fateh path in the election of the Islamist party, Hamas. It looked for a while as if the capitulationist Fateh line we discussed above was to be overturned by a government that challenged the received wisdom of the previous leadership. To the dismay of the Quartet members, a Palestinian leadership appeared which rejected Israel's 'right to exist', refused to abandon violence, or abide by previous peace agreements. Their success at the polls was widely seen as an indictment of the previous Palestinian leadership's corruption and failure to secure any improvement in people's daily circumstances. But it was also a statement about the futility of Fateh's line with Israel based on endless compromise without tangible results, and the need to return to basics. With Hamas's election, the most fundamental issue of all, Israel's legitimacy, was open to question. As the senior *Haaretz* commentator, Uzi Benziman, pointed out on 14 June 2006, the radical camp in Israel believed that the roots of the conflict with the Palestinians lay in their essential rejection of Israel's right to exist.

The Hamas victory provoked a determined campaign by Israel, the US and its Quartet partners to topple the new government. This was in line with Israel's wishes but also because the West had designated Hamas a terrorist organisation (again in line with Israel), and was caught in a dilemma: having to recognise it as the Palestinian people's democratic choice but having to refrain from dealing with 'terrorists'. So the US and Europe decided to subject the Hamas-dominated Palestinian Authority to a financial and diplomatic blockade unless it recognised Israel, renounced violence and accepted previous Israeli–Palestinian agreements.[57] This was a godsend for Israel since it shifted the onus for the stalled peace process away from its own stalling and prevarication onto the Palestinians, and, as long as the latter failed to comply with the West's conditions, Israel was at liberty to proceed unilaterally on the grounds that it had 'no Palestinian partner'. Accordingly, it suspended all contact with the Palestinian government, gas and fuel supplies were temporarily halted and Israel refused, not for the first time, to transfer the monthly $50,000 tax and customs receipts which it collected on behalf of the PA.

Soon thereafter all Western aid stopped as well, in line with the Israeli position.[58] The suspension of aid, which had been running at an annual $1 billion since the beginning of the second intifada, deprived the 160,000 government employees of their salaries, impoverishing their million dependents and bringing basic services to a halt. In February 2006, the US secretary of state warned Iran and the Arab states not to come to the PA's rescue. Several European member states, including Britain, Norway and Holland, also froze their individual contributions to the PA. I remember asking a European Union diplomat posted in Jerusalem as the withdrawal of aid was beginning to bite, how he could justify this cruelty towards a population he knew to be militarily occupied and highly vulnerable. Without blinking, he said, 'We're not obliged to give money to people we don't like. And if the Palestinians don't want to accept our conditions, it's their lookout.'

The suspension of aid led, quite predictably, to a deepening humanitarian crisis in the Palestinian territories. By the spring of 2006, 78 per cent of the Gaza population had sunk below the poverty line with rapidly rising rates of child malnutrition. Child beggars, never seen before, were out on the streets in Gaza, the most severely affected. The number of poor people in the Palestinian territories increased from 1.309 million to 2.733 million (out of a total population of 3.5 million) within three months of the imposition of sanctions against the PA.[59] According to the World Food Program (WFP), poor Palestinian families with no money to buy food were living on bread and herbs. Children were rummaging through rubbish for their one meal of the day. In Gaza, Israel's ban on fishing beyond the ten nautical miles limit it had imposed, prevented Palestinian fishermen from reaching the larger fish, cutting off another food source.[60] After March 2006, fishermen were confined to the harbour and the beach, a severe blow to a crucially important Gaza industry (*Guardian*, 11 November 2006). The International Committee of the Red Cross (ICRC) warned, in June 2006, that unless aid to the Palestinians was fully resumed, there would be a 'major humanitarian emergency' and that humanitarian organisations could not replace the government as a service provider.[61] This self-evident truth failed to dissuade the Western donors who were busily seeking ways to bypass the government.

Since a Hamas-led PA had been declared unacceptable, the West's only alternative was to bring about 'regime change', a policy that the Bush Administration had introduced to Iraq with lethal results and wanted to apply to Iran, Lebanon and Syria. No Hamas government, or one in which Hamas participated, was acceptable. Even before the Palestinian elections, the US had already tried to manipulate the result by shoring up the Fateh opposition's campaign with money, advice and a USAID-funded campaign to beautify Ramallah's streets in a belated effort to convince voters of the benefits of electing a Fateh government. When Hamas won in spite of this and tried to put together a coalition by inviting independents and other parties to join its administration, these came under covert US pressure not to co-operate.[62] The Quartet's political and economic boycott of Hamas crippled the government further. Not only was direct aid suspended, but all banks in the Palestinian territories and elsewhere were prevented from dealing with the PA for fear of threatened international sanctions. That made it impossible for donations from non-Western sources like Iran, the Arab League or the Gulf states, all of which offered funds to make up part of the shortfall, to be utilised.

The US/Israeli objective of this economic and diplomatic blockade
was to ensure the fall of the Hamas government and its replacement
with one more accommodating (to Israel).[63] Though Israel's unilateralist
policy had benefited from the Hamas victory for a while, the time would
soon come when a different Palestinian leadership was needed to sign
up to a final agreement advantageous to Israel and bound to be rejected
by Hamas. On the assumption that the browbeaten, corrupted Fateh
party was a safer bet for this purpose, secret talks reportedly took place
between Israeli and Fateh representatives under US auspices shortly
after the Hamas victory to find ways of marginalising the organisation
and dealing only with Fateh officials.[64] Suddenly, the (Fateh) Palestinian
president, whom Israel had declared a non-peace partner and refused
to meet after February 2005, became everyone's darling, reinvented
as the alternative Palestinian government. Efforts were made to help
him create a shadow administration that would enable Western donors
to bypass the elected government. The US started to train Abbas's
presidential guard, aiming to create a parallel military force to that
of the Palestinian Authority. Within five months it increased from
2,500 men to 4,000 with a US-donated budget of $20 million.[65] The
Quartet members agreed in April and again in June 2006 to donate a
temporary emergency aid package for essential services and worked
on a complicated formula for ensuring that the funds would not find
their way to government coffers. Rather than take the shortest and
most direct route for the aid to reach its humanitarian destination,
that is, via the government, they expended time and effort, scratching
their heads over finding other, circuitous and less efficient ways of
doing the same thing.

This US-inspired dirty tricks campaign, with which the other
members of the Quartet were complicit, had been devised with one
aim in mind: to help Israel save the Zionist project. What other reason
could there have been for the deliberately induced human suffering to
which the Palestinians were subjected, or the devious plots to topple
their government? The election of Hamas had brought back, as we
saw, fundamental questions about the legitimacy of the Zionist state
and its conduct no one wanted to confront. Should the Palestinians, for
example, be forced to recognise Israel's right to statehood when it had
never recognised theirs? And within which borders did Israel wish to
be recognised, since it was occupying Syrian and Palestinian land and

had never itself set its final borders with them? Diplomacy normally required states merely to recognise each other's existence, not their *right* to it; so wasn't asking that of Palestinians anything more than 'rubbing their noses' in it, forcing them to sanction their own dispossession? This was all made worse by the fact that they were aware of Israel's cynical use of this pretext as a ploy to delay peace negotiations.

More uncomfortably still, a Hamas government threatened to disrupt the carefully nurtured Palestinian compliance with a peace process that favoured Israel. Unlike Fateh, which had left itself with no cards to play against Israel, here was a political party with a sort of bargaining position able to trade it off: recognition of Israel and renouncing its aim to build an Islamic state in return for recognition of Palestinian rights from Israel. With Hamas in power, the Oslo Accords were starting to unravel and set the peace process on a dangerous path into uncharted territory. What had been a comfortable arrangement for the West, busily assisting the Palestinians to build a fantasy state and feeling virtuous about it, looked as if it was about to end. The only way to reverse this undesirable situation the Quartet could think of was to bring back the previous Fateh leadership, discredited though it was, in order to resume its previous function of compliance.

By May 2006, there were worrying signs of civil strife in the Palestinian areas, fuelled by hunger and unemployment for which the government was held responsible.[66] Angry Fateh men, without jobs or salaries, clashed repeatedly with Hamas fighters particularly in the suffocating hothouse that was Gaza. Several Palestinians lost their lives in this internecine fighting; there were pickets, sit-ins and attacks on government buildings. As the economic blockade worsened and the frustration mounted, violent street demonstrations erupted in early October 2006 and became gun battles between rival militias which claimed the lives of more than a dozen people. Communication between the Hamas and Fateh leaderships broke down and some Fateh militants even threatened to assassinate Ismail Haniyeh, the Hamas prime minister.[67] Some of this unrest was undoubtedly due to the frustration of those who had benefited from the previous Fateh administration and who could not come to terms with their removal from the centre of power (such as it could ever be in a colonial situation). The Israeli occupation had spawned a class of Palestinians accustomed to a host of petty privileges like travel permits or VIP status at checkpoints, which the Israeli authorities accorded them in a bid to divide and rule. Fateh ministers became accustomed to presenting themselves to the world as members of a government, as if it were true. The large budgets which international donors offered the PA added to this Palestinian sense of false empowerment, since the donors never once challenged the occupation that made their donations necessary. Many Palestinian officials benefited from these arrangements, a few became wealthy, and they acquired an army of security men, assistants and hangers-on who also benefited.

Such relative privileges in a context of general privation were not easy to relinquish or share and their loss led to scheming and subversion among the Fateh people in order to bring down the Hamas government. In September 2006, the Fateh members of the Palestinian Legislative Council considered resigning *en masse* in order to force elections for a new government. Israel and the West meanwhile observed these moves silently, hoping to encourage them. Such provocations in a suffocating Palestinian environment of prison-like, poverty-stricken enclaves, awash with weapons, and with a breakdown of central authority were bound to lead to an explosion. The only surprising thing was that it did not happen sooner, a tribute to the capacity for peaceful reconciliation amongst Palestinians that had kept them off each other's throats for so many years. It looked as if the cumulative effect of so many assaults had begun to overwhelm this capacity. The resulting civil war was dangerous and a tragedy for the Palestinians' future, that, rather than overthrowing their real enemy, Israel, they would end up overthrowing each other. People said wistfully that had Arafat lived, things would never have reached this pass. He would have known how to control the disaffected militants.

But even without Arafat attempts were made to try and heal the divisions between the factions. During June 2006, a rapprochement between the Fateh and Hamas leaderships briefly brought the Palestinians back from the brink, with an agreement over key aspects of the so-called 'Prisoner's Charter'. Drawn up by Fateh and Hamas prisoners in Israeli jails earlier that month, it set out the principles of a peace settlement with Israel, which were in essence a restatement of the old PLO position on a Palestinian state in all of the 1967 territories with Arab Jerusalem as its capital, the right to resistance and the right of return for the refugees.[68] But before anything further could happen, the Israeli army had moved in to attack Gaza in a massive bombing and invasive campaign in response, Israel claimed, to the capture of an Israeli soldier by militants operating from Gaza. In fact and as usual, the Israeli reaction was wildly disproportionate, prolonged and hugely destructive.

Gaza

An already wretched place, impoverished and overcrowded, Gaza suffered more than any other part of the occupied territories under Israel's repeated assaults. In the five months from the end of June 2006, when Israel launched its attack on Gaza, over 350 Palestinians were killed, many of them children. The death toll mounted amongst the wounded, since, as Reuter reported on 12 November, Israel went on to prevent their entry into Egypt through the Rafah crossing for treatment; Gaza's pitifully under-equipped and overcrowded hospitals could not cope. In just six days at the beginning of November, 50 people lost their lives in the small town of Beit Hanoun in northern Gaza, and in one attack on 9 November that shocked international opinion, the Israeli army killed 18 people, nearly all members of one family.[69] A Security Council Resolution on 11 November condemning the Israeli action was immediately vetoed by the US. The Israeli army moved to re-occupy the north of the Gaza Strip, and Gaza City's only power plant was bombed, cutting off electricity to a million people, that is, the majority of the inhabitants. Intensive bombing destroyed Gaza's few bridges and most of its infrastructure.[70] At the same time the closure regime imposed on Gaza intensified, cutting off all goods, including food, from entering. This, coupled with the cut-off of aid from the international donors after March 2006, created the most appalling humanitarian situation, prompting the *Haaretz* columnist, Gideon Levy, to describe Gaza as a second Calcutta (3 September 2006).[71] The Ramallah-based Centre for Middle East Consulting estimated that by November, 79 per cent of Gazans had sunk below the poverty line, 51 per cent of them in extreme poverty (*Al-Quds*, 15 November 2006).

Dire though it was, Gaza's situation in the second half of 2006 was but an extension of Israel's repressive policy against the Strip, especially after the second intifada. Despite the Israeli evacuation in 2005, Gaza remained encaged within electrified fences, shut off from the rest of the

Palestinian territories, unable to trade and its people denied entry or exit. It was easier for the proverbial camel to pass through the eye of a needle than for a Gazan to gain entry into Israel. Hardly any of the PA representatives elected in 2006 were allowed to travel the 50 miles to join their colleagues in Ramallah, making a travesty of the business of government. Even the Rafah crossing into Egypt, the only one not officially controlled by Israel, was still restricted to Gaza residents, guarded by a joint Palestinian/Egyptian force and overseen by EU monitors who shared surveillance data with the Israelis. It remained closed for a majority of the time and Gaza became one of the most inaccessible places on earth, only visited by aid agencies, journalists and selected officials. When I saw Gaza as a UN employee on the eve of Israel's 'disengagement' in August 2005, the situation was already bad enough, run-down buildings, dirty beaches and a society mentally stagnating for lack of contact with the outside world.

Inevitably, the Gazans resisted these harsh Israeli measures with what means they had, firing primitive, homemade (Qassam) rockets at Israel's border areas. These did little physical damage, but provoked an overwhelming Israeli military response. Israel rained thousands of shells onto northern Gaza and killed scores of Palestinians. According to the UN Office for Coordination of Humanitarian Affairs (OCHA), in less than two weeks in June 2006, the Israeli army killed 32 Gazans, ten of whom were children, and wounded 91 through air strikes and artillery shells. It bombed and blocked off roads and demolished acres of agricultural land, not to speak of the psychological damage its constant bombing was inflicting on a population almost half of whom were under the age of 15. But, as the veteran Israeli columnist, Danny Rubinstein, observed in *Haaretz* (12 June 2006), this only served to escalate the conflict. The Gazans reacted by making more and better rockets that would target Israel with greater precision, and before long, he opined, they would transfer this know-how to the Palestinians of the West Bank, where everyone was just as determined to resist.

Capitulating to Israel and the West

In November 2006, the Palestinian prime minister, Ismail Haniyeh, under tremendous pressure to accede to the wishes of the 'international community' (Israel and the Quartet) and accept their terms or be replaced b a new government, offered to stand down. This was because he placed the welfare of the people above his own position, that if the choice were between Haniyeh and lifting the blockade of the Palestinians then he would make that sacrifice (*Al-Quds*, 11 November 2006). His decision was the result of weeks of negotiation with Abbas and Fateh, forced on him by the incipient civil war, the widespread labour strikes, paralysis of public life and the growing and intolerable hardship that the Palestinians were suffering. A triumvirate of Arab states, Egypt, Jordan and Saudi Arabia, anxious (after Hizbullah's success in the 2006 Lebanon war) not to be seen supporting 'extremists', also urged Hamas to 'co-operate'. At the same time, Western machinations were also at work to help bring about the same result. In October 2006, secret meetings took place in London between British and Hamas officials to establish a channel of dialogue with 'moderate' Hamas elements. Some US figures previously involved in the Oslo process were included.

It was agreed that a 'national unity government' would be set up to replace the one elected at the beginning of the year and would be composed of politically neutral technocrats so as to quell the unrest and end the rivalry between the factions. Haniyeh insisted, however, on reciprocal Israeli moves in repaying the $50 million monthly tax revenues owing to the PA, and releasing Palestinian female and child prisoners. A new government would be set up, but in return for the lifting of international sanctions against the Palestinians. A new prime minister was found in the shape of a Gaza academic and a number of ministers representing Fateh and Hamas, as well as other Palestinian groups, were named. With a Fateh foreign minister appointed to the new government, the conditions imposed by Israel and the Quartet to recognise Israel's 'right to exist', abide by previous agreements and renounce violence, were likely to be fulfilled. (Despite this, it is worth noting that Israel and the USA immediately declared they would not deal with any Palestinian government that included Hamas members.) Haniyeh's defiant words notwithstanding, few were in doubt that they signified a defeat for the Hamas administration and a climb-down before Western pressure. The truth was, as Akiva Eldar argued in *Haaretz* (18 September 2006), it had been the reality on the ground (of sanctions and starvation), not politics, that had forced Hamas to swallow a political line as palatable to it as 'eating pork in Ramadan'. An editorial in *Al-Quds* on 15 September 2006, succinctly entitled

'Salaries in return for recognition', saw Hamas's agreement to a national unity government as a sign that the 'US/Israeli/Arab starvation plan' had started to deliver results. Indeed, no other conclusion was possible, and once again the Palestinians had succumbed to Israel and its sponsors' artful manipulation. What it would lead to was nothing more than a replay of the defunct Oslo process whose failure had led to the second intifada. But so alluring to Palestinians was the dream of statehood still that its pursuit justified almost any sacrifice.

Who Was to Blame?

The impetus to bargain away Palestinian fundamental rights, though they were unassailably enshrined in law and common humanity, was the logical consequence of a Palestinian fear of total annihilation by Israel. It was a despairing strategy to salvage something from which to regenerate the remnants of Palestine, even though the price was high. Without this sacrifice, it seemed to Arafat and his successors that Israel would finish what it had started in 1948: the destruction of the Palestinian people, the loss of the land that remained to them and possibly their expulsion. It was a case of saving what you could while the going was good – meaning, while the US and Europe supported the Palestinian case, including the creation of an independent state, and while Israel was prepared to negotiate. That matters should have come to this pass, of a people forced to de-legitimise their own national cause, renounce their legal rights and recognise the theft of their land by others as legally and morally acceptable (implied in their recognition of Zionism), was the result of several factors.

In the first instance was a determined Israeli policy to eradicate the Palestinians as a people with a legitimate national cause. The Palestinians never posed any physical threat to Israel. It was rather the fact of their moral power to invalidate Israel's claim to the same status – that of a legitimate nation in its own land – by their very existence as living witnesses to their own disinheritance. The near hysterical Israeli reaction to any mention of a refugee return to Israel is motivated by this fear. So long as their cause survived, a question mark would hang over the legitimacy of the Jewish state. Who would have imagined, with all of Israel's power and the strength of its support, that by the time of the second intifada, questions about its right to exist would be raised and that the old idea of a single state for Israelis and Palestinians (of which more later) would resurface? It was no wonder that Sharon was keen to ensure the Palestinians' total political annihilation while he was in office. Like the devoted servant of Zionism that he was, he understood that the future of the Jewish state needed a land 'cleansed' of Arabs, if not physically (though that was never to be ruled out), then in every other meaningful sense.[72]

There is no doubt that, in the second instance, Palestinian ineptitude and lack of leadership contributed to this depredation in Palestinian fortunes. For Arafat to have concluded that there was no alternative than to surrender to Israel's demands (though not all, as we saw), was a mistake. Palestinians had no formal power, it was true, but they had a negative power: to say 'no' to Israel's conditions at the Oslo talks and subsequently. The failure to exploit the fact that Israel would never have negotiated in 1993 had it not needed to – and it was that that gave the Palestinian veto its power – was a cardinal error. When the Oslo process (inevitably) broke down, the option of withdrawal from the process and mounting an effective resistance to occupation was the obvious alternative to a strategy of progressive capitulation to Israel's impossible conditions. By the time Arafat realised this in the second intifada, it was too late and too much had been ceded to Israel. Social breakdown and anarchic behaviour in the Palestinian territories had set in, making a cohesive resistance movement under one leadership difficult. The top cadres of Fateh and Hamas had been wiped out through treachery, a phenomenon bred by long-running, brutal occupations. As the Israeli secret service, the Shabak, freely admitted, these assassinations could not have happened without the help of Palestinian agents.[73] (Indeed, Israel strongly objected to the Abbas government's decision in May 2005 to execute the offenders, reviled by Palestinian society as traitors, because collaborators were important to Israeli security.)[74]

There is a whole story to be told about the mistakes, naivety and sheer folly of Palestinian conduct, not to speak of the ineptitude, self-absorption and timidity of the Arab governments – all of which played their deadly part in this tragedy. Even then, could the Palestinians' failure to defend themselves adequately against Israel have justified what was done to them? Where is it written that stupidity was a crime, deserving of punishment? Though not stupid, nevertheless, the

Palestinians had been required in the short space of 50 years or so to transform themselves from peasants and refugees into a modern people able to hold their own against the sophisticated challenges of dealing with Israel and its supporters. That they faltered and failed in various ways should not have been surprising. On the contrary, the only surprise was that they had come so far. Israelis saw it differently. At the Hebrew University in Jerusalem just before the outbreak of the second intifada, several Israeli academics told me that Israel had no apology to make for the refugee problem: 'You people were offered a state of your own under the UN partition plan [of 1947]. You turned it down; you and the Arabs then attacked us. So we had no choice but to defend ourselves. And people became refugees, as always happens in wars.' When I objected, 'Even if that were true, why didn't you let them come back?' they shrugged. 'Tough. That's what happens in the real world. You miss your chance, so you take the consequences.'

The most important cause of Palestinian degradation and near destruction, however, was the ceaseless support and indulgence showered on the Jewish state by the US and Europe since its inception and before. A reassessment of this misguided policy and of where the Zionist project could lead was possible at several junctures in the history of the conflict over the last 60 years. But no one bothered, since the action needed to rectify the problem involved some hard questions about the nature of what had been created in the Middle East and a reversal of Western policy towards the Jewish state. Thanks to this negligence, by 2006, Israel had succeeded in changing the occupied territories beyond recognition. It had colonised and cantonised them, erecting an impenetrable barrier wall to enclose and shut out these cantons – where there was no wall, as in Nablus, there was an electrified barbed wire fence instead and just as effective – and creating a series of ghettos inside which Palestinians festered, incapable of leading a normal life. Each community was separated from the other and scarcely anyone could visit Jerusalem any more. Moving about 'illegally' through tortuous unasphalted roads and tracks, the only alternative to being in a perpetual prison, took hours and carried considerable risks of discovery by Israeli checkpoints and patrols.

Generations of traumatised, uneducated and disturbed children who would be a long-term burden, were growing up, thanks to these conditions. In 2005, 55 per cent of Gaza's children were found to be suffering from acute post-traumatic stress disorder, and a sizeable proportion of them spoke of wanting to die because life offered them nothing. The effects on Palestinian adults were not much better.[75] Moreover, Israel's 'matrix of occupation', as Jeff Halper called it,[76] had wrought profound economic devastation. At the end of 2004, 65 per cent of the people of Gaza were below the poverty line (78 per cent in 2006) and unemployment ran at 35 per cent. The West Bank situation was only slightly better. The International Labour Organisation report in May 2005 estimated an overall unemployment rate of 50 per cent (in the age group 15–24 it was 40 per cent), with 50 per cent living in poverty.[77] A year later the UN Conference on Trade and Development (UNCTAD) assessed the Palestinian economy to be 'on the verge of collapse' (Dow Jones Newswires, 12 September 2006). By 2008, Israel plans to stop all Palestinians from working in the country, *Haaretz* reported (8 March 2005). Since the Israeli occupation had previously severely limited all forms of employment for Palestinians other than in Israel – all Nablus's industries were smashed in 2004 and the agricultural sector had shrunk due to the closures, blocks on exports of produce and the loss of land – these figures could be expected to double. Palestinians would then be forced to seek work through the only outlets they had left – to Egypt and to Jordan – countries with already stressed economies.

Meanwhile Israel's dumping of nuclear and other waste resulted in damage to the Palestinian environment, with unforeseen long-term consequences. *Al-Quds,* quoting several news agencies, reported on 6 July 2004 that nuclear waste from the Dimona nuclear reactor in the Negev was being buried at sites in the villages south of Hebron, polluting the mountain water aquifer, one of the largest in the West Bank. Not surprisingly, medical reports indicated that the number of new cancer cases amongst the people of the villages and the Negev had increased by 50 per cent, with sterility rates of 62 per cent recorded amongst men and women.[78] Israeli household refuse tipped into the area outside Nablus, including effluent from the nearby settlement of Bracha, had entered the water supply and was causing a burden of ill-health amongst villagers. *Al-Quds* (31 May 2005) cited Oxfam and Palestinian medical reports of a massive increase in cases of jaundice and amoebic dysentery. Using polluted water for agriculture in the area had also affected milk and cattle meat. The Palestinian environment was fragile enough as it was, with Palestinian rubbish tips all over the West Bank, since Israel did not allow modern waste disposal units to be built.[79]

Israeli trucks were shunting sand, clay and rocks on a daily basis out of Gaza and filling the space left with industrial waste.[80] A huge dump on the Palestinian side of the Green Line near the Kedumim settlement was to be set aside to receive tens of thousands of such waste.[81] In February 2005, 15,000 cubic metres of Israeli sewage were poured into the Gaza valley, polluting the offshore waters and poisoning the fish. At the Rafah crossing in Gaza, Israel set up an X-ray examination facility in May 2005, dubbed by Palestinians, 'the room of death', where travellers were routinely subjected to whole body X-ray examinations. Neither pregnant women nor children were exempted.[82] The quantity of radiation absorbed in this way would have far exceeded the limits allowed by the WHO and the IAEA, and the long-term effects of this practice can only be guessed at. For years, Palestinians had accused Israel of trying to poison them in a variety of ways, aiming to cause infertility or death with chemical and biological agents.[83] Whatever the truth of these allegations, it was impossible to doubt the deleterious multiple effects of poverty, malnutrition, environmental toxicity and lack of medical care on the health of the Palestinian population that the Israeli occupation had caused.

Ignorance or Cynicism?

Nothing presented in the foregoing account was new, mysterious or hidden. The information was all in the public domain, available to anyone who cared to look, and often exposed to public view through the media. How much better known it must have been to the myriad experts and specialists of the American and European governments. Israel never concealed (or halted) its colonisation programme of the Palestinian territories. It relentlessly judaised Jerusalem before the public eye, brazenly appropriating it as its capital and vociferously wearing down opposition to this illegal move. It succeeded in broad daylight in parcelling up the Palestinian territories into separate enclaves without physical means of connection. For decades it openly changed facts on the ground, as if there had been no international law and no peace process. The results could be clearly seen on the numerous published maps of the occupied territories, which showed a grid of Israeli settlements, bypass roads and the barrier wall that broke up the territory into a jigsaw of Israeli and Palestinian pieces. At the same time, Israeli human rights abuses against the Palestinians were shown on television, reported on by journalists, documented by human rights organisations, and observed by foreign diplomats, church and international groups, and a host of visitors.

Ariel Sharon's agenda before he was struck down by illness at the end of 2005 was plain to see. His and his close advisors' candid utterances about their plans were a matter of public knowledge. There should have been no surprises at a product of hardline Zionism like his, although it did not differ in essence from those of his more 'moderate' Zionist predecessors or that of his successor. Before leaving office, he fully intended to solve the problem of 'the other man' that the rabbis of Vienna had spotted more than a century before, by ensuring that the Palestinians were dealt with once and for all. The way to do that was to bring them to their knees and then force them into accepting 'peace' on his terms. That meant putting an end to their resistance and ensuring they had no political presence, and preferably no presence at all, in 'the land of Israel'.[84] An independent and viable Palestinian state was manifestly incompatible with these aims. So he developed and expanded the policy he had inherited of dividing up and fragmenting Palestinian land and robbing it of the bulk of its natural resources, making the creation of a state on any part of it an impossibility.

If a man from Mars had dropped down onto the West Bank in this situation, he would have understood Israel's strategy at once and drawn the obvious conclusion from it: that there was no possibility of the chequered landscape he saw becoming one contiguous state for anyone. Yet, the official Western discourse was that it was possible and would happen. Western powers persisted in speaking of a Road Map towards the creation of an 'independent, viable and contiguous' Palestinian state and went through the motions of trying to help create it. A host of academics, analysts and think tanks followed suit. A study by the prestigious American think tank, the Rand Corporation, published in May 2005, showed how a viable Palestinian state would look in 2015 with an ingenious plan of linking roads and a rail network, water conduits and power lines.[85] One could almost be persuaded that they were all being truthful, rather like the emperor's new clothes in Hans

Christian Andersen's story: two crooked tailors convince the emperor
and his people that they can make him a special suit, which only those
possessed of high intelligence, will be able to see. As he parades naked
before the populace wearing his new 'suit', everyone goes along with
the deception, affecting to see something that isn't there for fear of
being thought stupid. And it was rather the same with the Palestinian
state. The evidence of one's senses ruled out such a possibility, but
everyone pretended otherwise.

It was not credible that Western government officials and analysts did
not know the facts reviewed above. So, what was going on? Why did
they persist in the charade of making empty pledges to the Palestinians
about something they knew could not happen in the conditions as
given? While knowing that neither the American president nor a single
European leader was prepared to face Israel down or bring the slightest
pressure on it to co-operate? Was it some kind of cynical game to pacify
Arab and Muslim opinion and maintain a liberal peace-loving façade
for their own electorates? I recall a visit to the British foreign minister,
Baroness Symons, as part of a delegation in the summer of 2004 after
her return from a tour of the occupied territories. She spoke eloquently
about the human effects of the barrier wall on the Palestinians and of
the need to alleviate the suffering. When I asked what the government
was doing to stop the further building of the wall that was causing all
this suffering, she paused and then said, 'We leave that sort of thing
to the Americans.' When I persisted, 'But you know that they are
hamstrung by their domestic constituency and can't do anything', she
shrugged, and it was left at that.

If the West was playing a game, then it was a deadly one, played
at the expense of Palestinian lives and the stability and security of a
whole region. Indulging Israel's adventurism and greed had led to this
pass. Continuing the practice would be an act of callous indifference
and unforgivable irresponsibility. Whatever the explanation for
Western behaviour, by 2006, the charade had gone on long enough.
The Palestinians and the rest of the Arabs were entitled to know if the
West was serious about a proper settlement to the conflict, or if it was
playing games. If the former, then it would have to take the necessary
steps to bring that settlement about. If there was any possibility that it
was the latter, then the Palestinians would have to withdraw their co-
operation from a peace process set up on such terms. For far too long,

as it was, they had allowed themselves to be used as pawns in a game played for other people's convenience – Zionists fulfilling their dreams, Europeans expiating their post-Nazi guilt, Americans implementing their strategic aims and expressing their evangelical fervour, and Arab regimes legitimating their existence to their populations. Had the Palestinians appreciated their own strength – as potential destabilisers in an important region, as global icon for millions of oppressed people, as the key to defusing anti-Western Islamic rebellion and as the lynchpin of a peaceful resolution of the Arab–Israeli conflict – they would not have become so subservient to Israeli/Western designs.

This tragedy of errors was summed up for me in the conference, which the British government organised in London on 1 March 2005. The meeting was supposed to help the Palestinians practise good governance and financial probity, as if these were the real sources of the conflict. Israel, the arch cause of the problem, stayed away, like a disdainful schoolmaster waiting to hear better reports on badly behaved pupils. Listening to Tony Blair's and his ministers' unctuous homilies to the Palestinian president and watching their show of jocular friendliness towards him and his team, I was forcibly reminded of Britain's primal role in the creation of the Palestinian tragedy. The passage of nearly 87 years since the Balfour Declaration that helped the Zionists create a state at huge Palestinian expense had apparently changed nothing for Britain's establishment. Palestinians were still people to be patronised and pushed around. It saddened me to see Mahmoud Abbas and his colleagues meekly accepting their role, still intent, as it seemed, on pursuing the chimera of promised statehood. How many more 'compromises' would they be required to make in return for it? Was the economic blackmail the West had subjected the Palestinians to in 2006 to force them to remove their elected government the last act in this ignoble history of Western manipulation? And even then, with a Western world intent on keeping Israel happy, what sort of settlement could emerge from such a basis? And if the ongoing sham pretence of a 'peace process' were thrown aside, what would be the parameters of a durable and just settlement – not just a short-term political fix, which was all that was ever on offer? It is with these questions that the final part of this book is concerned.

6
Solving the Problem

There was a view prevalent in the West, especially amongst Zionist commentators, that the Israeli–Palestinian conflict was very complicated. Such people were fond of shaking their heads and saying that the dispute was impossible to understand because of history, the two sides' differing narratives, the mystical attachment to land, the Bible, the Holocaust, strong emotions, the Middle Eastern temperament and a host of other things thrown like so much dust in the eyes. Views predicated on this premise served not only to obscure the real situation but also forced on one the conclusion that the solution to such a problem was bound to be no less complex and probably impossible to define, let alone achieve. In reality, nothing was further from the truth. The issue was in essence quite simple: a European settler movement that ineluctably displaced an indigenous population and wilfully denied its basic rights, inevitably provoking resistance and incessant strife. The obvious way to end that strife was to redress the injustice done to the indigenous people as far as practically possible, and find a reasonable accommodation of the needs and rights of everyone involved. The parameters of such a solution were clear, and the only difficulty was how to implement them, not because of their complexity, but because of Israel's obdurate clinging to its settler, colonialist ideology, Zionism, and the Western support that allowed or even encouraged it to do so.

This chapter is concerned with the question of what constitutes that durable and just settlement between Palestinians and Israelis, irrespective of how attainable it was at the time of writing. The fact that something is right or wrong is independent of what can be done about it. There were in 2006 other proposed solutions more linked to political expediency and the reality of power than justice, and for that reason they seemed more possible to realise. But historical events were moving at so rapid a pace as to make such solutions either quickly redundant or in need of constant revision. Not the least significant events were the exit of Ariel Sharon from the Israeli political scene and his replacement with the weak and lacklustre Ehud Olmert, the rise of Hamas to the Palestinian leadership and changes in the wider region. The twists and turns in peace proposals that these events necessitated and the sometimes desperate lengths to which Israel and its Western backers went to preserve a status quo in keeping with their own agenda are illustrations of the triumph of hope over experience. The proper and durable solution to the conflict was obvious, but the major players, Israel and the West, preferred to inflict more bloodshed and greater pain in the pursuit of makeshift, short-term fixes rather than face it. There was no better illustration of this policy than the West's strong reaction to the rise to power of the Palestinian Islamist group, Hamas, as we saw in the previous chapter.

Israeli Ideas for a Solution

Israel had no new ideas for solving the conflict, only reworkings of the old Zionist formula for maintaining a Jewish state, that is, one with a Jewish majority. In over half a century it never managed to resolve its original dilemma with 'the other man', set out at the beginning of this book. Its attempts at obliterating the Palestinians in myriad ways – from their original dispersion to the denial of their history and existence, to their political marginalisation, to their imprisonment in ghettos – had failed to eradicate them as a physical and political reality. Yet the Israeli fantasy persisted that it was still possible to pursue a policy against the Palestinians that would make the problem go away. This can be summed up as a 'more of the same' strategy: nullifying Palestinian resistance by overwhelming force, forcibly confining the Palestinians in small, isolated enclaves so as to prevent their forming any sort of meaningful state, strangling their economy and society and so pushing them to emigrate (to Jordan or anywhere else, as long as it was outside what Israel considered to be its borders), and ignoring the rest – the refugees in camps, the other dislocated Palestinians, and those treated as unequal citizens of Israel. The difficulties of managing such scattered Palestinian groupings so as to ensure that none of them bothered Israel would have been a daunting prospect for anyone. But it seemed not to have deterred successive Israeli leaders from trying to make it happen.

The alternative, accepting the Palestinian presence as a reality that had to be addressed through genuine negotiations and a mutually agreed settlement, was not one that Israel apparently wanted to contemplate. The desire on the part of ordinary Israelis for 'peace' was widespread after the Oslo Accords, but it was not accompanied by an acceptance (or even an understanding) of the requirements that such a peace would demand from them. The majority accepted the need for Palestinians to have their state, but this was out of a desire to separate from them,[1] and most were unclear about the Palestinian state's exact geography and unprepared to relinquish land they had come to regard as theirs. In fact, as the Israeli commentator Gideon Levy pointed out in *Haaretz* (19 March 2006), had Israelis seriously supported the creation of a Palestinian state, they would soon have realised that it was not compatible with the carve-up of the West Bank they and their government contemplated. He identified this situation as 'Israel's national disease, to have their cake and eat it'. Israel's leaders paid lip service to the Palestinian state proposal, but secretly feared that the international community (including the USA), which had accepted the Palestinian demand for nationhood, might put pressure on the Jewish state to co-operate. The problem would then be how to accommodate Palestinian ambitions (and rights) in a way that did not impinge on Israel's own demands for land and security.

Reconciling these opposites had been a central preoccupation of all Israeli leaders ever since the acquisition of the 1967 territories and the emergence of the two-state proposition. This envisaged the creation of a Palestinian state on those territories, an idea Israel was able to ignore for decades, but which over time gathered such inexorable momentum as to make it impossible to reverse. Moreover, by its relentless policy of settling Jews in the Palestinian territories (more than 200 settlements dotted all over the West Bank, East Jerusalem and, until 21 August 2005, in Gaza), Israel was helping to bring about a situation it desired even less, the inextricable mixing of the two peoples. Rather than give up the settlements, the Israeli imperative became to remove those Palestinians caught in their way. By 2005, the demography issue had become an overt, publicly debated search for ways to clear Palestinians out of 'Jewish' land. Sharon (and most Israelis) was desperate to consolidate a Jewish majority, even if in a smaller Israel and even though it would entail the surrender of some of the land that he and most Israelis considered rightfully theirs (although one must not exaggerate the extent of the Israeli 'sacrifice' in settling for a smaller state; it would still leave Israel in possession of the best West Bank territory, discarding only the unwanted remnants).

These sentiments, openly discussed by Israeli politicians and leading figures, were regarded uncritically in the West as legitimate fears, as if it were acceptable for a nation to define itself exclusively by reference to ethnicity or religion and seek to exclude those who did not qualify on those counts. It was such ideas of course that had led to the expulsion of the non-Jewish (Palestinian) population from the country in the first place, and which continued to fuel the impetus to expel more. A particularly extreme example of this desire were the ultra-religious settlers, who claimed the whole land between the Euphrates in Syria and the Mediterranean Sea as Jewish, and cheerfully called for the eviction of some 40 million Arabs from it.[2] When secular politicians such as Avigdor Lieberman of the right-wing Yisrael Beitenu party called, in 2006, for the relocation of Israeli Arab citizens outside the borders of the state, offering them bribes to leave, or Shimon Peres, the Israeli 'elder statesman', proclaimed that Jerusalem could not be 'the capital of the Jewish people' while it contained 240,000 Arab inhabitants, or when the Israeli High Court passed a law, in 2002, prohibiting married couples from cohabiting in Israel if one of the spouses was a Palestinian from outside,[3] they were expressing a widely held social consensus in Israel.

This sought to segregate the Arabs of the West Bank and Gaza inside their own areas, and evict as many as possible of those who were citizens of the state. Opinion polls in 2006 showed a majority of Israeli Jews in favour of government-backed programmes to encourage these Arab citizens of Israel to emigrate; at the same time, only a small minority thought that relations between Jewish and Arab Israelis were 'stable'.[4] A 'land swap' was also proposed to persuade Israeli Arabs to leave; Arab localities in Israel like Umm al-Fahm or the area known as the Triangle could be added to the West Bank in exchange for the annexation of Jewish settlements to Israel. That such proposals found acceptance in Israeli society is indicated by the popularity of Lieberman's party which proposed it and came fifth in the elections.[5] Lieberman himself was appointed deputy prime minister in October 2006, as if to reward him for his views. These Israeli attitudes clearly reflected a combination of the anti-Arab racism that was an inevitable concomitant of Zionism and a feature of the Jewish state from the beginning, and the more recent Israeli fear of 'terrorism', for which the mass disappearance of Arabs was seen as the only remedy. The election in early 2006 of a new Palestinian government dominated by the Islamist party, Hamas, which Israelis viewed as terrorist, significantly aggravated these trends.

Israel's 'Peace' Plans

The parameters of the plan that would bring about the desired result of separation with the Palestinians while retaining large tracts of their land were drawn up, as we saw, under Sharon's premiership and adopted faithfully by his successor, Ehud Olmert. They were in reality reworkings of previous Israeli proposals for keeping the land and excluding their inhabitants. In 1967, Yigal Allon, Israel's deputy prime minister at the time, called for annexation of a third of the West Bank, the area north and south of Jerusalem, and a linking corridor running through the Israeli-controlled territory up to the Jordan Valley. Most of the settlements that were built shortly after the announcement of the plan were established in the areas designated for annexation by Allon.[6] The Sharon/Olmert plan's primary aim was to ensure a Jewish majority in the state by excluding the largest number of Palestinians possible, and envisaged the separation wall being built across the West Bank to be more or less Israel's final border with the Palestinian territories. When completed, the wall would encircle Palestinian towns to shut them off from contact with Israel. The major West Bank settlement blocs (Maale Adumim to the east of Jerusalem, Gush Etzion to the south and Ariel to the north) would be annexed to Israel, and the Jordan Valley would remain under Israeli control. The twelve settlements around Jerusalem with their 170,000 settlers were considered part of the city and not even mentioned (Maps 2 and 3).

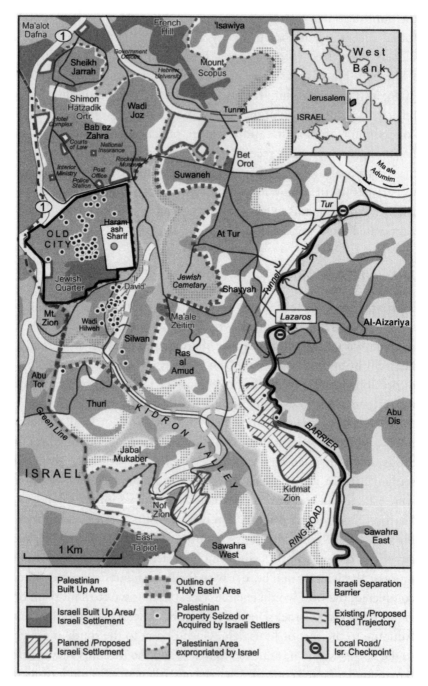

Map 2. Israeli settlements in and around Jerusalem, August 2006 (Source: The Foundation for Middle East Peace)

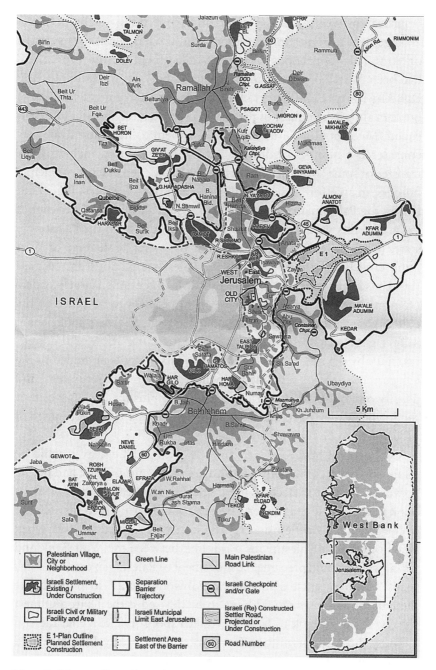

Map 3. Metropolitan Jerusalem, August 2006 (Source: The Foundation for Middle East Peace)

Jerusalem would be Israel's capital, but there might be some arrangement for Palestinian autonomy in the East Jerusalem suburbs or 'Arab neighbourhoods' as Israelis called them. Before 1967, these had been Arab villages outside Jerusalem's borders, for example, Abu Dis, Al-Aizariyya and Beit Hanina. But Israel's gerrymandering of the borders after its conquest of the city to create a larger capital for itself, called 'Metropolitan Jerusalem', added them to it. Israeli strategists considered a number of options for dividing the city, including the transfer of some 'Arab neighbourhoods' outside Jerusalem's municipal borders, in an effort to secure a Jewish majority.[7] The West Bank land left on the Palestinian side of the wall would shrink to 54 per cent at most, and this with the addition of Gaza would form the Palestinian state. (There is much confusion about the exact percentage of West Bank land Israel would leave to the Palestinians, not least because Israel has never provided a map to show its intentions.) Israeli leaders often misleadingly quoted a figure of 90 per cent to be ceded to the Palestinians, although in 2005 Ranaan Gissin, Sharon's spokesman, in fact gave a figure of 58 per cent.[8] An examination of the areas taken up by the large West Bank settlements, 8 per cent, added to the 9.5 per cent area of settlements included in 'Greater Jerusalem' and usually omitted from the Israeli calculation, plus the 28.5 per cent of the Jordan Valley Israel intended to keep, yields a total percentage of 46 per cent to be retained by Israel.[9]

A connection between Gaza and the West Bank enclaves could be established by a combination of bridges and tunnels. There had been a provision in the Oslo Accords for a 'safe passage' between the two areas but it never functioned properly because of intrusive Israeli surveillance over Palestinian traffic using it. The idea was revived in 2005 when Israel offered the Palestinians a rail link between the West Bank and Gaza, which would preclude the movement of Palestinian cars on Israeli roads.[10] Nothing came of it, but it was obvious that a system for linking the Palestinian areas would have to be devised if the Sharon/Olmert plan were not to look to Israel's Western sponsors like a charade.

Thus, the wall, permitting Israel to remain mostly Jewish, would exclude the bulk of the Palestinian population, and Israel could claim to have fulfilled the basic requirements of the Road Map: to create a Palestinian state that was 'contiguous' and, given sufficient international aid, could be viable as well. Olmert spoke openly about his vision of Israel's final borders, separating Israelis from the Palestinians and annexing West Bank land to Israel.[11] Like Sharon, he was prepared to act unilaterally, without consulting the Palestinians.[12] He thought the moment propitious, furthermore, since a Fateh government in place would have enjoyed international support and that could have forced Israel to abandon its plan and make peace not on its own terms. With the reviled Hamas, however, there was no such danger. And, provided Olmert was speedy with his plan's implementation before that most pro-Israeli of US presidents on record, George Bush, left office in 2009, it stood a good chance of succeeding. Mindful of this, Israel was pushing ahead with the wall's completion, the essential first step to fulfilling the plan.[13] Two visits to the Palestinian areas within months of each other in 2006 showed me how rapidly the wall was advancing around Ramallah and Bethlehem. Standing under its giant shadow near Rachel's tomb, the shrine that held the mythical remains of the mythical biblical character just outside Bethlehem, I could see that soon the wall would enclose it completely and sever it from the town it had always been a part of (Map 4).

Other ambitious scenarios for a future Israel, shorn of its Palestinians and safe for Zionism, were also under discussion. 'Our future in 2020', published in 2005, envisaged a demilitarised Palestinian state possibly federated with Jordan, with the right of return for the refugees abrogated, and full normalisation with the Arab and Islamic states. Joint Israeli/Arab projects would be dominated by Israel, with the Arabs providing the land and the manpower, the Arab trade boycott would be terminated and Israel would become the local agent for multinational companies in all parts of the region.[14] A year later, Giora Eiland, a former head of Israel's National Security Council, who did not believe that a Palestinian state in the 1967 territories was viable and might become unstable for that reason, proposed several grand measures to enhance Israel's future security. According to these, Israel would annex 12 per cent of the West Bank and ask Jordan to donate 100 sq km of its own land to compensate the Palestinians; 600 sq km of Northern Sinai would be taken from Egypt and joined on to Gaza to make it more viable, and Egypt could be compensated with 200 sq km of Israel's Negev desert. A tunnel should be dug under Israeli territory to connect Egypt with Jordan.[15] Eiland did not explain why either Jordan or Egypt should accept these encroachments on their land and security.

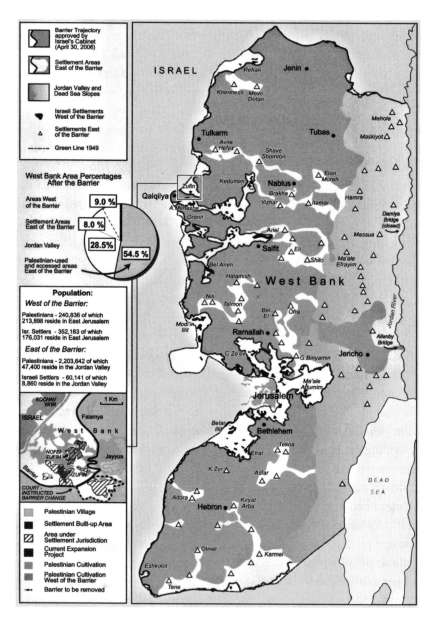

Map 4. The West Bank Separation Wall, July 2006 (Source: The Foundation for Middle East Peace)

The Jordanian Option

It was not clear in mid-2006 that Israel's plans for its future, as outlined here, would succeed in whole or in part. One could speculate about the possible outcomes and make plausible predictions based on Israel's history of successful unilateral initiatives and the Western support for them that was always forthcoming. But there were signs of other possible outcomes too. Ehud Olmert was no Sharon and lacked the authority needed to push through a unilateral programme so blatantly at odds with international law and human rights, not to speak of internal Israeli opposition to removing settlers from the West Bank. The American reception for it was lukewarm or ambiguous and the Quartet members were unhappy about it, stressing the need for co-ordination with the Palestinian side before taking any unilateral steps, and causing Olmert to convert his plan into a bilateral negotiation with the Palestinian president (while not changing its basic tenets).[16] Jordan was alarmed over the consequences if Israel were allowed to proceed with its strategy, which it thought could provoke a Palestinian influx from the West Bank into Jordan estimated at about half a million people.[17] Furthermore, there were anxieties about the plan amongst Israelis. Aluf Benn, writing in *Haaretz* (25 May 2005), questioned the wisdom of holding on to the large West Bank settlements and of retaining over 200,000 Arabs on the Israeli side of the separation wall, which would only perpetuate the conflict. Another of *Haaretz's* commentators, Zvi Bar'el, warned against antagonising Jordan and Egypt, both essential to Israel's border security, with unilateral Israeli moves that threatened both of them (11 June 2006).

Even so, who could tell if Palestinians might not end up accepting some version of the Olmert plan, if they had been so beaten down by the grinding misery of everyday life that almost anything was better, especially if the Western powers could elicit an improvement in Israel's terms? This might entail a more generous land swap for the large Jewish settlements, a deal on Jerusalem and, more probably, an arrangement with Jordan to facilitate Palestinian movement over the border. This would come about through a Palestine/Jordan confederation that would ease the pressure on the non-viable Palestinian state that Israel envisaged by extending it into Jordan as part of a formal interstate arrangement and not a 'Jordan is Palestine' deal, which Jordan would reject outright. Something like this had been in Sharon's mind when he produced his 'disengagement plan' as an essential safeguard against the possibility of its breaking down. The Israeli political analyst, Gary Sussman, who made a close study of Sharon's actions and pronouncements, came to the conclusion that Sharon foresaw the danger of creating a non-viable truncated Palestinian state without an outlet and planned accordingly.[18]

Jordan had always struck Sharon as the natural home for Palestinians, but he realised that it would not be willing to go along with this. He therefore envisaged that given time the Palestinian entity which had been created by his disengagement plan would itself agitate for a federation with 'the artificial kingdom', as he called Jordan. This allowed for a Palestinian demographic extension towards the east, away from Israel's border, and would need to be facilitated by Israel relinquishing parts of the Jordan Valley (although later his successor, Olmert, rejected any suggestion of easing Israeli control over this area). If this happened, Sharon foresaw it as inevitable that the West Bank Palestinians would meld socially and economically into Jordan (where at least 60 per cent of the population was Palestinian), and together they would form the Palestinian state. The advantage of this outcome for Israel was that the transition would happen peaceably and not appear to have been imposed by force, Amman might replace Jerusalem as the capital of the Palestinian state, and the refugee problem could be solved there. For a time the suggestion was that Iraq, until the insurgency against the US invasion of 2003 put paid to it, was another part of the solution to this Palestinian overflow. Those not accommodated in Jordan, and especially the refugees, could make their homes there. A man from Abu Dis told me in 2006 that every time the Iraqi situation worsened, the Palestinians, unlike all other Arabs, were relieved. 'At least they can't push us there yet', they said. In other words, the Israeli plan was to promote this solution by knowingly creating a fragmented, non-viable entity in the West Bank which was bound to look towards its Jordanian neighbour for a solution.

This was not as fanciful as it sounded. Many exiled Palestinians living in Western countries owned second homes in Jordan, went there regularly to see friends and relatives, arranged for local marriages for their children and aimed to retire there. Since a considerable number held Jordanian nationality, a leftover from the days when the West Bank was annexed to Jordan, it made these moves all the easier. One could see how plausible, even natural, it seemed for the Jordanian state to become the substitute homeland for Palestinians denied any other. While working in Ramallah during 2005, I tested out Sharon's Jordanian solution on a group of about 100 young women at a vocational training college.[19] I asked how they felt about being able to go to Jordan freely to visit relatives, study and perhaps work there or travel abroad, but on condition that the greater part of Palestine, including Jerusalem, was lost to Israel and the right of refugees to return was cancelled forever. All but two put up their hands in ready acquiescence, and, although I thought this response reflected little more than the craving for freedom that all prisoners have, it showed that Israel's policy of making life a living hell for Palestinians could drive them to consider relinquishing their basic rights and national cause.

No Other Way for a Zionist Israel

By 2006, Israel had taken every precaution it could devise to ensure the Zionist project's survival. The ethnic cleansing of Palestinians from the areas Israel wanted to keep was ongoing, and the Jewish state had successfully beaten off every attempt at peacemaking that did not ensure its retention of Arab land or maintain its hegemonic position in the region. As we saw, it turned down every Arab peace plan from the beginning, preferring to divide the Arab front with separate deals, and eventually succeeding with Egypt and Jordan. Even when the Arab states, in a restatement of their conviction that Israel's massively superior military power and huge international support gave them no alternative, put forward the rather modest Saudi peace plan in 2002, which gave Israel full Arab recognition and peaceful relations in return for its withdrawal from the 1967 occupied territories, Israel rejected it. Likewise with the Palestinians, who had significantly capitulated by recognising Israel, the usurper of their lands and cause of their dispossession, on 78 per cent of their original country and allowed it in the 1993 Oslo Accords to further fragment their territory, but whose every attempt at peacemaking Israel still felt impelled to discredit or foil. This it did through well-timed provocations, for example, assassinating important Palestinian figures as soon as Palestinians made a peace move, or undermining moderate Palestinian leaders who wanted a peaceful resolution, as happened with Yasser Arafat and later with Mahmoud Abbas, and then alleging it had no Palestinian negotiating partner.[20]

And yet, the Zionist project was not secure. The Sharon/Olmert plan still did not ensure an Arab-free territory, for untidy pockets of Palestinians like the 240,000 within the Jerusalem municipal borders, the thousands of villagers trapped on the Israeli side of the wall and the million-odd Palestinian citizens of Israel would still remain inside.[21] The inclusion of the villagers between the wall and the 1967 border, because the wall's route deviated from this line in many places, was unavoidable if Israel was to retain the best Palestinian agricultural land and water that it coveted. The villages, happening to be located on prime agricultural sites, some of them in the vicinity of the main West Bank water aquifers and immensely valuable to Israel, had to be included for that reason.[22] However, without land or residency rights, the villagers' blighted lives would push them into leaving altogether, thus removing another of its demographic obstacles. The Israeli hope was that a similar fate awaited the Palestinians of Jerusalem, who had lived for forty years under a restrictive Israeli regime of high taxes, poor municipal services, discrimination over housing, and an insecure legal status.[23] And indeed over the years, a slow exodus of Palestinians was effected through a variety of bureaucratic devices and methods by which the Israeli authorities evicted them. Israel's policy of cutting off Jerusalem from its West Bank hinterland left the Palestinians of the city ever more isolated and unable to support the public institutions that used to flourish there when it was the throbbing centre of Palestinian economic and cultural life.[24]

If, however, an effective ethnic cleansing of Arabs from Jerusalem did take place, and the villagers between the Green Line and the wall all left, it would still leave the impossibly difficult problem of the million Israeli Arabs to be dealt with. So blindly, however, did Israel's leaders pursue the aim of preserving a Jewish majority *and* keeping Arab land, that they were willing to ignore both reality and common sense. A combination of Arab weakness and American power and influence in the Middle East region, coupled with European inaction, reinforced them in this approach and persuaded them that there was no better time to impose the Israeli vision of the future. This conviction most likely pushed them into mounting the major Israeli assault on Gaza in June 2006, described in the previous chapter, aiming to crush all resistance in an area well known for its militancy. In a parallel political assault on the Palestinian Authority, Israel arrested 64 Hamas officials, eight of them government ministers. All this was done with the usual impunity from international action, and the humanitarian disaster that developed as a result did not prompt any intervention to protect the Palestinians, as if it had been no more than an unfortunate side-effect of an Israeli action that could be justified on the grounds of self-defence against Hamas terrorists.[25]

Why had it come to this, that Israelis could see no way to solve the conflict except through these drastic, morally degrading (and ultimately ineffective) means? As Danny Rubinstein pointed out in *Haaretz* (7 July 2006), Israel's destructive Gaza offensive only increased Palestinian anger and hatred for the Jewish state and strengthened Hamas, which refused to compromise on its demands. Why was it preferable to apply ever more stringent measures to harry the Palestinians out of existence, annex their territory and draw the borders unilaterally, risking international censure and potential failure at every turn, rather than envisage other solutions through, for example, negotiations with them or even through sincere adoption of the Road Map? After all, the latter still gave Israel the lion's share of the spoils in return for a small, demilitarised, non-sovereign Palestinian state, with Israel established as the vastly stronger party. The ostensible answer to these questions that Israel tirelessly promulgated was that its Jewish citizens had been so terrorised by Palestinian suicide bombings, they needed to put up defensive barriers against them. Undoubtedly many Israelis were genuinely afraid of Palestinians, especially after the second intifada, and hence their support for the building of the separation wall. But at bottom, there was also the ever-present fear that whatever acknowl-edgement was made of the Palestinians as a political presence, even the denuded one of the Road Map, could signify the start of an unstoppable unravelling of the Jewish state itself.

The real problem, as has repeatedly been noted here, lay with Israel's governing ethos and its inability to evolve. Zionism, which had been so resourceful in its early stages, ingeniously exploiting every opportunity to further its aims and intelligently debating its every move, showed itself in the end to be unimaginative and unable to adapt to new realities. The 'Iron Wall' philosophy of Vladimir Jabotinsky, articulated in the early decades of the twentieth century, remained more than 80 years later

Israel's only answer to the problem.[26] What else was the Sharon/Olmert plan that a majority of Israelis supported but a restatement of this philosophy? To deal with the Palestinian threat by building a wall, both physical and political, that would shut the Palestinians out – those, that is, whom draconian Israeli measures had not succeeded in pushing out of the country – was the only solution they could think of to forestall the inevitable consequences of their project. Basing Zionism inside another people's land without ensuring their effective annihilation, on the model of what happened, for example, in the settler colonialism of Australia or America, was a foolish mistake. This omission returns us to Benny Morris's regret, set out at the beginning of this book, that Israel did not expel the whole of the Palestinian population in 1948 and safeguard Zionism's long-term future.

In the event, it did not happen and Israel should have evolved ways over the decades of its existence to address the problem it had created other than by recourse to outmoded strategies, which were no longer feasible in a modern world concerned with democracy and human rights. Where the global trend was towards pluralism and the integration of minorities, Israel's struggle for ethnic purity was regressive and counter-historical. Nor was it likely that such strategies would work even on the practical level, for, as already discussed, the difficulties of removing so many Palestinians and ensuring that they did not return or resist the fate Israel had assigned to them, were formidable.

If the Sharon/Olmert plan, or some version of it, were implemented (and after the Lebanon war in 2006 it went into abeyance, at least temporarily), it would at best buy a little more time for Israel. Such had been the aim of all previous Israeli strategies which sought to postpone a settlement with the Arabs while 'creating facts' on the ground. The offer of any improvement in Palestinian life might arguably entice Palestinians to accept agreements they had always rejected. I remember briefly thinking that this outcome was more than likely, seeing the deteriorating human conditions in the West Bank cities in April 2006 (I was prevented from entering Gaza). It seemed to me that the adversaries Palestinians faced were simply too many for them to fight. How could they be expected to surmount such a formidable range of obstacles: an intolerable internal situation, an unrelenting Israeli colonisation bent on pushing them out, a highly partisan USA centre stage with a European supporting cast and an impotent UN? The Arab states, which could in theory have changed this situation, were also either impotent or effectively complicit by their inaction in the Western attack on the Palestinians. It was difficult to see how, with such concerted opposition, any way could be found out of the endless nightmare that had become Palestinian life. No wonder, I thought, that young Palestinians, at the end of their tether, saw no way out except to detonate themselves along with their tormentors.

Yet, the injustice of it all was so blatant and so persistent that I could also see that such acceptance would be short-lived, and as soon as the initial relief wore off, there would be a resurgence of resistance. As the head of UNRWA in Gaza, commenting on the effects of Israel's massive military operation at the end of June 2006, said, 'The [Palestinian] children see what goes on around them. I fear they will be the leaders of the third intifada, just as the children of the first intifada led the second.'[27] The Palestinian will to go on fighting against its oppressors, even if in fits and starts, was likely to continue. The empathy it drew from the rest of the Arab world could undermine the system of the Arab regimes' compliance with Western policy, while the Islamic movements, which had developed in the decades after the 1970s and for which Palestine was a mascot, were likely to become stronger with the danger that some of them could turn to terrorism. None of this would be orderly, focused or successful in its aims (setting up an Islamic state, reinstating the caliphate and the like). It was enough for it to create a situation so anarchic as to disrupt Israel's plans and those of its Western sponsors. Far from fantastic, this scenario looked inevitable as long as Israeli/Western political behaviour remained unchanged. Pursuing the same iron fist policy Israel had always used actually limited its options in the long run. The more it repressed the Palestinians, the harder they resisted; bombing and policing them constantly was militarily costly and invading them could never succeed in the narrow alleyways of Palestinian cities, especially not in Gaza. A Gazan once said to me, 'They've thrown everything at us, the only thing left is an atom bomb!'

The more the Palestinians suffered the greater was the sympathy for them worldwide. Nor could Israel's economy ultimately prosper in such an unstable situation. The tourist industry, which was hit hard during the second intifada, would decline again, as would foreign investment if the instability continued. The dead-end route that Israel's ideology had condemned it to is eloquently described in a *Haaretz* piece by Amir Oren ('Living by the sword, for all time', 2 May 2006). Referring to a 2004 Israeli army assessment of the conflict which concluded that it was 'irresolvable', he writes, 'This is our life (and our death) as far as the eye can see. Endless bloodletting until the end of time.' The army report noted that no Israeli policy to date had either worn down or vanquished the Palestinians. Oren recalls Moshe Dayan's grim prediction, cited at the beginning of this book, that Israel would 'live by the sword for all time'. While Israel clung to a Zionism that precluded any relationship with the Arabs other than one of master and slave, no comfortable outcome for Palestinians, Arabs or Israelis themselves was possible.

The Two-State Solution

We discussed above a number of Israeli 'solutions', which were really unilateralist ideas for preserving Zionism. They would not win the acquiescence of 'the other man' and had had to be imposed by bribery or coercion. By contrast, there were on the table other ideas which offered both sides to the conflict the possibility of a solution and were acceptable to the Palestinians. The most familiar of these was the two-state solution, which enjoyed wide Palestinian and international support. For those in the diaspora, 'Palestine', after the Oslo Accords, had made such a concept possible once again and, although so little of it had been liberated, became the focus of their efforts as a place of hope and the potential start of the journey back home. A Palestinian state was the first step in that direction. Most Palestinians anticipated a growing exchange with Israelis in the context of two neighbouring states at peace, and that this friendly contact would lead in time to a melting of the border between the two and a true mixing of populations. In this way, there could even be a sort of return for the refugees, but not as a way of taking over Israel. Some Palestinians believed strongly that the national quest for an independent state had to be coupled with a genuine and sincere acceptance of Israel's permanence, not a ruse for undermining it.

It was not that these ideas were articulated as such or even at the forefront of Palestinian preoccupations in the demand for statehood. The dominant need was to have the occupation lifted and attain a normal life, even though it meant dividing what had been Mandatory Palestine into two states, Israeli and Palestinian. This two-state aim was probably the best known and most internationally accepted solution of all for the conflict. Its support amongst Palestinians did not stem initially from any belief that it was in itself an ideal or even a desirable solution. But rather that it was the only way, as they saw it, of saving what little was left of Palestine, a place in which to recoup Palestinian national identity and social integrity. Israel's ghettoisation of Palestinian society had led to a social fragmentation and national disorientation that could only be reconstituted in a Palestinian state free of Israeli interference. Many Palestinians believed that without this crucial phase of healing and reintegration, there could be no advance for the national cause. As the Palestinian Knesset member, Muhammad Baraka, put it, Palestinian independence was a necessity if the 'criminal' expulsion of Palestinians from the land was to be halted; he saw Palestinian statehood as essential if a people who had been dispossessed, occupied and oppressed were to have any chance of developing their society and economy and to emerge from it free and whole.[28]

In addition, and given the massive power imbalance, on the one hand, and the international support for the creation of a Palestinian state on the other, the two-state solution acquired a 'most we can hope for' character that was unarguable. The fact that for a while it also looked to be potentially attainable added to its attraction. The Oslo Accords had nurtured in Palestinians inside and outside the occupied territories an aspiration to statehood, encouraged by Western-funded 'state building' projects, no less staunch than that which had animated the first Zionists (and with far greater legitimacy). Many wealthy Palestinians, in fact, consciously emulated the Zionist model by zealously investing in the Palestinian towns Israel had evacuated in order to build their state by incremental steps (though, as they said, without displacing anyone in the process).[29] Prominent among these was the Palestinian entrepreneur, Munib al-Masri, whose monumental palace built commandingly atop a hill in Nablus, struck me when I saw it as a statement of possession meant to defy the Jewish settlements encroaching on his city. These were all deliberately sited at hilltops in a crude bid to claim the Arab land below them for Israel.

Palestinians had always previously rejected the idea of partition, although it was a familiar one in Palestine's history as a device used by

Britain and later the UN for accommodating Zionist ambitions in the country. The Zionists first proposed it to the Mandate authorities as far back as 1928 when their numbers in the country were very small.[30] In 1937, the Peel Commission set up by the British government to find a solution for the conflict between Jews and Arabs in Mandate Palestine, recommended that the country be divided into Jewish and Arab states. In 1947, UN General Assembly Resolution 181 made the same recommendation and for the same reason. The story of how this resolution, which the UN was not legally entitled to table in the first place, was pushed through to a vote in its favour is an ignoble one. It is no secret that it took vigorous American and Zionist arm-twisting and intimidation to overturn the majority of states that would have voted against it.[31] It was passed against strong Arab opposition (some Palestinian communists accepted it, hoping it would put a brake on Zionist colonisation), not least because it was the first international recognition accorded to what was a blatantly unjust, settler colonialist enterprise in an Arab country, and which the Zionists used subsequently to legitimise their presence. It was seen as an extension of the original injustice perpetrated in 1921 by the League of Nations in conferring on Britain a mandate to encourage that settler colonialism in the first place. For the people of Palestine, partition was an outrageous assault on the integrity of their country and a gift to the Jewish immigrants of a statehood they did not deserve. This remained the Palestinian position after 1948, when the aim of the newly formed PLO was Palestine's total liberation, 'the recovery of the usurped homeland in its entirety', as the preamble to the Palestine National Charter of 1964 phrased it.

In 1974, however, the question of partition returned, at least implicitly, to the national agenda. At its twelfth meeting, the Palestine National Council (PNC) formally resolved to set up a 'national, independent and fighting authority on every part of Palestinian land to be liberated' from Israeli occupation. Although there was no mention of a Palestinian state and no recognition of Israel, the resolution paved the way to a new thinking about the future. This was reflected in the next PNC meeting in 1977, which called for 'an independent national state' on the land without referring to its total liberation. By 1981, the PNC had welcomed a Russian proposal for the establishment of a Palestinian state, and the idea of a two-state solution was becoming increasingly familiar.[32] In 1982, the Saudi-inspired Fez plan, which called for the creation of a

Palestinian state in the occupied territories and an implicit adoption of a two-state solution, also won guarded Palestinian endorsement. Jordan began to feature as the other part of a possible Palestinian/Jordanian confederation in the PNC meetings after 1983. Along with this went an increasing emphasis on the attainment of Palestinian goals by diplomatic means, including for the first time an endorsement of ties with 'democratic and progressive' Jewish and Israeli forces and the internationalisation of efforts to find a peaceful solution.

The outbreak of the first intifada and the PLO's isolation following its expulsion by Israel from Lebanon, in 1982, were important factors in accelerating the trend towards the two-state solution. Palestinian awareness of the realpolitik of Israel's power and the futility of military struggle against it convinced the PLO to adopt a political programme that reflected this reality. Hence it was that the PLO came to recognise Israel and propose the creation of an independent Palestinian state alongside it as the aim of the Palestinian struggle. It was a recognition that what was just was a separate issue from what was possible and attainable under the circumstances, and a decision to pursue the latter at the expense of the former. It would have been just for the whole of Mandate Palestine to revert to the dispossessed Palestinians and thus solve the refugee problem for good and for Israel to compensate them for their losses over the years. But the PLO saw this was impossible to realise and so opted for what was, they believed, attainable. At its 18th meeting in November 1988, the PNC accepted UN Resolutions 242 and 338 as the basis for negotiations with Israel. It also, and most significantly, accepted the previously rejected and humiliating UN Partition Resolution 181, finding itself acquiescing 41 years later to the division of Palestine and recognising Israel as a legitimate state. The Declaration of Independence that was the hallmark of this meeting set down the notion of a Palestinian state, implicitly to be established within the 1967-occupied territories with East Jerusalem as its capital. A month later, the PLO chairman, Yasser Arafat, reinforced this recognition of Israel in an affirmation of 'the right of all parties to the conflict to live in peace and security'.

The PNC was the dispersed Palestinian people's best attempt at a representative body in exile through which to reflect the broad range of their views. Even so, the 1988 decision voted in by the PNC was not uniformly welcomed, and the idea of a 'statelet' on 23 per cent of the land of the original Palestine was met with derision by many individuals and groups. The retreat from the original PLO goal of Palestine's total liberation, which had become evident since 1977, was regarded by this constituency as a craven capitulation to Israeli hegemony. I remember how angry my fellow activists in London felt at this betrayal of principle. They convened meetings, wrote defamatory articles and made speeches denouncing the 'statelet' and demanding a return to the PLO's original charter. The first London PLO representative, Said Hammami, posted there in 1975, strongly supported the creation of a Palestinian state and responded to these accusations with fierce condemnation. I recall him telling me with a chilling prescience he could not have been aware of at the time, 'So, you don't approve of what we [the PLO] are doing? Believe me, the day will come when all of you will rend your clothes with regret you did not fight for the "statelet", because even this small thing will be denied us, you will see!'

After the 1993 Oslo Accords made implicit the goal of creating a Palestinian state, which Palestinians and international agencies started to prepare for in the occupied territories with enthusiasm, the two-state solution dominated the international political discourse, even, as we saw, amongst Israelis. It was affirmed by UN resolutions, formed part of President Bush's vision for the future of the region and was central to the Road Map, the last but unimplemented international peace proposal. The international consensus was not *whether* a Palestinian state would be created but *when* and in what territory. The Palestinian doubters went into abeyance, waiting to see what would happen or half believing that their fears had been misplaced, and the return of Yasser Arafat and the PLO leadership to Palestine seemed to herald a new dawn.

Making the Two-State Solution Impossible

It was a false dawn, however. For, as we know, Israel's policy of 'creating facts' on the ground was the single most effective foil to these plans. It put the creation of a sovereign, viable Palestinian state out of reach, and thereby spelled the end of the two-state solution. As Israeli colonisation and segmentation of the West Bank proceeded unimpeded throughout the years since 1967, up to and including the period after the Oslo agreement, the Palestinian territories supposed to form the state were rendered unusable for that purpose by the jigsaw of Jewish colonies, bypass roads and barriers. Jerusalem was judaised beyond the possibility of its forming a Palestinian capital, and Gaza was left stranded in an Israeli sea, unconnected to anywhere. These logistical obstacles in the way of a viable Palestinian state had become so extreme by 2006 that most observers, including the most ardent supporters of the two-state solution, started to fear that it was not going to be realised. The UN Special Rapporteur on the situation of human rights in the Palestinian territories was forced to conclude: 'This vision [of a two-state solution] is unattainable without a viable Palestinian territory. The construction of the wall, the expansion of settlements, the de-Palestinization of Jerusalem and the gradual incorporation of the Jordan Valley are incompatible with the two-state solution.'[33] In their detailed report on the status of Jerusalem, the International Crisis Group considered that the Israeli measures to judaise the city were 'at war with any viable two-state solution'.[34]

Numerous studies and commentaries analysing this problem appeared, drawing the conclusion that a two-state outcome had been superseded.[35] The head of the Israeli Committee Against House Demolitions (ICAHD), Jeff Helper's concept of Israel's occupation as a triple layered 'matrix of control', military, territorial and bureaucratic is probably the most graphic of these and the best illustration of Israel's tenacious and irreversible hold on Jerusalem and the West Bank.[36] The geographer Jan de Jong's maps of the occupied territories, vividly demonstrated the impossibility of a Palestinian state arising in these segmented lands.[37] Given this situation, Palestinian Authority officials indicated that they would be forced to abandon the two-state solution and press for equal citizenship with Israelis.[38] The need to dissolve the PA and force Israel to deal with the Palestinians directly as a people under occupation rather than shielding behind the fiction of an independent government was openly debated.[39] Ahmad Qurei, the Palestinian prime minister, announced in January 2004 that if the two-state solution were made impossible to achieve then the Palestinians had no alternative but to aim for one state, a tactic meant to 'scare' the Israelis and their US sponsors into checking the growth of settlements and other obstacles to the creation of a Palestinian state.

These antics scared no one, however, since Israel had no intention of ever letting a viable Palestinian state come into being. Its colonisation

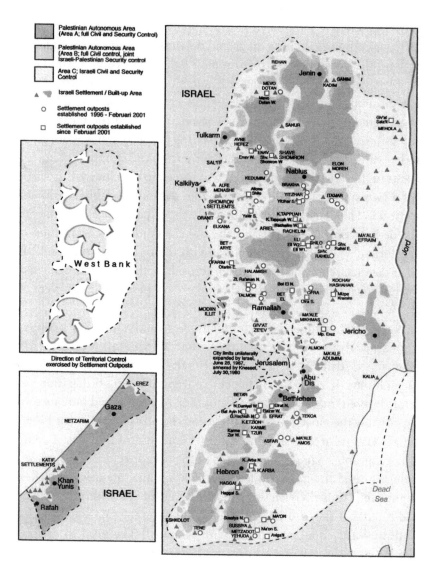

Map 5. Making the Two-State Solution Impossible: The West Bank After Oslo
(Source: The Foundation for Middle East Peace)

programme and studied avoidance of serious peace agreements or
meaningful negotiations were all designed to ensure that nothing other
than a truncated entity incapable of becoming anything more would
ever exist alongside the Jewish state. Had Israel conceded on this point
and a sovereign Palestinian state been created within the whole of the
1967 territories, a period of tranquillity might well have ensued. But

sooner or later, Israel feared, the basic issues would re-emerge and call for resolution: the initial dispossession that had led to the loss of most of Palestine and the expulsion of its people. Israel could no more abandon the West Bank settlements to allow for a Palestinian state there than it could leave Tel Aviv. As the left-wing Israeli activist, Haim Hanegbi, put it, 'Any [Israeli] recognition that the settlements in the West Bank exist on plundered Palestinian land will cast a threatening shadow over the Jezreel valley and over the moral status of Beit Alfa and Ein Harod [places in Israel pre-1967].'[40]

These issues would not be resolved in a territory forming one-fifth of the original Palestine and in the absence of a just solution for the refugees who could not be absorbed in such a small area. The proposed state was scarcely viable, as it was, without a further influx of refugees. (A Rand Corporation study, in 2005, found that it would need $33 billion capital investment in the first ten years for, among other things, the building of a corridor linking the northern West Bank and Gaza to make it territorially contiguous. But the new state could not accommodate the return of the refugees which would swamp its capacity.)[41] Israelis knew this as well as any Palestinian, which was why they resisted the creation of a sovereign, viable Palestinian state so fiercely and fought against any affirmation of the Palestinians as a people with a national cause. It was also why they needed almost just as much to set up a non-viable entity along the Sharon/Olmert lines they would call a state, as a fig-leaf to satisfy the international community, but in reality a dustbin for dumping unwanted Palestinians who could threaten their demography and, in consequence, a way of preserving Zionism.

Neither Feasible Nor Desirable

Israel was not wrong in its apprehensions. Those most anxious to bring about a two-state solution were Israel itself (on condition that the Palestinian state was no more than the collection of enclaves discussed above), and the Western powers, which wanted to save a project they had unwisely backed from the start and could not now abandon. To these may be added the pro-Western Arab states whose chief concern was a quiet life free from Western pressure to accommodate Israel and the wrath of their own populations for doing so. It was true that, in addition, there had grown amongst many Palestinians a genuine desire for a separate state, feelings nurtured by years of deprivation under occupation and the fear of losing the rest of Palestine if they held out for anything more ambitious. In recent years, a concern with recouping Palestinian identity and society, fractured by Israel's separation and closure policies, added powerfully to the desire for independence. Decades of cruel treatment at the hands of Israel had also led to considerable hostility towards Israelis, who seemed to them like an alien and not quite human species, and a longing to separate from them for good.

But those understandable reactions aside, what did the Palestinians really gain from a settlement that left the lion's share of their original homeland and its resources in the hands of a Zionist state that had robbed them of it in the first place? And what of the majority of their people, the millions of refugees and displaced, who had no access to that homeland? Why would anyone assume that such obvious injustice could be forgiven or forgotten? In a research study I carried out between 1999 and 2000, just before the outbreak of the second intifada, I interviewed 42 randomly selected Palestinian Arabs and 50 Jewish Israelis about the conditions for reconciliation between them.[42] These were people who came from various walks of life and, had it been a larger sample, might have been reasonably representative. Some 20 opinion formers from both sides (academics, politicians, journalists) were also questioned about the same topic. The results predictably showed that the greatest differences of view were over the issues considered basic to the Palestinians, the right of return for the refugees, Israel's acknowledgement of responsibility for their expulsion and the right to compensation. A 'historic reconciliation' with Israel, as the Palestinian respondents termed it, would require an Israeli apology and acknowledgement of its responsibility for the nakba and accepting the right of return with compensation as basic conditions. (The Israeli respondents, with a few exceptions, were unwilling to accept any of these terms.) Two-thirds of Palestinians were willing to accept the two-state solution, but only as a stage, and all of them considered the area pre-1967 to be Arab land. Was it possible, therefore, that such people could accept a Palestinian state, even had it been available, as anything other than a first stage to a retrieval of the rest of Palestine? Even if it took decades to accomplish, it had to be their final destination.

The Right of Return

The refugee issue was possibly the most cogent argument against a two-state solution. The refugees and their descendants living in camps, most run by the UN since 1948 and numbering 6.8 million (2005 figures),[43] formed the core of the Palestinian problem. They cherished the memory of the lost homeland and reared their descendants on a detailed knowledge of their towns and villages of origin in the old Palestine. On a visit to Bourj al-Barajneh refugee camp in Beirut in 1998, I was astonished to hear small children of four and five reciting the names of places they called their home towns in what is now Israel. The children all said they were 'going back' there when they grew up. Listening to them, I was both saddened and awed at the tenacity with which the Palestinians held on to the idea of return, despite decades of exile in the worst of conditions and the apparent hopelessness of their cause.[44] I wondered why, if it were the case that the international community had no intention of implementing the refugees' right to return, they were allowed to indulge their dreams in this way. It was no accident that these camps had provided the fighters of the PLO formerly and those of Gaza's Hamas activists latterly. The refugees, representing the bulk of Palestine's displaced population in 1948, also delivered a majority of the workforce that helped to build up the Gulf states from the 1950s onwards, and many went on to become successful entrepreneurs, journalists and other professionals. The prominent editor of the London-based *Al-Quds al-Arabi*, frequently cited in these pages, Abdul Bari Atwan, for example, started life in a Gaza refugee camp.

The right of return on which all these displaced people's hopes were pinned was a *cause célèbre* for Palestinians. Had there been no refugees and the Palestinian problem merely one of Israeli occupation, the conflict would have been easier to solve. But the 1948 dispossession was a fundamental part of Palestinian history, the legal backbone of the Palestine cause and the crucial basis on which the Jewish state was built. Few people in the West appreciated the importance of the right of return for Palestinians, which should have been enforced from the beginning, and it became customary for Western policy makers to view the Palestinian refugees as commodities that could be moved about as required, and not as human beings with needs and desires. The fact that this issue was of core importance to Palestinians was constantly ignored. But if there were to be a settlement it would reassert itself forcefully for all Palestinians, and no deal that did not address this issue would be considered just, legal or an end to the conflict.

The two-state solution stood no chance of solving this problem on any count. And strictly speaking, as some have argued, the creation of two states in itself logically rules out a refugee return to the Israeli state.[45] The two-state solution requires the Palestinians to recognise Israel *as a Jewish state*, that is, one with a Jewish majority, and therefore incompatible with an influx of non-Jews. That left the putative Palestinian state as the only option, but it could not hope to accommodate the number of returnees, and especially not the tiny, segmented entity Israel had in mind. Nor was it fair that people expelled from Haifa or Safad should have to make their homes in Ramallah or Jenin. Had the Palestinians, who were aware of all this, been less desperate for a way out of the dire situation of rapid Israeli encroachment on their land and existence, they would not have accepted a solution that abandoned the refugees to their fate. Their logic in doing this was to live to fight another day, for the basic injustice of the situation would remain and resurface at a later date. Not all the convoluted arrangements devised by Israel and the Western powers to dispose of the refugee issue could make Palestinians forget that it was their homes and land that had been usurped by a people who had no right to them and whose self-righteous ownership of a country that was not theirs was a constant affront.

7
The One-State Solution

In the previous chapter we saw how the two-state solution, whatever its merits or drawbacks, stood little chance of being realised in practice. The obvious alternative to it and to the variety of Israeli unilateralist proposals was the one-state solution. This was not simply a matter of logic, but of a fundamental difference in approach to solving the conflict. The two-state solution and its variants had as their sole object, no matter what the rhetoric about a 'comprehensive settlement', the termination of Israel's occupation and its damaging consequences for Palestinian civil life in the occupied areas. It left untouched the issue of the nature of the State of Israel and the damaging ideology it espoused. The previous sections of this book have reviewed this damage in some detail, the aggression and inherent anti-Arab racism of Zionism, which did not decrease over time. On the contrary, prominent Israelis were still publicly calling for the expulsion of Arabs from the country in 2006.[1] It was also noticeable that anti-Arab feeling increased sharply in the wake of the 2006 Lebanon war, as if Israelis, angry at their perceived defeat by Hizbullah, took revenge on an easier target, the Arab citizens of Israel. At the same time, moves to settle the country with more Jews at the expense of these citizens were as active as ever.[2]

Nor was the Jewish state in 2006 any more ready to integrate with its Arab neighbours than it had been in 1948. As an Arab writer commented in September 2006, 'Israel is still a foreign body and will remain so, for all its alliances, agreements and ties are external, outside the body politic of this region.'[3] The one-state solution aimed to address these problems by going to the heart of the matter: the existence of Israel as a Zionist state. If it was the case that the imposition of Zionism on the Arabs had been the cause of the Palestinians' dispossession, the rejection of their rights and the constant state of conflict between Israel and its neighbours, it made no sense for a peace agreement to preserve that status quo. The key date in the genesis of this conflict was not 1967, as the two-state proponents implied, but 1948. Israel's occupation of the 1967 territories was a symptom of the disease, not its cause. The problem was that the two-state solution did not merely just confine itself to dealing with the symptoms; it actively helped to maintain the cause. The roots of the conflict, as has frequently been reiterated in this book, lay in a flawed and destructive project that never stopped being so. It did not adapt to its environment or accept any limitations on its aspirations. Indeed Israel's very success encouraged this process, the more it took and escaped retribution, the more it wanted to take, and so on in a self-perpetuating cycle of aggression and expansionism. Only by bringing the Zionist project to an end would the conflict also be ended. Such an approach would be a radical challenge to decades of Arab pacification and coercion at the hands of those concerned to preserve the Zionist project.

The one-state solution meant the creation of a single entity of Israel/ Palestine in which the two peoples would live together without borders or partitions. Dividing a small country like Palestine with resources that respected no borders, especially not artificially constructed ones, was logistically unworkable if it was to be fair. All the partition proposals previously devised discriminated heavily in Israel's favour. The one-state solution was unique in addressing this and all the other basic issues that perpetuated the conflict – land, resources, settlements, Jerusalem and refugees – in an equitable framework. As such, it answered to the needs of common sense and justice, the sine qua non of any durable peace settlement.

In a single state, no Jewish settler would have to move and no Palestinian would be under occupation. The country's scarce resources could be shared without Israel stealing Palestinian land and water or the Palestinians left starving and thirsty. Jerusalem would be a city for both peoples, not the preserve of Israel to the anger of Arabs, Muslims and Christians and the detriment of international law. The Palestinian refugees would be allowed to return to their original homeland, if not to their actual homes. Their long exile and blighted existence would end, and the states that had played host to them could be relieved at last of a burden they had carried for more than 50 years. The long-running sore of dispossession that had embittered generations of Palestinians and perpetuated their resistance could heal at last. With the outstanding issues thus resolved, no cause for conflict between the two sides would remain, and the Arab states could then accommodate the Israeli presence in their midst with genuine acceptance. Such an outcome would, by extension, also dampen down the fires of Islamic rage against Israelis and Jews that had come to fuel violence and terrorism. The Arab hostility, real or imagined, which Israelis constantly faced and which forced them to maintain their state by superior force of arms and American patronage would end. Israel, which had become the unsafest place on earth for Jews, when transmuted into the new, shared state could be a place of real refuge for them. A normal immigration policy, once the returning Palestinian refugees had been accommodated, would operate under which Jews and others who wanted to live in Israel/Palestine could do so according to fair and agreed rules.

The one-state solution was the most obvious, direct and logical route to ending an intractable conflict that had destroyed the lives of so many people and damaged the Middle East region so profoundly. And for that reason it should have been the most actively pursued of all the options, but especially by the Palestinians, for whom it meant a reversal (as far as that was practically possible) of a process that had robbed them of their land and made them stateless refugees. People discussed the one-state solution as if it were a revolutionary idea. But it was no forward-looking innovation, rather more a way of going back, of restoring a land, deformed by half a century of division, colonisation and plunder into the whole country it had been before 1948. It was a healthy rejection of disunity in favour of unity and a humane desire for a life based on co-operation rather than confrontation. How much better for Israeli Jews to learn to live together with Palestinian Arabs in a relationship of friendship and collaboration that had the potential to be excitingly productive, rather than be condemned to the barren and dangerous dead-end future that Israel was driving them towards.

Sharing the Land

In spite of the obvious advantages of a one-state solution, its very mention was usually met with a variety of objections, the most cogent (and accurate) of which was that Israel would never agree to it and so it was dead in the water before it started. In fact, the idea of sharing the land between Arabs and Jews had a long and notable pedigree, far longer than that of the two-state solution, which was a recent notion in Palestinian history arrived at, as we saw, in response to a series of defeats for the Palestinian national liberation movement. There were two main ways in which Palestine could be shared: the binational model in which the two groups could share the country but remain ethnically separate, and the secular democratic, one-person-one-vote model, based on individual citizenship and equal rights irrespective of race, religion or gender. The binational model preserved the structure of two religious/ethnic communities, but the secular democratic model emphasised the individual rather than the community in the style of the Western liberal democracies. Thus binationalism enabled Zionism to survive, albeit in a reduced form, while the secular democratic alternative did not.

The Binational State

The various ideas for partition which were put forward during the Mandate period were really binationalist proposals that answered to the Zionist need to separate from non-Jews in a space which would permit a Jewish majority to exist. That was the reason for the acceptance of such proposals amongst Jews and their rejection by Arabs. By contrast, a small number of Zionists had argued from the start of Jewish immigration into Palestine at the end of the nineteenth century for an arrangement where two communities, Jewish and Arab, could live side by side co-operatively and in harmony.[4] They did not support the project to establish a Jewish state and considered the Arabs in Palestine to have an equally legitimate claim to it. Their aim was the revival of Jewish life in its 'ancestral homeland', as they phrased it, which should not be incompatible with Arab life in the same space. Judah Magnes, as we observed earlier, was the strongest proponent of this 'cultural Zionism'. His vision was of a binational state as part of a wider federation with the Arabs states, whereby Jewish immigration would not lead to Palestinian dispossession.[5] Such ideas led to the formation of the Brit Shalom organisation in 1925, which proposed adopting the Swiss or Finnish binational models for the putative shared state with the Arabs. Magnes later impressed the Anglo-American Committee of Inquiry, set up in 1946 to investigate postwar Jewish immigration to Palestine, with these binationalist ideas. With his fellow members of Ihud (union), the organisation he founded to promote binationalism, he went on to testify to the UN on the same subject.[6]

A number of other Zionist intellectuals also supported binationalism at this time, most prominently Martin Buber, Chaim Kalvarisky and Arthur Ruppin, all Zionist Jews living in Palestine.[7] Ruppin looked to a cultural rebirth in the East through co-operation between Jews, Arabs, Armenians and other 'Eastern peoples'. David Ben-Gurion, while chairman of the Jewish Agency in 1930, thought that a balance between Arab and Jews in a binational state was necessary in order to guard against the danger of one side ruling the other. Mapai, the main Zionist party of the time, adopted this view in 1931. Indeed, between 1921 and 1939 the Zionist leadership, including Chaim Weizmann, tended to be somewhat binationalist in orientation.[8] The socialist-Zionist organisation, Hashomer Hatzair, founded in 1946, also advocated binationalism as the means to realise the aims of Zionism. For the Zionists, who were nothing more than an immigrant minority, sharing the country would have been quite an achievement. The support of many of them for binationalism which would have brought them closer to their goal, was mainly based on that consideration. Needless to say, the vast majority of Palestinians felt differently. They did not share these binationalist ideas, which they saw as a means of forcing them to accept that a bunch of foreign colonists had equal rights with them in their own land.

But during the Mandate years, when Zionists were actively putting these binationalist ideas forward, a very small number of Palestinians did respond positively. Negotiations between these and the Jewish binationalists, which would have been a source of intense shame to the Palestinians had they been discovered, were normally held in secret. The Arab binationalists were motivated by a variety of reasons, not all of them noble, for example, accepting bribes in return for their support for Jewish Zionists, or because of internal rivalries between the prominent Palestinian families in which supporting the Zionists was used as a weapon in the contest. But a small number of them genuinely believed that the Jewish presence in Palestine could be beneficial by drawing in foreign capital to develop the country. It may also have been their sense that Zionism would prove difficult to dislodge and opted for the best arrangement in such circumstances.

One of these men was Ahmad Khalidi, head of the Government Arab School during the Mandate period, who in 1933 proposed a state divided into two cantons, Jewish and Arab, the latter to be linked to Transjordan, with Jerusalem, Hebron and Safad, left outside the cantons as 'free cities' belonging to neither. The cantons would have a joint ruling council of Arabs, Jews and British representatives; Jewish immigration would be confined to the Jewish canton and the three free cities.[9] Another was Musa Alami, a member of a prominent Palestinian family and Arab secretary to the British high commissioner, who also proposed a cantonal plan in the 1930s. The Jewish canton would include the Jewish colonies already established, and a national government with proportional representation would be set up which, inter alia, would restrict immigration to the Jewish canton. I met Alami in London during the 1970s when he was an old man but still active in running an agricultural project for Palestinian farmers in the West Bank. He was an impressive figure, despite his age, with sad eyes and a warm, intimate manner. Our meeting was short and the conversation inconsequential, and afterwards I wished passionately that I had asked him to share with me his memories of that special and crucial time in our unrecoverable history.

Fawzi Husseini, the head of the Filastin al-Jadida (The New Palestine) organisation that supported binationalism, was another Palestinian figure who believed that Jews and Arabs could develop the country together in a binational state. He went so far as to sign a formal agreement in 1946 with the League for Jewish–Arab Rapprochement and Co-operation, a coalition of several Zionist organisations that sought to build a programme for the binational state in Palestine. At the popular level, Palestinian villagers were in neighbourly contact with Jewish settlements in their vicinity and often had friendly relations with them. Shortly thereafter, fellow Palestinians assassinated Husseini for his pains, and the Zionists rejected the cantonal plans of his predecessors. Two years later none of it mattered much anyway, as most of Palestine's indigenous population was expelled and the Jewish state acquired the Jewish majority it had sought.

We will never know if the Jewish binationalists would have succeeded in the end, but it is unlikely. They were never anything more than a minority phenomenon and their basic aim was still to establish a European Jewish settler community in an Arab land in the belief that the indigenous population could come to accept or even be grateful for it. That such men as Magnes and Buber had the foresight and decency to appreciate that the Arab majority in Palestine had legitimate rights and could not be disposed of cannot be denied; indeed they were often held up as models of virtue. But this did not alter the fact of their unshakeable belief that European Jews like themselves, without a shred of connection to Palestine, except what was inside their heads, had an equal right to the country. Reading this history evokes for me memories of the European Jews I grew up with in Golders Green, who seemed as alien as, say, the Chinese to my native land (see Chapter 2). The idea that the forebears of such people thought they belonged in Palestine during the 1920s when the country was overwhelmingly Arab and the Jewish state no more than a gleam in Chaim Weizmann's eye, must have struck my forebears as wholly preposterous.

Later Binationalism

The binationalist idea became obsolete for decades as the Arab nationalists strove, at least initially, to reclaim the whole of Palestine, including the territory of the Jewish state. But the difficulties experienced elsewhere during the 1970s and 1980s in integrating ethnic groups harmoniously in one state were also not encouraging to the binationalist model. The break-up of Yugoslavia, the conflict in Cyprus between Greeks and Turks and the struggle for independence of Kurds in Iraq, were frequently cited as examples of the failure of this approach. But in Palestine, binationalism resurfaced in the last years of the twentieth century, as the pre-1948 problem of having to accommodate two communities living in the same space, returned. Thanks to Israel's colonisation of the West Bank and Gaza, the two peoples became inextricably mixed, making partition an impossibility and evoking the question of binationalism once again. Some observers in fact argued that the Oslo agreement itself was a binationalist arrangement because it set up a division of responsibility, based on ethnicity, between the Palestinians and the (dominant) Israeli groups.[10]

Impelled by the situation of ethnic separateness yet physical connectedness, a small number of Israelis and Palestinians began to discuss the binational idea in the 1990s as the only way for the two peoples to share a state and yet preserve their ethnic/cultural identity. This was of great importance to Jewish Israelis of course, but Palestinians also, aware of the need to reconstitute their society and identity, wanted to keep themselves apart for this purpose. Proponents of this solution argued that the two peoples had too strong a national affiliation and self-identification to accept any plan that ignored this important issue.[11]In a binational state, each community would be autonomous in terms of language, education and cultural life and would have its own administrative council to run such affairs. But for matters of common concern, such as national policy, defence and the economy, there would be joint institutions and a joint parliament with equal representation.

By the late 1990s an active debate on the one-state solution was taking shape with writers and political figures like Haim Hangebi and Meron Benvenisti, Azmi Bishara and Edward Said arguing for such an outcome.[12] (Said's position on this issue was in fact vague. His main concern was the co-existence on humanist grounds between Jews and Arabs in a shared homeland, without spelling out the mechanism that would achieve this.)[13] Long before that, in the aftermath of the 1967 war, the American political scientist, Don Peretz, had argued for a binational state as the preferred solution to the conflict.[14] He saw a Palestine–Jordan federation as a natural part of the plan, with this later becoming federated with Israel, an idea echoed in the 1971 Jordanian proposal for a 'United Kingdom' of Jordan and the West Bank, and also in the post-Camp David proposals of Menachem Begin and Jordan's King Hussein in the late 1970s to form a confederation or 'condominium'. Although the arrangement Israel and Jordan envisaged was for shared rule between them over the occupied Palestinian territories, such a suggestion hinted at the same idea of a Palestine–Jordan federation, whether consciously or not.[15]

The prominent American intellectual, Noam Chomsky, had been a committed binationalist before 1948. An opponent of the Jewish state as an entity, which could not be democratic, and was bound to discriminate against non-Jews, he saw binationalism as the only model for Arab–Jewish co-existence. However, the Jewish state having been created, he went on to believe that after 1967 there was still an opportunity to create a federal arrangement between Israel and the

Palestinian territories, which could make a closer integration between them possible over time. He thought this was a feasible idea up until the 1973 war, when the two-state solution became the adopted international position.[16] In the late 1980s, Sari Nusseibeh (later the head of Al-Quds university in Jerusalem), put forward the idea of a binational Jerusalem by encouraging Palestinian residents to apply for Israeli citizenship. This brought him much opprobrium from Palestinians at the time, although in fact he mainly supported the two-state solution.[17] But a similar idea appeared later, this time for all the Palestinians under occupation to become Israeli citizens.

Types of Binational State

The following remarks are meant in no way to provide an exhaustive analysis of binationalism. That is available in many studies elsewhere. A binational state could be configured as cantonal, federal, or, in an innovative variation latterly devised by the Swedish diplomat, Mathias Mossberg, as 'dual states' superimposed on one another. An earlier writer had described a similar idea as 'parallel sovereignty' for the two peoples in the same territory.[18] These proposals explored the possibility of Palestinians and Israelis sharing the same land by separating the concept of statehood from territory. Instead of two states alongside each other, Israelis and Palestinians would live in states superimposed on each other. Both of them would have the right to settle the whole area between the Mediterranean and the Jordan river as citizens of each state. But they also had the right to take the citizenship of each other's states if they so wished. Predominantly Jewish localities would belong to 'Israel' and Palestinian ones to 'Palestine', but Palestinian individuals living in an Israeli canton could opt to remain citizens of Palestine and vice versa. Each state would have its own administration and could maintain its separate ethnicity and culture. But there would be a common currency, taxation, labour market, joint defence and other shared services. In essence, this arrangement was similar to the Swiss cantonal system, and could become the truly globalised state of the twenty-first century where people did not need to be tied to a specific land for national definition.

Abu-Odeh saw the binational state as a federation of separate Jewish and Arab administrative units linked to a central government on the US model, as did Abboushi.[19] The units would be autonomous and could even develop their own economic strategies with help from the central government. Citizens had the right to move about freely and live in the units of their choice. Since all were supposed to be equal in such a state, resources would need to be transferred from the richer (Jewish) units to the poorer (Arab) ones to equalise their status. Such a transfer of funds could also serve as a way for Israel to make amends for the dispossession and exile it had caused generations of Palestinians. The refugees would have the choice of returning to the Palestinian or Israeli units, or be compensated for their losses and injuries over decades of dispossession. Abufarha proposed a binational configuration of two sovereign states in political and economic union.[20] The geography of these states would be based on demography, the Palestinian state to include areas of predominant Palestinian habitation, such as the West Bank, Gaza and the Galilee, and the Israeli state those of predominant Israeli residence, like Tel Aviv, Safad and Haifa. The sparsely populated areas would be part of 'Palestine', reserved for the returning refugees. Each state would have its own legislative council but would be federal in terms of political representation, external security and the economy. The residents of each state would be subject to its jurisdiction, regardless of ethnicity. Jerusalem would become a separate district to encompass Bethlehem and have its own independent council. It would grant equal residency rights to Israelis and Palestinians.

Several other federal solutions were proposed, all based on the concept of two territorially separate states, but without always delineating their exact borders. Belgium, Canada and Switzerland were frequently cited as models. The last was probably the most successful example of how ethnic communities could live peacefully with each other. All 26 Swiss cantons were self-governing, used their own languages and related to the federal government only in such matters as the judiciary, currency management, foreign policy and national defence. In Canada's case, the French- and English-speaking divide was managed by granting French-speaking Quebec virtual independence within the federal framework; Belgium was another example of a federal union between its Dutch- and French-speaking halves. This union of Flemish and Walloon communities, who were different culturally and had a long-standing history of conflict with each other, made Belgium seem a suitable model for a federated Israel/Palestine.[21] Its three regions,

Flemish, Walloon and that of the capital, Brussels, had their own parliament, language and culture, but citizens could travel and work anywhere in the country. Each ethnic community was responsible for the educational and cultural affairs of its members wherever they resided so as to maintain a communal cultural continuity outside of geographical space. In a similarly federated Israel/Palestine, Jerusalem would be the equivalent of Brussels. The federal constitution would protect the rights of Israelis and Palestinians, guarantee religious freedom and separation of church and state so as to guard against Jewish and Islamic theocratic extremism. Returning refugees could live in Israel as well as Palestine, but retain Palestinian citizenship.

One writer looked to the past for ideas, rediscovering the UN Special Committee on Palestine's (UNSCOP) binational proposal of 1947 as a model for a modern solution.[22] This proposed the creation of federated Jewish and Arab states with Jerusalem as the common capital. The federal authority would draw up a constitution that guaranteed equal rights for citizens irrespective of race or religion, and was responsible for defence, immigration, foreign policy, currency management and taxation. Another model was the Malaysian multi-ethnic state, which was a successful example of how to resolve years of inter-ethnic strife by intelligent economic and social policies.[23] Numerous other types of federal, confederal and cantonal arrangement, from Argentina to the Russian Federation to Switzerland, each with its own combination of self-rule and central authority, were discussed. Any of these examples could have provided inspiration and possible models for a federated or binational Israel/Palestine.[24]

Tamar Hermann has neatly divided the history of the binational idea into four stages.[25] First, the 'old school' of Jewish binationalists who did not regard this solution as ideal but as a way of defusing inevitable strife between the two communities. Second was the 'new school' of Jewish binationalists, individuals motivated by concern about the viability of Israel as a Jewish state and who saw this solution as the only way for saving Israeli Jews from themselves. Third were their Palestinian binationalist counterparts who sought a way in the present unfavourable power structure to realise Palestinian national rights. And fourth were the advocates of binationalism and secular democracy from the outside, influenced, in her view, by their experience of living under multicultural Western democracies and wishing naively to apply the same model to the situation in Israel/Palestine. None of these groups thought the binational solution desirable, she judged, but they advocated it because the reality on the ground precluded both sides from exercising their 'right' to statehood in the whole of the territory. In the end, they were a motley collection of intellectuals who were neither practising politicians nor decision makers, and hence detached from reality.

The 'Democratic Non-Sectarian State'

The idea of a secular democratic state, or at least its 'non-sectarian' antecedent, originated with the PLO in the late 1960s. As such, it was the first initiative for a future settlement to emanate from the Palestinians themselves. Up until then virtually all binationalist and partition proposals during the Mandate years came from British or Zionist sources, and the latter, as we saw, were confined to a small minority. By contrast, the one-state proposal espoused by the Palestinians was the position of their formal representative in exile, the PNC. At its fifth meeting in 1969 it envisaged a liberated Palestine that would be home to all its citizens, to live in a 'free democratic society encompassing all Palestinians, including Muslims, Christians and Jews'.[26] Later, 'society' was amended to 'state' and this 'Democratic State of Palestine' remained the theme of all PNC meetings until 1973. At its meeting that year, it resolved that all citizens would live 'in equality, justice and fraternity', in a state 'opposed to all forms of prejudice on the basis of race, colour and creed'. The international peace proposals put forward during this phase did not accord with this vision, nor did any of them make mention of Palestine's total liberation. Resolution 242 relegated the Palestinian issue to one of a mere 'just settlement for the refugees', the 1969 Rogers Plan was based on this resolution, and Jordan's 'United Arab Kingdom Plan', which was devised in 1972 and proposed a union between Jordan and an autonomous West Bank state, were all rejected on these grounds.[27]

The democratic Palestine state idea ('non-sectarian', not secular, was the term actually used, although Yasser Arafat referred to a 'secular state' on one occasion and retracted it soon afterwards),[28] was not just a slogan for the Palestinians. The PLO aimed to achieve it in practice through armed struggle and, after the 1971 PNC meeting, using diplomacy as well. Some PLO factions, notably the PFLP and PDFLP (the Popular Democratic Front for the Liberation of Palestine), thought the way forward was through a popular struggle to overthrow the pro-Western Arab regimes first. Otherwise they would only foil Palestinian efforts at liberation if they remained in power. (It was this that led to the 'Black September' confrontation with Jordan, which proved so costly to the PLO.) But, following the 1973 Arab–Israeli October War, the PLO's position became more pragmatic, hoping to reap some reward from a comprehensive Middle East settlement that looked possible in the aftermath of that war.

Although the Palestinian leadership had been considering the idea of setting up a Palestinian state on the West Bank and Gaza since 1971, at least as a first step towards total liberation, it was not until the twelfth PNC meeting of 1974 that it became an official position. Dropping the goal of a non-sectarian state for that of a 'National Authority' on any Palestinian land liberated by the armed struggle, the PNC signalled a fundamental change of direction that was to lead ultimately to the Oslo Accords. Nevertheless, the democratic one-state option was never formally renounced as the ultimate aim of the Palestinian Movement until 1988, when the PNC voted for an independent Palestinian state and recognition of Israel. In the intervening years it gradually faded from the debate and went quietly into abeyance as a noble dream or, as some Palestinians put it, a 'preferred outcome' that was unattainable in the circumstances obtaining at the time (and since).

By proposing the creation of one democratic state in Palestine, the PLO had taken an extraordinarily imaginative leap to map out a vision that acknowledged the Jewish presence *on equal terms* in the Palestinian homeland.[29] That the very people who had been dispossessed by the Jews should have devised a solution based on sharing with these Jews, rather than retaliatory expulsion and revenge, was a major concession that should have been acknowledged as such and applauded. Instead, and predictably, Israel rejected it out of hand, arguing that the Palestine National Charter, which defined the Jews as those living in Palestine before 'the Zionist invasion' and thus excluded most of Israel's population, made any accommodation with the Palestinians impossible.[30] This was a wilful misreading of the change in the Palestinian position by the Israelis. Dismissing what was a liberal and humane approach to the conflict, they were at pains to destroy it and discredit the motives behind it, even asserting that the one-state proposal was no more than a recipe for committing genocide against the people of Israel.[31] At the same time, and for no reason other than that they thought it premature, not one Arab or other country showed any interest in or even discussed the one-state proposal. The Palestinians themselves seem also not to have thought through the implications of such a solution or produced a plan for how it would be implemented. Obvious problems, such as the exact meaning of 'non-sectarian' in practice, or of introducing secularism to a largely religious society, or the issue of accommodating a vibrant and growing Palestinian nationalism, or the difficulties for Palestinians of co-existence with a people who had colonised and usurped their country, were glossed over or not addressed.

In reality, the Palestinian position on the democratic non-sectarian state was more complex than that apparently straightforward designation suggested.[32] The PLO was aware that, as a solution, it was most unlikely to be implemented in the short term, and in any case various Palestinian factions and leaders interpreted the concept differently. Most were agreed on the need to define what sort of Palestinian state they were seeking after liberation and that a democratic, non-sectarian state was the ultimate goal, but they differed over its precise meaning. Some leaders spoke of Jews having 'national rights' within such a state and the PDFLP, which promoted this position, was suspected of secretly aiming for a federal or two-state solution. Fateh wanted the state to be linked to the Arab world, something that Israeli Jews would be unlikely to accept, but it also spoke of building a country together with them in which the two peoples could live together and 'mutually interact'.[33] Other leaders thought a federal arrangement on the Swiss or Czech models might be acceptable. Two PLO factions, the Iraqi-backed Arab Liberation Front and the Syrian-backed al-Sa'iqa, by contrast, totally rejected the idea on the grounds that no resolution of the conflict could be independent of wider Arab agreement.

Why did the Palestinian movement put forward the non-sectarian democratic state proposal? Plausibly it was a way of opening up the debate on what would constitute an egalitarian solution to a conflict where justice was of paramount importance. The right of return was at the forefront of Palestinian preoccupations, especially those of the diaspora from where the PLO proposal sprang, and they thought that this was the only method of making it happen. At the same time, Palestinians recognised that no progress was possible without taking into account the presence of a strong and established Israeli Jewish society in their homeland. But they did not develop the non-sectarian state idea beyond the outline stage, probably because it struck them as futile when the concept itself had not been agreed by Israel or even amongst themselves, and so getting bogged down over the practical details was pointless. As Yasser Arafat said at the time, 'We do not debate the structure of the new state in detail because what we need now is the greatest possible national cohesion.'[34] Moreover, for many Palestinians, the unitary state was a theoretical notion they could not identify with and whose nature they were unclear about. The prospect of sharing the country with those who had usurped it and abused them struck them as intolerable. Thus the proposal was never adopted at the popular level, and the internal contradictions and lack of an agreed position amongst the leadership made it even less appealing. It was not followed up, even by its progenitors, and remained for decades as vague and unformed as when it was first proposed.

The Secular Democratic State: Later Developments

The secular, democratic one-state solution did not return to the political debate until the early 1990s, although it continued to inspire a small minority of Palestinian and other left-wing intellectuals.[35] Its later revival was roughly contemporaneous with that of the binational alternative, but initially, the Israeli adherents of the secular state were even fewer than those advocating binationalism. And even then their real numbers were obscured by the fact that the advocates of the one-state idea often did not distinguish between that state being binationalist or secular democratic, although the two were fundamentally different. Many Palestinian supporters of the one-state notion, especially those inside the occupied territories, came from the ranks of those who feared that the two-state solution was no longer feasible. This prompted demands for annexation to Israel if its colonisation of Palestinian territory continued to destroy the two-state solution. We pointed out earlier how Ahmad Qurei, the Palestinian prime minister, had warned of such an outcome in early 2004, but he was also echoing the popular and influential Fateh leader Marwan Barghouti's call – prior to his imprisonment in Israel

– for a one-state option for the same reason.[36] In this way the struggle against occupation would be converted into a demand for civil rights inside an expanded Israeli state, the last thing Israel wanted.

The more Israel colonised and fragmented the Palestinian territories, the greater the number of Palestinians demanding a one-state solution. It was even reported in 2003 (*Yediott Ahronot*, 28 November) that a Fateh leader and a supporter of the one-state idea, Qaddura Faris, was setting up a party to promote the proposal for annexation to Israel. Implicit in these moves was an undeclared desire for the demographic issue, so feared by Israel, to play to the Palestinians' benefit through a one-person-one-vote system where their numbers would make a difference. As Gary Sussman commented, Israel's greatest 'weakness' would become the Palestinians' greatest advantage.[37]

Ironically enough, annexation was not just a Palestinian demand. Hardline Israelis also wanted the Palestinian territories joined on to a greater Israel and proposed giving those Palestinians who refused to leave them 'residency' status or a sort of reduced citizenship as a mechanism for reducing the Palestinian presence.[38] Support for the secular state idea came mainly, however, from diaspora Palestinians, those opposed to Zionism and left-wing intellectuals who decried the principle of ethnic or religious states and had always held these views.[39] South Africa was frequently invoked as a model of a secular state that had made apartheid obsolete, and, by analogy, if such a state were to replace Israel it could do the same for Zionism. As the Washington-based journalist, Helen Cobban, pointed out, Israel would discover, like South Africa before it, that no amount of repression or fencing off or military attacks on neighbouring states could bring it peace, and so Israelis might have to settle for a one-person-one-vote unitary state.[40] Similarly using the South African model, the Israeli activist, Jeff Halper, argued that binationalism was logistically impossible given the physical intermingling of Israelis and Palestinians on the ground.[41] The only alternative, he believed, was a unitary, democratic state, and in order to attain this a South Africa-style anti-apartheid struggle against Zionism would be needed. Implicit in this was the acknowledgement that Israel's occupation was irreversible and all that was possible was to try and neutralise its controlling effects. He called for a campaign, not to end the occupation, which was a hopeless task, but for equal rights in a democratic, one-person-one-vote state.

Halper was one of the few prepared to outline a practical strategy for achieving the goal of the unitary state. Another was the Israeli writer, Daniel Gavron, an ardent Zionist turned unitary state supporter after the second intifada.[42] He saw that the only solution was a sharing of the land between Jews and Arabs and proposed a schedule for doing this, starting with the annexation of the Palestinian territories to Israel, followed by universal franchise, and then the creation of a multi-ethnic state. However, the main thrust of the argument of those advocating the one-state solution was still predominantly theoretical, especially amongst Jewish intellectuals like Tony Judt and Daniel Lazare, who did not distinguish between binationalism and its secular democratic alternative in their concern with the failure of Zionism and the Jewish state. Lazare summed up the objections to a state based on 'religio/ethnic polices elevating one group above all others' and hence increasingly abnormal in a modern world that shunned such practices.[43] In a later wide-ranging review of books on Israel and Zionism, he posed the question of whether Zionism was a failed ideology and raised the need for a binational solution.[44] The British Jewish historian, Tony Judt, had earlier written eloquently of his dismay at the Jewish state, which he saw as 'an anachronism' in a modern multicultural world that emphasised citizenship rather than race, religion or ethnicity.[45] Israel came into being, he thought, at a time when the notion of nation-states was past. He concluded that a two-state solution was inappropriate in such a situation, whereas the preferred outcome was a unitary, binational state. Judt was resoundingly attacked for this view by furious American Jews, who threatened his life and accused him of being a 'self-hating Jew', but this was an indication of the strength of the debate that was developing around the one-state solution after 2000.[46]

A Growing Debate

A new-found interest in the unitary state became apparent in the wake of the second intifada, largely provoked by Israel's refusal to abandon Palestinian land or respond to Palestinian demands for independence. Concern with the best way out of the impasse led to the creation of groups and individuals interested in reviving the one-state solution. In Israel, the Naturei Karta and the ultra-orthodox Satmar groups had traditionally supported such a solution, and indeed, in March 2006, some of them demonstrated in Jerusalem, declaring that they did not recognise Israel, only the Palestine of 1948.[47] In another demonstration by ultra-orthodox Jews in New York in December 2006, thousands protested against the existence of the State of Israel as a contradiction to the teachings of the Torah.[48] But the involvement of a wider range of actors was new. According to the US-based *Jewish Week* (23 November 2003), this 'alarming idea' had taken hold amongst Palestinians, American left-wing circles and on student campuses, and could garner global support. In 2003, a Swiss-based organisation, The Association of One Democratic State in Palestine/Israel, was set up by a Palestinian Swiss lawyer and soon acquired a membership of over 200 Arabs, Jews and others. By 2006, it had held two conferences, assembled a literature archive and attracted a range of international supporters, amongst them the Jerusalem-based Rabbis For Peace which joined the association in November 2003.[49] In the same year, a second group, the Right of Return Coalition (Al-Awda), active in other pro-Palestinian fields, formally adopted the one-state solution at its international conference in Toronto. A London-based association, The One-State Group, was established in early 2004 and another in Colorado named The Movement for One-Secular State.

By April 2004, 15 similar groups were operating, some in Israel/Palestine, but the majority in Europe and America.[50] Mainly they amounted to no more than email networks of interested activists, Jewish, Palestinian and others, and, as in the case of the London group, an Internet archive of relevant literature. They held sporadic meetings and conducted an active and intelligent debate via the Internet on all aspects of the binational and the secular democratic state. While working in Ramallah in 2005, I found such a group, Israelis and Palestinians who met to discuss the issue. Their numbers were small, and the Israeli members made regular visits to their Palestinian colleagues in Ramallah, since the latter were mostly prevented from entering Israel. Another group was centred on the Emil Touma Institute in Haifa, based on an initiative from fellow Israeli and Palestinian academics and activists, prominent amongst whom was the Israeli historian, Ilan Pappe. I was familiar with most of these groupings whose lively discussions produced valuable insights that developed the one-state concept well beyond the vague formulation of the PLO's non-sectarian state. One of the members of the London group, the

American historian Virginia Tilley, went on to publish a book on the one-state solution that reviewed its history and salient features, drawing comparison with the South African experience.[51]

Gradually, the one-state idea entered the mainstream debate, propelled by the discussions of such groups and the writings of a number of intellectuals and opinion formers. In 2004, the US Green Party adopted the principle of the single-state solution at its national convention, leaving the form of the state for the parties themselves to decide.[52] Hundreds of articles on the subject appeared in various mainstream publications, many of them quoted here, and it was no longer the preserve of a fringe minority.[53] In 2004, the then Iranian president, Hashemi Rafsanjani, called for unification between Israel and the Palestinian territories under one government which should be elected by 'Jews already present', Palestinian residents and refugees living in neighbouring countries. He spoke of harmony between Muslims, Christians and Jews in one land, thus taking a significant departure from the traditional Iranian line of refusing to recognise that Jewish immigrants had any rights at all in the country.[54] The Libyan head of state, Colonel Qadhafi, also put forward a proposal for one Israel/Palestine in his 'White Book', published in 2003. This document explained the reasoning behind his adoption of the one-state solution, for 'no other concept is capable of resolving the problem'.[55] 'Isratine', his proposed name for the new unitary state, would be home to Israelis and Palestinians, foremost amongst them the returning Palestinian refugees. He considered this the only just solution that would allow the two peoples access to a land they considered equally sacred. Qadhafi presented his idea to other Arab leaders at the Arab League Summit in Tunis in 2004, but there was no support for the proposal, prompting him to walk out in anger.[56]

Several opinion polls on the one-state solution demonstrated some support for it amongst Palestinians under occupation. According to the Palestinian Center for Policy and Survey Research, 27 per cent were in favour of one state (although that might have reflected Palestinian anxieties about the impossibility of attaining the two-state alternative). Indeed, a Jerusalem Media and Communication Centre opinion poll had found that in 1999 fewer than 20 per cent of West Bank and Gaza Palestinians and 15 per cent of Jewish Israelis favoured a binational solution if the attempt to establish two states failed. A Peace Index poll of Israelis in 2003 found that 73 per cent feared the emergence of a binationalist state, with only 6 per cent in favour.[57] In the survey of Palestinians and Israelis I conducted between 1999 and 2000, 22 of the 42 Palestinian respondents were willing to share a state with Israelis and 11 wanted this to be a democracy, asserting that 'Jews used to live with us before'. However, 24 wanted a two-state solution, qualified with such comments as, 'a first stage' or 'all we can have for now'. When asked explicitly about a secular democratic state, just three were in favour. Only 13 of 50 Israeli Jews on the other hand were willing to share the land, but only in the West Bank and Gaza (this was before the evacuation of the Gaza Strip by Israel). Nine were willing to share Jerusalem, but just its eastern half. Opinion polls after this date could well have found significant shifts in response to the question of one or two states, and possibly greater support for the one state.

How Acceptable was the One-State Solution?

Interesting as this evolution in thinking on the one-state debate was, it was nevertheless the case that its opponents were vastly more numerous than its supporters. In a conversation during the summer of 2005 with Amira Hass, the Israeli journalist and a woman known for her sympathies with the Palestinians, I remember her increasing irritation with the one-state position. 'You Palestinians can never learn to follow things through,' she exclaimed. 'Why change tactics in mid-struggle from something potentially attainable to run after something quite impossible?' The majority of Palestinians rejected the one-state option, and even thought it a dangerous idea because it would distract attention from the urgent struggle to end the occupation. Others were either mystified by the one-state idea or scathing about it. The sometime London head of the Palestinian Delegation, Afif Safieh, held such views with greater vehemence. 'If you believe in it,' he told me once, putting his fingers to his lips, 'never ever speak of it! It must remain secret until at least we've got our state.' The American Palestinian political scientist, Ibrahim Abu Lughod, regarded those of his countrymen who supported the one-state solution with great hostility. 'You people are little better than traitors to our cause', I remember him declaring when the issue came up at an Arab American University Graduates' conference in Jerusalem in 1993. 'You want to turn us into slaves in a second South

Africa!' During my researches amongst Palestinians in Gaza and the West Bank in late 1999, I found much initial puzzlement and scepticism about the question of the unitary state's actual application in practice. 'It won't work,' most people immediately said. But further discussion usually led to greater interest and more readiness to consider it as a possibility. By 2006, however, with Israel's brutal assault on Gaza in the background, reaction was angry and hostile to any suggestion of sharing with Israelis. At a meeting in London, several young Palestinian men, holding up pictures of bloody children lying dead in Gaza, told me angrily, 'If you want to let the occupiers into your house, that's your choice. But don't speak for the rest of us!'

The Palestinian sociologist, Salim Tamari, summarised these concerns in a cogent analysis that considered the binational option attractive but simplistic because it ignored the real situation on the ground.[58] He saw that there was no constituency on either side for such a solution; the Israeli state's established institutions and Zionist consciousness, as well as the material advantages its citizens enjoyed from exploiting Palestinian land and resources, would not be given up lightly; and Palestinians would resist the inevitably inferior position of their community within an advanced Europeanised, industrial state. Nor could one ask them to abandon their struggle for independence and the end of colonial occupation in order to have them struggle anew against hostile Israeli fellow citizens. If there was to be a binationalist arrangement, Tamari concluded, it should be with Jordan.

Jeff Halper reviewed a list of objections, many of which have already been mentioned, in an exhaustive study in 2002.[59] Israelis and Palestinians saw themselves as national entities that would not easily be accommodated in a common state; they would not give up their competing claims to self-determination, especially since for the Jews that was a basic feature of Zionism. If Palestinians were made to live with Israelis before they were ready – that is, before they had risen to an equivalent political, economic and social standard with Israelis – they could remain a permanent underclass.

According to Robert Keeley, a former president of the Middle East Institute in Washington, a one-state outcome was unimaginable while Israel continued to enjoy the unstinting support of the world's only superpower, the US.[60] He also thought that neither the Israeli Jews, who had worked so hard to create a Jewish state defined as one with a Jewish majority, nor the Palestinian Arabs, who had striven for a state of their own in which to rule themselves, would relinquish their positions. He concluded somewhat dramatically that the one-state solution was 'a recipe for disaster for Israel, for the Palestinians, for the entire Middle East' and for the whole world.

Israeli political figures likewise pointed to the futility of seeking a binational or one-state solution while there was such distrust and lack of good will between the parties. The seasoned Israeli writer and campaigner, Uri Avnery, thought it was foolish to abandon the fight for Palestinian independence in return for a chimera. In a well-argued essay he laid out a list of objections to the one-state solution hard to refute.[61] The struggle for a two-state solution had already gained the Palestinian movement a territorial base in the homeland, which, with patience and struggle, he argued, could be expanded, 'dunum by dunum', just as in the Zionist case. Binationalism, on the other hand, condemned Palestinians to life as an underclass in a vastly superior Israeli society, not much different from the fate of the 20 per cent disadvantaged Israeli Arabs already living there. For those who dreamed of a South Africa-type solution where Palestinians in a binational state would be an underclass only to begin with, later to attract worldwide support for their struggle against Israeli apartheid through their demographic dominance, he had few words of comfort. Unlike white South Africans, who were universally disliked and had few friends, Jews commanded the support of the powerful US Jewish community, they continued to excite Christian sympathy and guilt over the Holocaust, and it was the Arabs, not they, who were the world's bogeymen. The gravest objection to the binational state from an Israeli point of view, however, as Avnery explained, was that it would be a negation of Zionism, an outcome few Israelis were willing to even contemplate. And that doomed it from the outset.

Like Avnery, the PLO Executive Committee member and co-author of the Geneva Initiative, Yasserr Abed Rabbo, opposed binationalism on the grounds that Palestinians did not wish to live as second-class citizens in one state. But he did not rule out that, if forced to live in Bantustans as a result of Israel's barrier wall, they would demand a single state 'within a decade or two'.[62] At the same time, the PLO's foreign minister and head of Fateh, Farouk Qaddumi, was clear that a two-state solution was only a stage towards a single state to replace

Israel, in line, according to him, with the 1974 PLO incremental position on liberating Palestinian land and establishing Palestinian authority over it.[63] Though such bluntness was not the usual line adopted by Palestinian officials, Qaddumi was speaking for a majority of Palestinians. No Palestinian existed who did not harbour within him a yearning for the lost homeland in its entirety and an intention to return to it some day. No Palestinian accepted that the refugees should never be able to go home. This was made clear in my own small survey, but it was also an aspiration for diaspora Palestinians, who, after 1993, saw a real possibility (for the first time) of a return in the context of a two-state arrangement with open borders, that could lead to what would effectively be a common state with Israel.

Binational or Secular Democratic?

The distinction between binationalism and secular democracy was an important one, even though it was often blurred in one-state discussions. The binationalist solution permitted a degree of communal autonomy and identity but also of separation. In that sense it was another way of preserving for Jewish Israelis the concept on which the whole Zionist enterprise was founded: the self-definition of a group by recourse to a questionable religio/ethnic identity that entitled it to a specific territory. It maintained the Zionist myth that Palestinians did not accept and had fought hard to dispel, of a distinct ethnic Jewish community, which straddled borders and geography as one nation linked to one territory. These assumptions had underpinned the belligerent displacement of Palestinians at the founding of Israel, the Israeli 'law of return', and the fantasy of an unbroken historical link to the land that justified Israel's excesses. Proposing to create a binational state meant no more than preserving this structure of ideas but in a more limited space.

Moreover, binationalism permitted both communities to continue to believe they had an exclusive right to the whole land, and, since Israeli Jews were more advanced as a group, better organised and wealthier than Palestinians, they would assert that feeling of ownership in social dominance over them. Nor would they ever cease to strive for the 'ingathering' of more Jews to the state to strengthen their community's position. Thus Uri Avnery's forecast of a disadvantaged Palestinian community of second-class citizens ending up in an unequal society was likely to come true. Though there existed no real parallel for the case of Israel/Palestine, the Cypriot example of attempted binationalism between Greeks and Turks between 1960 and 1974 is instructive. There were Greek Cypriots who did not accept that Turks should have an equivalent status in the joint state, and who never gave up their view that Cyprus was Greek and a part of Greece, and so resented the Turkish presence. They showed this in vicious military assaults on the Turkish community and in numerous discriminatory ways. The whole experiment collapsed when Turkey, coming to the aid of its people, invaded Cyprus with consequences that are with us to this day.[64]

In a secular democratic state, on the other hand, citizens would have rights not derived from membership of an ethnic or religious group. They were equal before the law as individuals and not as groups, irrespective of race or religion. Such an arrangement would be useful in bypassing the difficulty of defining what in fact constituted the Israeli Jewish community. It was not homogeneous, indeed how could it be since it included people from places as culturally diverse as Morocco, Ethiopia and America, as well as a good number of non-Jews from Russia. Thus the secular state would reflect more closely the multicultural reality on the ground and help create a society into which Palestinians fitted more naturally as part of a cultural mosaic. It would also conform more closely to a tradition long familiar to Arab and Islamic societies, that of pluralism, interaction and tolerance towards different ethnicities and faiths in their midst. This was true, not only of the Islamic empire at its zenith, but also in more recent times. Jews, fleeing persecution in Spain in the fifteenth century, found refuge and prospered in the lands of the Muslim Ottoman Empire, and in our own time religious minorities, even under the totalitarian regimes of Saddam Hussein in Iraq and the Alawites in Syria, enjoyed equality with the rest. (It was only after the US/UK invasion of Iraq in 2003 and the resulting anarchy in the country that its Christian minority flocked to Syria for refuge and something more akin to the tolerance it had known before.)[65] Palestinian society in particular, before the mass immigration of European Jews imposed their exclusivist creed of Zionism and culturally alien philosophy on the country, had been a successful composite of Muslims, Christians and Jews as well as Armenians, Circassians, Europeans and others.

In such a state, religious practice and social customs were confined to the private sphere and did not inform state policy. Many Arabs feared that 'secular' meant 'atheist' and resisted this solution on that basis, but in fact it referred to nothing more than the separation of church and state, long familiar to Western liberal democracies like Britain or the USA. Unlike the binationalist state, a secular democracy was likely to be conducive towards helping its citizens develop a common national identity through a sense of belonging to each other and to the state. Their loyalty to their shared state and sense of social cohesion would, in theory at least, be greater in such a situation because it would not be competing with loyalty to their own communities.[66] In this environment, the supremacist ideas, discrimination on ethnic or racial lines and sense of exclusive ownership of the whole land that we referred to above would be discouraged from continuing and begin to fade, even if very gradually. In time, the hope would be that a new identity, developed as a result of this sharing, would permanently replace the previous ethnic or other definitions.

Such aims would of course directly conflict with Zionism and spell its end, and so would not be acceptable to the majority of Jews. Though Tilley has called this view into question, arguing that Zionism did not strictly require an ethnic state with a Jewish majority, and under the right democratic conditions, could be compatible with the creation of a unitary state, this seems improbable, given the present evidence.[67] From the Palestinian point of view, however, the secular democratic solution was the better option. Only then could the country be returned to a semblance of what it had been before Zionism overtook it. Who knows? It could even turn out better as a result of the amalgam of enterprising Jews and Arabs co-operating to build a new society. Aside from those who latterly argued for a period of separation in their own state while they recuperated from the ordeal of Israeli occupation, and so did not support a single state whatever its form, surely the only reason for Palestinians to choose binationalism over secular democracy was because they believed that the other solution was impossible to attain. The three Palestinian respondents in my survey who supported the secular democratic state thought it was 'utopian', and the 22 respondents who were willing to share a state with Israelis qualified their answer with: 'But only if they don't discriminate against us.'

A Formidable Challenge

There was no doubt that as a solution, the one-state proposition posed an enormous challenge to entrenched positions and established ideas about how the conflict should be solved. The combination of the cultural/psychological dependence of Jews worldwide on the idea of Israel and the Western addiction to supporting this dependence were formidable obstacles. The end of the Jewish state inherent in the creation of a unitary Israel/Palestine was unthinkable in a context of long-standing Israeli denial of its true history: how it came into being, the resulting injustice done to the Palestinians and the indifference to their sufferings over the last 60 years. That denial and the freedom from retribution allowed to Israel had enabled several generations of Israeli Jews to enjoy the privileges of a settler colonialist enterprise without bearing the costs. That and the anti-Arab racism that was an integral part of keeping the Israeli project viable would be difficult to give up. Discrimination in favour of Jews was structured into the very fabric of the Jewish state and its institutions.

How would one persuade a people reared on such privileges and feelings of superiority to abandon them in return for less prosperity and an uncertain future? And how could such people, with a history of being minorities in every society they had lived amongst and now found themselves a majority for the first time, relinquish that status to become a part of something once again? Equally problematic was the fact that, when implanted into the Arab region, Israel never saw itself as anything other than a Western state, and had no concept of or desire for being a part of the Middle East as would have to happen if it merged with Palestine. Such a situation would force on Israelis the unaccustomed prospect of revising their instinctive fear of and contempt for Arabs. Hillel Frisch, an Israeli academic I met at the Truman Institute in Jerusalem's Hebrew University in December 1999, told me without a trace of embarrassment that Arab civilisation had nothing to offer him or any other Jew. 'This so-called civilisation', he said, 'stopped in the fourteenth century and so what's there to learn from them now – democracy, technology, what?'

The one-state solution would signify the end of Zionism as a political ideology, but it would allow for the continuation of 'cultural Zionism', where Jews could maintain a Jewish cultural identity in the biblical homeland. One Israeli Zionist who seemed to have accepted this distinction was the former speaker of the Knesset, Avraham Burg, who wrote of his dismay at what Israel had become, the 'perversions of the Israeli soul', as he put it. Israelis could not assume that the existence of the state was assured, and he saw the need to re-establish the connection between Jews and 'the sources of Jewish culture' in an open, non-racist society that welcomed the Other.[68] However, so persuaded by political Zionism was the majority of Jews worldwide that they saw its demise as a sort of personal annihilation. It was an irony that in a situation where more than two-thirds of them did not live in Israel and apparently had no intention of doing so, they would still have fought for its survival to give them a psychological sense of being 'normal', like other minorities who had 'a country of origin'. Such sentiments were difficult to dispel and posed another significant obstacle.

At the same time, the Western powers, which had lavished moral and material support on Israel since its inception, balked at the prospect of confronting the disaster they had created for a Middle East bogged down by an intractable conflict with no end in sight. Far from solving the Jewish question through creating the Jewish state, as they had hoped, the problem would return to face them if that state were dissolved. They were as anxious as any Zionist to resist a one-state outcome that would signal the defeat of the project they had espoused and expose the folly of their strategy over many decades. Their near-hysterical reaction to the Iranian president, Mahmoud Ahmadinejad's provocative declaration in 2006, quoting the Ayatollah Khomeini that Israel should be 'wiped off the map', and the obsessive insistence that the Hamas government recognise Israel's 'right to exist' were indications of this sense of failure. The powerful Christian Zionists of America were no lesser champions of the Jewish state and, for their own fanatical reasons, would also fight any threat to its survival. Lastly, it would take considerable effort to reverse America's entrenched support for Israel, which had acquired the status of an adopted child for successive US governments. The American neoconservative agenda for the 'New Middle East' would go up in smoke if Israel were subsumed in a unitary state, reinforcing their determination to ensure its survival.

No wonder then that, despite an impressive revival of the debate over its various aspects, which had entered mainstream political thinking, the unitary state was still far from being adopted as the preferred solution by any official body or mass movement. Its proponents frequently looked to the example of South Africa, which had become a one-state democracy after the defeat of apartheid. In fact, the cases were not as close as some commentators wanted to believe.[69] While many of apartheid's discriminatory practices were replicated in Israel's restrictions on Palestinian life, the two projects had basic differences. In South Africa, blacks were in the majority and the whites sought to rule over them, not to replace them. The struggle between the two communities was over rights, citizenship and equality, not, as in the Israeli/Palestinian case, over the possession of land. The defeat of apartheid came about after the withdrawal of foreign, especially US, support caused by a large-scale, external anti-apartheid campaign and, most importantly, economic sanctions, of which there was no sign in the Palestinian case.

There was no doubt that Israel and the apartheid South African regime had forged a close relationship over decades and were agreed on similar discriminatory measures in dealing with their 'subject' populations.[70] But raising the South African parallel, though usually dismissed by Israel and its supporters as antisemitic,[71] was useful to the Palestinian struggle, even if it did not exactly mirror their own situation, mainly because it helped to stimulate a debate about the concept of exclusivist states and the one-state solution.[72] It was also useful in emphasising by example the importance of repentance, the need for the former oppressor to admit and make amends for the wrongs inflicted on his victim. This was as indispensable for the Palestinians as it had been for South Africa. The South African Truth and Reconciliation Commission established in 1995, after the defeat of apartheid, was set up to bear witness to and record the human rights violations perpetrated under the apartheid regime. It took testimony from thousands of abusers and their victims and allowed for a cathartic public exposure of unacknowledged crimes and unaddressed grievances. When it reported in 1998, the Commission set up a mechanism for victim reparation, including a compensation fund to which the beneficiaries of apartheid would be obliged to contribute.[73]

Although it might not have fulfilled all expectations or even been wholly successful – it was criticised for failing to achieve much reconciliation between the parties and for being weighted in favour of the abusers – the Truth and Reconciliation Commission nevertheless went to the heart of a psychological truth about human dealings. Conflicts rooted in injustice, as is the one in Israel/Palestine, need what the psychologists call 'closure', when the perpetrator acknowledges the injustice committed and makes visible and material reparation to his victim. It is only then that the conflict can definitively end and true reconciliation begin. From the start of their dispossession it was a bitter bone of contention for Palestinians that Israelis had never so much as apologised for what they had done, let alone make amends for it. The insistence on the implementation of their right of return had also to be understood in this context: that for Israelis it would constitute the fairest and most definitive act of repentance for crimes committed by Zionism, and in so doing they would have undone the state that it had created.

Desirable and Feasible?

The foregoing account has shown how difficult it was to implement the one-state solution. Yet that should not have been the starting point of the discussion. The question of whether this solution was *feasible* was frequently confused with whether it was *desirable*, and it was here that the struggle for hearts and minds should have started. Prolonged concentration on the two-state outcome as the only solution for the conflict had made it into a mantra that discouraged imaginative thinking. If one set aside the issue of feasibility, the advantages of the unitary state made it unarguably desirable. No other solution was able to satisfy the needs of justice for the Palestinians, including the refugees, and the needs of security for Israelis. Though these needs were frequently derided by Arabs who wondered why a state armed to the teeth and supported to the hilt by the world's one superpower should ever have felt insecure, Israeli Jewish fear was real. Whatever its source – and most of my Palestinian survey respondents put it down to the fact that, as they said, thieves never rested easy while their victims were close by – Israeli insecurity was an important factor. Indeed, it was frequently invoked by Israel to justify its attacks on neighbouring states. (One might have wondered why, given such a history of insecurity, the Zionists had insisted on putting themselves in a situation bound to create animosity.) My father, who had lost everything through the creation of Israel and yet who mainly blamed the British for allowing the tragedy to happen, viewed Jewish anxieties with humane concern. He saw the whole Zionist project as nothing more than a product of this Jewish fear. Arabs did not understand that, he often said, and it was one reason for their inability to deal with Israel.

Making the one-state solution happen was going to be hard and its supporters looked to a far distant future for its fulfilment. 'Not in my lifetime,' many of them said, or 'it will take a hundred years or more', or 'my children may see it, but their children more like', and so on. Whatever the truth, this solution could not come about in a rush or by a miraculous conversion to the view that it was the only way forward. Nor could it be imposed by force of circumstance (as will be discussed later). It had to be seen as a slow process of evolving political and social awareness, campaigning and preparation, all of them entailing arduous struggle.[74] It could not have been otherwise, given the monumental task of dismantling the structure and institutions of a state built on Zionism and replacing it with a genuinely democratic dispensation of equal rights and non-discrimination. The leap for Israelis from a world-view of supremacy and exclusivism imposed by force to a humanist philosophy of peaceable co-existence and opposition to racism and violence, would be huge. As would the leap for Arabs, from their rejection of any rights to Palestinian land for people seen as nothing more than colonisers, not to mention their enmity towards the Israelis developed over decades, to an unqualified acceptance of them as equal partners. It also required of Arabs the difficult task of redefining their own national identity and a readiness to embrace a new and unique entity in the region, an Israeli/Palestinian state without precedent. The role of regimes that had based their *raison d'être* on hostility to Israel with all the military and economic developments that that entailed would need to be revised. As such, the consequences for the region would be profound.

It is not the purpose of this book to set out a blueprint for building the unitary state. That has been ably discussed and reviewed by others.[75] One could write out a list of the traditional steps well known to all activists as to how one carries a political idea forward. This would include such things as political education, the creation of cadres and constituencies, enlisting the support of top politicians and decision makers, etc. But the main plank of the campaign was to start a debate amongst Palestinians and Jews about the one-state solution, to unify them around the concept and at the same time ensure that it became a part of the mainstream discourse. A two-state interim phase in which Palestinians replenished their shattered identities, regained normality and generally recovered from the Israeli occupation was a possible route to the end result, at least in theory (since the Palestinian state looked an unlikely eventuality, as discussed above). It was also a necessary aspiration to maintain in the short term so as not to create splits amongst the Palestinians. Too many Palestinians had become attached to the idea of having their own state and too many still believed that the international community would help them achieve it, to make them want to throw away the chance. Indeed, in the (unlikely) event of it happening, with borders hopefully opening up, allowing exchange and collaboration between the two states to grow, the time would come when integration became possible and, eventually, a one state. Likewise, a binational stage, reassuring Israelis and Palestinians that their national identities would not be subsumed in a single state before they were ready, was another possible route to the same end point.

The problem of course was not the dearth of ideas for solutions, but the absence of a political will to carry them through. In the case of the one-state solution, that was lacking on both sides, but much more on Israel's. Nor could one in all honesty deny that the obstacles in the way of such a project were so formidable as to make it nothing more than wishful thinking. If Palestinians had to be persuaded of its advantages for them, how much more difficult was it going to be to appeal to Israelis? And yet, there really was no way other than the one-state solution to resolve the conflict. This should have become clear from our discussions throughout this book. Once this fact was accepted, it would become possible to implement the one-state solution. To the charge that it was a utopian idea, one had only to recall Theodor Hertzl and the first Zionists. Once they were agreed on the aim of creating a Jewish state in Palestine, crazy as it must have seemed then and now, they exploited every opportunity to make it happen. It was not magic but strategic thinking. Creating a unitary state of Israel/ Palestine, far less implausible than the Zionist project ever was, should be no less successful.

Epilogue:
The End of the Zionist Dream?

This book has been devoted to an exploration of the various parameters of the Israel–Palestine problem and why, despite the many proposals put forward for its resolution, it has remained insoluble. It was shown that the major reason for this failure was the original and unresolved Zionist dilemma of how to create and maintain a Jewish state in a land inhabited by another people. Either the 'other man' had to be totally eradicated, or the Jewish state project had to be abandoned. Israel did not do either. Though it signally succeeded in expelling and keeping out a large number of Palestinians, it was never able to 'cleanse' the land of them entirely. On the contrary, their numbers have only increased and their political presence is ever more firmly established.

Yet, Israel has persisted in pursuing its original goal, in spite of this reality, which inevitably meant that no solution could have been possible. Nor is it at all likely that this pursuit, however determined, would have succeeded without the support and encouragement of the Western world. Israel, as we saw, was allowed to impose its own vision for the future, colonising Palestinian land and excluding or expelling its inhabitants, largely unencumbered by outside pressure or interference. The Zionist view, never concealed or amended, was that the entire land of Palestine was Jewish and the Arab presence in it a resented foreign intrusion. The consequences of such a position were not hard to predict and have unsurprisingly led to the present impasse. And yet, the Western powers that supported the creation of the Jewish state behaved as if in ignorance or denial of this fact. In the end, it was their permissive attitude and the inaction of the international community that led ultimately to the current problems. Had Israel's provocative enterprise been checked at any stage, the situation would not have deteriorated to the point where a solution became virtually impossible even to visualise.

What outcomes are possible in today's situation? The options available are limited: a) to allow the present situation to continue; b) to partition the land into an Israeli state and a collection of Palestinian enclaves; or c) to share the land in one unitary state. The first two options, as discussed in previous chapters, were clearly unsustainable in the long run. Only the third option, as was argued at length in Chapter 7, stood any chance of enduring. That is because it was the only just arrangement to resolve a conflict whose essence was injustice. Its root causes, the Palestinian dispossession and its consequences were never addressed. It was shown that all peace proposals other than that of the unitary state were inherently flawed because they were inequitable, ignored or downgraded the importance of the refugee problem, and, for that reason, could not have been durable even had they been implemented.

The most persistent of these 'non-solutions' was the proposal that took shape after 1974 to partition the old Mandate Palestine into two states, one Israeli on four-fifths of the land and the other Palestinian on the remaining fifth. This inequitable solution continued to be put forward, despite the reality on the ground that decimated the part allotted to the Palestinians: the near-annexation to Israel of almost half the West Bank territory, the barrier wall which was relentlessly drawing a new border between the two sides in Israel's favour and nothing like the 1967 lines supposed to delineate a Palestinian state, and the total isolation of Gaza. Crucially, the solution provided no countercheck on the power imbalance between the two sides, so huge as to ensure that the stronger party, Israel, could always determine events in its favour and render it under no obligation to accept any proposal with which it disagreed. The two-state solution in the form advocated by the Palestinians and the international community was the last thing Israel wanted, and it had the power to refuse. US support for Israel, which had increased almost exponentially in the 1990s to reach its apogee with the Bush Administration, ensured that it had carte blanche to do anything it desired. This omnipotence was vividly illustrated by the total impunity with which the Israeli army destroyed Gaza and Lebanon in the summer of 2006.

It was simply beyond belief that the people of Gaza could have been subjected at that time to the inhuman conditions of a deadly siege, without electricity or clean water and on the brink of starvation, without the least attempt on the part of the world community to stop it. And equally unbelievable that the world stood by while Israel's air force bombed Lebanon's airport, most of its infrastructure, roads and bridges, hundreds of civilian homes, and polluted its coastline with a massive oil spillage from wantonly targeted attacks on its fuel depots. Such gross abuses of power have led me to wonder more than once why it was that Israel did not go the whole way, bomb Gaza to smithereens, for example, deport all the Palestinians and raze their towns and villages to the ground. Who would have stopped Israel had it done so? Certainly not the European powers, which meekly followed the American lead, and not the Arab states, which were incapable of independent action. And of all the Muslim states which supported the Palestinians, only Iran espoused it fully, but whether it would ever be in a position to challenge the US–Israeli axis on their behalf was unknown and unlikely.

Not once in the last half-century has Israel failed to accomplish what it wanted, if not immediately then later, as its steady progression from fledgling state to regional superpower convincingly shows. That success was like an intoxicating drug for Israelis, making them impervious to the need for their leaders to seek peaceful relations with their neighbours. So long as Israel was powerful enough to smite the Arabs if they showed the slightest opposition, it had no interest in a deal except on its own parsimonious terms. We saw how the other side shifted considerably to accommodate the Israeli position, as the Oslo Accords and other Arab peace proposals showed. For Israel, however, that was not enough and it continued to take more and offer less.

While that remains the case it is evident that the two-state solution, flawed though it is, cannot succeed, and, so long as Israel remains a Zionist state enjoying unabated Western support as such, things will never be any different. The Jewish state must by its very nature fight on to maintain itself as ethnically separate, supremacist and privileged. Any retraction from this position, however small, would open a Pandora's box of unpalatable questions that no one has wanted to answer. Why, for example, should such an anomalous state, out of step with the regional culture, language, religion and *Weltanschauung* ever have been set up in the Middle East? It was inevitable that a people who saw mankind as divided into Jews and eternally hostile Gentiles whom they had to protect themselves against (no matter what the origin of these sentiments) could never have merged into the region or made for normal neighbours.[1] More importantly, most Israelis held the Arabs and particularly the Palestinians in contempt. This was a theme running through Zionist history from the start. Such people would fight every attempt to integrate them – the sine qua non of any proper solution – would reject it as an attempt to 'Arabise' them, and would maintain their special bond with the Jews outside and the West. Only through such links could they maintain their sense of themselves as the centre of world Jewry and a part of Western civilisation.

That a state with such an ethnically biased, exclusivist ideology can survive in this rigid form indefinitely must be open to question. But the logic of allowing Israel to remain in its present hegemonic state means that there can be no long-term peaceful settlement, and the short-term future is bleak indeed. It is possible that this could take the form of Ariel Sharon's revived Jordanian option, a last desperate effort to salvage the two-state solution from the wreckage of Israel's leavings in the West Bank. The parts remaining after Israel annexes its settlements, bypass roads and other areas it wishes to keep would be joined onto Jordan in a federation. This plan, or some version of it, which was rumoured at the time of writing to be under consideration by Western politicians and acceptable to a number of Palestinian leaders, raises more questions than it answers.[2] How would the West Bank enclaves be connected to each other and skip the Jordan Valley (annexed to Israel) to be joined to Jordan? What would happen to Gaza, which Egypt has refused to become its extension across the border between them as the pressure of population rises? Had Jordan agreed to the plan and did the Palestinians of the occupied territories accept the loss of half the West Bank and their connection to Gaza? If the strategists who supported this option had some sorcery to make it happen, then they have kept it secret from the rest of us.

But what if none of this happened, if most Palestinians refused to accept meekly the fate being concocted for them, and an alternative scenario took shape, a nightmare descent into violence and anarchy? The signs of widespread Palestinian frustration and resistance were already in evidence, and perhaps foreseeing this, an Israeli writer described the situation today as 'explosive, unstable and impractical' and carried within it 'the beginnings of an intifada of resistance which will be more violent than those before and which will put Israel before choices that threaten its very existence'.[3] In a last-ditch stand to defend Zionism, Israel would continue to build the wall, would try to expel or starve out the Palestinians to thin their numbers and they, with nothing left to lose, would resist by every means, including terrorism and suicide bombings. Thanks to Israel's obduracy and aggression, something of this sort was already happening with the rise of the radical, fundamentalist movements, Hamas in Palestine and Hizbullah in Lebanon.

Both of these had agendas that referred back to the origins of the conflict and questioned the very legitimacy of the Jewish state. Neither was prepared to surrender fundamental rights, despite Israel's overwhelming power, and both had shown they were prepared to fight for their principles. Israel responded to this new phenomenon in the same old way: violence and more violence, and would be likely to continue along the same path. Even if Hamas were removed from power by Israel and its allies' machinations, as looked to be the case at the end of 2006, it could not be eradicated as an opposition force. The Palestinian territories would become more radicalised, ungovernable and unviable. Those Palestinians who had not emigrated, the majority, would find ways of penetrating into Israel for work or food, and fighters would continue to take revenge, perhaps in ways that cannot be imagined now. This would obviously be more difficult when the barrier wall was built completely – only a third had been built by 2006 – and it was still porous enough then to permit the infiltration of illegal Palestinian workers and several suicide bombers to the other side. Israel would retaliate with greater savagery and military violence and the Palestinians would fight back harder. The Palestinian community inside Israel meanwhile might become drawn in, either because of internal repression against it or by identification with fellow Palestinians under occupation, or both.

Eventually, and after much bloodshed, the barriers erected by Israel would disintegrate and a binational situation, if not a state, would come about, not in an orderly way but willy-nilly. The entry of Palestinians into what Israelis had always wanted to be an exclusive club for Jews might prompt those who had the means to leave the country. Those would most likely be the Jews of European origin who always saw themselves as part of the Western world anyway, and those for whom life with Arabs was unpalatable (often the same people). Emigration from the Jewish state at times of crisis had often been a well-kept secret feature of Israeli life. During the short-lived conflict with Lebanon in July 2006, for example, the rate of emigration from Israel increased five-fold and the US and Canadian consulates were flooded with visa applications.[4] As the Israeli writer, Irit Linur, lamented in *Haaretz* (24 September 2004), 'Life in Israel is of a trial period, and anyone who can get his hands on more glittering options abroad should take advantage of them ... We, the aware and the correct, all too often see the State of Israel the way it is seen in Europe: a country on probation, a home on probation.'

The Israeli population remaining would be composed of the poor, the ultra-religious, the oriental Jews and many of those born in the state who felt they belonged nowhere else. So a new situation would be born, a state for Jews and Palestinians, not through a managed process of orderly transition, but through chaos, displacement, the creation of new refugees and the deaths of many people on both sides. And in the end all that the Zionist experiment would have accomplished would be to have postponed the inevitable for 60 years or so. The Middle East has absorbed myriad communities, no matter what their origins, and the hotchpotch of European and oriental Jewish migrants and their descendants who had formed the Israeli community would be no exception. In time, they too would become part of the region, as if the State of Israel had never been. The pity of it was that it should have taken so much destruction, death and suffering to return history to its initial point of departure.

The fact, of course, is that the Zionist project was flawed from the start and the Israeli state should never have been set up. The best solution to this intractable problem is to turn back the clock before there was any Jewish state and rerun history as from there. I recall making this remark at a meeting in London in 1978, one of the first of its kind between a few of us Palestinians and a handful of Israelis who defined themselves as anti-Zionist or non-Zionist. Their shock and surprise at such sentiments was evident, and all of them rejected my comment as a personal attack on them. What made them think,

I remember wondering, that Palestinians could ever have wanted a foreign immigrant community to set up a state in their country?

It was perverse to believe that 'the other man', the Palestinians, could ever have vanished or become irrelevant. As Meron Benvenisti put it, 'The Zionist dream was maimed from the outset. It didn't take into account the presence here of another national group. Therefore, from the moment the Zionist movement decided that it was not going to exterminate the Arabs, its dream became unattainable.'[5] But Benvenisti did not see that even had Israel eradicated the Palestinian population, there was still the Arab world hugging its every border to contend with. 'If Israel remains a colonialist state in its character, it will not survive,' wrote Haim Hanegbi. 'In the end the region will be stronger than Israel, in the end the indigenous people will be stronger than Israel.'[6] Zionism's ethos was not about peaceful co-existence but about colonialism and an exclusivist ideology to be imposed and maintained by force.

All the same, the clock will not go back and, although the Jewish state cannot be uncreated, it might be, so to speak, unmade. The reunification of Palestine's shattered remains in a unitary state for all its inhabitants, old and new, is the only realistic, humane and durable route out of the morass. It is also the only way for the Israeli Jewish community (as opposed to the Israeli state) to survive in the Middle East. To quote Haim Hanegbi once more, 'Anyone who wants to ensure the existence of a Jewish community in this country has to free himself from the Zionist pattern . . . Because as things are now, there is no chance. A Jewish nation-state will not take hold here.'[7] Our review of the tremendous obstacles facing the one-state solution may be daunting to some of those who support it in theory. But the fact that something is difficult to realise does not make it any less desirable. Nor does the attainment of the one-state solution hinge solely on the wishes of Israel and its supporters. Other factors, though now unforeseen or thought improbable, could intervene and alter the situation dramatically, for example, a change in US foreign policy or a renaissance of Arab power, or some other extraordinary circumstance. There are predictions of coming changes in the world order, the decline of America, the rise of China and South East Asia, the revival of Russia, even regional shifts after the Lebanon war and its destabilising effect on pro-Western, regressive Arab regimes.[8] Any of these could make a radical difference to Palestinian fortunes, although none of them has yet fully happened and some might never do so.

If and when they do, such events will merely dictate the pace and timing of the one-state solution. But the concept itself must have been established long before, not as an immediately attainable goal but as a vision, an aspiration and a belief in the ultimate humanity of Jews and Palestinians and all those who wish to see them prosper.

Notes

Introduction

1. Z. Jabotinsky, *Writings: On the Road to Jerusalem* (Jerusalem: Ari Jabotinsky, 1959), cited in A. Shlaim, *The Iron Wall: Israel and the Arab World* (London: Allen Lane, 2000), pp. 13–14. See also Lenni Brenner, *The Iron Wall: Zionist Revisionism from Jabotinsky to Shamir* (London: Zed Books, 1984), pp. 73–5.
2. Moshe Dayan, *Milestones: An Autobiography* (Hebrew) (Jerusalem: Edanim Publishers, 1976), cited in Shlaim, *The Iron Wall*, p. 101.
3. Cited in D. Ingrams, *Palestine Papers, 1917–1922: Seeds of Conflict* (London: John Murray, 1972), p. 73.
4. Akiva Orr, *The Un-Jewish State: The Politics of Jewish Identity in Israel* (London: Ithaca Press, 1983), pp. 228–9.
5. '218 Indians officially converted in India', *Ynetnews*, 5 October 2006.
6. Israel Ministry of Foreign Affairs, 'Jewish Agency plans fast-track conversions for immigrants from CIS', 7 March 2003.

1 The Cost of Israel to the Arabs

1. Ilan Pappe, *A History of Modern Palestine: One Land, Two Peoples* (Cambridge: Cambridge University Press, 2004), pp. 131–6.
2. D. Neff, *Fallen Pillars: US Policy towards Palestine and Israel since 1945* (Washington, DC: Institute of Palestine Studies, 1995), p. 3.
3. D.Hirst, *The Gun and the Olive Branch* (London: Faber and Faber, 2003), p. 106.
4. M. Arakie, *The Broken Sword of Justice: America, Israel and the Palestinian Tragedy* (London: Quartet Books, 1973), pp. 1–16, 25.
5. Neff, *Fallen Pillars*, pp. 24–6.
6. C. Rubenberg, *Israel and the American National Interest: A Critical Examination* (Chicago, IL: University of Illinois Press, 1986), pp. 10, 27–8.
7. Avner Cohen, 'US knew about nuke plans', *Ynetnews*, 6 February 2005; D. Hiro, *Inside the Middle East* (London: Routledge & Kegan Paul, 1982), pp. 214–30.
8. N. Balabkins, *West German Reparations to Israel* (New Brunswick, NJ: Rutgers University Press, 1971), pp. 174, 185.
9. L. G. Feldman, *The Special Relationship between West Germany and Israel* (Boston, MA: George & Allen Unwin Publishers, 1984), p. 89; also see pp. 96, 99.
10. Hiro, *Inside the Middle East*, p. 216.

11. Ibid. pp. 97, 157.
12. G. Lavy, *Germany and Israel: Moral Debt and National Interest* (London: Frank Cass, 1996).
13. Hiro, *Inside the Middle East*, pp. 97, 157.
14. Francis Nicosia, *The Third Reich and the Palestine Question* (London: I. B. Tauris, 1985), pp. 29–49.
15. Ibid. p. 42.
16. Hiro, *Inside the Middle East*, pp. 231–45.
17. Y. Govrin, *Israeli–Soviet Relations, 1953–1967* (London: Frank Cass, 1998), p. 326.
18. Benny Morris. *The Birth of the Palestinian Refugee Problem Revisited*, 2nd edn (Cambridge: Cambidge University Press, 2004); Ilan Pappe, *The Making of the Refugee Problem 1947–9* (London: I.B. Tauris, 1992), p. 96.
19. J. Dash, 'Doing good in Palestine: Magnes and Henrietta Szold', in W. M. Brinner and M. Rischin (eds), *Like All the Nations? The Life and Legacy of Judah L. Magnes* (New York, NY: State University of New York Press, 1987), pp. 99–111.
20. Y. Porath, *In Search of Arab Unity, 1930–1945* (London: Frank Cass, 1986), pp. 600–1.
21. Ben-Gurion never accepted the part relating to the creation of a Palestinian state. See Simha Flapan, *The Birth of Israel: Myths and Realities* (New York, NY: Pantheon Books, 1987), p. 37.
22. David Ben-Gurion, *Letters to Paula* (London: Vallentine, Mitchell, 1971), cited in Shlaim, *The Iron Wall*, p. 21.
23. Exact figures for the totality of the world Palestinian population are hard to obtain. Statistics in use are based on a mixture of UN refugee numbers and estimates for the rest. The Palestinian Central Bureau of Statistics estimated a world Palestinian population of 10.1 million at the end of 2005 (Wafa News Agency report, 31 December 2005); the Palestinian researcher Salman Abu Sitta's estimate (excluding those in Israel) for 2000 was 8,270,509 (personal communication, 2005). See also, Abu Sitta, *The Palestinian Nakba: The Register of Depopulated Localities in Palestine* (London: Palestine Return Centre, 1998).
24. The Hamas victory in the Palestinian Legislative Council elections of January 2006 led to new attempts to revive the PLO's old role.
25. International Bank for Reconstruction and Development, *Disengagement, the Palestinian Economy and the Settlements* (Washington, DC: July 2004).
26. Meron Benvenisti, *Sacred Landscape: The Buried History of the Holy Land since 1948* (Berkeley, CA: University of California Press, 2000), pp. 11–43.
27. 'Suppression of Jerusalem's Arab and Islamic identity accelerates', *Al-Quds*, 14 January 2005.
28. W. Khalidi, *All That Remains: The Palestinian Villages Occupied and Depopulated by Israel in 1948* (Washington, DC: Institute for Palestine Studies, 1992); Salman Abu Sitta, *Atlas of Palestine* (London: Palestine Land Society, 2005).

29. See review of Hillel Cohen's 2006 book, *Good Arabs* (Hebrew) by Amira Hass in *Haaretz*, 20 September 2006. The book lays out these facts as derived from recently released Israeli security archives.

30. Amongst these may be cited a number in various countries: Ilan Pappe of Haifa University is engaged with others in a current oral history project about the nakba of 1948; Rosemary Sayegh has also worked on oral history taken from Palestinian refugees in the Lebanese camps; May Saykali in the US has worked on an oral history of Haifa; and there are ongoing projects by Mahmoud Issa in Denmark on the history of Lubya, one of the destroyed Palestinian villages of 1948.

31. Salman Abu Sitta's Testimony, <www.al-awda.org>; researchers are analysing the newly released Israeli archive documents for this period.

32. See also Hazem Saghiyeh, 'The Year of Iraq, one year', *Al-Hayat*, 31 December 2003.

33. Awni Farsakh, *Al-Quds*, 12 January 2005.

34. United Nations Development Programme, *The Arab Human Development Report, 2002–3*; N. Fergany interview in *Al-Ahram Weekly*, 14 July 2002.

35. M. LeVine, 'The Arab Human Development Report: a critique', *Middle East Report*, 26 July 2002.

36. A. Hewedy, *Militarisation and Society in the Middle East* (London: United Nations University Press, 1989).

37. David Ben-Gurion, *Rebirth and Destiny of Israel* (London: Thomas Yoseloff, 1959), p. 419.

38. Cited in Hirst, *The Gun*, p. 320.

39. Shlaim has meticulously reviewed these overtures in *The Iron Wall*, pp. 62–9, 117–23.

40. Flapan, *The Birth of Israel*, pp. 122–33.

41. <www.arableagueonline.org>

42. Shlaim, *The Iron Wall*, pp. 71–6, 84–7.

43. For a full account of the Suez affair, see Keith Kyle, *Suez* (London: Weidenfeld and Nicolson, 1991).

44. Nasser ordered the withdrawal of the UN force, UNEF, stationed in Sinai since the end of Suez war, and closed the Straits of Tiran through which a proportion of Israeli shipping passed.

45. K. Firo, *The Druze in the Jewish State: A Brief History* (Leiden: Brill, 1999), p. 58. See also L. Parsons, *The Druze between Palestine and Israel: 1947–1949* (Wiltshire: Anthony Rowe, 2000). The relationship between Israel and the Druze community is complex and by no means based on Israeli respect for Druze rights, nor were all Druze willing to accept Israel's patronising and discriminatory policies despite its avowed support for them.

46. Firo, *The Druze*, pp. 245–6.

47. Ibid. pp. 220–1.

48. Oded Yinon, 'A Strategy for Israel in the 1980s', *Kevunim* (Hebrew) (Jerusalem: World Zionist Organisation, No. 14, February 1982), cited in Hirst, *The Gun*, p. 534.

49. Shlaim, *The Iron Wall*, p. 172.

50. K. E. Schultze, *Israel's Covert Diplomacy in Lebanon* (London: Macmillan Press, 1998).

51. Seymour Hersh, 'Plan B', *The New Yorker*, 28 June 2004.

52. Jim Lobe, 'Democracy and the neocons: marriage of convenience', *Daily Star*, 21 July 2004; Stephen Sniegoski's series of articles on the neocons, Israel and the Iraq war, www.thronwalker.com, 2005.

53. Philip Gordon, 'Bush's Middle East vision', *Survival*, Vol. 45, 2003, pp. 155–65.

54. Patrick Cockburn, 'Iraq diary', *London Review of Books*, March 2006.

55. Rima Allaf, Ali Ansari, Maha Azzam, Rosemary Hollis, Robert Lowe, Yossi Mekelberg, Soli Ozel, Gareth Stansfield and Mai Yamani, *Iraq in Transition: Vortex or Catalyst?*, Chatham House Middle East Programme Briefing Paper (London: Royal Institute of International Affairs, 2004).

56. 'Lebanese militiamen complain Israel abandoned them', *Reuter*, 12 May 2004.

57. 'Cluster bombing of Lebanon "immoral" UN official tells Israel', *Guardian*, 31 August 2006; 'When rockets and phosphorus cluster', *Haaretz*, 13 September 2006.

58. 'Amnesty urges UN to probe Israel strategy', *Financial Times*, 22 August 2006; Amnesty International Press Release, 23 August 2006.

59. 'Historic Byblos polluted by war', *BBC News*, 22 August 2006.

60. According to Amnesty International (23 August 2006), these were estimated at 118 soldiers and 43 civilians. To this should be added that about a million Israelis were temporarily displaced people with loss of property and economic damage in northern Israel.

61. Rami Khoury, 'A new man for the Mideast?', *Newsweek International*, 21–8 August 2006.

62. UN Security Council Resolution 1559, passed in 2004, demanded the disarming of all Lebanese militias, and the UN ceasefire agreement in August 2006 made the same stipulation.

63. *Al-Quds*, 12 and 17 March 2005.

64. Meir Yoav Stern, *Maariv*, 31 October 2005.

65. This report originally appeared in Hebrew in the Israeli daily *Yediott Ahronot* in September 2006, cited by Zuhair Andraws, *Al-Quds*, 6 October 2006.

66. 'Rice visits Egypt after Saudi Arabia to strengthen "the moderate coalition" against Iran', *Al-Quds*, 3 October 2006.

67. A row over changing the Iraqi flag to one that used blue and white erupted during 2005 because it was too reminiscent of the Israeli flag's same two colours.

68. '$2.5 million the size of Israeli exports to Iraq', *Al-Quds*, 11 August 2004.

69. Jacob Abadi, 'Israel and Sudan: the saga of an enigmatic relationship', *Middle Eastern Studies*, Vol. 35, No. 3, 1999; G. Warburg, 'The Sudan and Israel: an episode in bilateral relations', *Middle Eastern Studies*, Vol. 28, No. 2, 1992.

70. Since 2004, Turkey has objected to Israeli secret agents operating in the Kurdish areas of northern Iraq; see Hersh, 'Plan B'.

71. J. Abadi and J. Krischer, 'Israel and the Horn of Africa – the strategic and political imperatives', *Journal of South Asian and Middle Eastern Studies*, Vol. 25, 2002, pp. 41–64.

72. May Shamaa, 'Eritrea in the age of Afewerki: an Israeli strategic triumph' (Arabic), *Shu'un Filistiniyya*, Vol. 64, 2005, pp. 95–109.

73. S. Decalo, *Israel and Africa: Forty Years 1956–1996* (Gainesville, FL: Florida Academic Press, 1998); A. Oded, *Africa and the Middle East Conflict* (London: Lynne Rienner, 1987).

74. 'India, Israel joint high-tech projects can bring thousands of jobs – India, Israel set up joint study group to boost trade ties', *India Daily*, 9 December 2004; 'A Banner Year For Israeli Arms Exports', *Business Week Online*, 7 March 2005; Amy Waldman, 'The bond between India and Israel grows', *New York Times*, 7 September 2003.

75. Manoj Pundit, 'Why is Israel betraying India?', *Jerusalem Post*, 5 September 2005; see also *Haaretz*, 1 and 5 September 2005.

76. Graham Usher, 'Musharraf's opening to Israel', *Middle East Report Online (MERIP)*, 2 March 2006.

77. Ephraim Dowek, *Israeli–Egyptian Relations, 1980–2000* (London: Frank Cass, 2001).

78. The so-called Copenhagen group, set up in 1997 and composed of Egyptian and Israeli scholars, was one of the best known of these. Little is now heard of this, but in 2005 the Egyptian writer, Ali Salem, was awarded an honorary doctorate by Israel's Ben-Gurion University for his 'services in the cause of normalisation'; see Zuhair Andraws, *Al-Quds*, 24 May 2005.

79. The Moroccan Solidarity with the Palestinian People Committee denounced the conference as 'an insult to the Moroccan people'; see Shawqi Amin, *Al-Quds*, 27 May 2004.

80. 'A past Israeli official: we hear in secret from Arab leaders the opposite of what they say in public', *Al-Quds*, 18 May 2004.

81. This claim was made by Mithal al-Alussi, head of the Iraqi People's Party, who had visited Israel and called for normalisation with it; see *Al-Quds*, 17 January 2005. He narrowly escaped several assassination attempts in 2005.

82. Zuhair Andraws, *Al-Quds*, 27 May 2005.

83. Lawrence Wright, 'Helping Mohammed', *The New Yorker Online*, 27 May 2002. The Muslim Brotherhood is an Islamic organisation established in Egypt in 1928 and is considered the mother organisation of all modern Islamist movements. It has branches in Syria, Jordan and Palestine. Its work has been both charitable and political.

84. Thoraya Obaid's statement to the Washington Institute for Near East Policy, 25 April 2002 (UNPF website).

85. Ali Salem, 'My drive to Israel', *The Middle East Quarterly*, Vol. 9, No. 1, 2002.

86. T. C. Niblock, *Saudi Arabia: Power and Legitimacy* (London: Routledge, 2006), pp. 148–50.

87. Akram Hijazi, *Al-Quds*, 31 September 2006.

88. Andrew Hammond, 'Political Islam takes center stage since 9/11', *Reuters*, 5 September 2006.

89. B. Milton-Edwards, *Islamic Politics in Palestine* (London: I. B. Tauris, 1996), pp. 103–44.

90. Robert Dreyfuss's *Devil's Game: How the United States Helped Unleash Fundamentalist Islam*, American Empire Project Series (New York, NY: Metropolitan Books, 2005) is highly illuminating on the Israel–Hamas relationship.

91. S. Kedourie and S. G. Haim (eds), *Arab Nationalism: An Anthology* (Berkeley, CA: University of California Press, 1976), pp. 3–72.

92. The US had imposed various types of sanctions on the Syrian regime in 1979, and again in 1986 and 1989. In 2003, Congress passed the Syrian Accountability Act which gave the president the power to impose a range of further sanctions. Only some of these have been implemented.

93. Jim Lobe, 'The Neo-Cons: are they serious about Syria?', *Inter Press Service*, 17 December 2004.

94. In fact, bringing about a collapse of Syria's government in the drive towards destabilising it might not have benefited Israel at all. A weak Assad regime, intimidated into compliance with US–Israeli plans, would have been preferable to the alternative, almost certainly a hardline Islamist government far less compliant.

95. Although Kuwait had been assisted to gain its independence by the British in 1899, under the Ottoman Empire, it was regarded as part of the district of Basra. Much later, in 1956, the pro-British Iraqi prime minister, Nuri al-Said, wanted it federated with Iraq; see William Cleveland, *A History of the Modern Middle East* (Boulder, CO: Westview Press, 2004), pp. 201–11.

96. Ibid. pp. 203–4.

97. See, for example, Said Aburish, *A Brutal Friendship: The West and the Arab Elites* (London: Victor Gollancz, 1997), pp. 13–35. Also N. Ayyubi, *Over-Stating the Arab State: Politics and Society in the Middle East* (London: I. B. Tauris), p. 86ff.

98. US Congressional Budget Office official website.

99. Shirley McArthur, 'Congress passes foreign aid, appropriations, keeping most unhelpful provisions', *Washington Report on Middle East Affairs*, Vol. 25, No. 1, January/February, 2006, p. 26.

100. Egypt was reportedly negotiating a $2 billion deal to supply Israel with natural gas over the next 15 years, *Haaretz*, 12 February 2004.

101. The 'Bridging the Rift Centre', set to be a truly massive and ambitious undertaking, was to be built on 15 acres of land straddling the Israeli–Jordanian border and was backed by four major US universities, *Jordan Times*, 26 February 2004. Such 'normalisation' initiatives were sharply criticised by Jordanian civil society institutions, Arabic News.com, 12 April 2004.

102. Editorial, *Al-Quds*, 11 May 2005.

103. 'Yemeni "respect" for Jews', *Jewish Chronicle*, 3 September 2004.

104. Yusuf Nur Awad, 'The Algiers summit and the renunciation of principles', *Al-Quds*, 24 March 2005.

105. Zuhair Andraws, 'Enough! Enough! We have reached the end', *Al-Quds*, 5 April 2005. *Al-Quds* is a rare example of an Arab newspaper unafraid to publish opinions unpalatable to the authorities in some Arab states and has consequently been boycotted by them from time to time.

106. 'Arab rulers are part of the aggression against their people', reader's letter, *Al-Quds*, 1 March 2005.

107. Saleh Suleiman, 'Servile followers', *Al-Quds*, 22 March 2005.
108. Shlaim, *The Iron Wall*, pp. 68–71, 73–6.
109. Ibid. pp. 79–81.
110. Noam Chomsky, *The Fateful Triangle: The United States, Israel, and the Palestinians* (London: Pluto Press, 1983), p. 64.
111. Ibid. pp. 65, 68.
112. Neil Lochery, *The View from the Fence: The Arab–Israeli Conflict from the Present to its Roots* (London: The Continuum International Group, 2005), pp. 143–7. In 2006, Syria's president tried to make a fresh start by offering to hold peace talks with Israel without tangible result.
113. Yehuda Litani, *Yediott Ahronot*, 3 June 2004.
114. Ghada Karmi, *In Search of Fatima: A Palestinian Story* (London: Verso, 2002), pp. 139–40.
115. Ghalia Ali, *Jordan Times*, 30 May 1998; see also US Committee for Refugees, *Country Report: Jordan* (Washington, DC: 22 November 2002).
116. The Israeli government reportedly set up a committee to asses the claims of Jews who fled Arab countries against those countries. In particular, Israel demanded the restitution of property for the 100,000 Iraqi Jewish refugees, *Jewish Week*, 1 February 2004.
117. A strong Moroccan movement of solidarity with the Palestinians had been in existence for many years, and at various stages in the conflict Moroccans have taken to the streets in mass demonstrations. which the authorities were unable to suppress. The largest of these took place during the second intifada.
118. Maintaining Israel's 'strategic edge' was a declared US policy. The preferential trade tariff agreement between the EU and Israel, as well as European funding for Israeli research institutions and numerous academic and cultural exchange programmes to the benefit of Israel, were part of the same effort.

2 Why Do Jews Support Israel?

1. Karmi, *In Search of Fatima*, p. 184.
2. Melanie Phillips, 'Can Israel disengage?', *Prospect Magazine*, February 2004.
3. N. W. Cohen, *American Jews and the Zionist Idea* (Tel Aviv: Ktav Publishing House, 1985).
4. 'Economist tallies swelling cost of Israel to US', *Christian Science Monitor*, 9 December 2002.
5. Ibid.
6. Tony Bayfield, 'We need a new kind of Zionism', *Guardian*, 23 March 2005.
7. US aid to Israel in 1997 alone was estimated at $5.5 billion; see Richard Curtiss, *Washington Report on Middle East Affairs*, December 1997; Jewish National Fund, <www.jnf.org>.
8. 'No one knows the full cost of Israel's settlement ambition', *USA Today*, 14 August 2005.
9. Scott Wilson, 'Golan Heights land and lifestyle lure settlers', *Washington Post*, 30 October 2006.

10. The Israeli National Insurance Institute found that in 2002 32.8 per cent of the population was in poverty or 17.7 per cent of families, and that the percentage of poor children out of a total number of children was rising. After the Netanyahu government was elected in 1997, 1.4 million Israelis were living in poverty and the divide between rich and poor had grown; see 'Finished with Likud, it was poverty not disengagement that determined the outcome of the Israeli elections', *Al-Ahram Weekly*, 1 April 2006.

11. See, for example, David Kretzmer, *The Legal Status of the Arabs in Israel* (Boulder, CO and Oxford: Westview Press, 1990), and Uri Davis, *Apartheid Israel* (London: Zed Books, 2003), pp. 82–124.

12. Shalom Dichter and As'ad Ghanem (eds), *The Sikkuy Report July 2002 and 2003*, <www. Sikkuy.org>; 'Settlements get more aid money than other towns', *Haaretz*, 20 October 2004.

13. Sami Chetrit, *The Mizrahi Struggle in Israel* (Hebrew), translated to Arabic by A. Shalhat (Ramallah: Madar, 2005); 'Racism within the ranks', *Al-Ahram Weekly*, 2–8 September 2004.

14. '218 Indians officially converted in India', *Ynetnews*, 5 October 2006.

15. Dina Porat, ' "Amalek's accomplices", blaming Zionism for the Holocaust: anti-Zionist ultra-orthodoxy in Israel during the 1980s', *Journal of Contemporary History*, Vol. 27, No. 4, 1992, p. 698.

16. 'Jewish extremists seek Sharon's death', *Daily Star*, 21 July 2004.

17. I. Shahak and N. Mezvinsky, *Jewish Fundamentalism in Israel* (London: Pluto Press, 2000), pp. 96–112.

18. According to the Israeli Central Bureau of Statistics, the proportion of those born in Israel in 1996 was 61.6 per cent. In 1960, it was 37.4 per cent.

19. Ian Lustick, 'Recent trends in emigration from Israel: the impact of Palestinian violence', Paper presented to the annual meeting of the Association for Israel Studies, Jerusalem, June 14–16, 2004; '750,000 Israelis left the Jewish state', *Al-Quds*, 9 December 2003.

20. Noam Arnon, *Haaretz*, 28 August 2002.

21. John Rose, *The Myths of Zionism* (London: Pluto Press, 2004), pp. 41–3; M. Goodman, *The Ruling Class of Judea: The Origins of the Jewish Revolt Against Rome AD 66–70* (Cambridge: Cambridge University Press, 1987), pp. 62–4, 250.

22. Norman Cantor, *The Sacred Chain: A History of the Jews* (London: Fontana Press, 1995), pp. 61–2.

23. Rose, *Myths*, p. 43.

24. C. Abramsky et al., *The Jews in Poland* (Oxford: Blackwell, 1986); Ilan Halevy, *A History of the Jews Ancient and Modern* (London: Zed Books, 1987), pp.102–11.

25. Cantor, *Sacred Chain*, pp.162–7.

26. Arthur Koestler, *The Thirteenth Tribe: The Khazar Empire and Its Heritage* (London: Hutchinson, 1976); D. M. Dunlop, *The History of the Khazars* (Princeton, NJ: Princeton University Press, 1954).

27. Halevy, *A History*, pp. 93–102.

28. Kevin Brook, *The Jews of Khazaria* (Northvale: Jason Aaronson, 1999). *The Jewish Chronicle*, that foremost organ of British Jewry, reported the view

that Ashkenazi Jews were predominantly descended from 'Turkish and Slav converts' ('Hunt is on for the missing link in Yiddish', 7 February 1997).

29. Marc Ferro, 'Les Juifs: tout des Sémites?', a chapter in his collection, *Les Tabous de l'histoire* (Paris: Nil Editions, 2002), pp.115–35.

30. Milton Himmelfarb, 'The history of the Khazars by D. M. Dunlop', *Commentary Magazine*, Vol. 6, 1955.

31. 'Origins of Old Testament priests', *Nature*, Vol. 394, 1994, pp. 138–9.

32. Mazin Qumsiyeh has given an authoritative review of the genetic evidence in his, *Sharing the Land of Canaan: Human Rights and the Israeli–Palestinian Struggle* (London: Pluto Press, 2004), pp. 24–30. But see also the early work of E. Koblyansky, S. Micle, M. Glodschmitt-Nathan, B. Arensburg and H. Nathan, 'Lewis blood groups and ABH secretor systems in some Jewish populations of Israel', *Acta Anthropogenetica*, Vol. 6, No. 3, 1983, pp. 133–40; and E. M. Wilsman, 'Techniques for estimating genetic admixture and applications to the problem of the origin of the Icelanders and the Ashkenazi Jews', *Human Genetics*, Vol. 67, No. 4, 1984, pp. 441–8; R. A. Reyment, 'Moors and Christians: an example of multivariate analysis applied to human blood groups', *Annals of Human Biology*, Vol. 10, No. 6, 1983, pp. 505–21; 'In the blood', a BBC series, shown in 1996, reported on genetic research amongst Yemeni Jews which found few differences between them and non-Jewish Yemenis, suggesting that they were more likely to have descended from Arabian converts.

33. Thomas Kolsky, *Jews Against Zionism: The American Council for Judaism 1942–1948* (Philadelphia, PA: Temple University Press, 1990).

34. 'A Jewish genesis in Africa', *Jewish Chronicle*, 7 February 1997.

35. 'How 90 Peruvians became the latest Jewish settlers', *Guardian*, 7 August 2002; Israeli Ministry of Foreign Affairs, 'Jewish Agency plans fast-track conversion for immigrants from CIS', 7 March 2003.

36. Isaac Deutscher, *The Non-Jewish Jew and Other Essays* (London: Oxford University Press, 1968), p. 25.

37. Quoted in K. Sabbagh, *Palestine, a Personal History* (London: Atlantic Books, 2005), p. 160.

38. Personal communication with Joachim Martillo, a specialist in the subject, to whom I am indebted for the remarks in this section; see also Deutscher, *Non-Jewish Jew*, p. 96; and 'Racism within the ranks', *Al-Ahram Weekly*, 2–8 September 2004.

39. Chetrit, *The Mizrahi Struggle*; 'Racism within the ranks', *Al-Ahram Weekly*, 2–8 September 2004; 'A democratic state with equality for all its citizens', *Maariv*, 30 December 2003.

40. For example, Hebrew has no letter corresponding to the Arabic *ghain* (pronounced like the French 'R'). But because Europeans pronounced their Rs in this way, they introduced a sound that was alien to the language and not part of the Hebrew alphabet, but which the Eastern Jews imitated.

41. Cited in Brook, *The Jews of Khazaria*, p. 220.

42. Deutscher, *Non-Jewish Jew*, pp. 62, 86–7.

43. 'Haskalah', *Encyclopaedia Judaica* (Jerusalem: Keter Publishing House, 1971), pp. 139–51; 'Assimilation', *Encyclopaedia of Judaism* (Jerusalem: The Jerusalem Publishing House, 2002), pp. 85–7.

NOTES   277

44. Halevy, *A History*, pp. 127–34.
45. Rose, *Myths*, p.102.
46. Deutscher, *Non-Jewish Jew*, pp. 96–7.
47. Michael Novick, *The Holocaust in American Life* (New York, NY: Houghton Mifflin, 1999), p. 149.
48. Cited in Joseph Massad, 'Deconstructing Holocaust consciousness', *Journal of Palestine Studies*, Vol. 32, No.1, 2002, pp. 78–89.
49. Akiva Orr, *The Un-Jewish State: The Politics of Jewish Identity in Israel* (London: Ithaca Press, 1983).
50. 'What the left won't give up', *Haaretz*, 28 September 2004.
51. 'Anti-Zionism is anti-Semitism', *Guardian*, 29 November 2003.
52. Bob Drogin and Greg Miller, *Los Angeles Times*, 3 September 2004; David Shipler, *New York Times*, 22 December 1985; see also Kathleen and Bill Christison, 'Dual loyalties: the Bush neocons and Israel', *Counterpunch*, 6 September 2004; and a 1997 detailed review of this issue by Sami Husseini, 'A long history: Israeli espionage against the US', *Counterpunch*, 30 August 2004.
53. Mark Sherman, 'FBI: Pentagon analyst passed secret info', *Associated Press*, 5 May 2005; see also Helena Cobban, *Al-Hayat*, 6 September 2004, and *International Herald Tribune*, 7 September 2004.
54. 'Franklin to testify against former AIPAC officials', *Haaretz*, 30 September 2006; James Petras, 'Them or us: AIPAC on trial', *Counterpunch*, 7/8 January 2006.
55. *Jewish Chronicle*, 3 September 2004.
56. John Whitbeck, 'The great Israeli spy affair', posted on his website on 20 September 2004.
57. 'Anti-semitic attacks rise to a record level', *Guardian*, 11 February 2005.
58. There was a question mark over the origin of several attacks perpetrated on Jews in France. In September 2004, a 52-year-old French Jew was reported to have committed an arson attack on a Jewish soup kitchen in central Paris (*Jewish Chronicle*, 3 September 2004). In July of that year and also in France, a young woman with a baby claimed she had been attacked while on a suburban train because she was Jewish. The story, which caused a public outcry, turned out to be a total fabrication, much to the embarrassment of French Jewish leaders who had imputed all such incidents to anti-semitism.
59. European Monitoring Centre on Racism and Xenophobia, 'Racism and xenophobia in the EU member states', *Annual Report 2003/2004*.

3   Why Does the West Support Israel?

1. John Kerry, 'An Unwavering commitment to reform the Middle East', *Forward*, 27 August 2004.
2. 'Kerry position paper outlines support for Israel', *Haaretz*, 2 July 2004.
3. Paul Findley, *They Dare to Speak out: People and Institutions Confront Israel's Lobby* (Westport, CT: Lawrence Hill & Company, 1985), pp. 16–23.
4. *Washington Report on Middle East Affairs*, November 2004, pp. 24–5.

5. C. Rubenberg has an excellent section on this subject in her *Israel and the American National Interest: A Critical Examination* (Chicago, IL: University of Illinois Press, 1986), pp. 353–76. It is still relevant and the power of the Israel lobby is, if anything, greater today.

6. J. Mearsheimer and S. Walt, 'The Israel lobby and U.S. foreign policy', *London Review of Books*, Vol. 28, No. 6, 2006. This is a shortened version of the full paper which is available online.

7. James Petras, *The Power of Israel in the United States* (Atlanta, GA: Clarity Press, 2006).

8. Reported by Daphna Berman in *Haaretz*, 4 October 2004.

9. Bernard Gwetzman, *New York Times*, 22 March 1984.

10. 'Middle East studies under scrutiny in U.S.', *Washington Post*, 13 January 2004.

11. 'Reforming the campus: Congress targets title VI', *National Review Online*, 14 October 2003.

12. Norman Finkelstein, *Beyond Chutzpah: On the Misuse of Anti-Semtism and the Abuse of History* (London: Verso, 2005), pp. 69–70. Finkelstein himself has been the victim of discrimination by US academia for his critical stand on Israel.

13. See Stephen Green, 'Neo-Cons, Israel and the Bush Administration', *Counterpunch*, 28 February 2004, for a detailed account.

14. Reported in Jewish Global News, <www.jta.org>, 8 October 2004.

15. 'Iraq was invaded "to protect Israel" – US official', *Asia Times*, 31 March 2004; *Los Angeles Times*, 3 September 2004.

16. Quoted by Justin Raimondo, 'Senator Hollings is right. It's all about Israel', <www.Antiwar.com>, 21 May 2004.

17. 'White man's burden', *Haaretz*, 5 April 2003. This fascinating article includes interviews with leading neoconservatives on their ideas for the Middle East.

18. Stephen Zunes, 'Don't blame Israel', AlterNet, 14 January 2006.

19. Mearsheimer and Walt, 'The Israel lobby'.

20. Posted on the Internet on 29 June 2004; see Kennett Love Papers in <http://infoshare1.princeton.edu/libraries/firestone/rbsc/finding_aids/kennlove>.

21. 'Nader: White House is Israel's puppet', *Jerusalem Post*, 30 June 2004.

22. *Al-Ahram Weekly*, 27 September 2000.

23. *Guardian*, 5 October, 2004.

24. 'Some US backers of Israel boycott dailies over Mideast coverage', *New York Times*, 23 May 2002.

25. Alison Weir, *Censored 2005: The Top 25 Censored Stories*, <http://ifamericansknew.org/media/sides.html>, 15 September 2004.

26. This tract, written in the nineteenth century, has been shown to be a fabrication of Tsarist Russian provenance.

27. Noam Chomsky, *The Fateful Triangle: the United States, Israel and the Palestinians* (London: Pluto Press, 1983), pp. 17–32.

28. See also Jeff Halper, 'Israel as an extension of American Empire', *Tikkun*, 19 June 2006.

29. Ibid.

30. D. Little, 'The making of a special relationship: the United States and Israel', *International Journal of Middle East Studies*, Vol. 25, 1993, pp. 562–85.
31. Rubenberg, *Israel and the American National Interest*, pp. 63–7, 68–84.
32. Stephen Zunes, 'Understanding the U.S.–Israel relationship', *Fellowship Magazine Online*, January/February, 2003.
33. Joseph Massad, 'Blaming the lobby', *Al-Ahram Weekly*, 23 March 2006.
34. Shlaim, *The Iron Wall*, pp. 309–10.
35. *International Herald Tribune*, 21 August 2004; Aluf Benn, *Haaretz*, 29 September 2004; *Jerusalem Post*, 30 September 2004.
36. *Reuters Report*, 16 October 2004.
37. Interview with the Iranian defence minister, Ali Shamkhani, Al-Jazeeranet. com, 30 October 2004.
38. Paul Findley, 'Washington's fateful cover-up of Israel's attack on the USS Liberty', *Washington Report on Middle East Affairs*, August 2005, pp. 16–18.
39. For an exhaustive analysis of these, see George Ball and Douglas Ball, *The Passionate Attachment: America's Involvement with Israel, 1947 to the Present* (New York, NY: W. W. Norton, 1992), pp. 256–94.
40. Reported by the BBC World Service, 25 April 2004.
41. 'Rice says US irked by Israeli arms sales to China', *Associated Press*, 16 June 2005.
42. Y. Malachy, *American Fundamentalism and Israel* (Jerusalem: Hebrew University Press, 1978); this book is useful for its account of the early period in America.
43. Hani al-Raheb, *The Zionist Character in the English Novel* (London: Zed Books, 1983).
44. Barbara Tuchman, *Bible and Sword: England and Palestine from the Bronze Age to Balfour* (London: Alvin Redman, 1956), pp. 113–33.
45. Quoted in Tuchman, *Bible*, p.124.
46. Rose, *Myths*, p. 121.
47. Malachy, *American Fundamentalism*, pp. 134–50.
48. Stephen Sizer, *Christian Zionism: Road Map to Armageddon?* (London: Inter-Varsity Press, 2004), pp. 23–4.
49. Norton Mezvinsky, Personal communication, in 2004, based on research for his forthcoming book with Stephen Sizer on Christian Zionism.
50. 'Christian Zionism: an egregious threat to Middle East understanding', *ZNet*, 28 October 2006.
51. Craig Nelson, 'America's Christian Zionists Take Israel by Storm', *Austin American Statesman*, <www.statesman.com>, 4 January 2004.
52. For an exhaustive analysis of the power and effect of Christian Zionism in the US, see various writings of Stephen Sizer, in particular, his *Christian Zionism*. See also Grace Halsell, *Prophesy and Politics: Militant Evangelists on the Road to Nuclear War* (Westport, CT: Lawrence Hill & Company, 1986).
53. Nelson, 'America's Christian Zionists'.
54. Quoted in Phyllis Bennis and Khaled Mansour, 'Praise God and pass the ammunition', *Middle East Report* Fall 1998.
55. Sizer presents many examples of these opinions, put forward by highly influential American fundamentalists, in his *Christian Zionism*.

56. 'Evangelical Christians hail rightist's call to oust Arabs', *Forward*, 18 October 2002.
57. Greg Philo and Mike Berry, *Bad News from Israel* (London: Pluto Press, 2004).
58. Hani Abu Asaad's remarkable film, *Paradise Now,* made in 2006, broke through into the mainstream market, but it dealt specifically with the subject of Palestinian suicide bombing.
59. *The Garden of the Fitzi-Continis*, the beautiful film of the famous Italian film director Visconti, tells the touching story of a genteel Italian Jewish family destroyed by Mussolini's alliance with the Nazis. *Life is Beautiful* is a humorous and deeply moving depiction of another Italian Jewish family in a Nazi concentration camp. It would be impossible to see these films and remain unmoved.
60. G. Simons, *The Ethnic Cleansing of Palestine* (London: Palestine Return Centre, 2006), pp. 337–8.
61. 'Churches debate pro-Palestinian divestment', *Associated Press*, 18 February 2006.
62. Several Michigan universities were starting divestment campaigns to the alarm of the Jewish community; see 'News: anti-Israel activities at Wayne State', *Detroit Jewish News*, 18 October 2006; divestment in Israel was also being considered by the five million-strong Evangelical Lutheran Church and the smaller United Church of Christ in the US, *Reuters*, 10 August 2005.
63. <http://ec.europa.eu/comm/external_relations/israel/intro/index.htm>.
64. <http://ec.europa.eu/world/enp/index_en.htm>.

4   The 'Peace Process'

1. For details of the deplorable conditions in the West Bank and Gaza, see the UN regular reports on the human rights situation by the UN Office for Coordination of Humanitarian Affairs (OCHA); the excellent reports of *The Palestine Monitor* are to be found on its website; Amnesty International, *Israel and the Occupied Territories: An Ongoing Human Rights Crisis*, 31 May 2005; B'tselem, the Israeli human rights organisation's reports; and a host of others.
2. There was a courageous and decent minority of Israelis who did not hold these views. Some of them formed specific groups like the Marxist Matzpen, set up in the 1960s, or the later Uri Avnery-led Gush Shalom group. Many others operated as individuals, like the Haifa academic, Ilan Pappe, or the courageous *Haaretz* journalists, Amira Hass and Gideon Levy.
3. The Arab policy of preventing Palestinian attacks on Israel, which started in 1949 and has continued ever since with varying success, is a case in point. In 1970, the Jordanian army attacked PLO guerrillas in Amman who had established themselves (the so-called Black September). Further examples are to be found in Lebanon's stringent restrictions on the civil rights of the Palestinian refugees in the camps, not allowed to work or receive education or health care from the state, and could not even repair their own dwellings in the camps. Kuwait's expulsions of its Palestinian residents, many of them established for decades, in 1991, as mass punishment for their leadership's

alleged links with Saddam Hussein, is a particularly striking example. There is, in addition, a whole string of minor restrictions, humiliations and discrimination practised routinely against Palestinians by Arab officials.

4. This was the armistice line drawn after the 1948-9 Arab–Israeli wars between what became Israel and the previous Mandate Palestine, the so-called Green Line. The territory on the Arab side of it after these wars comprised the Gaza Strip, the West Bank and East Jerusalem.

5. Niall Ferguson, *Guardian*, 9 March 2005.

6. Osama bin Laden had used exactly this terminology in his call for a jihad against 'the Jews and the crusaders', cited in Council on Foreign Relations, 'Terrorism Q&A', 28 February 2005, <http://cfrterroism.org/causes/israelsupprtprint.html>.

7. I visited Pakistan between 28 February and 7 March 2003 at the invitation of the Pakistani daily, *Dawn*. I spoke at universities and public places in Karachi, Lahore and Islamabad, where the sentiments were much the same.

8. *Agence France Press*, 17 April 2005.

9. Council of Foreign Relations, 'Terrorism Q&A'. The report sets out evidence for the rise of anti-Americanism in the Middle East as largely stemming from US support for the Jewish state.

10. Quoted in the magazine, *Nida'ul-Islam*, October/November 1996. See also 'Usama bin Laden v. the U.S.: edicts and statements', *Frontline*, 1 March 2005, <http://www.pbs.org/wgbh/frontlint/shows/binladen/who/edicts.html>.

11. Osama bin Laden and others, 'Jihad against Jews and crusaders', *World Islamic Front*, 23 February 1998, <http://www.fas.org/irp/world/para/docs/980223-fatwa.htm>.

12. <http://ec.europa.eu/comm/external_relations/mepp/decl/>.

13. In further appeasement, the Jordanian monarch condemned Syria, Iran and Hizbullah as the causes of regional instability and supporters of Palestinian terrorist acts against Israel, *Haaretz*, 23 March 2005.

14. For much of the material in this section, I am indebted to Charles Smith's excellent book, *Palestine and the Arab–Israeli Conflict* (Basingstoke: Macmillan Education, 1994); also to William Quandt's *Decade of Decisions: American Policy toward the Arab–Israeli Conflict 1967–1976* (Berkeley, CA: University of California Press, 1977).

15. Smith, *Palestine*, p. 506.

16. Quandt, *Decade of Decision*, p. 278.

17. Moshe Dayan reputedly threatened, in October 1977, to state publicly that the American president refused to undertake not to pressure Israel into accepting a Palestinian state, to which Carter caved in quickly. Zbigniew Brezhinski, *Power and Principle: Memoirs of the National Security Adviser*, cited in Adel Safty, *From Camp David to the Gulf: Negotiations, Language & Propaganda and War* (Montreal: Black Rose Books, 1992), p. 63.

18. Quoted in G. Ball and D. Ball, *The Passionate Attachment: America's Involvement with Israel, 1947 to the Present* (New York, NY: W.W. Norton, 1992).

19. David Hoffman, *Washington Post*, 27 June 1992.

20. See Smith, *Palestine*, pp. 437ff; Naseer Aruri, *The Obstruction of Peace: The US, Israel and the Palestinians* (Monroe, ME: Common Courage Press, 1995); Edward Said, *Peace and Its Discontents: Gaza–Jericho 1993–1995* (London: Vintage, 1995); Tanya Reinhart, *Israel/Palestine: How to End the War of 1948* (New York, NY: Seven Stories Press, 2002), pp. 13–21; and much else.
21. Said, *Peace*, Introduction.
22. Wilton Park is situated in Sussex where regular conferences take place on international issues. Such meetings attract international participants, usually official government representatives and prominent experts and scholars. Though initially set up by the Foreign Office, Wilton Park has no connection with it, but the conference reports it produces are influential with an elite community of opinion formers and decision makers.
23. The Jordan/Israel Peace Treaty, <www.kinghussein.gov.jo>.
24. Shahak and Mezvinsky, *Jewish Fundamentalism*, pp. xiii–xiv.
25. Hirst, *The Gun*, pp. 86–7; Shahak and Mezvinsky, *Jewish Fundamentalism*, pp. 96–112.
26. The Rev Michael Prior worked, until his death in 2004, at St Mary's College, Strawberry Hill, to the south of London. He became prominent for his critiques of the Hebrew Bible, which he saw as providing sanction for the Zionist theft of Palestinian land. See his, *The Bible and Colonialism: A Moral Critique* (Sheffield: The Continuum International Publishing Group, 1997); and his essay, 'The moral problem of the land traditions of the bible', in Michael Prior (ed.), *Western Scholarship and the History of Palestine* (London: Fox Communications and Publications, 1998), pp. 47–81.
27. B'tselem report on Hebron, 19 August 2003; see also *Haaretz*, 16 March 2005.
28. According to these plans, a wall was to be built, separating the old city, where the settlers and also the Ibrahimi mosque were situated, from the rest of Hebron. If this happened, it would almost certainly lead to an exodus of the Arab inhabitants out of the old city, thus leaving it to be totally judaised. See *Al-Quds*, 2 May 2005.
29. The Israeli-only roads were intended to connect the settlements with each other and with Israel, bypassing Palestinian towns and forbidden to Palestinian drivers, while appropriating acres of West Bank land in the process.
30. The Institute of Palestine Studies, *The Palestinian–Israeli Peace Agreement: A Documentary Record* (Washington, DC: The Institute of Palestine Studies, 1994).
31. For example, no lawyers were present in the Palestinian negotiating team at Oslo and no maps were used to agree to Israel's division of the territories into areas A, B and C after the Oslo 2 agreement.
32. Palestinian National Authority, *the Wye River Memorandum*, <www.pna.gov.ps/Goevnement/gov/wye_river_memorandum.asp>; Naseer Aruri, 'The Wye Memorandum: Netanyahu's Oslo and unreciprocal reciprocity', *Journal of Palestine Studies*, Vol. 28, 1999.
33. See, for example, Naseer Aruri, *Dishonest Broker: The US Role in Israel and Palestine* (Cambridge, MA: South End Press, 2003), pp. 117–24.
34. For the Sharm al-Sheikh Memorandum (Wye II) and related documents, see *Journal of Palestine Studies*, Vol. 29, 2000.

35. Egypt offered Israel, ahead of its anticipated July 2005 withdrawal from Gaza, a force of 3,500 men, tanks and helicopters to police the Egypt–Israel border to prevent Palestinians from smuggling arms and men into Gaza; see *Haaretz*, 8 February 2005. This offer was followed up with a request to Egypt from the Israeli foreign minister, Silvan Shalom, for help in facilitating normalisation of relations between Israel and the Arab states which had no peace treaties with it; see *Al-Quds*, 20 April 2005 and also *Haaretz*, 12 April 2005.
36. Cited in Reinhart, *Israel/Palestine*, p. 75.
37. The Foundation for Middle East Peace, *Report on Israeli Settlement in the Occupied Territories*, Vol. 9, No. 6, 1999 and Vol. 10, No. 4, 2000.
38. Akram Hanieh, 'The Camp David papers', *Journal of Palestine Studies*, Vol. 30, 2001, pp. 75–97; William Quandt and Ann Lesch, 'Clinton and the Arab–Israeli conflict: the limits of incremenatlism', *Journal of Palestine Studies*, Vol. 30, 2001, pp. 26–40; Reinhart, *Israel/Palestine*, pp. 21–61; Robert Malley, *New York Times*, 10 July 2001; Hussein Agha and Robert Malley, 'Camp David: the tragedy of errors', *New York Review of Books*, 9 August 2001.
39. Akram Hanieh, *Al-Ayyam*, 29 July 2000–10 August 2000. As a senior advisor close to Arafat, Hanieh was in a special position and privy to the events at Camp David.
40. Reinhart, *Israel/Palestine*, p. 60.
41. Hirst, *Gun*, pp. 71–2; Smith, *Palestine*, pp. 498–9.
42. J. Pressman, 'Visions in collision: what happened at Camp David and Taba?', *International Security*, Vol. 28, No. 2, 2003.
43. Palestinian National Authority, *The Mitchell Report on Israeli–Palestinian Violence*, Official Website <www.pna.gov.ps>.
44. Palestinian National Authority, *The Tenet Plan: Israeli–Palestinian Ceasefire and Security Plan*, Official Website, <www.pna.gov.ps>.
45. Bush had already spoken of his vision for the day when 'two states – Israel and Palestine – live peacefully together within secure and recognised borders' in his November 2001 address to the UN General Assembly, and reiterated the position on several occasions thereafter. See Aluf Ben, *Haaretz*, 12 April 2005.
46. 'A performance-based road map to a permanent two-state solution to the Israeli–Palestinian conflict', <www.bitterlemons.org>.
47. Smith, *Palestine*, p. 516.
48. Palestine Liberation Organisation, Negotiations Affairs Department, *Israel's Wall*, 9 July 2005.
49. This was UNGA Resolution ES-10/L.18/Rev.1, passed on 20 July 2005.
50. The Foundation for Middle East Peace, *Report on Israeli Settlement*, Summer 2006.
51. Ever since President Bush's declared support for the creation of a Palestinian state, Israeli leaders became constrained to respond. At his meeting with Ariel Sharon in April 2004, Bush made clear his wish to see a 'democratic' Palestinian state established under the leadership of Mahmoud Abbas. He asked that Israel should cease settlement activity; see Aluf Ben, *Haaretz*, 12 April 2005.

5 Destroying the Palestinians

1. *Haaretz*, May 2005.
2. The documentary evidence for this section is well summarised in Reinhart, *Israel/Palestine*, pp. 133–42.
3. Interview with Sylvain Cypel, *Le Monde*, 24 December 2001.
4. *Yediott Ahronot*, 30 June 2004.
5. *Jane's Foreign Report*, 12 July 2001.
6. This was Raed Karmi from Tulkarm, killed after an Israeli army unit tracked him down in his hideout.
7. The total destruction of the Jenin refugee camp in April 2002 was one of the worst atrocities of this campaign. See Reinhart, *Israel/Palestine*, pp. 152–70; Human Rights Watch Report, 'Jenin: IDF military operations', Vol. 14, No. 3, May 2002.
8. *Yediott Ahronot*, 4 June 2004. This was in the context of Israel's refusal to deal with Arafat over its withdrawal plan from Gaza. Egypt as usual was playing the role of the mediator between the US/Israel and the Palestinians.
9. Arafat was elected as Palestinian president in January 1996 in elections that were attested to be free and fair (within the confines of a military occupation) by international observers.
10. Ghada Karmi, 'Who killed Yasser Arafat?', *Al-Ahram Weekly*, 14 November 2004. The massive international media coverage of his final illness and the cast of kings, presidents and senior dignitaries who attended his funeral are telling indications of his world stature.
11. Roman Bronfman, 'Israel must accept the Saudi initiative and integrate into the Middle East if it wishes to survive', *Haaretz*, 19 May 2005.
12. Reuters, quoted in *Al-Quds*, 9 February 2005.
13. Conal Urquhart, *Guardian*, 25 February 2005.
14. *Middle East International*, No. 747, 1 April 2005, p. 6.
15. *Haaretz*, 28 April 2005.
16. *Al-Quds*, 13 April 2005.
17. *Jerusalem Post*, 2 May 2005.
18. *Al-Quds*, 13 April 2005.
19. Zeev Schiff, *Haaretz*, 6 May 2005.
20. WAFA (the Palestinian news agency) report, 4 May 2005.
21. According to the Palestinian National Information Centre, these comprised incursions into Palestinian territory, house demolitions and destruction of thousands of dunums of farmland in Bethlehem, Qalqilya, Jerusalem and Hebron. See *Palestine Report*, No. 29, 2–8 May 2005.
22. <www.humintarianinfo.org/opt/docs/UN/OCHA/ochaClosureRpt260405.pdf>, 5 May 2005.
23. UN assessment, cited in *Al-Quds*, 13 April 2005.
24. They comprise groupings of the largest settlements, joined to smaller ones, in three locations in the north, centre and south of the West Bank. With the bypass roads and military areas, they occupy 17 per cent of the West Bank.
25. AFP, cited in *Al-Quds*, 29 March 2005.

26. Israeli officials affected to be astonished by this accusation, stressing that Maale Adumim had been recognised (by the US) as part of Israel, and what they did on their land was their business (UPI, 25 March 2005).

27. Al-Quds, 4 June 2005, citing Palestinian and Israeli sources.

28. Meron Benvenisti, Haaretz, 29 July 2005; Yehuda Litani, Yediott Ahronot, 29 July 2004.

29. Chris McGreal, Guardian, 5 April 2005.

30. Danny Rubinstein, Haaretz, 31 May 2005; Amira Hass, Haaretz, 31 March 2005.

31. 'The Israeli occupation plans to partition Hebron with a separation wall', Al-Quds, 29 March 2005.

32. It is not known who, if anyone, is buried at these ancient sites, almost certainly places of veneration from Canaanite times. Benvenisti, Sacred Landscape, pp. 273–85.

33. Al-Quds, 9 May 2005.

34. Ibid. 2 March 2005.

35. Haaretz, 1 May 2005.

36. Aluf Benn, Haaretz, 18 February 2005; Palestine Media Centre Report, 1 April 2005.

37. Akiva Eldar points out that a considerable number of Israelis thought 'Gaza first meant Gaza last'. Haaretz, 23 May 2005.

38. Al-Quds, 3 May 2005.

39. Al-Quds, 17 March 2005; Maariv, 2 May 2005.

40. For example, Tanya Reinhart, 'Behind the smokescreen of the Gaza pullout', Electronic Intifada, <http://electronic intifada.net/v2/article3768.shtml>, 19 April 2005.

41. Human Rights Watch, World Report, 2005, pp. 473ff and its earlier report, Razing Rafah: Mass Demolitions in the Gaza Strip, 2004; Jennifer Lowenstein, 'The disengaged: Gaza and the fragmentation of Palestinian nationhood', Electronic Intifada, April 2005.

42. Foundation for Middle East Peace, Report on Israeili Settlement in the Occupied Territories, Vol. 15, No. 1, January–February 2005; Lowenstein, 'The disengaged', note 41.

43. Report on Israeli Settlement, Vol 15, No. 2, March–April 2005.

44. Interview with The Palestine Report Online, 26 March 2005.

45. Uri Avnery, The Other Israel, No. 117/8, January 2005.

46. Gadi Ta'ov, Maariv, 23 May 2005.

47. Ghada Karmi, 'Vanishing the Palestinians', Counterpunch, 17/18 July 2004; Uzi Arad, a prominent Israeli analyst at the Herzliya Interdisciplinary Institute, has agreed that a Palestinian majority does not threaten the Jewish state because Israeli governments have succeeded in evacuating the Palestinian centres. What happens there is 'no longer relevant' to Israel, Haaretz, 6 August 2004.

48. Baruch Kimmerling, 'Fenced in all round: Sharon's master plan', Le Monde Diplomatique, 6 June 2004; Mahmoud Sueid, 'Sharon's plan to cancel the Palestinians' (Arabic), Majallat al-Dirasat al-Filistiniyya, Vol. 52, 2002, pp. 31–56.

49. Amnesty International report, BBC World News, 24 April 2005; 'Palestinians accuse the settlers of poisoning their flocks', *Al-Quds*, 7 April 2005.

50. The Christian Arab community has traditionally been well educated and entrepreneurial. See also Reinhart, *Israel/Palestine*, pp. 126–9.

51. The regular reports from the Gaza-based Palestinian Centre for Human Rights, The Palestine Monitor, UNRWA, the International Solidarity Movement, B'tselem, the Israeli Committee Against House Demolitions, and personal narratives posted on the Internet are a few examples.

52. Several articles in *Al-Quds* dealt with this quarrel and its implications: 14 March 2005, 28 April 2005 and 9 May 2005.

53. The Beilin–Abu Mazen plan of 1995, agreed between the then Israeli justice minister, Yossi Beilin, and Mahmoud Abbas (Abu Mazen), stipulated that the Palestinians would recognise West Jerusalem as the capital of Israel, and Israel would recognise Palestinian sovereignty over the Haram al-Sharif and a Palestinian capital in the village of Abu Dis, with some other disparate areas of East Jerusalem, the whole to be called 'Al-Quds'; see Reinhart, *Israel/Palestine*, pp. 26–9.

54. After 1995, discreet negotiations took place amongst North American, European and Arab officials to work out a package for the refugees, consisting of patriation into the current host country, emigration to a third country – Canada, Australia and some European states – and financial compensation. Canada offered to take in 75,000 refugees from Lebanon at a rate of 15,000 a year (*Al-Quds*, 22 April 2005).

55. 'After the war is over', *The Economist*, 1 April 2002.

56. Zuhair Andraws, *Al-Quds*, 21 March 2005.

57. Craig Smith, 'Europe stops all payments to Hamas-led Palestinians', *New York Times*, 7 April 2006; 'US suspends aid to Palestinians', BBC News, 7 April 2006.

58. Steven Erlanger, 'Israel to allow aid that does not reach Hamas', *New York Times*, 10 May 2006.

59. Accessible Information Development Activities (AIDA), 'Humanitarian situation in Gaza continues to deteriorate six months after Gaza redeployment', *Fact Sheet*, 18 April 2006; Palestinian National Authority Central Bureau of Statistics, '1.4 million new paupers in the Palestinian territories in last three months', Ramallah, 12 June 2006.

60. 'Still some food in the garbage', IPS News Service, 2 June 2006.

61. AFP, 'Palestinian humanitarian crisis deepens amid aid freeze: ICRC', 12 June 2006.

62. Harvey Morris, 'US tells moderates to stay out of Hamas cabinet', *Financial Times*, 10 March 2006.

63. 'US and Israel "trying to destabilise Hamas"', *Guardian*, 15 February 2006; Ori Nir, 'US seen backing Israeli moves to topple Hamas', *Forward*, 7 July 2006.

64. Uzi Mahnaimi, 'US holds secret talks to weaken Hamas', *Sunday Times*, 19 February 2006; Zuhair Andraws (citing Aluf Ben in *Haaretz*), 'US and Israeli sources: Washington prepared a comprehensive plan to strengthen Abbas at Hamas' expense', *Al-Quds*, 17 May 2006.

65. Nidal al-Mughrabi, *Al-Quds*, 7 October 2006.

66. Sam Bahour, 'Why Palestinian strife is escalating', *Philadelphia Inquirer*, 11 May 2006.
67. 'Palestinian coalition talks fail as Rice flies in', *Guardian*, 5 October 2006.
68. 'The principal clauses of the "Palestinian National Charter"', *Al-Quds*, 7 June 2006.
69. Donald Macintyre, *Independent*, 11 November 2006.
70. UN Office for Co-ordination of Humanitarian Affairs (OCHA), *Situation Report*, 24 August 2006.
71. See also J. Egeland and J. E. Eliasson, 'The human catastrophe of Gaza is a time bomb', *Le Figaro*, 3 September 2006.
72. Ilan Pappe details this Israeli policy in *The Ethnic Cleansing of Palestine* (Oxford: Oneworld Publications, 2006).
73. Danny Rubinstein in *Haaretz*, 5 March 2004. Most of these agents spy for Israel in return for trifling payments, or travel permits or other forms of government favour; many do so because of threats to their families or intimidation.
74. *Al-Quds*, 1 June 2005.
75. Sandra Jordan, *Observer*, 3 April 2005; Eyad el-Sarraj and Samir Qouta, 'Disaster and mental health: the Palestinian experience', *Occupation Magazine*, <www.kibbush.co.il>, 14 March 2005; see also various reports and studies of the Gaza Mental Health Programme, Gaza.
76. Jeff Halper is the co-ordinator of the Israeli Committee against House Demolitions. He has written widely on this subject. See 'Paralysis over Palestine: questions of strategy', *Journal of Palestine Studies*, Vol. 34, No. 2, 2005, pp. 55–69.
77. International Labour Office, *The Situation of Workers in the Occupied Territories* (Geneva: May 2005). See also 'Stagnation or revival? Israeli disengagement and Palestinian economic prospects', *World Bank Report*, 1 December 2004.
78. 'Dimona's nuclear waste spreads cancer and sterility in Southern Hebron and Negev', Palestinian Authority International Press Service, 6 December 2006.
79. Palestine Monitor Report, <www.palestunemonitor.org/new_web/april05_archive.html>.
80. *Al-Quds*, 19 May 2004.
81. *Haaretz*, 4 April 2005.
82. Arab Media Internet Network, 28 March 2005; Islamonline.org, 2 April 2005.
83. Jamil Hamed summarises the evidence, citing the newspaper, *Maariv*, and *Jane's Foreign Report* on the making of a noxious gas bomb by the Sharon government, which was capable of killing thousands of Palestinians. *Al-Quds*, 17 September 2004.
84. The idea of 'transfer' had not left the Israeli public discourse. An opinion poll in October 2005 found that 60 per cent of Israelis favoured expulsion of the Palestinians from both side of the Green Line, Zuhair Andraws in *Al-Quds*, 23 October 2004; also, Martin van Creveld, 'Sharon's plan is to drive Palestinians across the Jordan', *Daily Telegraph*, 24 October 2004.
85. See Donald Macintyre, 'Welcome to Palestine, 2015', *Independent*, 24 May 2005, reporting on the Rand Corporation study.

MARRIED TO ANOTHER MAN

6 Solving the Problem

1. 'The majority in Israel now support two states for two nations', *Maariv*, 21 March 2005.
2. Yossef Harmoni, 'Calls to expel the Arabs to Saudi Arabia, Kuwait and Yemen', *Maariv*, 6 October 2004.
3. 'Israeli High Court upholds unification law', *Associated Press*, 14 May 2006. In fact the law is supposed to apply only to women over 25 and men over 35.
4. 'More than half of Israelis want govm't to help Arabs emigrate', *Haaretz*, 9 May 2006.
5. 'Israelis ponder a land swap', *Christian Science Monitor*, 5 April 2006.
6. Michael Palumbo, *Imperial Israel: The History of the Occupation of the West Bank and Gaza* (London: Bloomsbury, 1992), pp. 60–2.
7. Nadav Shragai, 'Five options to divide the Jerusalem cake', *Daily Star*, 20 March 2006.
8. Gary Sussman, 'Sharon and the Jordanian option', *Middle East Report (MERIP)*, No. 231, March 2005.
9. Extrapolated from Jeff Halper, *Obstacles to Peace: A Critical Tour of the Jerusalem/West Bank Interface* (Jerusalem: The Israeli Committee against House Demolitions, 2003), pp. 19–27; and International Crisis Group, 'The Jerusalem powder-keg', *MERIP*, No. 44, 2 August 2005.
10. Aluf Benn, 'Israel offers PA rail link between West Bank and Gaza', *Haaretz*, 7 June 2005.
11. 'Olmert: talks with US, Israelis to precede pullout', *Haaretz*, 26 March 2006; 'Permanent borders in four years', interview with Olmert, *Jerusalem Post*, 9 March 2006.
12. Karby Leggett, 'Olmert to call for global support of Israel's West Bank pullout plan', *Wall Street Journal*, 12 April 2006.
13. 'Olmert wished to finish building the separation wall in the West Bank as soon as possible', *Al-Quds*, 1 May 2006.
14. 'Our future in 2020', *Nativ*, May 2005; report by Zuhair Andraws, *Al-Quds*, 23 May 2005.
15. Interview with Ari Shavit, *Haaretz*, 4 April 2006.
16. 'Western diplomats worried by prospect of Israeli unilateralism', *Haaretz*, 11 May 2006; 'PM drafting alternative to convergence plan', *Haaretz*, 13 June 2006.
17. *Yediott Ahronot*, 22 October 2004.
18. Sussman, 'Ariel Sharon and the Jordan option'.
19. The college belonged to the Palestinian NGO, In'ash al-Usra, founded in 1983 by a great Palestinian patriot, Sameeha al-Khalil. The girls ranged in age from 18 to 21, nearly all wore headscarves and came from poor families.
20. B. Michael, 'Sharon and his assistant Mofaz destroyed every Palestinian leadership that sought peace', *Yediott Ahronot*, 23 December 2005.
21. 'Life in the armpits of Palestine', *The Economist*, 7 April 2005; '55,000 Palestinians to be cut off by Jerusalem fence', *Haaretz*, 10 July 2005.
22. Avraham Tal, *Haaretz*, 20 April 2006; Fareed Taamallah, 'A thirst for West Bank water', *Nation*, 9 June 2006.

23. Palestinians constituted 33 per cent of Jerusalem's population, but received 12 per cent of the welfare and service budgets, and they rarely got planning permission to build homes, see Angela Godfrey Goldstein, 'The choice is now', *Challenge*, May/June 2006.

24. According to the Israeli organisation, Hamoked, Israel was stopping Jerusalem ID holders from renewing their permits, except if they resided continuously in the city, <www.hamoked.org>, 28 February 2006.

25. UN Office for the Coordination of Humanitarian Affairs (OCHA), *Gaza Strip Situation Report*, 4 July 2006; 'Europe's response to the siege of Gaza is shameful', *Guardian*, 6 July 2006.

26. Shlaim, *The Iron Wall*, pp. 12–14.

27. Karen Abu Zayd, Interview with Akiva Eldar, *Haaretz*, 11 July 2006.

28. Muhammad Baraka, 'Between the one-state and two-state solution independence is not a luxury, it is a necessity', *Al Majdal*, Badil Resource Centre for Palestinian Residency and Refugee Rights, Winter 2005, pp. 20–24.

29. 'Munib al-Masri follows in Zionism's footsteps to build the Palestinian state', *Al-Quds*, 13 January 2005.

30. Ilan Pappe, *A History of Modern Palestine*, pp. 86–7.

31. Henry Cattan, *Palestine and International Law: The Legal Aspects of the Arab–Israeli Conflict* (London: Longman, 1973), pp. 42–56.

32. Muhammad Muslih, 'Towards an analysis of the resolutions of the Palestine National Council', *Journal of Palestine Studies*, Vol. 19, No. 4, 1990, pp. 3–29. This paper contains a detailed analysis of the formal Palestinian position on the two-state solution.

33. *Report of the Special Rapporteur on the Situation of Human Rights in the Palestinian Territories Occupied by Israel since 1967*, UN Doc. E/CN.4/2006/29, 17 January 2006.

34. International Crisis Group, 'The Jerusalem powder-keg', *MERIP*, No. 44, 2 August 2005. The ICG is an NGO specialising in conflict resolution with headquarters in Brussels.

35. An excellent summary of these logistical problems is provided by the PLO Negotiations Affairs Department study, *Israelis' Pre-Emption of a Viable Two-State Solution* (Ramallah: 2002); see also, 'Israel redraws the roadmap, building quietly and quickly', *Guardian*, 18 October 2005; and, 'Is this the end for a Palestinian state?', *Guardian*, 4 March 2003.

36. Jeff Halper, 'Obstacles to peace', pp. 8–18; 'A Palestinian prison state?', *Boston Globe*, 11 April 2005.

37. Jan de Jong, 'The end of the two-state solution – a geo-political analysis', in Mahdi Abdul Hadi (ed.), *Palestinian–Israeli Impasse: Exploring Alternative Solutions to the Palestine–Israel Conflict* (Jerusalem: PASSIA, 2005), pp. 315–41.

38. Michael Tarazi, 'Two peoples, one state', *New York Times*, 5 October 2004.

39. Ali Jarbawi, 'Remaining Palestinian options', *The Arab World Geographer*, Vol. 8, No. 3, 2005.

40. Cited by Ari Shavit, 'Cry the beloved two-state solution', *Haaretz*, 8 August 2003. I will have recourse to cite this excellent article several times in what follows.
41. 'Thinktank: Palestinian state viable', *Aljazeera.Net*, 27 April 2005.
42. Ghada Karmi, ' Reconciliation in the Arab-Israeli conflict', *Mediterranean Politics*, Vol. 4, No. 3, 1999, pp. 104–14; the article, which preceded the survey, provides an account of the issues to be investigated. The survey results have not been published.
43. Badil Resource Center *Survey of Palestinian Refugees and Displaced Persons 2004–2005* (Bethlehem: Badil Resource Center for Palestinian Residency and Refugee Rights, 2006).
44. The Ramallah-based Near East Counselling Institution found that 71 per cent of West Bank refugees were living in extreme poverty, <www.imemc. org>, 20 November 2006.
45. This is the view of the Palestinian academic, Sari Nusseibeh, expressed in 'Pushing Mideast peace', *New York Times*, 1 November 2003.

7 The One-State Solution

1. Effi Eitam, a former Israeli minister with explicitly racist views, provoked a storm of controversy when he talked of the need to expel 'the Arabs' from the West Bank, *Maariv*, 14 September 2006.
2. 'Increasing Israeli racism: its aim is to expel the Arabs', *Al-Quds*, 25 October 2006.
3. Muhammad Ajlani, *Al-Quds*, 20 September 2006.
4. As'ad Ghanem, 'The binational idea in Palestine and Israel: historical roots and contemporary debate', *Holy Land Studies*, Vol. 1, No. 1, 2002, pp. 59–82; Nick Kardahji, 'Dreaming of co-existence – a brief history of the bi-national idea', in Mahdi Abdul Hadi (ed.), *Palestinian–Israeli Impasse: Exploring Alternative Solutions to the Palestine–Israel Conflict* (Jerusalem: PASSIA, 2005), pp. 1–19.
5. William Brinner and Moses Rischin (eds), *Like All the Nations? The Life and Times of Judah L. Magnes* (New York, NY: State University of New York Press, 1987); Arthur Goren, *Dissenter in Zion: From the Writings of Judah L. Magnes* (Cambridge, MA: Harvard University Press, 1982), pp. 307–67.
6. J. L. Magnes, M. Reiner, Lord Samuel, E. Simon. M. Smilansky, *Palestine – United or Divided? The Case for a Bi-National Palestine before the United Nations* (Westport, CT: Greenwood Press, reprinted 1983); M. Buber, J. L. Magnes, E. Simon (eds), *Towards Union in Palestine: Essays on Zionism and Jewish–Arab Cooperation* (Jerusalem: Ihud, 1947).
7. Martin Buber, 'The land and its possessors', in his collection, *Israel and the World: Essays in a Time of Crisis* (New York, NY: Schoken Books, 1948), pp. 227–34; Paul Mendes-Flor (ed.), *A land of Two Peoples: Martin Buber on Jews and Arabs* (New York, NY: Oxford University Press, 1983).
8. Noam Chomsky, *Middle East Illusions* (Lanham, MD: Rowman and Littlefield, 2003), p. 67.
9. Susan Lee-Hattis, *The Bi-national Idea in Palestine during Mandatory Times* (Haifa: Shikmona, 1970).

10. Meron Benvenisti, 'The binational question', *Haaretz*, 7 November 2002.

11. As'ad Ghanem, 'The binational solution: conceptual background and contemporary debate', in Abdul Hadi (ed.), *Palestinian–Israeli Impasse*, p. 36.

12. Ari Shavit, 'Cry the beloved two-state solution', *Haaretz*, 8 August 2003; Meron Benvenisti, 'The binational option', *Haaretz*, 7 November 2002; see also his book, *Intimate Enemies: Jews and Arabs in a Shared Land* (Berkeley, CA: University of California Press, 1995), p. 31ff; Edward Said, 'The one-state solution', *New York Times*, 10 January 1999; Azmi Bishara, *New Realties, Old Problems* (London: Pluto Press, 1998), pp. 212–26.

13. Interview with Edward Said, 'My right to return', reported by Ari Shavit, *Haaretz Magazine*, 10 August 2000.

14. Don Peretz, 'A binational approach to the Palestine conflict', *Law and Contemporary Problems*, Vol. 33, No. 1, 1968, pp. 31–43.

15. Daniel Elazar, *Two Peoples, One Land* (Lanham, MD: University Press of America, 1991), pp. 180–5.

16. 'Justice for Palestine? Q and A on prospects for a solution', *Znet*, 30 March 2003; Chomsky, *Middle East Illusions*, pp. 39–71.

17. Mark Heller and Sari Nusseibeh, *No Trumpets, No Drums: A Two State Settlement of the Israeli–Palestinian Conflict* (London: I. B. Tauris, 1991).

18. Mathias Mossberg, 'Superimposing a solution', *Foreign Policy*, 27 June 2006; Deb Reich, 'Beyond the onion of blame', *Counterpunch*, 30 October 2002.

19. Lama Abu-Odeh, 'The case for binationalism', *Boston Review*, 14 March 2005; Tarif Abboushi, 'New road map: one state, modelled after US', *Houston Chronicle*, 11 June 2003.

20. Nasser Abufarha, 'Alternative Palestinian agenda – proposal for an alternative configuration in Palestine–Israel', in Abdul Hadi (ed.), *Palestinian–Israeli Impasse*, pp. 145–87.

21. Andrew Reding, 'Call it "Israel–Palestine" – try federal solution in Middle East', *Pacific News Service*, 26 June 2002.

22. Issam Nashashibi, 'Back to the future: is there a more equitable Palestinian–Israeli solution in UNSCOP's "Minority Plan"?', *Washington Report on Middle East Affairs*, January–February 1999.

23. Israel Shamir, 'The Malaysian solution', posted on his website, 15 January 2003.

24. Elazar, *Two Peoples*.

25. Tamar Hermann, 'The bi-national idea in Israel/Palestine: past and present', *Nations and Nationalism*, Vol. 11, No. 3, 2005, pp. 381–401.

26. M. Muslih, 'Towards co-existence: an analysis of the Resolutions of the Palestine National Council', *Journal of Palestine Studies*, Vol. 19, No. 4, 1990, pp. 13–16.

27. William Quandt, Fuad Jabber and Ann Mosley Lesch, *The Politics of Palestinian Nationalism* (Berkeley, CA: University of California Press, 1973), p.144.

28. *Time Magazine*, 21 December 1970.

29. Alain Gresh, *The PLO: The Struggle Within: Towards an Independent Palestinian State* (London: Zed Books, 1983), pp. 7–50.

30. Article 6 of the Palestine National Charter, as amended in 1964, stipulated this.
31. Yehoshafat Harkabi, *Fedayeen Action and Arab Strategy*, Adelphi Papers, No. 53 (London: International Institute for Strategic Studies), 1968.
32. Quandt et al., *Politics*, pp. 100–12.
33. Reported by *Newsweek*, 27 April 1970.
34. Gresh, *The PLO*, p. 50.
35. Fouzi al-Asmar, Uri Davis and Naim Khader (eds), *Towards a Socialist Republic of Palestine* (London: Ithaca Press, 1978).
36. 'Palestinians ready to push for one state', *Associated Press*, 9 January 2004.
37. Gary Sussman, 'The challenge to the two-state solution', *MERIP*, No. 231, March 2005.
38. Effi Eitam's vision, reported in *Haaretz*, 4 November 2002.
39. For example, Tikva Honig-Parnass, 'Bi-nationalism versus secular-democratic state', *News from Within*, 13 March 2002, and her interview with Eli Aminov in the same publication, 'A secular–democratic state', July 2002. See also Ghada Karmi, 'One land two peoples', *Haaretz*, 9 July 2002; 'A secular democratic state in historic Palestine: an idea whose time has come' (Arabic), *Al-Adab*, July 2002; 'The right of return and the unitary state in Israel/Palestine', *Race Traitor*, No. 16, Winter 2005.
40. Helena Cobban, 'A binational Israel–Palestine', *Christian Science Monitor*, 9 October 2003.
41. Jeff Halper, 'Preparing for a post-Road Map struggle against apartheid', Paper given to the UN International Conference on Civil Society in Support of the Palestinian People, New York, 5 September 2003.
42. Daniel Gavron, *The Other Side of Despair: Jews and Arabs in the Promised Land* (Lanham, MD: Rowman and Littlefield, 2003); Peter Hirschberg, 'One-state awakening', *Haaretz*, 12 December 2003.
43. Daniel Lazare, 'The one-state solution', *Nation*, 11 October 2004.
44. Daniel Lazare, 'The one-state solution: however utopian, binationalism may be the last hope for Israeli–Palestinian peace', Book Review, *Nation*, December 2003.
45. Tony Judt, 'Israel: the alternative', *New York Review of Books*, Vol. 50, No. 16, 23 October 2003.
46. Nathaniel Popper, 'Embattled academic Tony Judt defends call for binational state', *Forward*, 26 December 2003.
47. <www.nkusa.org>, 28 March 2006.
48. Ibid. 8 November 2006.
49. Financial support for this association was rumoured to have come from Libya, a fact which antagonised many potential members.
50. Mortaza Sahibzada, convenor of the London One-State Group, <www.one-state.org>, last accessed in January 2005. Also see the list of one-state groups in Abdul Hadi (ed.), *Palestinian–Israeli Impasse*, pp. 341–2.
51. Virginia Tilley, *The One-State Solution: A Breakthrough for Peace in the Israeli–Palestinian Deadlock* (Michigan, MI: University of Michigan Press, 2005); see also her article, 'The one-state solution', *London Review of Books*, Vol. 25, No. 21, 6 November 2003.

52. <http://greens.org/platforms/us/draft democracy>.

53. The London one-state group website, <www.one-state.org>, had a comprehensive archive of single-state articles.

54. 'Rafsanjani proposes uniting Israel, Palestine under one govm't', *Jordan Times*, 14 November 2004.

55. *Isratine*, Gaddafi Official Website, 8 May 2003.

56. 'Gaddafi walks out, boycotts Arab summit', *Reuters*, 22 May 2004.

57. For the Peace Index poll of October 2003, see Tami Steinmetz Centre for Peace Research, Tel Aviv University, <http://spirit.tau.ac.il/peace index/2003>; 'Peace Index – demographic fears favour unilateral separation', *Haaretz*, 7 December 2003.

58. Salim Tamari, 'The dubious lure of binationalism', in Abdul Hadi (ed.), *Palestinian–Israeli Impasse*, pp. 67–73.

59. Halper, 'A Middle Eastern confederation: a regional "two-stage" approach to the Israeli–Palestinian conflict', *Arab Media Internet Network*, 15 December 2002.

60. Posted on John Whitbeck's website, 7 October 2004.

61. Uri Avnery, 'A binational state? God forbid!', *Journal of Palestine Studies*, Vol. 28, No. 4, 1999, pp. 55–60.

62. 'Abed Rabbo rules out bi-national state', Palestine Media Centre Official Website, January 2004.

63. 'New Fatah chief al-Qaddumi goal is to eliminate Israel in "second stage"', *Middle East Newsline*, 23 December 2004.

64. Nancy Crawshaw, *The Cyprus Revolution: An Account of the Struggle for Union with Greece* (London: Allen and Unwin, 1978), pp. 364–97.

65. William Dalrymple, 'The final place of refuge for Christians in the Middle East', *Guardian*, 2 September 2006.

66. The Palestinian political scientist, As'ad Ghanem, disagreed with such notions. His view was that the ethnic nature of the Jewish and Palestinian national movements was too strong to permit the development of a common civil identity. See his article, 'The binational idea', in Abdul Hadi (ed.), *Palestinian–Israeli Impasse*, p. 59.

67. Yoav Peled, 'Zionist realities', *New Left Review*, Vol. 38, March–April 2006, pp. 21–36, and Tilly's replies to it, 'The secular solution', pp. 37–57.

68. Avraham Burg, 'End of an era', *Haaretz*, 5 August 2005.

69. Mouna Younis, *Liberation and Democratization: The South African and Palestinian National Movements* (Minneapolis, MN: University of Minnesota Press, 2000), pp. 1–21.

70. 'Brothers in arms – Israel's secret pact with Pretoria', *Guardian*, 7 February 2006.

71. 'Worlds apart', *Guardian*, 6 February 2006.

72. 'A one-state solution for Israel/ Palestine: inevitable or pie in the sky?', *Media Review Network*, 2 March 2004.

73. *Truth and Reconciliation Commission of South Africa Report*, Official Website, 21 March 2003.

74. Abd al-Alim Muhammad, *The Future of the Arab–Israeli Conflict: The Palestinian Unitary Democratic State* (Arabic) (Cairo: Centre of Political and Strategic Studies Publications, 1999), p. 59.

75. A good example is the paper by Fadil Kiblawi, 'Towards a sustainable solution: alternative constructions for an Israeli–Palestinian peace', in Abdul Hadi (ed.), *Palestinian–Israeli Impasse*, pp. 73–144.

Epilogue: The End of the Zionist Dream?

1. Yehoshafat Harkabi, *Israel's Fateful Decisions*, p. 209.
2. Walid Awad, interview with Khalil Toufakji, *Al-Quds*, 8 September 2006.
3. 'Israel has shown its capability for military retaliation, but it is no solution for two million hungry Palestinians', *Yediott Ahronot*, 6 September 2006.
4. Zuhair Andraws, *Al-Quds*, 1 September 2006.
5. Reproduced by Ari Shavit, 'Cry the beloved two-state solution', *Haaretz*, 8 August 2003.
6. Ibid.
7. Ibid.
8. The US National Intelligence Council predicted in 2005 that within 15 years the emergence of new global powers, for example, China, India, Brazil and Indonesia, would erode America's current dominance; Fred Kaplan, 'A CIA report predicts that American global dominance could end in 15 years', *Slate*, 26 January 2005.

Bibliography

Newspapers, Periodicals and Electronic Resources

Al-Ahram
Al-Ahram Weekly
Acta Anthropogenetica
Arab Media Network
Asia Times
Associated Press
Al-Ayyam
Boston Globe
Boston Review
Challenge
Commentary Magazine
Counterpunch
Daily Star
Detroit Jewish News
Financial Times
Forward
Guardian
Haaretz
Al-Hayat
Houston Chronicle
International Herald Tribune
InterPress Service
IPS News Service
Jerusalem Post
Jewish Chronicle
Jewish Week
Jordan Times
Le Monde Diplomatique
Los Angeles Times
Maariv
National Review Online
Newsweek International
New Yorker
New York Times
Occupation Magazine
Pacific News
Philadelphia Inquirer

Prospect
Al-Quds
Tikkun
Time
USA Today
Wall Street Journal
Washington Post
Yediott Ahronot

www.alternet.com
www.aljazeeranet.com
www.antiwar.com
www.arabicnews.com
www.jta.org
www.merip.com
www.ynetnews.com
www.princeton.libraries/kennlove
www.ifamericansknew.org
www.statesman.com/nation
www.sikkuy.org
Palestine Report Online

Reports and Documents

AIDA Fact Sheet, 2005
Amnesty International Reports, 2005
Badil Resource Centre Reports, 2004–5
B'tselem Reports, 2005
Gaza Situation Report, 2005
Human Rights Watch World Report, 2005
ICRC, 2006
Jane's Foreign Report, 2001
The Sikkuy Report, July 2002 and 2003
UN Office for the Coordination of Humanitarian Affairs Report, 2006
Washington Report on Middle East Affairs, 1997
World Bank Report, 2004

Articles

Abadi, J. 'Israel and Sudan: the saga of an enigmatic relationship', *Middle Eastern Studies*, 35 (1999).
Arthur, S. M. 'Congress passes foreign aid, appropriations, keeping most unhelpful provisions', *Washington Report on Middle East Affairs*, 25 (2006).
Aruri, N. 'The Wye Memorandum: Netanyahu's Oslo and unreciprocal reciprocity', *Journal of Palestine Studies*, 28 (1999).
Avnery, U. 'A binational state? God forbid', *Journal of Palestine Studies*, 28 (1999).

Baraka M. 'Between the one-state and two-state solution independence is not a luxury it is a necessity', *Al Majdal* (Winter 2006).

Cobban, H. 'A binational Israel–Palestine', *Christian Science Monitor* (2003).

Cockburn, P. 'Iraq diary', *London Review of Books* (March 2006).

Cohen, N. W. 'Economist tallies swelling cost of Israel to US', *Christian Science Monitor*, (2002).

Findley, P. 'Washington's fateful cover-up of Israel's attack on the USS Liberty', *Washington Report on Middle East Affairs* (August 2005).

Ghanem, A. 'The binational idea in Palestine and Israel: historical roots and contemporary debate, *Holy Land Studies*, 1 (2002).

Gordon, P. 'Bush's Middle East vision', *Survival*, 45 (2003).

Halper, J. 'Obstacles to peace: a critical tour of Jerusalem/West Bank interface', *Israel Committee Against House Demolitions* (2003).

—— 'Paralysis over Palestine: questions of strategy', *Journal of Palestine Studies*, 34 (2005).

Hanieh, A. 'The Camp David Papers', *Journal of Palestine Studies*, 30 (2001).

Jarbawi, A. 'Remaining palestinian options', *The Arab World Geographer*, 8 (2005).

Judd, T. 'Israel; the alternative', *New York Review of Books*, 50 (2003).

Karmi, G. 'Reconciliation in the Arab–Israeli Conflict', *Mediterranean Politics*, 4 (1999).

—— 'The right of return and the unitary state in Israel/Palestine', *Race Traitor*, 16 (2005).

Krischer, J. A. 'Israel and the Horn of Africa: the strategic and political imperatives', *Journal of South Asian and Middle Eastern Studies*, 25 (2002).

Levine, M. 'The Arab Human Development Report: a critique', *Middle East Report* (2002).

Little, D. 'The making of a special relationship: The United States and Israel', *International Journal of Middle East Studies*, 25 (1993).

Malley, H. 'Camp David: the tragedy of errors', *New York Review of Books*, 9 August 2001.

Mearsheimer, J. and Walt, S. 'The Israel lobby and U.S. foreign policy', *London Review of Books*, 28 (2006).

Muslih, M. 'Towards an analysis of the resolutions of the Palestine National Council', *Journal of Palestine Studies*, 19 (1990).

Peled, Y. 'Zionist Realities', *New Left Review*, 38 (2006).

Peretz, D. 'A binational approach to the Palestine conflict', *Law and Contemporary Problems*, 33 (1968).

Porat, D. 'Amalek's accomplices blaming Zionism for the Holocaust: anti-Zionist ultra-orthodoxy in Israel during the 1908s', *Journal of Contemporary History*, 27 (1992).

Prusher, I. 'Israelis ponder a land swap', *Christian Science Monitor* (2006).

Quandt, W. and Lesch, A. M. 'Clinton and the Arab–Israeli conflict: the limits of incrementalism', *Journal of Palestine Studies*, 30 (2001).

Reinhart, T. 'Jenin: IDF military operations', *Human Rights Watch Report*, 14 (2002).

Salem, A. 'My drive to Israel', *Middle East Quarterly*, 9 (2002).

Sussman, G. 'The challenge to the two-state solution', *MERIP*, 231 (March 2005).

Shamaa, M. 'Eritrea in the age of Afewerki: An Israeli strategic triumph', *Shu'un Filistinyiya*, 64 (2005).

Sueid, M. 'Sharon's plans to cancel the Palestinians', *Majallat al-Dirasat al-Filistinyiya*, 52 (2002).

Tamari, S. 'The dubious lure of binationalism', in Abdul Hadi, M. (ed.), *Palestinian–Israeli Impasse* (Jerusalem: Palestinian Academic Society for the Study of International Affairs, 2005).

Usher, G. 'Musharraf's opening to Israel', *Middle East Report Online* (2006).

Walt, J. M. S. 'The Israel lobby and US foreign policy', *London Review of Books*, 28 (2006).

Warburg, G. 'The Sudan and Israel: an episode in bilateral relations', *Middle East Studies*, 28 (1992).

Wilsman, E. M. 'Techniques for estimating genetic admixture and applications to the problem of the origin of the Icelanders and the Ashkenazi Jews', *Human Genetics*, 67 (1984).

Yinon, O. 'A Strategy for Israel in the 1980s', *Kevunim*, World Zionist Organisation (14 February 1982).

Books

Abdul Hadi, M. (ed.). *Palestinian–Israeli Impasse: Exploring Alternative Solutions to the Palestinian–Israel Conflict* (Jerusalem: PASSIA, 2005).

Abramsky, C. et al. *The Jews in Poland* (Oxford: Blackwell, 1986).

Aburish, S. *A Brutal Friendship: The West and the Arab Elite* (London: Victor Gollancz, 1997).

Abu Sitta, S. *The Palestinian Nakba: The Register of Depopulated Localities in Palestine* (London: Palestine Return Centre, 1998).

—— *Atlas of Palestine* (London: Palestine Land Society, 2004).

Arakie, M. *The Broken Sword of Justice: America, Israel and the Palestinian Tragedy* (London: Quartet Books, 1973).

Aruri, N. *The Obstruction of Peace: The US, Israel and the Palestinians* (Monroe, ME: Common Courage Press, 1995).

—— *Dishonest Broker: The US Role in Israel and Palestine* (Cambridge, MA: South End Press, 2003).

Al-Asmar, F., Davis, U. and Khader, N. (eds). *Towards a Socialist Republic of Palestine* (London: Ithaca Press, 1979).

Ayyubi, N. *Over-Stating the Arab State: Politics and Society in the Middle East* (London: I. B. Tauris, 1996).

Balabkins, N. *West German Reparations to Israel* (New Brunswick, NJ: Rutgers University Press, 1971).

Ball, G. and Ball, D. *The Passionate Attachment: America's Involvement with Israel, 1947 to the Present* (New York, NY: W. W. Norton, 1992).

Ben-Gurion, D. *Rebirth and Destiny of Israel* (London: Thomas Yosseloff, 1959).

—— *Letters to Paula* (London: Vallentine Mitchell, 1971).

Benvenisti, M. *Intimate Enemies: Jews and Arabs in a Shared Land* (Berkeley, CA: University of California Press, 1995).

—— Sacred Landscape: The Buried History of the Holy Land since 1948 (Berkeley, CA: University of California Press, 2000).

Bishara, A. New Realities, Old Problems (London: Pluto Press, 1998).

Brenner, L. The Iron Wall: Zionist Revisionism from Jabotinsky to Shamir (London: Zed Books, 1984).

Brinner, W. M. and Rischin, M. (eds). Like All the Nations? The Life and Legacy of Judah L. Magnes (New York, NY: State University of New York Press, 1987).

Brook, K. The Jews of Khazaria (Northvale: Jason Aaronson, 1999).

Buber, M. Israel and the World: Essays in a Time of Crisis (New York, NY: Schoken Books, 1948).

—— et al. (eds). Towards Union in Palestine: Essays on Zionism and Jewish–Arab Co-operation (Jerusalem: Ihud, 1947).

Cantor, N. The Sacred Chain: A History of the Jews (London: Fontana Press, 1995).

Carey, R. and Shainin, J. (eds). The Other Israel: Voices of Refusal and Dissent (New York, NY: The New Press, 2004).

Cattan, H. Palestine and International Law: The Legal Aspects of the Arab-Israeli Conflict (London: Longman, 1973).

Chetrit, S. The Mizrahi Struggle in Israel, transl. from Hebrew by Shalhat, A. (Ramallah: Madar, 2005).

Chomsky, N. The Fateful Triangle: The United States, Israel and the Palestinians (London: Pluto Press, 1983).

—— Middle East Illusions (Lanham, MD: Rowman & Littlefield, 2003).

Cleveland, W. A History of the Modern Middle East (Boulder, CO: Westview Press, 2004).

Cohen, N. W. American Jews and the Zionist Idea (Tel Aviv: Ktav Publishing House, 1985).

Crawshaw, N. The Cyprus Revolution: An Account of the Struggle for Union with Greece (London: Allen and Unwin, 1978).

Davis, U. Apartheid Israel (London: Verso, 2002).

Decalo, S. Israel and Africa: Forty Years 1956–1996 (Gainseville, FL: Florida Academic Press, 1998).

Deutscher, I. The Non-Jewish Jew and other Essays (London: Oxford University Press, 1968).

Dowek, E. Israeli–Egyptian Relations, 1980–2000 (London: Frank Cass, 2001).

Dreyfuss, R. Devil's Game: How the United States Helped Unleash Fundamentalist Islam, American Empire Project Series (New York, NY: Metropolitan Books, 2005).

Dunlop, D. M. The History of the Khazars (Princeton, NJ: Princeton University Press, 1954).

Elazar, D. Two Peoples, One Land (Jerusalem: University Press of America, 1991).

Encyclopaedia Judaica (Jerusalem: The Jerusalem Publishing House, 2002).

Encyclopaedia of Judaism (Jerusalem: Keter Publishing House, 1971).

Feldman, L. G. The Special Relationship between West Germany and Israel (Boston, MA: George & Allen Unwin Publishers, 1984).

Ferro, M. Les Tabous de l'Histoire (Paris: Nil Editions, 2002).

Findley, P. *They Dare to Speak out: People and Institutions Confront Israel's Lobby* (Westport, CT: Lawrence Hill & Company, 1985).

Finkelstein, N. *Beyond Chutzpah: On the Misuse of Anti-Semitism and the Abuse of History* (London: Verso, 2005).

Firo, K. *The Druze in the Jewish State: A Brief History* (Leiden: Brill, 1999).

Flapan, S. *The Birth of Israel: Myths and Realities* (New York, NY: Pantheon Books, 1987).

Friedman, M. *Jewish Intellectuals and the Shaping of Public Policy* (Cambridge: Cambridge University Press, 2005).

Gavron, D. *The Other Side of Despair: Jews and Arabs in the Promised Land* (Lanham, MD: Rowman and Littlefield, 2003).

Goodman, M. *The Ruling Class of Judaea: The Origins of the Jewish Revolt against Rome AD 66–70* (Cambridge: Cambridge University Press, 1987).

Goren, A. *Dissenter in Zion: From the Writings of Judah L. Magnes* (Cambridge, MA: Harvard University Press, 1982).

Govrin, Y. *Israeli–Soviet Relations, 1953–1967* (London: Frank Cass, 1998).

Gresh, A. *The PLO: The Struggle Within: Towards an Independent Palestinian State* (London: Zed Books, 1983).

Halevy, I. *A History of the Jews Ancient and Modern* (London: Zed Books, 1987).

Halsell, G. *Prophecy and Politics: Militant Evangelists on the Road to Nuclear War* (Westport, CT: Lawrence Hill & Company, 1986).

Harkabi, Y. *Fedayeen Action and Arab Strategy*, Adelphi Papers, No. 53 (London: International Institute for Strategic Studies, 1968).

—— *Israel's Fateful Decisions* (London: I. B. Tauris, 1988).

Heller, M. and Nusseibeh, S. *No Trumpets, No Drums: A Two-State Settlement of the Israeli–Palestinian Conflict* (London: I. B. Taurus, 1991).

Hewedy, A. *Militarisation and Society in the Middle East* (London: United Nations University Press, 1989).

Hiro, D. *Inside the Middle East* (London: Routledge, 1982).

Hirst, D. *The Gun and the Olive Branch* (London: Faber and Faber, 2003).

Ingrams, D. *Palestine Papers, 1917–1922: Seeds of Conflict* (London: John Murray, 1972).

Karmi, G. *In Search of Fatima: A Palestinian Story* (London: Verso, 2002).

Kedourie, S. and Haim, S. G. (eds). *Arab Nationalism: An Anthology* (Berkeley, CA: University of California Press, 1976).

Khalidi, W. *All That Remains: The Palestinian Villages Occupied and Depopulated by Israel in 1948* (Washington, DC: Institute for Palestine Studies, 1992).

Koestler, A. *The Thirteenth Tribe: The Khazar Empire and Its Heritage* (London: Hutchinson, 1976).

Kolsky, T. *Jews Against Zionism: The American Council for Judaism* (Philadelphia, PA: Temple University Press, 1990).

Kretzmer, D. *The Legal Status of Arabs in Israel* (Boulder, CO and Oxford: Westview Press, 1990).

Kyle, K. *Suez* (London: Weidenfeld and Nicolson, 1991).

Lavy, G. *Germany and Israel: Moral Debt and National Interest* (London: Frank Cass, 1996).

Lee-Hattis, S. *The Bi-National Idea in Palestine during Mandate Times* (Haifa: Shikmona, 1970).

Lochery, N. *The View from the Fence: The Arab–Israeli Conflict from the Present to its Roots* (London: The Continuum International Publishing Group, 2005).

Love, K. *Suez, the Twice Fought War: A History* (London: Longman, 1970).

Magnes, J. L. *Towards Union in Palestine: Essays on Zionism and Jewish Arab Cooperation* (Jerusalem: Ihud, 1947).

Reiner, M., Lord Samuel, E. S., Smilansky, M. and Magnes, J. L. *Palestine United or Divided? The Case for a Bi-national Palestine before the United Nations* (Westport, CA: Greenwood Press, 1983).

Malachy, Y. *American Fundamentalism and Israel* (Jerusalem: Hebrew University Press, 1978).

Mendes-Flor, P. (ed.). *A Land of Two Peoples: Martin Buber on Jews and Arabs* (New York, NY: Oxford University Press, 1983).

Milton-Edwards, B. *Islamic Politics in Palestine* (London: I. B. Tauris, 1996).

Mohammed, A. *The Future of the Arab–Israeli Conflict: The Palestinian Unitary Democratic State* (Cairo: Centre of Political and Strategic Studies Publications, 1999).

Morris, B. *The Birth of the Palestinian Refugee Problem Revisited*, 2nd edn (Cambridge: Cambridge University Press, 2004).

Neff, D. *Fallen Pillars: US Policy towards Palestine and Israel since 1945* (Washington, DC: Institute of Palestine Studies, 1995).

Niblock, T. C. *Saudi Arabia: Power and Legitimacy* (London: Routledge, 2006).

Nicosia, F. *The Third Reich and the Palestine Question* (London: I. B. Tauris, 1985).

Novick, M. *The Holocaust in American Life* (New York, NY: Houghton Mifflin, 1999).

Oded, A. *Africa and the Middle East Conflict* (London: Lynne Reinner, 1987).

Orr, A. *The Un-Jewish State: The Politics of Jewish Identity in Israel* (London: Ithaca Press, 1983).

Palumbo, M. *Imperial Israel: The History of the Occupation of the West Bank and Gaza* (London: Bloomsbury, 1992).

Pappe, I. *The Making of the Refugee Problem 1947–9* (London: I. B. Tauris, 1992).

—— *A History of Modern Palestine: One Land, Two Peoples* (Cambridge: Cambridge University Press, 2004).

—— *The Ethic Cleansing of Palestine* (Oxford: Oneworld Publications, 2006).

Parsons, L. *The Druze between Palestine and Israel: 1947–1949* (Wiltshire: Anthony Rowe, 2000).

Petras, J. *The Power of Israel in the United States* (Atlanta, GA: Clarity Press, 2006).

Philo, G. and Barry, M. *Bad News from Israel* (London: Pluto Press, 2004).

Prior, M. *The Bible and Colonialism: A Moral Critique* (Sheffield: The Continuum International Publishing Group, 1997).

—— (ed.). *Western Scholarship and the History of Palestine* (London: Fox Communications and Publications, 1998).

Porath, Y. *In Search of Arab Unity, 1930--1945* (London: Frank Cass, 1986).

Quandt, W. *Decade of Decisions: American Policy toward the Arab–Israeli Conflict 1967–1976* (Berkeley, CA: University of California Press, 1977).

Quandt, W., Jabber, F. and Lesch, A. M. *The Politics of Palestinian Nationalism* (Berkeley, CA: University of California Press, 1973).

Qumsiyeh, M. *Sharing the Land of Canaan: Human Rights and the Israeli–Palestinian Struggle* (London: Pluto Press, 2004).

Al-Raheb, H. *The Zionist Character in the English Novel* (London: Zed Books, 1983).

Reinhart, T. *Israel/Palestine: How to End the 1948 War* (New York, NY: Seven Stories Press, 2002).

Rischin, M. *The Life and Times of Judah L. Magnes* (New York, NY: State University of New York Press, 1987).

Rose, J. *The Myths of Zionism* (London: Pluto Press, 2004).

Rubenberg, C. *Israel and the American National Interest: A Critical Examination* (Chicago, IL: University of Illinois Press, 1986).

Saad-Ghorayeb, A. *Hizbullah, Politics, and Religion* (London: Pluto Press, 2002).

Sabbagh, K. *Palestine: A Personal History* (London: Atlantic Books, 2005).

Safty, A. *From Camp David to the Gulf: Negotiations, Language & Propaganda, and War* (Montreal: Black Rose Books, 1992).

Said, E. *Peace and Its Discontents, Jericho–Gaza, 1993–1995* (London: Vintage, 1995).

Schultze, K. E. *Israel's Covert Diplomacy in Lebanon* (London: Macmillan Press, 1998).

Shahak, I. and Mezvinsky, N. *Jewish Fundamentalism in Israel* (London: Pluto Press, 2000).

Sharif, R. *Non-Jewish Zionism: Its Roots in Western History* (London: Zed Books, 1983).

Shlaim, A. *The Iron Wall: Israel and the Arab World* (London: Allen Lane, 2000).

Simons, G. *The Ethnic Cleansing of Palestine* (London: Palestine Return Centre, 2006).

Sizer, S. *Christian Zionism: Road Map to Armageddon?* (London: Inter-Varsity Press, 2004).

Smith, C. *Palestine and the Arab–Israeli Conflict* (Basingstoke: Macmillan Education, 1994).

Tilley, V. *The One-State Solution: A Breakthrough for Peace in the Israeli–Palestinian Deadlock* (Michigan, MI: University of Michigan Press, 2005).

Tuchman, B. *Bible and Sword: England and Palestine from the Bronze Age to Balfour* (London: Alvin Redman, 1956).

Younis, M. *Liberation and Democratization: The South African and Palestinian National Movements* (Minneapolis, MN: University of Minnesota Press, 2000).

Index

Compiled by Sue Carlton